The Enjoyment of Theatre

Eighth Edition

Jim Patterson
University of South Carolina

Jim Hunter
University of South Carolina

Patti P. Gillespie
University of Maryland

Kenneth M. Cameron

Allyn & Bacon

Boston Columbus Indianapolis New York San Francisco Upper Saddle River
Amsterdam Cape Town Dubai London Madrid Milan Munich Paris Montreal Toronto
Delhi Mexico City Sao Paulo Sydney Hong Kong Seoul Singapore Taipei Tokyo

Editor-in-Chief: Karon Bowers
Acquisitions Editor: Jeanne Zalesky
Assistant Editor: Megan Lentz
Development Manager: David Kear
Associate Development Editor: Angela G. Pickard
Media Editor: Megan Higginbotham
Executive Marketing Manager: Wendy Gordon
Managing Editor: Linda Mihatov Behrens
Associate Managing Editor: Bayani Mendoza de Leon
Senior Operations Specialist: Nick Sklitsis
Operations Specialist: Mary Ann Gloriande
Art Director, Cover: Anne Bonanno Nieglos
Designer, Cover: Ilze Lemesis
Production Coordination, Text Design, and Electronic Page Makeup: Elm Street Publishing Services
Cover Image: Photograph by Bruno Vincent

Library of Congress Cataloging-in-Publication Data
The enjoyment of theatre / Jim Patterson...[et al.].
p. cm.
Earlier eds. by Kenneth M. Cameron and Patti P. Gillespie.
Includes index.
ISBN 0-205-73461-8
1. Theater. I. Patterson, Jim (Jim Aris)
PN2037.C27 2009
792dc22 2009041060

---

10 9 8 7 6 5 4 3 2 1 CRK 12 11 10

Allyn & Bacon
is an imprint of

www.pearsonhighered.com

ISBN-13: 978-0-205-73461-0
ISBN-10: 0-205-73461-8

CONTENTS

PREFACE

The Enjoyment of Theatre's balanced coverage of performance and history provides a comprehensive and accessible introduction to theatre for both majors and nonmajors. This text covers the full span of theatre's 2,500-year history, establishes the aesthetic underpinnings of theatre art, and explores performance/production topics such as playwriting, acting, directing, design, and the theatre industry. The authors make theatre come alive for students by showing them how theatre is relevant to their everyday lives.

NEW TO THIS EDITION

The emphasis throughout this comprehensive revision has been to make theatre accessible to today's students and to underscore the relevance of theatre to contemporary life. For the first time, this new edition of *The Enjoyment of Theatre* offers an engaging, **full-color design complemented by rich images and lively features**. We believe that students in the introductory theatre course will enjoy the visual appeal of a full-color text that is in keeping with the visual nature of our culture. For instance, pictures of theatre productions will more fully reveal the directors' and designers' intent. As a result of a new publishing process, this edition of *The Enjoyment of Theatre* will **sell for less** than the previous edition and for less than most competitive texts on the market today, making this edition accessible to all students through its content, coverage, design, and price. The eighth edition includes twenty-five *Spotlights*, new features in which key questions of theatre's art and history, as well as significant individuals, are discussed in greater detail. In addition, examples are **updated and several recent developments added, along with a new chapter on U.S. theatre since 2000**. Our approach to this edition is, as always, to deliver clear and accessible writing, avoiding jargon.

We believe that the book's clear and logical presentation of material, augmented by carefully chosen illustrations and images, will appeal to students as much as other editions of *The Enjoyment of Theatre*. The photographs include many productions at colleges and universities that we believe will give students an insight into the theatre produced by schools very much like their own. There are also photographs from Broadway plays and musicals as well as from important regional theatres throughout the country. The caption for each image clarifies and enriches the text. We believe that the pictures in *The Enjoyment of Theatre* can and should be used as teaching tools.

ORGANIZATION

The Enjoyment of Theatre is organized in three parts: "Locating Theatre, Experiencing Plays: Theory and Criticism," which establishes the aesthetic underpinnings of theatre art; "Today's Theatre and Its Makers: Theatre Practice," which examines the artists who make theatre; and "Theatre of Other Times and Places: Theatre History," divided into three sections, which surveys theatre history from the perspective of stage practice. Throughout, we examine theatre as an artifact of culture. Instructors may opt to use *The Enjoyment of Theatre* in its totality for a course organized as a survey of theatre past and present, or they may make selective use of any combination of sections, emphasizing certain aspects of theatre while omitting others.

SPECIAL FEATURES

This edition builds on proven features from past editions. Students are told at the beginning of each chapter, under "Objectives," what they should take away from that chapter. At the conclusion of each chapter there is a listing of Key Terms to alert the student to significant, and probably testable, concepts. The Glossary includes definitions of all Key Terms with notation of the page on which the term first appears.

The eighth edition introduces the *Spotlight* feature to explore key questions and significant individuals in greater detail. Some of the twenty-five Spotlights were formerly sidebars called "The Story of the Play" that, expanded, now include information about the author and genre.

ANCILLARY SUPPORT

We offer both instructors and students material to enrich the course. Students can access an author-supported Web site called Study Guides (www.theatrestudyguides.com) that includes sample true/false questions (along with correct answers), study tips, and practice essay questions to answer or think about. There is a Study Guide for each of the twenty-one chapters. For more practice, students can also access the Pearson Allyn & Bacon Introduction to Theatre Study Site (www.abtheatre.com), which features introduction to theatre study materials for students, including learning objectives and a complete set of practice tests for all major topics. Students will also find Web links to valuable sites for further exploration of major topics.

For the instructor, the authors have written a comprehensive Instructor's Manual and Test Bank available electronically via Pearson's Instructor's Resource Center at www.pearsonhighered.com/irc. (Instructors should contact their local Pearson representative for access). This teaching resource provides a brief explanation of the text's content and organization, suggested course organizations for semester or quarter courses, and approaches to teaching each chapter (chapter goal, key questions, important concepts, activities, and assessments).

ABOUT THE AUTHORS

The eighth edition of *The Enjoyment of Theatre* continues the collaboration of Jim Hunter and Jim Patterson, both of the University of South Carolina, with Patti P. Gillespie and Kenneth M. Cameron, the originators of this popular textbook. Each author is an experienced teacher and theatre artist. Jim Hunter, a member of the national theatre design union United Scenic Artists, works regularly in theatres across the country. He is also chair and artistic director of the Department of Theatre and Dance at the University of South Carolina. Jim Patterson, a member of the Stage Directors and Choreographers Society, has directed plays across the United States in summer festivals and at colleges and universities. For many years, he headed the MFA program in direction and was artistic director of the University of South Carolina Summer Repertory Theatre.

ACKNOWLEDGMENTS

We are indebted to Tim Donahue for much of this edition's visual impact; his collages and other art have greatly enhanced *The Enjoyment of Theatre*. Our editors at Allyn & Bacon made possible this color edition of *The Enjoyment of Theatre*, especially Karon Bowers, editor in chief. We are indebted to Jeanne Zalesky, acquisitions editor, and Angela Pickard, associate development editor, who were instrumental in seeing this edition to press and especially Martha Beyerlein of Elm Street Publishing Services, who worked directly with us. We would also like to thank the reviewers who helped us with the development of this project, including Peter Lach, Fairmont State University; Kevin P. Kern, University of Florida; Professor Thomas Murdock, College of the Siskiyous; and Hugh Murphy, Barry University.

Note on Colorization: Certain illustrations were originally in black and white and have later had color added; the colors may therefore be inaccurate. These figures are: 16.3, 16.5, 18.7, 18.9, the Chapter 21 Spotlight, and the drawing on page 287.

PART

I

LOCATING THEATRE, EXPERIENCING PLAYS

Theory and Criticism

Part I focuses on ways of understanding theatre, ways usually called theory and criticism. **Theory** is an attempt to explain the nature of something and tries to answer such fundamental questions as, what is it? how does it work? **Criticism** develops a considered judgment or discussion about the qualities of a specific play or performance. What does this particular play mean and how does it convey that meaning by its form and structure? How does this particular production present the play to this audience? Why were these particular choices about acting and directing and design made? How does this production try to communicate its ideas to the audience? How well did it succeed? Part I ends by considering some of the people who use theory and criticism as they work with and in today's theatre.

CHAPTER

1

Theatre

Performance and Art

OBJECTIVES

When you have completed this chapter, you should be able to:

- Define *performance* and list traits shared by performances
- Define *art* and list traits shared by arts
- Discuss how theatre differs from other kinds of performance (e.g., lectures, games, parades, rituals)
- Discuss how theatre differs from other kinds of arts (e.g., painting, sculpture, opera, dance)
- Discuss, using specific examples, similarities and differences between art and life; performance and life; dramatic character and real person; dramatic character and actor; performing art and visual art; performing art and sport
- List and explain the traits that constitute theatre
- Explain in what sense theatre is a system of relationships (rather than a thing)
- Explain how theatre resembles and yet differs from film and television

WHY THEATRE?

People choose to go to the theatre for many reasons. Theatre's immediacy, relevance, and engagement appeal to people in many different ways simultaneously.

Part of theatre's appeal is social: It's a good place to be part of a great event. Part of its appeal is sensuous, for theatre pleases the senses through the talent of its actors, the spectacle of its visual display (scenery, costumes, lighting), and the beauty of its language and music. It appeals, too, by engaging the imagination with its stories and characters, which offer us experiences we have never had—and may never have—but which we recognize as possible: exotic yet familiar, good and evil, funny and sad. And theatre appeals intellectually because it engages the audience with the issues relevant to people. The immediacy of theatre is exciting because it is happening now, right in front of us, not recorded and projected for us to view.

Theatre is both a performance and an art. Most of today's theoretical work sees theatre as a kind of performance; earlier theories saw it as a kind of art. Both views are correct. By shifting between the two perspectives, we can understand more about the theatre than would be possible from either one alone.

FIGURE 1.1

Street Performance

Theatrical moments abound around the world. The leaning statue performs in Chicago; the mud couple perform in Madrid. No matter where the street performers work, they create a makeshift "stage" in hopes of earning money.

THEATRE AS PERFORMANCE

An activity in which some people do something while other people watch is a performance.

Many different kinds of performance exist, on a continuum from humdrum and everyday to formal and special. People perform in everyday life—that is, they shift their actions, and sometimes even their appearance, depending on what they are doing and for whom. For example, they might dress and behave one way when applying for a loan but dress and behave differently when competing in a triathlon. They may perform many informal roles in life—student, parent, athlete, and consumer. These informal roles are constantly shifting because people change their behavior for other people in certain situations.

On the other hand, some performances in life are formal and clearly structured, and may seem even more special because they do not happen every day. In such performances as religious services and weddings, there are usually agreed-on sequences of events and predetermined sets of words. In games and sports, there are rules that must be followed and time constraints that must be observed. More highly structured still are such performances as circuses and fairs, where people come together on special occasions to watch trained people do things for their enjoyment as audience. Most formal of all are performances of the sort found in theatre, opera, and dance, for, in these instances, people gather to watch specially trained people perform in highly structured works of art—hence the name performing arts to describe this special group.

Traits Shared by Performances

All performances, both informal and formal, share certain traits. They have:

- Doers (performers, actors)
- Something done (a speech, ritual, or play)
- Watchers (spectators, audiences)
- Performance sites (a stadium, church, theatre, or street)
- Movement through time (beginnings and ends)

In a fight between spectators at a hockey game, the fighters are the doers (performers or actors); fighting is the something done; the crowd that turns its attention from the ice to watch the fight is the audience, the watchers or spectators; the performance site is the stands where the fight is taking place. The fight begins and ends. In a theatrical performance, the actors do a play for an audience, usually in a theatre building, and the performance takes time.

Immediate and Ephemeral The relationship between the doers and the watchers leads to one of performance's greatest appeals—its immediacy. Because it happens in real time, with the performer and spectators brought together in the event, performance has a compelling sense of "now."

The same interaction that gives live performance this power of immediacy, however, also makes it ephemeral—fleeting, nonrecoverable. In performances, as in life, events happen and are gone, never to be recaptured. Although a storyteller (another kind of performer) may repeat a story for different audiences, the storyteller is a human being and not a machine. For this reason, each time a storyteller works, the performance is different, the more so because audiences affect performance and audiences change at every performance.

An exception to this generalization is when performances exist in such media as radio, film, television, and video. Such recorded performances exist physically on film stock as images or as electronic impulses and so can be recovered exactly as they were made and repeated unchanged many times. Live performances do not leave a record. Exact copies do not exist. They cannot be played again and again without change. When the moment in performance is gone, it is entirely gone. Thus, performance is ephemeral.

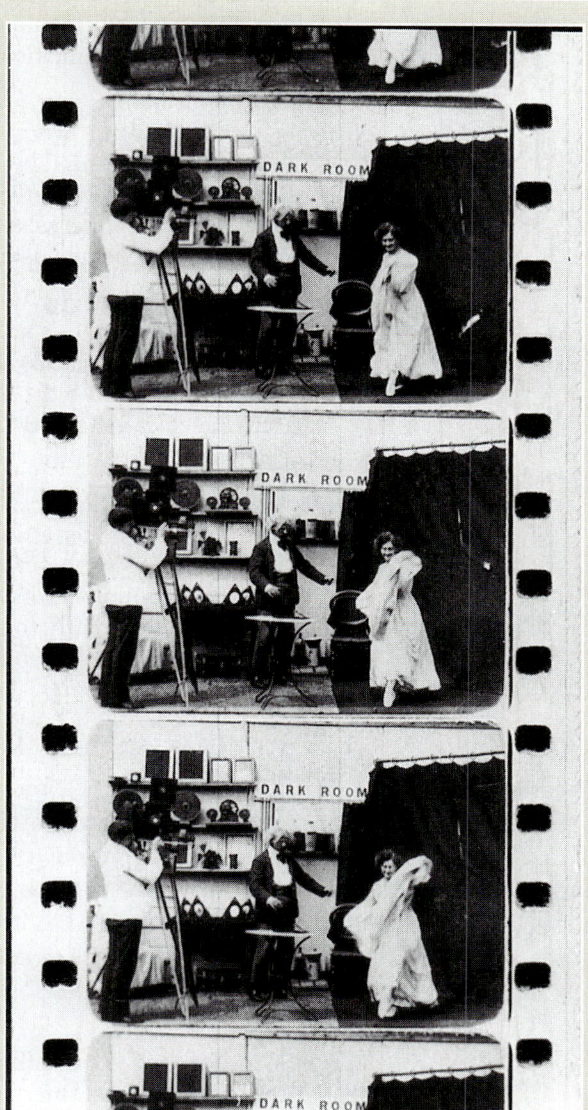

FIGURE 1.2

Film

Film, like theatre, often uses actors and scripts; unlike theatre, it gives its audiences projected images, not actual people. Film, unlike theatre, can be shown repeatedly without change.

Traits Causing Differences among Performances

Different types of performances, although sharing some traits, do not share all; that is, performances are not identical. They differ according to their:

- Purposes (the reasons for which they are done)

  Church services are held so that people can worship; games, so that someone can win; auctions, so that people can exchange goods and money.

- Relationships between doers and watchers

  At spectator sports, the watchers (fans) interact often with one another—talking, buying drinks—but they seldom interact with the players, except indirectly, to scream at a player's mistake or to cheer for a score. At a parade, on the other hand, watchers interact often and directly—waving, smiling. Spectators may watch for a while or even leave to do other things, coming back only in time to catch the end of the parade. In a recorded performance (radio, film, TV), performers and spectators aren't even at the same site: They don't occupy the same time or place and *so cannot interact*.

- Organizing principles (the reasons performances begin and end and seem all to be part of the same event)
  Auctions are organized by the things to be bought and sold; they begin when the auctioneer holds up the first item for sale and end when the last item has been sold. Church services are organized neither by rules nor by items to be sold but by a schedule determined by custom, symbolism, and doctrine.
- Self-awareness (the degree to which the people involved know they are at a performance and why)
  In street fights, spectators do not come together purposefully; they encounter the fight by accident. But people come to a boxing match or circus specifically to watch trained people perform. Boxing matches and circuses, then, are self-aware in a way that street fights are not.

Obviously, none of these traits (purpose, relationship, organizing principles, and self-awareness) is better than another; each is simply different, and from different combinations of these differences come different types of performances. A final, extended example of one kind of performance—**ritual**—may clarify how traits can combine differently to produce a kind of performance.

Rituals share many elements across cultures. They often incorporate such elements as masks, costumes, dance, music, and some sort of text, although the texts are often improvised and transmitted orally rather than in writing. Rituals usually have as their purpose some sort of cultural outcome—to heal, to honor, to mourn. An identifying element is the community bonding of those present; that is, one of the results of a ritual is to bind members of a community together. Such bonding is probably enhanced because ritual lacks any clear separation between performers and audience—those attending participate regularly and directly in the activities. In addition, rituals often lack a dedicated space and can take place over an extended period of time.

Summing Up

Theatre is a kind of performance that shares some traits with other sorts of performances: It has doers and watchers, a place of performance, and movement through time; it is immediate and ephemeral. Although resembling other kinds of performances, it is not identical with any of them; it has its own purposes, relationships, principles, degree of self-awareness, and relation to time.

Spotlight

Life/Art/Performance: *Frost/Nixon*

President Richard Nixon resigned in disgrace in 1974 over the crime called "Watergate." In 1977, the British journalist David Frost interviewed Nixon on television about his presidency—many hours of tape were cut down to four 90-minute shows. In 2006, dramatist Peter Morgan turned the story of those interviews into a play, *Frost/Nixon*. In 2008, director Ron Howard turned the play into a film, using Morgan's script and the same two actors who had played Frost and Nixon in London and New York.

A chain of life, art, and performance was thus forged: Hours of interviews were shaped into four TV shows; the televised interviews and their backgrounds were turned into a play; the play was turned into a movie. At the heart of the play was what National Public Radio critic Bob Mondello called "a David and Goliath mismatch" based on the idea that Frost was a TV lightweight, Nixon a power hitter: "It could almost have been called Froth-Nixon." It also, according to Ben Brantley of the *New York Times*, "blithely rejiggered and rearranged facts and chronology," including "the show's high point, a late-night phone call Frost receives from a drunken Nixon," a "pure fabrication."

Ron Howard's film used Morgan's script but was seen as different from the play. Manohla Dargis, also from the *New York Times*, found it "a talkathon embellished with camera movements." Mondello, however, cited Howard's "semi-documentary approach, [which] has the effect of giving Frost more heft on screen. . . ." To Mondello, it was less the supposedly lightweight Frost who brought Nixon to near-tears and a near-admission of guilt than television itself—"that unblinking eye. . . ." He pointed out that the play made the same point intellectually, but the film made it visually and in close-ups, "theater being a medium of words, and film a medium of images. . . ."

There is no question that the original interviews, the play, and the film were effective. Terms like "theatrical smackdown," "briskly entertaining," and "the aura of a boxing bout" were used. Supposedly real events, therefore, were turned into successful art, both theatrical and cinematic, in which "larger-than-life seems truer-to-life than merely life-size ever could." (Brantley)

But were the televised interviews of 1977 "real" events, or were they, too, art? Surely the winnowing of thirty hours to six comprised manipulation, compression, pointing, "dramatizing"—art.

Were, then, the unedited thirty hours of taped interviews the "reality?" Were Frost and Nixon any less performers in them than the actors in the film and the play? Both Frost and Nixon were paid well for those hours; both had reputations at stake. When were they not performing? Were they ever in their adult lives not performing? Where in the chain of life, art, and performance was their "reality"?

THEATRE AS ART

In addition to being a kind of performance, theatre is also a kind of art. Just as there are many different kinds of performances, there are many different kinds of art—poetry, novel, painting, sculpture, architecture, music, dance, theatre, to mention only the most obvious.

Traits Shared by Arts

Just as all performances share some traits, all arts, however different they may be in some ways, share certain traits. For example, all art:

- Is artificial
  That is, art is made rather than natural (existing in nature). This idea is at first difficult to grasp because we often prize art for how closely it resembles nature, thrilling to a portrait or a painting precisely because it so closely resembles the thing it copies. Still, an artist makes art; it does not just happen.
- Stands alone
  Art may have but does not need any practical use in real life. An advertising jingle may be arresting and tuneful, but it is not normally considered a work of art, because its purpose is to sell something. For many, a piano sonata has no practical use in the world and may not even be hummable, but it is an example of musical art.
- Is self-aware
  Artists know in a general way what they are trying to do, and they possess a preparation and a discipline that allow them, within limits, to accomplish what they attempt.
- Produces a certain kind of response
  The response is aesthetic: An aesthetic response includes an appreciation of beauty and some understanding that goes beyond the merely intellectual or the merely entertaining.

Traits Causing Differences among Arts

Although all arts share certain traits, they also differ in certain ways, and it is these differences that allow us to distinguish among the kinds of art. Arts differ in:

- Their relationship with time and space
  Some arts unfold through time; for example, music or novels require time to move from their beginnings to their ends. Other arts exist in space. A building or a piece of sculpture occupies space and does not move from a beginning to an end over time; it is best seen when a person walks around it, looking at it from several sides.
- Their principles of organization
  Some arts are organized by stories; in them, lifelike characters seem to be thinking and talking and doing things very much the way people do them

in real life. Other arts do not use stories but instead are organized by patterned sounds (music) or patterned colors (painting).

- Their idea of audience
  Novels and paintings, for example, assume they will be enjoyed by solitary individuals; opera and dance, on the other hand, assume that groups of people will assemble to enjoy them. The ways by which arts reach their audiences also differ.
- Their mode of presentation
  Some arts, such as novels, are transmitted by the printed page; others, like film, rely on mechanically produced images; still others, like opera, dance, and theatre, require live performers in the presence of a live audience.

FIGURE 1.3
Choices
Artists make quite different production choices. While realistic approaches are often seen in the theatre, this production of *Big Love* from Virginia Commonwealth University makes abstract choices.

Theatre's Relationship with Other Arts

Theatre's relationship with other arts is complex. Sometimes it contains them, other times it merges with them, and often it transforms other arts for its own purposes (and vice versa). Scenery and costumes routinely use techniques of painting and sculpture, and plays so often include songs and dances that we have the expressions *theatre music* and *theatre dance*. Works such as *Porgy and Bess* or *Sweeney Todd* so completely merge opera with musical theatre that they are performed by both theatre companies and opera companies, and songs such as "The Impossible Dream" become famous simply as songs, having lost all association with the play in which they first appeared.

Sometimes, too, the same story rests at the center of several different arts. *Romeo and Juliet,* for example, has been staged as a play, a ballet, an opera, several films, and *West Side Story,* a Broadway musical. In each case, the artists made quite different choices, selecting from *Romeo and Juliet* those elements that could be best communicated through their own art. For opera the composer selected those moments best communicated through music; for dance the choreographer selected the moments best communicated through movement; and so on. Such choices focus the audience's attention in different ways.

Shakespeare's play leads us to watch and listen to the actor speak Shakespeare's poetic dialogue, but opera leads us to listen to the music, perhaps barely following the story, and dance may ask us to watch movement only, almost ignoring story and character.

Summing Up

Theatre resembles other arts in being artificial and self-aware and in intending to evoke an aesthetic response rather than to produce an immediately useful item. It differs from other arts in its relation to time and space, its principles of organization, its anticipated audience, and its mode of presentation, and it has a complicated relationship with many other arts.

THEATRE AS PERFORMING ART

From what we have examined about theatre as a particular kind of performance and a special kind of art, we can now say more about the major characteristics of theatre.

- Theatre uses a special kind of performer—the actor.

  An actor is a performer who impersonates, that is, who uses the pronoun *I* and means somebody other than him- or herself. Thus, actors differ from street fighters, for example, who neither intend to perform nor pretend to be someone other than themselves. Actors differ even from jugglers and music-video stars, who do not say "I" and mean someone other than themselves.

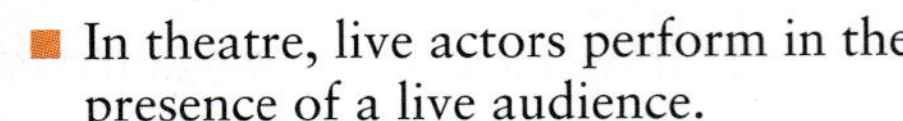

- In theatre, live actors perform in the presence of a live audience.

  A live actor in the sense used here is not the opposite of a dead actor but rather an actor who is in the physical presence of the audience. Thus, theatre actors differ not only from other kinds of performers but also from other kinds of actors. Theatre actors differ from actors in film or television, for example, because in those media the picture or image of the actor (rather than the actual actor) is offered to the audience.

  Theatre actors must both impersonate and be physically present, for it is these two traits—**impersonation** and **presence**—that separate them from various other performers, on the one hand, and from actors in other media, on the other.

Craig Schwartz

FIGURE 1.4

The Actor as Performer

The actor is a performer who impersonates a character who is different from himself or herself. Here, in *Minsky's* at the Center Theatre Group, an actor "sells a song," that is, performing a song as a character in a musical. This character is partly defined by clothing.

- Theatre is both immediate and ephemeral.

  Because in theatre actors and audiences share both space and time, theatre is both an immediate and **ephemeral art**: that is, it has a strong sense of *now*, and it cannot be repeated exactly.

- Theatre depends on action (which for now we can think of as stories and characters) to organize and bind the theatrical event.

  We can think of stories as worlds created for artistic purposes, worlds that resemble (but are distinct from) the actual world in which we live: *virtual worlds*, an expression that recalls the invented worlds of the computer's virtual reality. Part of the reason that theatre's virtual worlds resemble our own real world so convincingly is that these virtual worlds are inhabited by **characters**. Characters might be thought of as virtual people because characters are artistic creations intended to resemble people. Well-created characters are often so compelling, so lifelike, that we feel as though we know them personally. We may even begin to talk of them as though they were real people. But characters are not real people; they are created by a playwright for the play, just as any virtual world is created.

- Theatre's virtual world is more intense and concentrated than the world in which we live.

  Because everything on stage has been selected and placed there by someone for a purpose, everything on stage is important—it has meaning for an audience. Therefore, everything on stage gains a significance that it may lack in real life. For example, it is not unusual for theatre audiences to be captivated by an onstage scene in which an actor cooks a meal or uses a

FIGURE 1.5

Live and Immediate

Theatre actors and audiences share both space and time. The stories unfold in the audience's presence in the here and now. This immediacy sets theatre apart from the recorded performances of film and television. This moment is from Virginia Commonwealth University's staging of *The Civil War*.

washing machine. Obviously, cooking or using a washing machine is not very interesting in real life, but, on stage, these simple actions can provide insight because theatre transforms them from ordinary to meaningful activities.

- The theatre uses a real performance space, but usually with artificial (that is, made-for-the-purpose) settings.

Theatre uses a defined performance space that is physically in the presence of the audience and limited by existing architecture. It can give us representations—replicas—of actual places (e.g., outer space), but it can give them only on a scale appropriate to its own scale and to the actors working in or in front of the scene. Film, on the other hand, can take us anywhere and show us images of actual places, even on a vast scale (the Grand Canyon, outer space). Because film shows images of places rather than real places, it can range far in its presentation of objects and spaces.

Many kinds of activities easily shown on film (horse races, car crashes) are difficult to present on stage. Film and television can show not only races and crashes, but also selective close-ups that direct our attention and heighten the impact of the events: speeding hooves, snorting nostrils, exploding gas tanks, collapsing fenders. Theatre has no exact equivalent to film's close-up on stage, but theatre can heighten focus by the use of staging, lighting, and sound.

Theatre audiences love spectacle, like horse races presented on stage, even though they know they are seeing an obvious trick; they seem to appreciate the skill required to create the illusion. Indeed, it is one of theatre's paradoxes that the very restrictions of theatre's real space seem to increase the audience's enjoyment of difficult scenes produced there.

- Theatre proceeds at its own pace through time.

We cannot play a performance again, nor can we play it backward, nor can we fast-forward it to see how it will come out. We cannot put a theatrical performance aside for a while and pick it up later. If we don't like a performance, we cannot jump to another station or change channels. If we don't understand a moment in the theatre, we cannot stop and go back to it, hoping to grasp its significance the second or third time through. In other words, as members of a theatre audience, we do not control the way the theatrical performance unfolds as we can control the pace at which we watch a DVD or read a poem or a book. For better or worse, the theatre performance proceeds at its own pace and must be followed at that pace.

- Theatre is not a thing (an object) but a process, a system of constantly altering relationships among actor, action, audience, time, and space.

Changing even one of these relationships changes the whole. We might be tempted to think, for example, that a play in the theatre and a play on film have only mechanical differences, but a filmed play has no live actor and can be stopped and replayed, and the camera "sees" for the audience.

These changed performance-audience relationships change the whole process.

- Theatre is lifelike, but it is not life.

Because theatre is an art, it is artificial—made by artists. Theatre's artificiality, however, is sometimes more difficult to see than the artificiality of other arts because theatre is also a performance. Theatre uses real human beings pretending to be other human beings engaged in actions that look very much like those we see in life. So convincing is it that sometimes people have confused a theatre performance with real life. There are many apparently true stories about people attending their first play who have rushed on stage to save a character who is being threatened, like the man who tried to save Desdemona from Othello.

Theatre in fact sometimes seems so lifelike that it has often been used as a metaphor for life. The most famous example of the metaphor is probably Shakespeare's "All the world's a stage / and all the men and women merely players," but there are others, such as "This world is a comedy to those that think, a tragedy to those that feel. "We need to remember, however, that a metaphor is a special kind of comparison, one that implies but does not use the words *like* or *as*. We know that the real sense of these quotations is that the world is like a comedy or like a tragedy. And, clearly, the metaphor comparing life and theatre is apt.

Life and theatre move forward through time. Just as life has a past, a present, and a future, plays have a beginning, middle, and end, and in

Jason Ayers

FIGURE 1.6

A Heightened Vision

Theatre artists create worlds more intense and concentrated than the world in which we live our everyday lives. Here, two quite different worlds require actors to create a reality appropriate to the play: (left), *Lilly's Purple Plastic Purse* at the Alabama Shakespeare Festival and (right) *Mother Courage and Her Children* at Theatre South Carolina.

plays, as in life, these stages are defined through time. Life and theatre exist in space; that is, men and women in life take up space and move through space, like actors on a stage. Life and theatre have men and women doing and saying things: While some people act and speak, others listen and watch. Those who act and speak in life are *like* actors in the theatre, whereas those who listen and watch in life are *like* audiences in the theatre. And the lives of real people that we know often don't seem very different from the actions or stories that we see when we go to a play.

Despite such similarities, however, life and theatre are different in many ways, only a few of which need be suggested. Most lives last for years; most theatre lasts a few hours. Life often seems diffuse, confused, and inexplicable; theatre appears concentrated, orderly, and meaningful. Life may be dangerous, but theatre is safe in a special way. Although theatre may bring us up close to a human activity (like a murder) that is terrifyingly *like* life in its immediacy, we as audience are separated from it and so can watch it in relative safety, experience it without physical danger.

Spotlight

Study Alert

There is one Web site, supported by the authors of *The Enjoyment of Theatre*, that students should visit regularly: www.theatrestudyguides.com. There students will find sample true/false questions (along with the correct answers), study tips, and sample essay questions to answer and/or think about. There is a Study Guide for each of the twenty-one chapters.

In addition, a regular visit to the *New York Times* theatre Web site will lead to recent articles, reviews, and video clips or slide shows about important theatre artists and events: http://theater.nytimes.com/pages/theater/index.html.

Four other sites will provide informative material related to the first ten chapters of *The Enjoyment of Theatre*. Information about the actors' union can be found at http://www.actorsequity.org/; the directors' and choreographers' union, at http://www.sdcweb.org/; the scenic artists' union at http://www.usa829.org/; and the professional stagehands' union, the International Alliance of Theatrical Stage Employees, Moving Picture Technicians, Artists and Allied Crafts of the United States, at http://www.iatse-intl.org/home.html. Each of these sites can be used to learn more about the arts and crafts of theatre in America.

KEY TERMS

Check your understanding against this list. Brief definitions are included in the Glossary; persons are page-referenced in the Index.

aesthetic response 8
art 8
audience 4
characters 11
criticism 1
ephemeral art 11
impersonation 10
performance 4
performing arts 4
presence 10
ritual 6
theory 1

CHAPTER

2

Theatre

The Performing Audience: Three Roles

OBJECTIVES

When you have completed this chapter, you should be able to

- Describe ways in which theatre audiences are social
- Explain how the size and arrangement of audiences affect their ability to be social units
- Explain how permission and self-image promote the social quality of audiences
- Explain how theatre audiences are interactive
- Explain why theatre audiences can serve as an index to culture
- Describe how business and theatre interact
- Explain the fundamental tension between theatre as art and theatre as business
- Describe funding patterns in today's theatre in the United States

Theatre is not only a performance and an art; it is also an expression of the time and place that produce it, an expression of its culture. Often, too, theatre is a business, and, in our own time, a very big business.

As keys to culture and engines of finance, audiences are central to understanding both how theatre works as an expression of its culture and how it works as a business. For this reason, we begin by discussing this important part of every theatrical performance, its audience.

Tim Donahue

FIGURE 2.1

Social Theatre

Going to the theatre can be an exciting shared experience. This sense of a special collective experience is critical to unleashing the full power of theatre.

THEATRE AS PERFORMING ART: THE ROLE OF THE AUDIENCE

Social Audiences

Most people enjoy the companionship of others—they are social beings who enjoy feeling they are members of a group. Every good theatre audience is a group in which the response of each audience member depends both on the performance and on the responses of other members of the group. If a theatre audience fails to coalesce as a group, the performance itself will be less successful. A sense of groupness in the audience, then, is critical to unleashing the full power of the theatre. Although there are no hard-and-fast rules about how to build an audience's sense of itself as a group, several factors are at work.

Size and Arrangement Both size and seating arrangement are important. One person in a theatre audience is not enough. To enhance a performance, a theatregoer's response needs to be amplified, joined by the responses of others. Forty thousand people in a theatre won't work either, because so many people can't relate intimately with the stage. Although there's no magic number for a theatre audience, some numbers are clearly too small and others are too large. Probably the number is about right if the audience fits well within the space, and each person can easily hear and see the performance. The best audience space for a theatre is, therefore, one small enough to define an audience (help it see itself as part of a group) but not so small as to confine it (make it physically uncomfortable). A hundred people in a very large theatre will feel uncomfortable, but the same number in a small space will easily enjoy the play. Also, the arrangement of seats interacts with the number of spectators and the size of space to affect the audience's sense of itself as a social unit.

FIGURE 2.2

Stage-to-Audience Relationship

Audience size and seating arrangement are important. An audience member's experience is amplified by the presence and responses of others in the audience. Audiences at small "studio" productions enjoy a special intimacy. Here the actress is surrounded by the audience, seated on four sides.

Permission There is an unspoken agreement in theatre between actors and audiences that what the actors embody on stage is not real life and that it is permissible to respond to it in unusual ways (laughing out loud at a character who is crying, for example, or applauding when a sympathetic character shoots one who threatens). This agreement gives audiences permission to respond in safety to whatever transpires on the stage; that is, no audience member will be harmed by onstage threats or sanctioned for responding to onstage actions. This shared permission contributes to shaping the audience into a social unit. Permission is thus a social phenomenon that bolsters theatre-going as a social experience.

Self-Image Each theatre audience develops a self-image, which also enhances the audience's sense of itself as a group. An audience's self-image influences its behavior, including its dress. Part of the self-image comes from society's expectations. Members of a theatre audience do not wear pajamas, although they watch television in them comfortably. Part of the self-image comes from specific expectations set up by the particular theatre or production, often as a way to enhance the enjoyment of a performance. For a special celebration in the theatre or a special play, for example, the theatre might encourage audience members to dress formally, but for another kind of play at a different theatre, audience members might be encouraged to wear T-shirts and jeans. These two

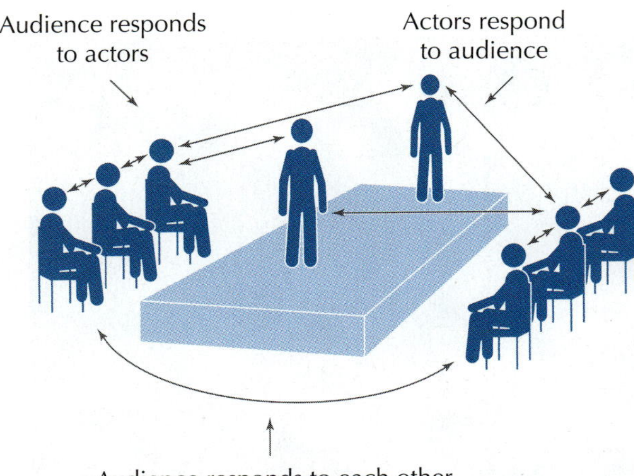

FIGURE 2.3

Theatre's Interactive Nature

Audience members affect one another; actors affect and are affected by the audience.

audiences would likely expect different experiences from their night out at the theatre, and they will behave accordingly.

Interactive Audiences

Audiences are not just social units; they are *interactive* social units, with individual audience members interacting both with the performers on stage and with one another. Obviously, no one can say for certain precisely how an audience will respond during a play or how any individual in an audience will respond at a given moment. Performances differ, audiences differ, and individuals in audiences differ.

When performances are successful, however, most members of the audience behave similarly much of the time. That an audience is a group rather than a collection of individuals or a mob suggests that audience members will respond to many of the same things in roughly the same ways—and indeed they do.

Audience Approval

- Applause. Audiences usually clap their hands at any point during the performance that warrants response and usually at the end of each scene or section.
- **Laughter.** When something is funny, audiences usually laugh, anything from a belly laugh to a snicker. Sometimes audiences will laugh because they're uncomfortable—nervous laughter. Actors dread hearing this kind of laughter because it shows the performance is not working.
- **Silence.** When something is sad, audiences may cry, although today's theatre audiences do not shed tears as easily as they once did—or as easily as they now laugh. Although we associate applause, laughter, and tears with success, silence is often a sign of a successful performance: "You could hear a pin drop." Especially at the end of a well-performed serious play, silence is often the audience's response, as if applause were too frivolous for the moment.
- **Curtain Call.** At the end of a play, actors take a bow for as long as the applause continues (although to milk an audience—try to make the audience extend its applause—is considered bad form).
- Standing Ovation. To show exceptional approval, audiences may stand and applaud.
- Encore. In past times, audiences might clap so long that actors gave an encore—a repeated piece—just as many musicians do today.

Audience Disapproval

- **Withhold Applause.** To show disapproval, audiences may simply withhold the usual responses of approval.
- **Noise.** More likely, though, they will become noisy. Coughing, shuffling feet, whispering, and rattling programs are all signs of unease or boredom; each person may think he or she is being quiet, but many people moving at once, however unconsciously, can become quite loud—and horribly revealing.
- **Protest.** More aggressive signs of disapproval come when members of the audience boo or leave the theatre. In some ages, audiences were even more aggressive, yelling at the actors and even throwing things on stage.

Joan Marcus Photography

FIGURE 2.4

Audience Response

Theatre, because of its immediacy, can have powerful effects on audiences. This moment from the Broadway revival of *South Pacific* is romantic and isolated, a contrast to the boisterous tone of other moments in this classic musical.

An audience's disapproval most often signals a bad performance (about which we say more in Part II), but it may signal instead an audience that fails to enter into the created world prepared by the playwright and the actors. Occasionally such an audience just doesn't understand theatre well enough to enjoy it. More often, though, audience members refuse to enter the created world because they are alienated from the particular performance. Sometimes they are encountering a performance they did not expect from reading the play's title or the reviews of the performance. More likely, members of the audience are embarrassed, shocked, or angered to find a play whose political, religious, or ethical views they deplore. They may be reacting to particular scenes whose language, violence, or nudity they find shocking.

THEATRE AS CULTURAL EXPRESSION: THE ROLE OF THE AUDIENCE

Culture

The idea of culture is a complex one. For our purposes, **culture** is that set of beliefs, values, and social behavior that a group shares. People have called the culture of the twenty-first century a consumer culture (one that values the acquisition of goods), a popular culture (one that prefers reality TV, hip-hop, and graphic novels to ballet, opera, and Jane Austen), a communication culture (one saturated with such means for sharing ideas as texting and blogging), and a mass culture (one produced by the media and intended for the greatest number of people). The point is that there are always several layers of culture—cultures within cultures. Still, it is possible to distinguish in a general way U.S. culture from, say, Afghan culture or Ugandan culture. One writer has argued, "Language is culture." As we use the word *culture,* then, we are trying to suggest a complex web of traits that compete, merge, and exist alongside one another and that constitute a recognizable cluster—a gestalt or worldview.

Culture and Audience

In preparing their art, theatre artists must make decisions that are meant to touch the audience's culture—to enhance its enjoyment by touching its central concerns. In deciding what play to produce, for example, producers will consider the needs of the likely audience; in deciding where to produce it, they will match the size of the likely audience with the configuration of available spaces. Playwrights must write plays that will bring real audiences with real cultures into the theatre and affect them once they get there. Designers and directors must figure out ways to guide the responses of audiences through visual cues, so that the play "means" for audiences what they want it to mean; that is, they must provide visual clues that give the play appropriate cultural resonances. Actors must imagine how audiences will respond to moments of performance and then perform in ways that prompt appropriate responses, based in part on shared cultural understandings of vocal and physical meaning ("body language"). When an audience has a shared culture with the performance, they have a shared context in which to experience and understand it.

Mirror of Culture

By studying both the choices of theatre artists and the responses of the audience, we can glimpse something about the world existing outside theatre—the culture. Through the choices made by theatre artists, we can begin to infer what they think their audiences—and therefore the larger culture—seem to want or need. It is in this way, and because of these linkages, that theatre, probably more than any other art, expresses and partakes of the culture of which it is a part. For such reasons, theatre has been called, metaphorically, a "mirror of life." But we must be cautious in any conclusions that we draw, for several reasons.

First, theatre is at the *center* of some cultures but peripheral to others. Cultures in which theatre was central include those of Greece in the fifth century BCE and of western Europe in the Middle Ages. These theatre performances were part of major civic and religious festivals that were held on important days. At these times, the entire community was involved, and most citizens attended and supported the festivals, including the theatrical performances embedded in them.

FIGURE 2.5

Theatre and Culture

By studying the choices of theatre artists, we can glimpse something of the world existing outside the theatre—the culture. Audiences attending this production of *A Midsummer Night's Dream* eavesdrop on a dream.

Today, however, most Americans don't attend theatre. Many can't afford it, some don't have access to it, and a few don't like it. Were we to study theatre in an attempt to understand the culture of fifth-century BCE Greece or western Europe during the Middle Ages, we could be fairly confident that the audience in the theatre fairly represented most living in that same time and place (the culture). Studying theatre to grasp traits of our own culture, however, would require us to remember that theatre now appeals to only a limited group, and so its audience may represent only a small subset of today's larger culture. Still, by the very act of asking the question, "Who goes to the theatre and why?" we can glean something about a culture's values and interests.

Second, although theatre is a "mirror of life," we must remember that a mirror can be distorting instead of accurate. A bathroom mirror shows a person his or her physical appearance, and some theatres do seem to show life more or less as it is lived at a particular time and place. A fun-house mirror, however, stretches, compresses, and otherwise distorts the image, and some theatres show the audience just such a distorted image of itself, highlighting its horrors or poking fun at its foibles—interpreting and critiquing rather than merely presenting the culture. The point is that theatre can offer important insights into people and cultures so long as inferences are drawn carefully, cautiously, and tentatively.

Third, changes in audiences, theatres, and cultures are connected. When performances are free or inexpensive, people from all economic classes can attend, a

Summing Up

Because theatre audiences are interactive social units, theatre artists shape performances in ways calculated to achieve certain responses from them. For the same reason, we can use theatre as one probe into the culture of a particular time and place.

Craig Schwartz

FIGURE 2.6
Mirror of Life
Theatre can offer important insights into people and cultures. The mirror may show a raucous interlude in a zany musical (*Minsky's* from Center Theatre Group, Los Angeles.)

circumstance that influences the choice of play, for example. When a single ticket costs several hundred dollars (as they sometimes do in today's theatres), affluent patrons will probably be overrepresented, again influencing the choice of plays. When men and women are equally free in a culture, both can be expected in theatre in roughly equal numbers, but in cultures in which women are thought to need protection (in the 1800s in the United States, for example), gender differences within audiences may be striking. Race and ethnic heritage may also figure significantly, both because all cultures do not prize theatres equally and because some people may be segregated or denied access to theatres based on race or ethnicity. Then, too, theatre audiences expect different things from the performance, often because of their level of education. Audiences are to a degree self-selected—that is, some people will want musicals; others, comedies; still others, plays that are politically challenging or sexually free. All such factors must be weighed before generalizing about the relationship between a theatre's audience and its culture.

THEATRE AS BUSINESS: THE ROLE OF THE AUDIENCE

Just as audiences are important to theatre as art and cultural expression, so audiences are important to theatre as business. In a commercial theatre (that is, one run as a business), the audience pays the bill. For much of theatre's early history, theatre was not a business—that is, it was not a commercial opportunity for people to make a living. Rather, theatre was a communal celebration in which volunteers did most of the work, and bills were paid by the community or church or wealthy citizens as their religious and civic duty.

Since the Renaissance (c. 1500s), however, many theatres in the West have been a business; subsidy has given way to pay-as-you-go, and audiences have provided the money that pays the bills. Some people argue that thus theatre places too much emphasis on making a profit and not enough on artistic expression. But someone has to pay, and it has yet to be demonstrated that the effects of commercialism on theatre are worse than the effects of patronage, when a king or church subsidized performances. Other people argue that the business side of theatre should simply be ignored. But the business side of theatre cannot, in fact, be ignored. Actors, designers, and playwrights have to make a living, just like bankers and secretaries and autoworkers, so paying the bills is surely as important as other factors affecting theatrical art.

Balancing Business and Art

The role of audience in the business of theatre sets up tensions almost at once with its role in the art of theatre. As we have seen, for theatrical performance to work, a theatre audience must have a sense of itself as a social group. But a major force in theatre tugs against this idea of a coherent group, and that force is money. The economics of theatre demands that the audience be big enough to pay for the scenery and costumes, actors, support personnel, the rent on the building, the author's royalties, the maintenance of the space. A desire for profit—income over and above expenses—demands that audiences be bigger still: bigger audience, more profit. Therefore, although the art of the theatre may suggest that the best-sized audience for a particular play in a particular space is two hundred, the business of the theatre may demand an audience of three thousand, a size that will almost certainly degrade the audience as a social unit. Some tension between theatre as art and theatre as business is almost inevitable. Some compromise on both sides is inescapable. Such a compromise, however, must be a careful one.

Bringing Business to Art

The language of business dominates talk about wholly unrelated fields. It is not uncommon to hear students described as *consumers* at a university, and the graduates described as the university's *products*. We routinely speak of *spending* or *saving* or even *banking* something as elusive as time. We ask governments and doctors to be more *efficient,* and we expect agents for athletes to *negotiate* megasalaries and advertising contracts. The talk and decisions around theatres

Craig Schwartz

FIGURE 2.7

Theatre and Money

Large-scale productions such as musicals often require that the box office generate enough income to pay for the performers, the orchestra, scenery, lighting, costumes, and author royalties. Here, a moment from *My Fair Lady* (Center Theatre Group, Los Angeles).

now, not surprisingly, are as much about profit, loss, bottom line, and labor relations as about the meaning of plays and the aesthetics of production.

Similarly, business executives now lead all sorts of organizations, including those not usually considered businesses, like charities or not-for-profit arts organizations. Such people bring with them the outlook and practices of corporations. Their skills in policymaking and management often allow them to transfer from one sort of enterprise to another: first CEO of a corporation, then governor of a state, and later president of a university or health maintenance organization. University presidents, for example, are now seldom drawn from the world of scholarship, and managers of hospitals may or may not have training in medicine. Just so, Broadway theatres are run by a loosely tied group of executives drawn mostly from business and real estate, many of whom have little experience in theatre.

Businesses now take considerable interest in the arts for their contributions to the quality of life as well as possible commercial benefit. They, or the foundations growing out of them, give major support to the visual, musical, and performing arts. A luxury home builder, for example, underwrites weekly radio broadcasts of the Metropolitan Opera, and the Ford Foundation funds a program to support emerging playwrights. Businesses routinely support theatres in cities around the country, buying blocks of tickets and advertisements in the programs, awarding grants for specific projects, or even sponsoring selected productions. Not only are such ventures believed to be excellent advertisement for products, but they are also thought to be good ways of demonstrating that businesses are good corporate citizens. Event-related spending by audience members for such things as hotels, restaurants, parking, souvenirs, and refreshments makes a considerable impact on local businesses. As a bonus, businesses have come to believe that having a professional symphony, ballet, or theatre company in a city makes it easier to recruit managers and executives.

Changing Patterns in Business and Theatre

Just as audiences changed over time to embody a changing culture, so, too, has the business of theatre shifted to embody changes in business. For example, when businesses outside the theatre were small and often home based, theatre companies were centered on one or two families who put on plays and shared expenses, income, and work. Such sharing companies were among the earliest ways that theatre organized itself to do business.

Shareholder Companies When cities grew large enough to house a theatre company more or less permanently, several unrelated people formed larger and more complex **sharing companies**, with the most valuable members of the company owning several shares and the least valuable owning a share or less. Members of such companies tended to specialize, performing only certain kinds of roles or undertaking only certain tasks of production, such as playwriting or costuming. Such companies even hired other people, paying them a salary rather than allowing them to join the company. The theatre company in which Shakespeare worked was of this sort. He owned shares in the company as well as in the building in which the company performed, making him (like the other shareholders) both businessman and theatre artist.

By the late 1800s, business outside of theatre had changed its ways of organizing, and so had theatre. In such countries as Germany, theatre had come to be thought of as a cost of government, and so all major German cities subsidized—and continue to subsidize—theatres, allowing tax dollars to join with ticket sales to pay expenses. In several countries, notably France and England, government-supported theatres existed alongside commercial theatres.

The Commercial Producer in the United States The United States set a different pattern. Here, private enterprise mostly ruled. The old sharing system, in which theatre artists participated directly in the business of the company, gave way to a system of for-profit corporations headed by entrepreneurs who saw theatre mostly as a way to make money. Businesspeople (as distinct from theatre people) began to invest money, sometimes in a theatre company but more often in a single production, and they expected to recover their investment, with interest, from ticket sales. When, outside the theatre, great monopolies formed in railroads and steel, and the so-called robber barons (such as the Carnegies and the Rockefellers) dominated the economy in the United States, theatres also became monopolies headed by powerful men. In New York City and on the road, these **producers** controlled theatre buildings and the productions playing in them. The commercial producer typically found investors, planned and ran the show, and paid the theatrical personnel (who then became mere employees). Ticket sales were needed not only to pay the bills but also to make a profit for the investors, who were no longer theatre artists themselves. As ticket sales alone proved unable to equal the rising costs of production, paid advertising and public relations became an important part of theatre's business, just as they had become important tools of other businesses.

FIGURE 2.8

Commercial Theatre

Musical theatre is the most popular kind of theatre in the United States today. Broadway ticket prices for this production of *Hair* range from $122 to $37, depending on seat location. For *Hair*, "premium seating," the best seats in the orchestra section, was priced at $252.

Joan Marcus Photography

Spotlight

Perseverance Theatre

Macbeth (2004) was set in the context of southeast Alaska's indigenous Tlingit culture and was performed by an all–Alaskan native cast. This piece later toured the state and, in March 2007, was remounted a third time for performances at the new Smithsonian National Museum of the American Indian in Washington, D.C., in association with the citywide Shakespeare in Washington festival. Photo courtesy Perseverance Theatre.

Perseverance Theatre, Juneau, Alaska

Theatres are born because people feel a need for artistic expression for themselves, their communities, or some underrepresented group. That is, people start theatres to reflect a culture in which they live, as with the Perseverance Theatre in Alaska.

When Molly Smith graduated from American University, she dragged fifty old theatre seats with her back to Juneau, Alaska, determined to start a theatre. In 1979, she borrowed ten thousand dollars from her grandmother and looked around for talent. Smith has said, "If I needed an actor, I'd go into a bar and pull somebody off of a bar stool and say, 'Do ya wanna be in a play?'" She interviewed thirty-five old-timers, casting six of the best storytellers for her first production, *Pure Gold*. "They were people who'd come up with the gold rush or it was Filipinos who were working in the mines or of course it was the Native Americans, the Tlingit people, who've been there for centuries. And the audiences were hungry for it. They were hungry for it because it was part of what had drawn people to Alaska. So this theatre company was very much about really plumbing the resources of what there was in Alaska."

Perseverance Theatre began, then, from the impulse to reflect Alaska's culture. Molly Smith is now the artistic director of the Arena Stage in Washington, D.C., but the theatre she founded in Juneau still prospers.

Perseverance Theatre is now the largest not-for-profit professional theatre in Alaska. It has a budget of more than one million dollars, small when compared to other not-for-profit professional theatres in the United States. Its mission statement remains unchanged: to tap the potential of Alaska through the passionate creation and presentation of theatre. The theatre is dedicated to "engaging community, pursuing excellence, embracing risk, and inspiring self-discovery."

Perseverance has premiered more than fifty new plays by Alaskan and other American playwrights, among them *The Long Season*, a musical about the Filipino Alaskan experience, and *columbinus*, an exploration of adolescence and the phenomenon of school shootings. The 2007–08 season included two productions that reflected Alaska's culture—*Battles of Fire and Water*, based on the Russian and Tlingit wars over the land where Sitka now stands, and *8 Stars of Gold*, celebrating Alaska's fiftieth year of statehood.

Corporations Recently, the costs of production have escalated so dramatically that ticket sales and paid advertisements alone no longer generate enough money, and so the sale of film, television, and video rights has become an increasingly important source of funding. Businesspeople and mid-level managers increasingly assumed responsibility for producing theatre, bringing with them the ideas and techniques of business and management. Too, these businesspeople, lacking experience in theatre, transferred much of the artistic power—once belonging to actor-sharers—to directors and designers. The once centralized power of the producer has dispersed among others: the director, the general manager, and other co-investors, many of whom are now major entertainment corporations (like Disney) rather than, as previously, wealthy individuals.

Not-for-Profit Experiments When, in the early 1900s, government trust-busting broke up the monopolies outside theatre, forces inside theatre also broke the monopolies of the most powerful for-profit producers, and so business practices changed. Starting about fifty years ago, severe pressures on the commercial theatre led to cautious experimentation in ways of producing theatre other than as a strictly profit-making enterprise.

As a result, most professional theatre in America (not New York) is now produced by not-for-profit organizations. The contrasts between these commercial **for-profit** and **not-for-profit** professional theatres are significant:

- A commercial theatre production is formed as a business partnership to produce only one production. When that show closes, the partnership ends. A not-for-profit theatre is organized as an ongoing enterprise. It produces a series of plays each season and intends to do so indefinitely.
- Commercial productions are usually planned as open-ended runs to be performed as long as enough theatregoers buy tickets to make the run profitable. A not-for-profit theatre plans a slate of plays with a fixed number of performances allotted to each production.

Almost all of the income for commercial productions is generated by ticket sales. Not-for-profit theatres, however, generate only about 60 percent of income from ticket sales; the remainder comes mostly from donations. The federal tax code is structured to give tax breaks to not-for-profit contributors. That same code generally views commercial productions as it does any business partnership.

Not-for-profit theatres throughout the country as well as the four not-for-profit theatre organizations that produce on Broadway give the American theatre new plays, revivals of important older plays, and musicals in revival. Clearly, the quality of their offerings is high, rivaling that of the for-profit productions. Between 2000 and 2006, more than 60 percent of "Best of . . ." Tony Awards went to not-for-profit productions or not-for-profit-originated productions.

Educational Theatre **Educational theatres** are subsidized. Although the out-of-pocket costs of their productions must often be defrayed by the sale of tickets and program advertisements, the salaries of the faculty (who usually direct, design, manage, and mount the productions) are almost always paid by the university. Because the students who act and crew the productions are seldom paid, the majority of the labor costs associated with producing plays is charged to the college or university, not to the production. This substantial subsidy allows such theatres to be somewhat adventurous in their selection of plays and the ways in which they are presented.

THE NATIONAL ENDOWMENT FOR THE ARTS With an occasional exception, government funding for theatre in this country has been conspicuously absent. Therefore, one closely watched development was the establishment in 1965 of the **National Endowment for the Arts (NEA)**, whose purpose was to encourage the development of the arts throughout the country. It did so in two major ways: by establishing state arts councils as coordinating and funding units and by subsidizing some existing performance groups. To receive grants, theatres had to be organized as not-for-profit theatres, a departure from the commercial Broadway model.

The NEA continues to be controversial. Not all citizens agree that government should fund art when urgent social problems remain unsolved and unfunded. Not all citizens agree that taxpayers should pay for art that some find offensive. The latter issue led to a threatened cutoff of the NEA's funding in 1990 and 1995. Both issues promise to be debated for some time to come.

The precedent set by the NEA may help account for a relatively new phenomenon: Cities and counties are supporting theatre as a form of recreation for citizens who seek an alternative to well-established programs in sports and crafts. By contributing both advice and money, local governments strive to improve the work of local community theatres, which they view as an important resource for the participants and their audiences. Community leaders increasingly see the arts, including theatre, as important to a community's quality of life and attractiveness to newcomers and new businesses, comparable to other amenities, such as parks, libraries, and schools.

Summing Up

Since the 1500s, most theatres in the West have been run as businesses, a focus that places theatre audiences in the crucial role of providing the money needed for productions. Because the needs of theatre as business often conflict with its needs as art, compromises are necessary. Just as the values of business now pervade Western cultures, they also permeate those theatres' cultures.

KEY TERMS

Check your understanding against this list. Brief definitions are included in the Glossary; persons are page-referenced in the Index.

applause 18
culture 19
educational theatres 27
encore 18
for-profit 27
milk an audience 18
National Endowment for the Arts (NEA) 28
not-for-profit 27
producers 25
sharing companies 24
standing ovation 18

CHAPTER

3

How to Read a Play

OBJECTIVES

When you have completed this chapter, you should be able to

- List and explain Aristotle's six parts of a play
- Explain the interrelationships among the six parts
- Describe different kinds of plot
- Explain "wholeness of action"

SEEING VERSUS READING

Seeing a play and reading a play are different experiences. They require different tools and different approaches. Seeing a play is the only complete theatrical experience. Reading a play sensitively means understanding what it is and how it works.

First, a play is not theatre; that is, reading a play from a book offers an incomplete experience. Because of the incompleteness of the written text, some theatre artists talk of the play's script as a "notation" for production, others as "a pretext rather than a text." To make an analogy with music: A written play is like musical notes on a page; the performed play is like the music heard when a musician turns the notes into music. The incompleteness of the written play makes reading a play different from reading a newspaper or a novel. The newspaper and novel are both complete in themselves; their language fills them out. A play, on the other hand, is only a part—although an important part—of a different kind of experience.

Second, reading a play means understanding that playwrights create plays by making choices. The playwright, to be successful, must persuade an audience, convince it of the truth of the play. A playwright's goal is not simply to tell a story but to tell it in a certain way. The playwright, using only words, must shape characters and actions that allow actors to perform and designers to design so as to produce certain effects in audiences. Playwrights, then, are always shaping, although indirectly, the meanings and pleasures that audiences glean from the play. Both of these traits have implications for how to read a play.

Filling in the Blanks

Because the play is intended for performance, its written text leaves large areas blank. The play reader must learn to fill in these blanks through clues embedded in the text (such clues are, in fact, clues to performance). For example, in a novel, many paragraphs may be devoted to describing the place where the novel takes place; in plays, such lengthy descriptions are absent because the place of the play will be shown visually, through scenery and lighting, in the theatre. A play reader must visualize the place from clues.

Because the playwright, through choices, is constantly shaping the perception of the audience, a reader's job is to discover how. That is, a reader must locate the choices made by the playwright and from these choices try to infer what the playwright wanted to do to audiences, using actors. The task is not always easy, because the tendency of any reader is to "believe" the story, to see it as "the way things are." To guard against this tendency, a reader should remember that every play begins as a stack of blank paper and that any story can be told in several different ways, each having quite different results. It is the task of the reader to discover which way the playwright decided to tell the story and what the anticipated results of that decision are.

Thinking Critically

Reading a play means making the effort—and knowing how to make the effort—to understand the play, both how it will appear in the theatre and what choices the playwright made and why. These ideas are often

Courtesy Anita Tripathi Easterling

FIGURE 3.1
Creating the World: Environment
A script may call for a specific location or merely suggest an environment. In John Steinbeck's play, *Of Mice and Men*, a bunkhouse is the setting for a number of scenes. The reader must then imagine what this bunkhouse looks like. Here, in a production at the Virginia Stage Company, the designer presents an abstracted version of a bunkhouse.

hard to keep in mind because the written play can be read with pleasure *as if* it were self-contained, and it can be so convincing that it is hard to imagine it being any other way. But it is important to remember that the written play is only one part of theatre (a play is not self-contained) and that the play results from choices made by a playwright specifically to affect audiences in certain ways.

Reading a play, then, requires techniques of critical thinking that can be learned. In this chapter, we examine the process of play reading in three stages: preliminary work, play analysis, and organizing a coherent response.

PRELIMINARY WORK

Before beginning to read the play, some preliminary work will more than repay the time. The idea here is to get ready to enter a new world: What does the world look like? Who are the "people" living in this world?

Title

Reading begins at the beginning—with the title, the first piece of information. The author believed that the title said something important about the play; therefore, it is a clue to at least one important part of the play. Titles like *Richard II* and

Cats are straightforward; on the other hand, titles like *Half Off* and *Top Girls* are mysterious until well into the play.

Cast of Characters

This list provides vital information about the size and traits of the cast—their names, ages, gender, and relationships. Introductions are as important in reading a play as they are in entering a room at a party.

Opening Stage Directions

The description of the play's setting (the place where the play takes place) is usually given here, as are descriptions of the play's opening moments. In plays that have been produced, these stage directions often reflect the actual Broadway or London production; in other plays, they give the playwright's vision. Reading them, we may be able to visualize (and hear) the play's opening.

Time for Questions

The reader should think about the information so far and begin to ask questions. What kind of theatre is being used? What is the historical period of the play? What did buildings, furniture, clothing look like in this period? What is the opening mood—joyful or somber, tense or relaxed? How do characters get on and off the stage? Is the setting indoors or outdoors? Are there doors, and if so, where? Where do the characters enter from?

First Reading

Then, with the beginning as strongly visualized as possible, the reader begins to read the play, underlining and making notes on:

- What happens in the play
- Who makes things happen and who tries to stop things from happening; also, what is the relative importance of the characters
- What key words, images, and ideas run through the play (including the relevance of the title)

Ending

It is important to pause briefly over the ending to contemplate the outcomes of the story. Did the characters achieve their individual goals? Were the outcomes serious or playful? Who ended the play better or worse off than they began it?

After the first reading, the reader is familiar with the play and has a sense of what it is about and what happens in it, as well as who its characters are. The next stage aims at an orderly and informed analysis of the play. Such an analysis may finally result in a judgment about the play.

PLAY ANALYSIS USING THE PARTS OF THE PLAY

Plays can be analyzed from many different points of view. A historian, for example, might read a play to discover something about the period in which it was written; a linguist might read it to study ways in which language is used or ways in which the use of language has changed over time. Many critical methods are available to help with an analysis of plays, and several are discussed in Chapter 5.

Aristotle

A theatre person most often reads a play for information about how it will appear in the theatre. One useful method of extracting this sort of information was first offered by the Greek Aristotle, whose ideas are adapted here for modern use.

Aristotle identified the following six parts of a play:

1. Plot
2. Character
3. Idea
4. Language
5. Music
6. Spectacle

Two points need to be made here. One, the order of the parts is important because it suggests the precise nature of the relationship among them. Two, the six parts should not be thought of as boxes into which sections of the play are placed; rather, they are parts of a system, a network of interrelationships so connected that a change in any one can have important effects on all others. These relationships are exceedingly complex, but, in brief, reading down the list gives a sense of control (e.g., the nature of the plot controls the kind of characters that must appear in it; the kinds of characters control the kinds of ideas possible in the play, etc.). Reading up the list suggests source materials (e.g., music, in the sense of sounds, is the material out of which language is made; ideas are the material out of which characters are made, etc.)

Although very old, this breakdown is still useful. We can go through almost any play and show how every aspect of the play—every speech, movement, event—relates to these six parts.

Plot

Plot is the ordering of the incidents in a play. This means that plot is not only what happens in the play, but it is also the order in which things are made to happen and the reasons why things are put in that order by the playwright.

Parts of Plot Plot is itself made up of many parts. Aristotle and later critics have offered names for the most common of these parts.

- **Exposition.** The giving of information about past events. The greatest amount of exposition often comes at the beginning of the play, when

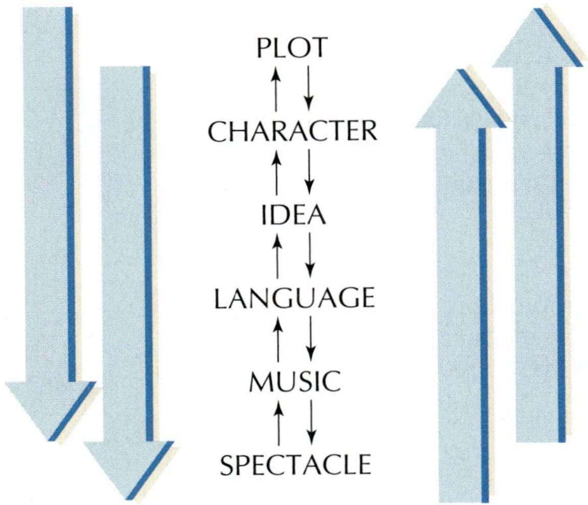

FIGURE 3.2
Parts of a Play
The six parts of a play constitute a system; a change in any one changes all the others. As the arrows show, the relationships are reciprocal: In other words, plot determines the kind of character needed; character is the stuff out of which plot is made.

audiences know least about events and characters. In some plays, however, important exposition is delayed until very late; in a murder mystery, for example, the most important facts about past events ("whodunit") come at the end.

- **Point of Attack**. The place in the *story* where the playwright begins the *plot*. Greek playwrights tended to begin their *plots* late in the story and so are said to have a late point of attack; Shakespeare tended to begin his plots toward the beginning of his stories and so is said to use an early point of attack.
- **Action**. The central chain of events in the play, particularly as those events are the central character's attempt to achieve an important goal. Action and character are tightly bound and are understood through each other, so that an answer to the question "What is the play's action?" always requires the inclusion of character.

Successful action in most plays has wholeness, that is, it has a beginning, middle, and end (in terms of logic, not time). The beginning of a play means that nothing necessary comes before it. A play's action usually begins when a character makes a **discovery**. When characters discover, they usually are led to decide (to act). Discovery therefore propels action and moves a play from its beginning to its middle, during which characters will make other discoveries, some of which will result in a **reversal** (a change in the direction of the action, usually occasioned by a discovery that is contrary to the character's expectation). The end of a play comes when no necessary action remains.

If the action is not a logical whole, the play will not be understandable to the audience as a work of art. Wholeness is fundamental. It is one of the most important aspects that distinguish art from life, which it imitates.

Unlike a play, a life is not perceivable as a whole, especially while it is being lived. Our lives are diverse and complicated; we carry on several "actions" of which we perceive only dimly (and often incorrectly) the beginnings; the ends are always over life's horizon. People often say they do not understand their lives; they are confused or have lost control or are having an identity crisis. They do not see the whole of their lives.

In a play, on the other hand, wholeness is visible and allows the audience to understand, and so to learn. A dramatic character might be confused or out of control or in an identity crisis, but the audience sees the whole of the situation (beginning, middle, and end) and so is not confused. It is important to remember that drama is able to reveal life to us because it is an invention and not real life.

- Complication. The opposing or entangling of the action. Often at the beginning of the play the action seems simple: A character desires to accomplish something. Obstacles then complicate this desire, particularly the efforts of other characters to frustrate the action, or even to destroy the central character. Complications are most often revealed as discoveries by characters and reversals in the course of the action.

  A common kind of complication, one that is central to most (but not all) plays, is conflict. In situations in which one or more characters try to thwart the ideas and actions of another, conflict results. Conflict between characters may provide an easily understandable moral or philosophical opposition (e.g., good versus evil), but other conflicts are between a character and a force (e.g., society, fate, or gods, which may be personified).

  Most plots have many complications. Each complication changes or threatens to change the course of the action because the character must deal with the complication before pursuing the original goal. Complications are either caused (by some agency like another character or a god or a force) or accidental (the result of something like a storm, a flood, or a chance meeting of characters). Caused complications are usually thought to be better than accidental ones, especially in serious plays.

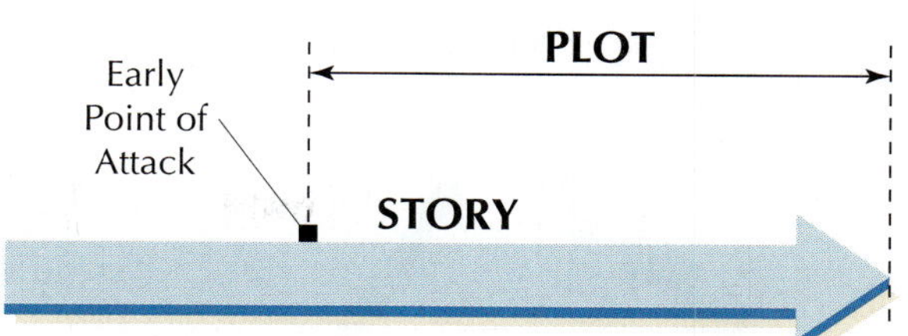

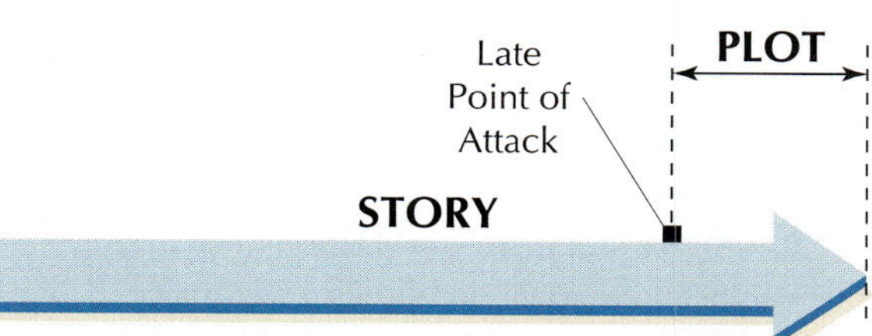

FIGURE 3.3
Plot and Story
Plot is the arrangement of the incidents, the way the story is told. When plot and story begin at about the same point, the play has an early point of attack. When the plot begins late in the story, the play has a late point of attack.

- Rising Action. Action of increasing complication.
- Crisis. Derived from the Greek word for decision, crisis means "decisive moment," a turning point in the action. Crisis usually results when the play's major discovery leads to the major reversal. We expect to find rising action from complication to crisis; after the crisis, we anticipate falling action.
- **Falling Action, Resolution, or** Dénouement. "The untying"—the unraveling of complication, the declining action as crisis is passed and complication is resolved.

Kinds of Plot In one sense, there are as many kinds of plots as there are plays, but some basic patterns tend to repeat and so have been given names. Two in particular can be cited.

Causal Plot (also known as linear, or climactic, or antecedent–consequence plot). The incidents of linear plot can be seen to lie along a line of causality from

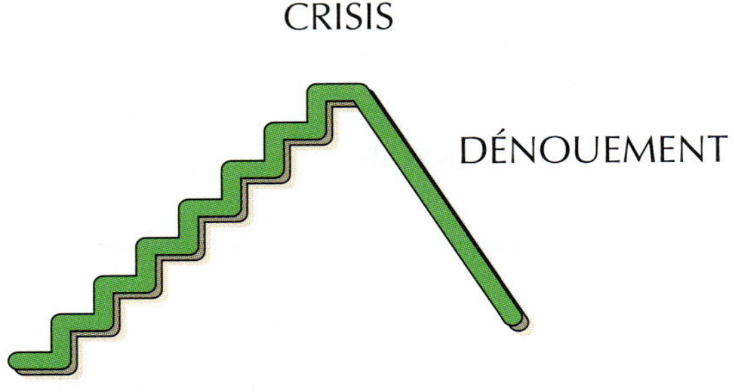

FIGURE 3.4
Complication, Crisis, and Dénouement
Rising action typically comprises many smaller complications. The turning point (crisis) initiates the falling action (dénouement).

beginning to end. The word *climactic* is sometimes used because such plots build to a **climax**, the most exciting moment of the plot for the audience. (Note that the term differs from *crisis; climax* refers to an audience's response to plot and not to a part of the plot.)

Causal plots are of two major types: single line of development, with no subordinate lines (for example, Sophocles' *Oedipus the King*), and multiple lines of development, consisting of a major line and several subordinate ones, often called "subplots" (for example, Shakespeare's *Hamlet*).

Episodic Plot (also known as contextual or thematic plot). The incidents (episodes) of episodic plot do not follow one another because of causality; rather, they are usually ordered by the exploration of an idea, with each scene exploring a new aspect of a problem or enlarging the study made to that point. Many contemporary plays often employ a nonlinear structure to link scenes by thematic or emotional associations.

Only the imagination of playwrights limits the way plots are organized. Nontraditional and experimental arrangements are constantly being tried, and old organizations, like plots of spectacle, language, or character, are occasionally still used.

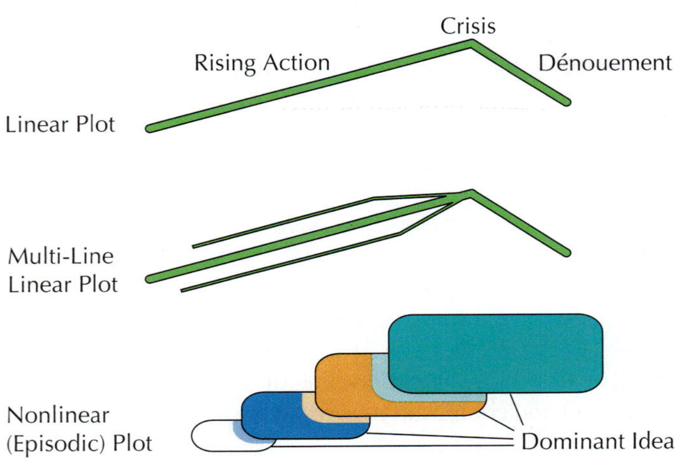

FIGURE 3.5
Kinds of Plot
Greek tragedy typically has a simple linear plot. Shakespearean tragedy a multilinear plot. Many contemporary plays have episodic plots.

Character

A dramatic **character** and a real human being are not the same thing. Dramatic characters are inventions of playwrights. The fact that dramatic characters pursue human goals, speak human words, and embody human responses means only that dramatic characters are part of an artistic creation that is *about* life, not life itself. Dramatic character is, at best, an imitation of selected aspects of humanity.

In addition to being imitations of people, dramatic characters are functions within a plot. That is, they were created by the playwright to perform certain tasks within the plot. Each character can be analyzed in every scene for its function, using the play's parts: for example, to further the plot, to reveal information about character, to express ideas, to contribute to spectacle. To understand what function a character performs in the plot, it is often helpful to ask *what would not occur* in the story if the character were removed.

KINDS OF CHARACTERS Some kinds of characters repeat often, and so critics and scholars have designated them as follows:

- **Protagonist**. The central figure in the main action
- **Confidant(e)**. A character in whom the protagonist or another important character confides
- **Antagonist**. In a play with conflict, the character who opposes the protagonist
- **Raisonneur**. Or author's character—one who speaks for the author, directly giving the author's moral or philosophical ideas; usually not the protagonist
- **Foil**. One who sets off another character by contrast: comic where the other is serious, stupid where intelligent, shrewd where naïve

In many plays, characters can be divided into sympathetic and unsympathetic, the former created to appeal to audiences, the latter to repel them. The fate of these groups at the end of plays usually embodies the major moral stance of the play and so should be noted.

CLUES TO CHARACTER Because playwrights cannot describe characters to us directly, we must seek clues about their appearance, motivations, and behaviors. A reader must remain alert for such clues, especially noting places such as these:

- Stage directions, although some playwrights do not discuss characters in stage directions.
- What other characters say; however, we must understand these other characters in order to know how to interpret what they say.
- What the characters say about themselves, with the same problem of interpreting what they say.
- What the characters do—their acts.
- Relationships between characters; under increasing complications, the real nature of relationships—hate, love, friendship, dependence, forgiveness—shows more clearly.
- Most important, the plot itself—for example, decision reveals character; complication forces decision. Characters often change as the plot develops; leading characters often behave and think differently at the end of the play; they have "learned." Accounting for such changes helps one gain understanding of both character and play. Some critics even say that "the play is understood by its ending," a great oversimplification but often a useful notion.

Idea

No play is without meanings. A play does not have to be filled with intellectual speeches to offer meanings, and a careful reader learns how to find and understand

Spotlight

Marlon Brando and Vivien Leigh played in *A Streetcar Named Desire* in London and in the film version of the play.

Reading a Play and Organizing a Response

A Streetcar Named Desire may be America's most often-produced play Written by Tennessee Williams (1911–1983) and first produced on Broadway in 1947, *Streetcar* has remained popular with both critics and audiences. The play has been variously interpreted—as the collapse of the Old South and the rise of the New, as a struggle between civilization and savagery, as a clash between the sexes. Its most famous scene is the rape of Blanche DuBois by Stanley Kowalski (the husband of Blanche's sister, Stella). The critical excerpt that follows focuses on that scene:

> Because [Blanche] refused to become the woman in the traveling salesman joke, the stereotype of the nymphomaniacal upper-class girl, [Stanley] rapes her. His famous line rationalizing the rape, "We've had this date with each other from the beginning," summarizes both the struggle for mastery in which he and Blanche have engaged, leading to the crucial combat, and his ultimate reduction of her to the whore of his history, who provokes and enjoys yet another encounter. . . . If it ended with the rape, the play might justifiably be regarded as representing post-war life in the South, where the most provocative problem was the shift from the aristocratically dominated tenor of social intercourse to the first-generation, lower-middle-class urban mores brought to the fore by the returning soldiers. But the troubling focus of *A Streetcar Named Desire* is not that a drunken man, left alone in a two-room flat of the French Quarter with his drunken sister-in-law, subdues and violates her, but that the act becomes public and the woman is punished. She is taken away under the consenting gaze of all the characters on stage, who constitute most of the characters in the play. . . . She had been victimized by Stanley's—and implicitly patriarchy's—historical discourse.

This short excerpt (from a longer piece of criticism) illustrates how an analysis of a scene can be organized into a written response. The subject [the rape scene] is introduced by explaining why Stanley rapes Blanche [she won't demean herself by becoming a joke or a stereotype]. Stanley's line of dialogue is used as evidence to bolster the claim that Stanley and Blanche have been engaged in a struggle for dominance and that Stanley plans to win through violence. That the play does not end with the rape is used as evidence to conclude that the play is not about a changing South (the critic thus rejects as inadequate another common interpretation of the play). A final bit of evidence—the play's punishment of the raped woman rather than the rapist—is used to argue a sociopolitical point: that this play, by showing a woman overcome by male violence, can be generalized to a world outside the play where women are victimized by patriarchy.

The issue is not whether you agree with this reading of the scene. The issue is that this evidence supports this reading. Another reader could have a different response to the scene and organize another essay.

FIGURE 3.6

Creating the World: Character

The play reader may get only a name and sex and age but must imagine the character. Such clues help actors to create fully realized characters, such as (left to right) Pantalone, a gentleman, *Macbeth* at the University of Texas at Austin, and a street youth in *Polaroid Stories* at Theatre South Carolina.

them. Even the silliest comedy has meaning because it imitates human action and because it expresses a time and a society. Not all playwrights set out to teach, but we can extract meaning from their plays nonetheless.

Plays seldom offer single, simple meanings. The best offer many meanings, and any attempt to reduce these to "the idea of the play" or "the theme of the play" greatly oversimplifies the work. Meanings fall into two major categories: idea—meanings contained entirely within the play; and extrinsic meaning—those meanings (perhaps wholly unintentional) in the society and the period of which the play is an expression. We are concerned here with idea.

The play's idea comes in part from its plot. We tend to generalize from example, and the playwright, by choosing and ordering events, has created an example (the play). We can then generalize from that example, seeing that (in this playwright's view) certain causes lead to certain (good or bad) events.

In plays organized by conflict, the victor in the conflict may embody the "good" way of behaving, whereas the loser embodies the "bad." They are rewarded or punished accordingly, through (for example) money, love, promotion, or pardon. For example, comedies often end with the formation of a new society; by discovering who is included and who is excluded from this society, a reader can often grasp the major idea of the play by asking questions: Why were these people included and those excluded? What were the traits of each group? The behaviors of each group?

The play's idea comes also from character. In an effective play, the major ideas are embodied in the character and action of the protagonist. If the character is positive (approved by the author, "good"), then the protagonist embodies a good. These "goods" and "bads"—the defining elements of the play's moral world—are best understood through the system of rewards and punishments in the play. Typically, the protagonist explains his or her own idea near the play's crisis; rewards and punishments usually appear in the play's dénouement.

The play's language can also reveal idea. Important characters' speeches before and after crises are especially revealing, as are important characters' speeches when they are on stage alone or with a confidant(e). The speeches of raisonneurs, especially when close to the complications and crises, often reveal idea, as do many speeches during the dénouement when the playwright (through the characters) is tying up questions and resolving issues raised by the play.

Language

As we have seen, language through the speeches of characters is an important carrier of meaning. But language as an act, separate from the meaning of the words, can also reveal idea, as, for example, whenever words or images repeat often in a play. The frequent appearance of the word *death* in a play about love would suggest that the play's idea is probably not "Love conquers all." Similarly, repeated images or metaphors carry meaning. One such image in *Hamlet* is of weeds, which support an idea about the protagonist as fighting against an evil, choking, destructive environment.

As an "act" separate from the meaning of the words, language is also one of the most revealing clues to character. The choice of words and the length of sentences can tell the reader something about the circumstances of a character—social class, level of education, complexity of thought, for example. As well, the rhythm of a character's speech may indicate something about mood or lifestyle.

Music

In musical plays, the importance of music to character, mood, and rhythm is clear. In nonmusical plays, the reader must understand that the language itself embodies music, because language in plays is intended to be spoken aloud. Spoken language inevitably has pitch and rhythm and itself is musical.

Like language, music reveals clues about plot, character, and idea. For example, regular, slow rhythms create very different moods from sharp, staccato ones. Verse, especially rhymed verse, is usually more formal than prose; in serious plays, verse seems to add weight to the action, whereas in comedy it often enhances the wit of a line by accentuating a word or nuance.

Spectacle

In reading, it is especially important to try to visualize the action so that the contribution of spectacle to the performance can be imagined. To be sure, much of the spectacle in today's theatre is the work of designers, whose individual genius cannot be predicted from the page. The cues for their work are there, however, in the same text the reader uses. The imagination must work to keep spectacle in the mind's eye while reading.

Spectacle, like language, can embody idea, clarify character, and forward plot. A burning cross on stage captures a racial situation that needs no words to describe; two female characters, one dressed in red and the other in pink, predispose us to think of them as differing in their degree of "feminine propriety"; a pistol drawn from a purse may be enough to cause the antagonist to retreat in defeat and the protagonist to prevail, without any words being spoken, because in this instance what is seen (the spectacle) is enough to communicate the idea.

Spectacle—which on stage is always working on the sense of sight—is the hardest of the six parts to understand from the text. It is necessary to imagine it as fully as possible, but the imagined spectacle of the reader will probably prove quite different from the actual spectacle of performance, although both should probably suggest the same meanings.

Craig Schwartz

FIGURE 3.7
Spectacle
The imagined spectacle of the reader will probably prove quite different from the actual spectacle of performance. Here lights, costume, singers and dancers provide the spectacle for the Center Theatre Group/Deaf West Theatre production of *Pippin*.

ORGANIZING A RESPONSE

The result of a play analysis should be an organized response to the text. An organized response should be *informed* (based on a knowledge of drama and theatre), *orderly* (consistent and well reasoned), and *defensible* (based on the evidence offered by the text and capable of explanation to somebody else).

Response Based on the Parts of a Play

Analysis should reveal how the parts work together in the play. A response probably should not simply begin with plot and then move to each part in turn, but any response will want to be based on answers to questions about the parts, questions like:

- Is the plot internally consistent? How is the plot organized? What is its point of attack? Its crisis? Its major complications?
- Is each character active, interesting, and consistent? Does each have a function throughout? What would or would not happen if the character were removed from the play?
- Are the play's ideas important, and are they embedded in character and plot?
- Is the language interesting and expressive?
- Does the play's music (including its spoken language) support and enrich character and idea?
- Is the spectacle interesting and appropriate? Does it support rather than overwhelm the other parts of the play? What opportunities for spectacle are suggested?

Response Based on Genres

The word genre means simply a kind or type. In general literature, the word customarily refers to such types as novel, poetry, and drama. Within drama, the word is used to distinguish recurring types (specifically recurring forms) of drama—tragedy, comedy, and so on.

Generic criticism is a major branch of dramatic criticism, so much so that whole books have been written about, for example, the nature of tragedy. Our understanding of genres often changes under historical pressure, so that within any one category we can have several kinds—neoclassical tragedy, Romantic tragedy, heroic tragedy, and so on. Here it is possible to give only the broadest useful definitions of five major genres:

1. **Tragedy.** A work of the highest seriousness, with a serious protagonist in a serious action with serious consequences. Human decision is central to tragic action.

Summing Up

Using an analysis based on the parts of a play and its genre, a reader should be able to organize an informed, orderly, and defensible response, either in speech or in writing. Such a response should go beyond personal response to the play (although personal response is important). It should demonstrate an understanding of the play and how it might work in the theatre; it should not be merely a gut reaction. Certainly, part of the enjoyment of theatre depends on gut reaction—but only part.

2. **Comedy.** A work whose issues are usually social and mundane (rather than spiritual or moral), with a protagonist involved in an action without deeply serious consequences. Usually, as well, human decision is limited, comic characters being comic because they are locked into types or into intense self-interest.
3. **Tragicomedy.** A work that mixes elements of tragedy and comedy, often by giving otherwise serious plays a happy ending, or vice versa, but often by conferring a degree of seriousness on characters and subjects usually not so treated.
4. **Melodrama.** A work of apparent seriousness with issues cast in terms of extremes (good and evil), the actual issues being less profound than the language suggests. Endings often show good rewarded and evil punished, in keeping with characters who are aligned according to morality; good (hero, heroine) and evil (villain).
5. **Farce.** A comic work whose aim is laughter, from a non-English word meaning "to stuff," indicating that farce is stuffed with laughter-producing elements. The typical protagonist in farce pursues a mundane, often trivial action, and characters often lack decision. Both the characters and the plots of farce have been called mechanical, and it is in the working out of its machinery that farce often provokes its best laughter.

KEY TERMS

Check your understanding against this list. Brief definitions are included in the Glossary; persons are page-referenced in the Index.

CHAPTER

4

How to See a Play

OBJECTIVES

When you have completed this chapter, you should be able to:

- Describe major differences between reading and seeing a play
- Explain how an experienced audience member can both participate in and observe a performance
- Explain differences between actor and character and between real person and dramatic character
- Explain differences between plot and story
- Explain differences between dramatic and theatrical style and discuss how they may be related

EXPERIENCING THE PERFORMANCE

The play text comes to us only as words on a page. The performance that we see results from putting together several arts—the written text, the actors, the scenery, costumes, and lighting. Text is repeatable, but performance is not—we watch it moment by moment, responding to many stimuli (sensual, emotional, and intellectual) and unconsciously fusing them into a whole. The written text appeals to our intellect and emotions; performance in the theatre appeals most immediately to our senses and only through them to our intellect and emotions.

Taking It In

Studying a play is, therefore, different from studying a performance. In studying a play text, we analyze—we take a play apart to see how it *might* work on stage. In studying a performance, we "take it in" through our senses (mostly sight and hearing) and see and hear how it *does* work on stage. In analyzing a play, we can stop to think, or return to a difficult passage to reconsider it. In studying a performance, we watch and hear a moment go by—in real time; later we can only *recall* (not retrieve) that moment.

For such reasons, criticism of performance requires an approach somewhat different from that of play analysis.

Performance criticism can use, cautiously, Aristotle's six parts of a play text, but with the understanding that the nature of theatre radically alters the relationships between these parts. For example, spectacle takes on more importance because theatre is visual. Modern theatre especially has endowed spectacle with great meaning—in the ability of light to focus attention and create mood, in the ability of setting and costume to give information about time and place, and so on.

In the analysis of a play text, plot, character, idea, and language dominate. But in the analysis of a performance, these four parts (residing mostly in the play) *are submerged within and expressed through music and spectacle, through being spoken by actors and appearing physically on stage* (see Figure 4.1).

An example can clarify this point: Character in a play text is revealed only through written words. Character in performance, however, is revealed through the work of the actor, for whom the written text (and its six parts) is the basis of the artistic creation *but is not the artistic creation itself*. Character in performance depends not only on what the words of the play *say* but also on what the actor *does*—with voice, body, costume, and makeup. To discover character in performance (to understand what the actor is doing with and to the text) means to ask not only the questions asked during play analysis but

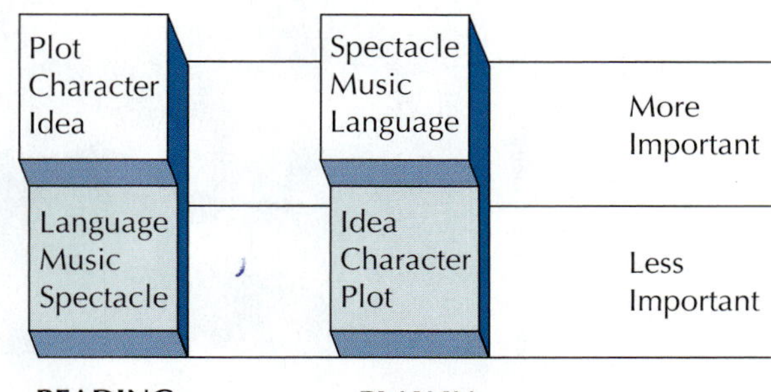

FIGURE 4.1

Parts of Performance

In reading a play, plot, character, and idea claim first attention; in watching a play, spectacle, music, and language dominate.

another set as well, including such questions as these: How does the actor say the words? How does the actor react to the words and actions of others? How does he or she stand? move? wear costumes? create rhythms? create images?

New Questions

Performance criticism thus introduces a whole new set of questions to textual analysis: What are the arts of the actor, the scenic designer, the costume designer, and the lighting designer? And how are these arts fused with the written play?

- Play analysis examines only the art of the playwright; performance criticism, however, examines the arts of the other theatre makers as well. For this reason, Aristotelian analysis remains a good starting point for thinking about performance, but it is only a starting point; it must be supplemented.
- Performance criticism means looking in two directions at once—at the play and at the audience, because performance binds the written play to a particular audience. Play analysis and performance analysis are thus inevitably linked, but they are different.

Rita Hoeppner as Hedda Gabler. Photo: Lenny Cohen

FIGURE 4.2

Point of View

The script is the foundation for a production, but the director's approach can startle an audience. This production at Triad Stage of Ibsen's *Hedda Gabler* upends many of the conventions associated with the original production.

In analyzing play texts, we saw that playwrights made decisions aimed at shaping the perceptions of the reader. In analyzing productions, we see that each theatre artist is also making such decisions. That is, actors build their performances through a series of decisions, each aimed at promoting a certain understanding and eliciting a specific response from the audience. Designers envision and then build their costumes and settings, their stage lighting and sound tracks, so as to communicate certain ideas to their audiences and to evoke certain kinds of responses from them. Whereas playwrights have only a general audience in mind, theatre artists must prepare their productions for specific audiences that will be physically present in the theatre. Just as play analysis requires an effort to remember that a playwright is trying to persuade the reader to a certain point of view about a series of events, a performance analysis requires us to remember that theatre artists have made decisions to create *this* performance as it is.

Any play carries within it possibilities for many different productions, some similar, others wildly different. One production might try to reproduce the play more or less as the playwright created it; another production might try to modernize the play, bringing its appearance and approach more in line with contemporary values; still another might use the elements of production to comment on or even critique the world of the play (the world created by the playwright) exposing its ideas as unworthy or unjust. Just as play analysis requires an effort to discover and understand the choices of the playwright, performance analysis means trying to see and understand the choices made by theatre artists, who want us to accept the performance as they have envisioned it.

Just as play analysis requires us to think critically about what we read, performance analysis requires us to think critically as we watch the performance unfold in the theatre. We can consider the techniques of performance criticism in three parts: preliminary work, performance analysis, and organizing a response.

PRELIMINARY WORK

The preliminary work of performance criticism begins before the audience member arrives at the theatre and continues to the opening of the curtain. The preliminary work includes considering:

- The art of theatre itself
- The nature of the work itself
- The program distributed to the audience
- The clues offered by the theatre's physical surroundings

The Art of Theatre

Analyzing a performance means in part knowing enough about theatre to do so. Knowing the role of each theatre artist, for example, enhances the ability to understand a performance. Understanding the role of the theatre audience in performance—that it can affect performance and so has some responsibility to "work" with actors in creating the event—suggests a need to consider responses as a part of the critique of performance.

Thus, knowledge of the art of theatre supports a critique of any single performance. Attending theatrical performances, taking courses in theatre arts, and reading books about theatre provide this general knowledge. In a lifetime of attending plays and reading about theatre, a person becomes a knowledgeable member of an audience and so is better equipped to engage in performance criticism.

The Work Itself

An audience member should take the time to learn something about the material to be performed before arriving at the theatre. Some people like to read a play before seeing it; others prefer simply to learn something about it through reviews and advertisements. From whatever source, audience members should arrive at the theatre with a general idea of what they are going to see—because expectations will affect the way a performance is perceived. Just because *Cat on a Hot Tin Roof* has a funny-sounding title does not make this play a comedy, and anyone arriving at the theatre expecting a comedy might be angered or confused by the performance. Taking children to see *Who's Afraid of Virginia Woolf?* because it sounds like a children's story will probably result in an unhappy shock.

The Program

An audience member should read the program before the play begins. It almost always indicates the place or places where the action will unfold and introduces the characters who will appear on stage, giving their names and major relationships. Programs often include a synopsis of the play's major action, highlighting the most

FIGURE 4.3
What to Expect
The title of the production and signs advertising it give a hint about what to expect. *We Will Rock You* promises raucous music and romance, according to this sign outside a Madrid theatre.

important moments and thereby suggesting where the audience's attention should focus. Sometimes in the program there will be notes written by the director, designer, or dramaturg. Such notes may be especially helpful, for they sometimes point to the major issues with which the production grapples or explain the director's special point of view in staging this play. (Programs also often offer helpful, if inessential, information, like what good restaurants are close to the theatre and what attractions are coming next to that theatre.)

The Physical Surroundings

An audience member will be repaid for spending a few minutes looking around the theatre and listening to sounds, because theatre artists will often try to establish a proper mood for a play even before it begins. Country-and-western music in the background probably reveals something important about the production and sets a mood quite different from that established by a Bach concerto or a rap song. Lighting may be used to establish mood, and scenery (where visible) may suggest things like time, place, and social class.

Sometimes oddities (for example, small platforms with scenery or lighting stands) appear in an area normally reserved for audience seating. Such spaces alert an audience member that the performance may spill over from the stage and into the auditorium, a signal that the play may be unusual in other ways as well.

The purpose of the preliminary work is to become prepared for the moment when the performance itself begins. The more prepared for the performance, the better able the audience is to follow the performance as it moves at its own rate through time.

PERFORMANCE ANALYSIS

The goal of performance analysis is to help the audience member reach greater enjoyment through understanding—not merely a statement like "I really liked that," or "I was bored." Rather, the audience member needs to be able to explain the reasons behind such responses. These reasons usually have to do with the selection of the play, the appropriateness and skill of the actors, the suitability of the visual elements, and so on. Much of the rest of this book deals with ways of understanding and evaluating the several arts involved in performance. The purpose of this section, however, is to offer a way of looking at the contributions of these arts, to serve as an introduction to issues involved in the complex problem of performance analysis.

Watching while Participating

To analyze a performance, an audience member must do two things at once: participate in the performance (entering into the action, empathizing with the characters, and so on) and watch the performance ("standing back" from the story and characters in order to observe how the effects are being achieved). This dual view of performance is as rewarding as it is difficult to achieve, but with practice any audience member can learn to participate and observe simultaneously. Again, if carefully used, Aristotle's ideas can help us think through this dual view, and the vocabulary in Chapter 3 can, with adaptation, serve us here as well. The play's central values in performance are its story, characters, and ideas, reached through language, music, and spectacle, as expressed in acting, scenery, costumes, lighting, and sound.

Values of the Play

Drama, as imitation of human action, allows audience members to generalize from particular stories, characters, and ideas to more general human truths. Because the stories, characters, and ideas are invented and concentrated for the play, they seem even more important than similar events (unselected and unfocused) seem in real life. Thus, the concentration of theatre art accounts for much of its power, but that same concentration complicates the task of performance analysis.

STORY Plays, as imitations of human actions, are compelling because they tell stories. **Story** is similar to, but not identical with, Aristotle's plot. While experiencing theatre, we cannot analyze plot—we cannot perceive the ordering of the incidents and the reasons for that ordering—we can only follow and respond to the story of the play, to the tale of "what happened."

Stories are made up of incidents that have coherence; that is, the incidents are related to one another for a reason. Stories are not only compelling in themselves (we are interested in what happens), but they are also compelling because they serve as the framework within which the characters, words, ideas, and values of the play unfold. In a sense, then, we understand the characters, ideas, and values of a performed play through the story that it tells.

Suspense. **Suspense** is the unfolding of events in such a way that audiences want to know what happens next. "And then what happens?" they ask. Suspense requires preparation—curiosity must be created. And suspense must be satisfied—the audience must learn what happens, and what happens must be understandable in terms of what the audience expected might happen. *Suspense, then, requires preparation, connectedness, and resolution.*

Surprise. **Surprise** is a happening that is unexpected at the time but quite logical when viewed in retrospect. Therefore, surprises, to work, must be prepared for within the world of the performance; that is, surprises are not the same as mistakes or accidents. For example, if during a love scene on stage a bed collapses, it is a surprise if the bed was supposed to collapse (perhaps for purposes of comedy); if the scenery simply broke down, it is not a surprise but an accident.

CHARACTERS In performance, characters and story are interrelated, as characters and plot are in a play. We understand each through the other, although they remain independent. But characters in performance, unlike characters in a play, are created by the actors' choices of vocal and physical traits as well as by the words printed on the pages of the play text and the decisions and actions in that text. Characters in performance are therefore very complex creations that are based on the characters in the play but are nonetheless different from them.

Spotlight

Hagen receives a Tony award.
Photo: Ray Stubblebine/
Getty Images.

Seeing a Play: Performing Character

Blanche DuBois in *A Streetcar Named Desire* is one of the great roles in America's theatrical repertory. The first two women to perform it were Jessica Tandy and Uta Hagen; both received rave reviews on Broadway. Because they appeared within months of one another, people compared them. What the comparisons revealed was that two very different Blanches could come from the same script. One critic described their differences:

> In Miss Tandy's acting Blanche's mental collapse was closer to the surface throughout the play and the agony of the last act [which includes the rape scene] was implicit in the preliminary scenes. Blanche had slipped into the limbo of the psychopathic world before the time of the play.... Although [Miss Hagen's] Blanche is overwrought from the beginning, the evil furies attack her at specific moments in the narrative and she slips over the borderline in the course of the play.
>
> This is a point of view that leaves the first act with less significance than it had in Miss Tandy's performance. But it fills the last act with terrifying wildness. Hagen is a decisive actress of great strength and power who has constructed the part with lucid deliberation, artfully underscoring the meaning of individual scenes. When the malevolence of the world tortures Blanche beyond the point of endurance, Miss Hagen reaps the reward of her method and vividly describes the agony, fright and loneliness of a woman who has been pushed out of human society into the pitiless seclusion of madness.

Some of these differences came from the techniques of the actresses themselves, but some too came from quite different views of the play. Elia Kazan, who directed Tandy, wrote that, from Stanley Kowalski's point of view, Blanche was a destructive and dangerous woman who, if left alone, could wreck his home. (Kazan adopted Stanley's point of view, even confessing that he hated Blanche.) When Hagen took over the role, she disagreed with this interpretation and requested a different director (who, incidentally, never got credit). Together they found a Blanche who "was the victim of a destructive society rather than a madwoman disrupting a healthy world." The result was that "Hagen's Blanche... left audiences feeling they had watched a delicate woman driven insane by a brutish environment epitomized by Stanley Kowalski. Tandy's Blanche... left audiences feeling that a madwoman had entered an alien world and after shaking that world had been successfully exorcised."

Clearly, drama and performance differ. In *Streetcar*, both actresses spoke the same words, wore identical costumes, and moved within the same stage settings, but their characters were different because their interpretations of the play were different. One script can contain many performances. Analysis of drama and of performance also differs. In dramatic analysis, scripts can be consulted repeatedly for evidence, but in performance analysis, evidence exists in seeing the performance or relying on accounts of others who saw the performance.

FIGURE 4.4
Character
Audiences are attracted to some characters because they seem recognizable, whereas other characters are inviting because they represent something exotic. Here are scenes from *The Civil War* at Virginia Commonwealth University (left) and *Adventures of a Black Girl* (right) at Wayne State University.

Audiences respond to characters for different reasons. Often a character is appealing because audiences can identify with it. "I recognize myself in that character" or "I can identify with her" are strong sources of pleasure or suffering in the theatre. We like to see the mirror held up so that we can watch those like ourselves. Some characters are said to have universal appeal (or to be a universal character); the appeal of such characters is that they are recognizably like human beings of many different times and places.

Some characters appeal to feelings deep within us. Such characters, we say, appeal to us at a subconscious level, through some subconscious reference. For example, the Greek tragedy *Oedipus Rex* has survived for 2,000 years. One critic said it causes us to "think the unthinkable"—a man who has children by his mother and murders his father. All these things are in the play text. But in performance they are given a terrible immediacy that gives them life, size, and horror—*this* man and woman, *this* bloodshed, *this* scream.

Still other characters appeal because we recognize others in them, a trait especially clear in the case of historical characters. Seeing an actor portray a character we think we know offers a special treat for audiences, who will often flock to see an actor portray former luminaries in works like *Abe Lincoln in Illinois* or *Picasso at the Lapin Agile*. Here the delight is not only in enjoying the character in the performed play but also in watching to see how closely the actor meets our preconceptions of the real person. To take advantage of this associative response, the performance must depict people with whom the audience has strong ties and must present them in convincing—and perhaps visually recognizable—ways.

IDEA Often the ideas that are revealed through a performance are given the least thought while we sit in the theatre and watch, but they are what we talk about most once we leave the theatre. There is a good reason for this phenomenon. Performance is transitory; theatre is "the home of the Now." When we leave the theatre, the vividness of the acting—the onstage images and sounds—fades. We seldom remember sensory stimuli clearly; afterward we can only describe them. We are therefore left with the intellectual content of the play in performance, which is verbally expressible and so may remain fresh and sharp in our minds.

In fact, the ideas within the performance may become more important with the passing of time. If experiencing the immediacy of the performance has moved us, it has become part of our lives, and now we want to know what it means to us.

Ideas are embedded in all play texts and performances. Some ideas are more interesting and more important than others, to be sure, but ideas exist in all. Whereas the ideas of play texts come mostly through the plot and dialogue, ideas in performance come most immediately through the specific choices made by the actors and designers (of scenery, costumes, lighting, and properties). For example, images in performance can communicate ideas vividly, even without words (although words, of course, deepen and extend the ideas). For example, an actor with a shaved head, wearing paramilitary garb, quite clearly communicates an ideology even before he speaks. A set that positions a computer so that it looms menacingly above the actors makes a clear (although nonverbal) statement of a power relationship, a statement that the actors' words and performance enhance and modify. It is through such means that specific performances of Shakespeare's *Julius Caesar* have offered ideas about Nazi Germany and South American dictatorships, even though the play's ideas were about the nature of rule in Republican Rome and, perhaps, Elizabethan England.

Ideas that are not well integrated into the performance are distracting and theatrically unsatisfying. Indeed, to update an old theatrical adage, "If you want to send a message, use a fax." The saying means that ideas are not the end-all or be-all of performance. Ideas are only one important element in judging the importance of a play in performance, even though they tend to dominate later discussions of performance, lingering after the immediate, sensory elements of performance have faded from memory.

Idea in performance succeeds only if other, theatrical values of the play succeed, because ideas come to audiences through the other elements of specific performance.

Values of the Specific Performance

Story, character, and idea reside mostly in play text; music (what we hear) and spectacle (what we see) reside in performance. Indeed, the word *theatre* literally means "seeing place," and auditorium "hearing place"; the spectator is one who watches, audience those who listen. Therefore, audience members will also want to ask questions about the elements of performance that may be distinct from the play text itself. Three such elements are central to understanding most performances: the given circumstances of the performance, its theatrical conventions, and its style.

Given Circumstances We may define the **given circumstances** of a performance as those basic traits that determine the world of the stage: the age, sex, social class, and physical health of the characters; the time and place of the action; the mood established on the stage; and so on.

Usually, the written play determines the given circumstances, but not always. For example, the play *Everyman* comes from the English Middle Ages, and so the performance usually proceeds as if it were unfolding then and there. But a director may wish to emphasize the timelessness of this action and so perform it as if it were taking place in England of the 1990s or in the American west during the gold rush. In producing a French comedy of the 1660s, a director might want to do it "authentically," making it as close as possible to what the original production might have looked like. Or the director might decide that the fun within the play is more important than the circumstances of its original production and so select materials based on their brightness and color, even using techniques of cartoons or caricatures as guiding principles. Clearly all such decisions will necessarily affect not only the visual aspects of the production but also the sounds selected as background and the techniques used by the actors.

Making It Clear Whatever the decision about given circumstances, the circumstances for every production must be made clear to the audience through the visual aspects of production (scenery, costumes, lighting, properties), the sounds and music of the production, and the work of the actors. An audience member engaged in performance criticism must determine what the given circumstances of production are and then examine how those circumstances were communicated through the arts of production. Only then can some evaluation of this aspect of production be made, through answering questions like these:

- What seem to be the source and purpose of the production's given circumstances?
- Are the circumstances clear?
- Are they consistent throughout the production?

Conventions A **convention** can be thought of as a contract between theatre artists and audiences, an agreement to do things a certain way for the good of all. It is a shortcut between what is meant and what is done. Each of the arts within theatre has conventions. Several examples can clarify.

In today's theatre, it is a convention that months or years can pass between the acts of a play, even though common sense tells us that, in fact, only a few minutes have passed.

A convention in scenic design is the agreement between actors and audience that when a setting depicts a room of a house, a door in that room leads to another room of the house or to the outdoors. Common sense tells us that the door actually leads to an area backstage. Another sort of scenic convention allows a yellow cardboard circle hung aloft to represent the sun.

An acting convention from the eighteenth century was that a hand raised to the forehead, palm out and the eyes cast upward, indicated suffering.

In musicals, characters sing their emotions. This use of music is a convention, because common sense tells us that music neither accompanies our lives nor changes as we shift activities and moods.

Such agreements between artists and audiences enhance performance and so work for the good of both. Audience members trying to understand and evaluate a performance need to watch for the conventions operating in a production:

- Are the conventions clear?
- Are the conventions similar to other, familiar theatrical conventions? To conventions on television? Or are they in some way distinctive?
- Do the conventions seem aimed at promoting the view that the onstage world is quite like real life, or do they aim rather to call attention to the differences of the stage from life?

STYLE The word **style** is one of the most useful and yet one of the most confusing that is applied to any art. Part of the confusion comes from the word being used in so many ways in daily life: Clothes are "stylish"; there is "New Orleans–style" jazz, different from "Chicago style"; there are kosher-style dill pickles; many performers are said to have their own personal "style."

In art, including theatre art, the word *style* is used to describe a recurring cluster of traits that seem to set one type off from another type of the same art—two styles of painting, for example, or two styles of music. Style, then, is the mode in which the art is presented. Dramas (written texts) have style, and so do performances. It is therefore possible to speak both of dramatic style and theatrical style.

Generally, a play written in a particular style will also be performed in that style; that is, the dramatic and theatrical style are the same. But in some instances (for reasons we return to later), theatre artists may decide that the performance should be in a style different from that of the written play.

Styles tend to change over time. For example, seventeenth-century plays and productions displayed something we now call a Neoclassical style, while early nineteenth-century plays and productions generally showed what we call a Romantic style. Contemporary theatre is marked by its tendency to use many different styles among its productions, but, for a single production, there is usually a single style.

Abstraction. **Abstraction** is removal from observable reality. An artist can choose any point along a continuum from quite abstract to wholly lifelike. For example, a painting that is simply a splash of red interrupted by dots of black is quite abstract, whereas a near-photographic portrait of Marilyn Monroe is quite lifelike.

Similarly, a theatre artist can either:

- Reproduce observable reality
- Render parts of reality as generalized but understandable shapes
- Abandon reality almost entirely

For example, scenic designers might choose to reconstruct a room on stage, making it as much like a real room as possible; or they might make all walls transparent and use furniture specially made of steel; or they might choose to show only an open space with platforms and geometric shapes. Lighting designers might, through color and angle, suggest real sunlight, or they might choose to flood the acting area with blue light. Costume designers might use real clothes taken from a thrift shop, or they might construct a covering of metal and cardboard in such a way as to disguise the shape of the human body.

Decisions about the level of abstraction are choices about style and are themselves often closely related to the selection and use of detail.

Detail. At issue here are both the *amount* and the *kind* of detail. Again, an artist can choose anything along a continuum from no detail to overwhelming detail, and along various continua of kinds of detail: natural/artificial, expensive/cheap, urban/rural, and so on. For example, the abstract painting could be a splash of solid red with a single black dot, or it could be highly textured layers of many shades of red with numerous black dots of varying textures. The portrait of Marilyn Monroe might show her dressed in a solid fabric or in a highly patterned one, wearing no jewelry or bedecked in brooches and rings.

Similarly, theatre artists can make choices about amounts and kinds of detail. An actor, for example, can move often, crossing the stage, sitting and standing, gesturing nervously (much detail); or she might remain quite still, using no gestures, and speak in a monotone (little detail). A scenic designer may fill a room

FIGURE 4.5

Abstraction

This setting has been greatly abstracted even though it is recognizable as an office. The hanging panels add color and serve as projection screens for *Push* at Pennsylvania State University.

with furniture and bric-a-brac (much detail) or leave the same room utterly unadorned except for a single chair stage center (little detail). The costume designer might choose a rich silk dress covered with dollar signs sewn in brilliants (much detail) or a plain black leotard (little detail).

Again, all such decisions are matters of style, and they often interact with the materials selected for rendering the details.

FIGURE 4.6
Style: Detail
Costume designers help establish character by the details they provide. Here, eyeglasses, a colorful scarf, pronounced freckles, and a zany kitchen colander hat help the actor communicate his role as a happy-go-lucky weirdo in this University of Texas at Austin production of *The Very Persistent Gappers of Frip.*

Material. Choosing material means making decisions about such things as mass, line, color, and texture. Different materials produce different effects. An oil painting differs from a charcoal sketch; a building in stone differs from one in brick.

In theatre, too, certain kinds of materials predispose audiences in certain ways. For example, a setting built entirely of aluminum tubing calls on an audience's association with science or industry, perhaps, and invites a sense of detachment, coldness, cleanness. Such a setting is different from an otherwise identical setting made of bare wood, which an audience might associate with an earlier time and so derive a sense of tradition, comfort, and warmth. Similarly, costumes made of burlap will "say" something to an audience quite different from otherwise identical costumes made of satin or wool or cotton, each of which encourages its own set of associations.

Production Style. In examining visual elements in production, performance critics must therefore ask such questions as:

- Are the colors pastel or saturated?
- Are the textures smooth and shiny or rough and pocked?
- Are lines curved or jagged?
- Are masses large and unbroken or broken up?

Actors. Although more difficult, similar questions about actors can lead to an understanding of their style:

- Do the actors seem to be real people involved (unknowingly) in a real situation, or are they clearly aware of themselves as performers (perhaps they address the audience directly from time to time)?
- Are the actors using many small details of voice and movement, or are they relatively still, both vocally and physically?
- What materials of voice and body have the actors selected for the performance (soft or loud voices, erect or slouching posture, and so on)?

ORGANIZING A RESPONSE

The result of critiquing a performance should be an organized response to the performance itself. Because most performances are based on plays, a piece of performance criticism will most often need to address two related questions:

- What are the major values of the play?
- How are these values revealed or transformed through performance?

As with play-text analysis, performance criticism should be *informed* (based on knowledge of theatre), *orderly* (consistent and well reasoned), and *defensible* (based on evidence offered by the performance itself and capable of explanation to someone else).

Good performance criticism often synthesizes the values of play and performance; that is, the critic does *not usually* begin with a discussion of story, characters, and idea and then move to a discussion of given circumstances, convention, and style. Rather, the critic tries to communicate how the performance (the work of the actors, director, and designers) reveals the story, characters, ideas, and values of the play. In the course of the discussion, many of the questions given earlier in this chapter will be answered for the particular production.

Some other guiding questions might be the following:

- Are the given circumstances of the production clear? How do they relate to the given circumstances of the play itself? How are these given circumstances made clear?
- What are the conventions of the production? Do they seem to work with those of the play? How or how not?
- What is the style of the production, and how is that style achieved? Is it the same style as that of the written play (if that question is answerable)? Are the various theatrical arts in the same style?
- Is the story clear? How do the several elements of production enhance its suspense and surprises?
- Are all characters clear? Are they interesting? How has each actor made the character clear? Interesting? How have the several elements of design contributed to these goals?
- Are the ideas clear? Compelling? What elements of production have worked to further these goals?
- Did the audience seem attentive and appreciative, and how did the audience responses fit with my own?

KEY TERMS

Check your understanding against this list. Brief definitions are included in the Glossary; persons are page-referenced in the Index.

abstraction 55
auditorium 53
convention 54
given circumstances 54
story 50
style 55
surprise 50
suspense 50

CHAPTER

5

Mediating the Art and Business of Theatre

OBJECTIVES

When you have completed this chapter, you should be able to:

- Distinguish between those who influence the art of the theatre and those who influence the business of theatre
- Explain what constitutes a good theory
- Discuss the kinds of questions that theorists ask
- Distinguish between a critic and a reviewer
- Discuss what a dramaturg does
- Describe what experts in marketing, public relations, and advertising do
- Compare modernism and postmodernism
- Describe the roles of agents and casting directors

Mediators indirectly shape audiences and performances. They "mediate" because they stand between entities—art and business, play and audience, and so on. They influence which plays and performances are available and how plays are read and performances are seen. Mediators may not work directly with artists or performances in the theatre, but they nevertheless help mold the perceptions of audience members and sometimes those of theatre artists as well. Mediators, then, are intermediaries who link an audience to a performance or an artist to a production.

Mediators both produce and use theory and criticism, sometimes only to explore intellectual possibilities, sometimes to sell tickets. They sometimes act as consumer advocates, suggesting which plays are worth seeing.

Theorists, critics, reviewers, and dramaturgs mediate the art of the theatre. Agents, casting directors, and marketing people—public relations experts, advertising agencies, publicity specialists—mediate the business of the theatre.

MEDIATORS OF THEATRE ART

Theorists

A **theory** is an intellectual construct that seeks to explain a phenomenon. In theatre, there are two kinds of theories: dramatic theory, which deals with plays (Aristotle's theory of tragedy, for example) and performance theory, which deals with live performance and has no example comparable to Aristotle.

Theorists seek to answer such questions as, What is theatre? and What is drama? They may seek to answer questions about genre as well: What is tragedy? What is comedy? They may seek to answer social or political questions: What role has theatre played in the maintenance of the status quo? How is drama implicated in racism?

An ideal theory meets several requirements. It should be:

- Systematic, meaning that it is reasoned and orderly
- Internally consistent, meaning that no one part of it would contradict any other part
- Sufficient, meaning that it would give all the information necessary to understand the phenomenon
- Congruent, meaning that it would account for all available evidence and contradict none

Theories are thought better still when they offer their dense explanations both briefly and clearly.

Theatrical Theories Today There are no ideal theories. One can examine, for example, a play through any number of theories.

Theories of drama and theatre have multiplied in the postmodern period—that is, the period since just after World War II, when many previous assumptions about the nature of truth as "scientifically verifiable" and "objective" have come under

Courtesy NyghtFalcon

FIGURE 5.1

Modernism and Postmodernism

Productions of *Tobacco Road* and *The Diary of Anne Frank* at Triad Stage in North Carolina illustrate the sharp contrasts of modern and postmodern staging. With a run-down trailer as a background, *Tobacco Road's* setting is crammed with realistic detail, clearly a modern approach. The steeply slanted overhead nonrealistic structure and a random array of non-period furniture for *The Diary of Anne Frank* signal a postmodern approach.

serious attack. Most postmodern theories rest on new assumptions about the world and people's place in it, which the following comparisons may help clarify:

Modernism rests on:	**Postmodernism rests on:**
The industrial age	The information age
Reason, science	Nihilism, meaninglessness
Causality	Randomness and probability
Hierarchy and authority	Participation, dialogue
Autonomous individuals	Socially shaped people
History as progressive	History as nonlinear, discontinuous
Dualities, opposites	Differences rather than opposites

The multiplication of theories of drama and theatre is itself an expression of postmodernism, which prizes difference and chance.

Among the most important current theories are the following:

- **Feminist Theory**. An amalgam of film theory and a branch of psychoanalytic theory, with various goals: for example, to study a historically male theatre vis-à-vis women, to examine gender in performance, to define a feminist aesthetic.
- **Marxist Theory**. An attempt, influenced by the philosophy of Karl Marx, to explain links between art and economics by asking some version of questions such as these: Who profits by the current arrangements for publishing and

producing plays? Why do audiences approve of plays and productions that seem to endorse an oppressive status quo? How can audiences be persuaded to see and act on their own oppressions?

- Semiotics. The study of signs, an attempt to understand how audiences make meanings from the auditory and visual clues given in a performance; a potentially powerful theory for explaining theatre and its effects because semiotics endorses the essence of theatre as a "seeing and hearing" place.

The Importance of Theories Theories and theorists of theatre are important because they influence the practice of theatre. Theories shape artists and the audience's expectations and responses. At the extreme, theories affect what is and is not acceptable. Granted, it is not easy to say which comes first—the theory or the practice; that is, it is unclear whether theory leads practice by urging theatre artists in one direction or another, or whether theory follows practice by codifying after the fact what audiences find satisfying in plays and production practices, or whether theory and practice simply change along parallel paths, both influenced by some larger force.

When a once-accepted theory begins to fall into disfavor, competing theories and practices jostle around until some new theory gains widespread acceptance, after which patterns of plays and productions again begin to coalesce. Until a new theory gains dominance, however, both plays and productions are remarkable for their blends of styles. We are living in such an age.

The creation of theory, then, is an activity of major importance, one now located mostly in universities, where whole courses are sometimes devoted to the work of a single theorist—"Aristotle on Tragedy," for example. From universities, theories filter into the general consciousness through the work of other mediators and artists.

Tim Donahue

FIGURE 5.2
Marketing
This quotation from a newspaper review makes a promise to the theatregoer, one of fun and escape. Producers often feature quotes outside the theatre to attract ticket buyers.

Critics

Criticism is a considered examination of a play or group of plays, usually by applying theory. The line between criticism and theory is not always clear, however, because many theorists are also critics, and many critics make theoretical statements. Like theory, criticism has two branches: dramatic criticism (the study of plays) and performance criticism (the study of performances).

Probably because theories of drama are more fully developed than theories of performance, dramatic criticism continues to be the more widely practiced.

Today, different dramatic critics focus on quite different subjects—a play's form and structure, its images and metaphors, its politics and sexuality, and so on; their focus usually depends on what theories guide the critic's inquiries. Critics and their criticisms are often labeled by the issues they address: formal critic(ism), Marxist critic(ism), feminist critic(ism). Most performance critics, absent well-developed theatrical theories, often seek to describe and explain the complex impacts of discrete moments of performance.

Criticism today, both dramatic and performance, unfolds mostly in university classrooms and academic publications. Like theory, criticism is a serious intellectual undertaking, needing reflection that militates against deadlines and other pressures. For this reason, most of the best modern critics have academic connections; only a few of today's best critics are also theatre artists.

Because of its academic home, criticism might be expected to affect mostly scholars and students. But criticism reaches a larger public—theatre audiences—because theatre artists (especially directors and dramaturgs) routinely read criticisms of past productions to help them think about the play they are preparing. Through such research, criticism affects the work of theatre artists directly and, through them, audiences. Because today's audience members seldom read criticism, however, its influence on them is indirect, filtered through theatre directors and dramaturgs (see below). Like theorists, then, critics are important because they influence theatrical practice and so, indirectly, audiences, both in how to see plays and what plays to see.

Dramaturgs

A **dramaturg** is a specialist in dramatic literature and dramatic and theatrical history who works with theatrical production. Dramaturgs need strong grounding in theory and criticism, for they are regularly called on to explain plays and justify decisions made about their productions. Although long active in European theatres, dramaturgs became common in the United States only after World War II. They now work on the staffs of many resident theatre companies. Most gain their training in universities, some of which now offer graduate degrees in dramaturgy.

The tasks of dramaturgs differ from theatre to theatre. Most perform some combination of the following functions:

- Assisting in the selection of plays
- Reading and evaluating new plays
- Providing historical and literary background to directors, designers, and actors
- Assisting directors, sometimes by advising on the production
- Working on plays—adapting, restructuring, translating
- Writing notes for theatre programs
- Preparing materials for use in advertising, public relations, and education
- Devising educational materials for schools

Clearly, dramaturgs influence both productions and audiences directly: productions, by participating in decisions about what plays are produced and how they are produced; audiences, by writing program notes and educational and public relations materials aimed at preparing audiences to appreciate the production. By shaping plays and productions, dramaturgs influence audiences indirectly as well as directly.

Reviewers

Reviewers see plays and then write about them for publication in magazines, newspapers, television, radio, and the Web. Their orientation is toward consumer protection; that is, presenting themselves at best as an "ideal audience," they recommend or warn against performances on the basis of a taste shared with their readership.

Spotlight

Walter Kerr (right), president of the Drama Critics' Circle, presents Tennessee Williams with the Circle's 1955 Best American Play Award for *Cat on a Hot Tin Roof*. Photo © Bettmann/CORBIS. All Rights Reserved.

The *New York Times* Theatre Reviewers

Today's theatre audiences have an almost unlimited supply of sources to find reviews and opinions of theatre performances. In addition to traditional sources like newspapers, the Web has unleashed a vast array of sites, some with editorial oversight and experience, but most consisting simply of individual viewpoints. When looking for useful information, it is important to know the reliability and experience of each source. Knowing the reputation of a writer and the quality of editorial oversight is important to substantiate the review. As a focal point of American theatre, New York has no shortage of voices from all corners, yet the undisputed center for New York theatre reviews is the *New York Times*.

Many reviewers, even many publishing under the editorial aegis of the *New York Times*, approach the review as entertainment rather than critical insight. Yet the *Times* has had a number of widely esteemed theatre critics over the years.

Brooks Atkinson served as theatre critic for the *New York Times* for more than fifty years, beginning in the 1920s. His long tenure made him one of the most powerful reviewers of his era and he is credited with making and breaking many productions. In 1961, a Broadway theatre was renamed the Brooks Atkinson Theatre in his honor. Atkinson died in 1984.

Walter Kerr worked as a *Times* theatre critic from 1966 to 1983 and received the Pulitzer Prize in 1978 for his work. He was also an author, professional stage director, and playwright. Kerr wrote the musical *Goldilocks* with his wife, Jean Kerr. In 1990, a theatre on Broadway was renamed the Walter Kerr in his honor. Kerr died in 1996.

Two of the more prominent recent *New York Times* critics are Frank Rich and Ben Brantley. Rich served as the chief theatre critic from 1981 to 1994 and currently writes an opinion column. Brantley, chief critic since 1996, continues with others on the theatre review staff to hold considerable influence over New York theatre.

Reviewers are seldom critics. They do not rely consistently on theory; they rarely pretend to objectivity. They lack the time to process and reflect on what they have seen, their work usually appearing in a daily or weekly medium. Sometimes a review must be written in hours, depending on the deadline. Often, the format is so limited (one minute on radio or television) that little can be said at all. Reviewers may popularly be called critics, but the two words are not synonymous.

Reviewers evaluate both the play and its performance. They do not attempt to tell readers or listeners what performance is or how it works, however, but they do tell them whether the performance is likable within certain limits.

Some reviewers have theatrical backgrounds or education. Some do not. Experienced reviewers have trained themselves to recognize their own responses and to turn them into interesting, often witty prose, one of the functions of reviewing being to entertain.

Some reviewers develop power within their communities. The New York reviewers were once said to have life-or-death power over Broadway productions; recent research shows, however, that reviewers influence only about 10 percent of Broadway ticket purchases. Reviewers' mediation extends beyond the review itself, nonetheless, whenever quotations from the reviews are included in theatrical advertising. Because of this practice, some reviewers may try to write quotable reviews, eager, perhaps, to see their names on theatre marquees with those of the actors. They have then crossed the line between mediation and participation.

Some powerful reviewers may unknowingly influence the choice of plays that get produced. Reviewers, then, bridge the gap between the mediators of theatre art and business.

MEDIATORS OF THEATRE BUSINESS

Marketing

Marketing is a business discipline that oversees public relations and advertising. The chief precept of marketing is that a business should be focused outward to its various markets. For a theatre, marketers may break down the audience into various niches—by age, educational level, racial and gender makeup—and target them accordingly. A knowledgeable producer may realize that the theatre has, as well, smaller but important market groups—reviewers, donors, investors, local government officials, even artists it wishes someday to hire.

Developing customer subgroups within a general audience population may require changes in dates and times of performances, ticket prices, special amenities for special donors, public relations, and advertising. Some theatres, for example, have designated certain performances as "singles' nights" to appeal to one such subgroup. Some theatres have changed traditional days of performances: Theatres did not used to perform on Sundays, until marketing surveys revealed that Sunday matinees were attractive to many customers. Some productions, especially musicals, now perform twice on Sundays. Other marketing research has

Tim Donahue

FIGURE 5.3
Selling the Brand Name
The Disney Corporation announces three productions, all established titles, in this 25-story-high sign in the Broadway theatre district.

suggested that advertising copy can be adapted to other niche audiences: Teacher guides, for example, are used to attract school groups; discounted day-of-performance ("student rush") tickets can appeal to a subset with more time than money; a play with African-American or Hispanic or gay and lesbian content can use special public relations and advertising approaches.

PUBLIC RELATIONS AND ADVERTISING A specialist in **public relations** strives to position a theatre organization vis-à-vis its several publics—town, neighborhood, business community. **Advertising** does the same thing. The difference is that public relations seeks free media coverage, while advertising pays for its placement in media. As a result, advertising will always say what the theatre wants said about the production when the theatre wants it said; public relations cannot be so controlled. A schedule for advertising can be precise; usually, public relations cannot dictate when, or even if, media will cover a theatre's offerings. Public relations and advertising are sometimes lumped together and called *publicity.*

The tools of public relations include press releases, artist interviews, photos and video clips, and the staging of public events that attract free media coverage. "Broadway Barks," for example, is an event to promote pet adoption and support animal shelters by having stars from current Broadway shows meet the public. The media coverage it draws calls attention to the productions in which the actors appear.

Advertising consists of posters, direct mailings, billboards, flyers, television and radio spots, and advertisements in newspapers, magazines, and even other theatres' programs.

Theatres differ radically in the funds they can devote to public relations and advertising. A student director may well handle all advertising personally, probably by photocopying posters and flyers made on a home computer. New York producers customarily contract with an advertising firm to promote their productions, and stars often have their own press representatives. University theatres often have somebody to coordinate marketing, including publicity; when money is available, advertising may include some combination of radio and television spots, newspaper ads, posters, and flyers.

THE HOOK At whatever level, publicity campaigns try to capture the attention of potential audiences and lure them to the production. For each production, publicity people search for an angle, a "hook," that will set this production apart: the actor who goes on with a broken ankle, the actor whose mother played the same role in the original Broadway production. With the director and, if such a person exists, the producer, the person in charge of advertising will create an image—a logo—or phrase for the production. This image or phrase will grow out of the interpretation governing the production and will inform the graphics and text used in advertising it. (For a play about love, will we emphasize the rose or its thorns? A pink rose or a black one? Will we use the word *love* or the word *passion*?)

A well-conceived advertising campaign will not aim to bring everybody to the theatre but to bring those people likely to enjoy and understand the production. In fact, one responsibility of public relations and advertising is to alert people to productions that might be unsuitable for certain groups, e.g., parents with young children. Thus, with the concept of markets firmly in mind, a sophisticated theatre will create different advertising campaigns for different potential audiences.

Agents and Casting Directors

Agents are mediators between artists and the commercial theatre. **Casting directors** work for the producing entity and sift through an acting pool to find the most suitable actors for a production (most of whom are represented by agents). Agents and casting directors serve both for-profit and not-for-profit theatres.

Agents link professional theatre artists (not only actors, but also playwrights, directors, and designers) with the businesspeople who hire them. Theatre artists pay a part of their income, usually 10 to 15 percent, to the agent who successfully connects them to the job. In addition, the agent negotiates favorable terms for contracts, helps sort out disputes, and collects and distributes money.

An unspoken assumption, whether true or not, is that actors or playwrights who don't have agents lack the skill to succeed. Often, they are merely beginners with no track record. Inescapably, agents usually guard the gate of the commercial theatre; getting in without one is hard.

Tim Donahue

FIGURE 5.4
Advertising
It can cost from $5 million to $25 million to open a musical on Broadway. Extensive (and expensive) advertising helps to protect this investment.

Play Readers

Play readers mediate between playwrights and producing entities. They read unproduced plays, both unsolicited scripts and those submitted by agents, to discover possible plays for the producing organization. Major New York not-for-profits may receive as many as a thousand scripts a year for a four- to six-play season. Artistic staff members can't read this many scripts and practice their craft. The work, therefore, is assigned to readers, who winnow the list, leaving the most promising scripts for the artistic staff to choose from. The play reader needs at least the skill to reject the absolute duds and not to throw away the rare masterpiece.

Summing Up

A large number of people—mediators—affect which productions are available to audiences, how those productions are conceived, and how audience members relate to them. Theorists shape understanding and acceptance of plays; critics and dramaturgs analyze plays and performances to increase understanding of theatre and drama; reviewers warn certain audiences away and encourage others to attend; marketers and public relations and advertising staff try to pull people into the theatre. Mediators stand between the theatre's component parts and negotiate their relationship: art and business, business and audience, audience and artists, artists and art.

KEY TERMS

Check your understanding against this list. Brief definitions are included in the Glossary; persons are page-referenced in the Index.

advertising 66
agents 67
casting directors 67
criticism (dramatic and performance) 62
dramaturg 63
feminist theory (of theatre) 61
marketing 65
Marxist theory (of theatre) 61
mediators 60
modernism 61
play readers 67
postmodernism 61
public relations 66
reviewers 64
semiotics 62
theory (dramatic and performance) 60

PART

II

TODAY'S THEATRE AND ITS MAKERS

Theatre Practice

After briefly introducing the many kinds of theatres that exist today, Part II explores theatre artists—playwrights, actors, directors, designers, and technicians—as they train and as they work. It tries to to answer questions such as: What is the nature of the artist's work? What skills do the artists need to practice their craft? Where do they gain such skills? In what venues can they practice their craft? How are they rewarded?

All the artists of the theatre have differing skills, acquired through differing means. Together they must collaborate if the production is to be a success. As in a sports team, one great athlete without teamwork from the rest of the players will rarely win a game, so in the theater: All the artists must share a collaborative strategy to lead the show to success.

CHAPTER

6

Making Theatre Today
The Context

OBJECTIVES

When you have completed this chapter, you should be able to:

- Identify the principal theatre configurations and stage shapes
- Differentiate among the main producing structures in the United States, with an understanding of the strengths of each
- Explain several types of theatre funding

Before studying the people who make theatre happen, we need to examine the contexts in which they work in the United States. In what kinds of spaces can they make their plays? Are some arrangements of actors and audiences better than others for certain sorts of plays? What kinds of producing arrangements are available, and what are their strengths and weaknesses? Finally, how can theatre productions be financed, and what are some implications of the different funding sources?

THEATRE SPACES

Given the diversity of theatres around the country, it should not be surprising that theatre artists choose different sorts of physical spaces in which to work. With various elaborations, three basic theatre spaces now dominate: proscenium, thrust, and arena stages. In addition to these three, a few less common arrangements can be named and briefly described.

Proscenium Stages

The most popular theatre shape in western Europe and the United States since the seventeenth century, proscenium theatres are marked by a proscenium arch or frame that separates the stage and the auditorium.

The stage behind the proscenium arch is typically equipped with a rigging system, which allows scenic pieces to "fly" (be lifted out of sight above the stage floor), and a trap system, which allows objects and people to sink below the stage floor or to rise from it. Some are equipped with wagons or "slip stages" that allow scenery to be moved into place from the wings, the spaces on each side of the stage. In most proscenium theatres, there is an area that extends a few feet in front of the arch, an area called the apron or forestage.

The area on the audience side of the proscenium—the auditorium, or front of house—is arranged so that almost all seats face the stage. Ground-level seats are orchestra seats. Above them are balconies (also called galleries), which may curve around at least part of the side wall. Older proscenium houses have small,

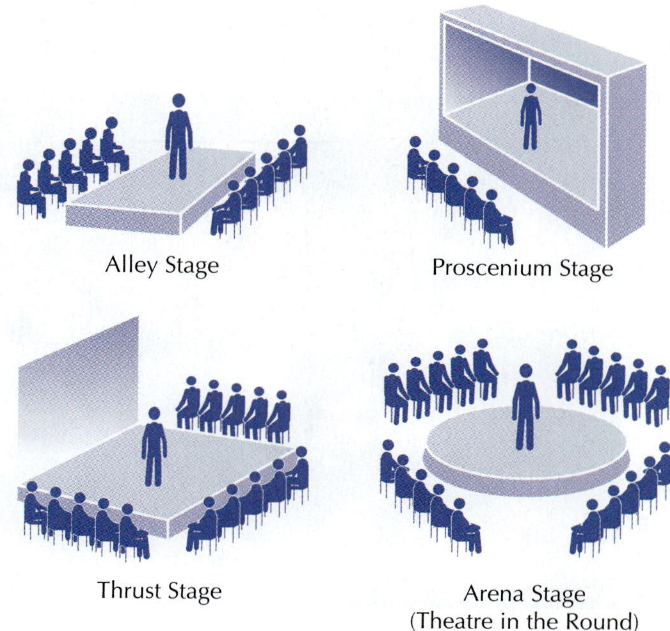

FIGURE 6.1

Basic Theatre Spaces

Actor–audience relationships in four configurations; alley (audience on two sides of the actor); proscenium (audience on one side); thrust (audience on three sides); and arena (audience surrounding actor).

separate balconies, called boxes, usually on the side walls of the theatre near the stage. These boxes were at one time the most prized seats in the theatre, but they are now usually avoided because of their bad angle for viewing the stage (bad sight lines) and are often used as lighting positions instead.

Thrust Stages

Some plays, especially those of Shakespeare and his contemporaries, were not written for production in a proscenium theatre. For this reason, several theatre companies, especially those whose repertory stresses plays from the past, have sought a variation of the theatre used in Shakespeare's day. Such groups have built theatres with thrust stages (also called Elizabethan, or Shakespearean, or three-quarter-round stages).

In such theatres, there is no arch separating the actors from the audience. Instead, audience members are placed on three sides of the action, usually on a raked (slanted) floor to improve sight lines, and in balconies. Actors enter the playing area from the back or through vomitories (tunnels that run through and under the audience and open near the stage itself—also called Voms). Because in this theatre elaborate stage machinery cannot be concealed behind a proscenium arch, and because, too, of the close physical relationship between the actors and the audiences, thrust stages tend to rely on acting, costumes, and properties rather than complex scenic effects. Indeed, in such theatres, without a front curtain and proscenium arch to mask them, all scene changes and all actors' entrances must be made in full view of the audience.

Of the many thrust theatres, perhaps the best known are those at the Festival Theatre in Stratford, Ontario, Canada, and at the Guthrie Theatre in Minneapolis, Minnesota, both of whose repertories stress revivals of masterpieces from the past.

Jason Ayers

FIGURE 6.2
Arena Theatre
For staging in the round, both actors and scenery need to be visible to all audience members no matter their seating location. This arena stage has four vomitories (actor tunnels used for entrances and exits). Only three are visible here.

Arena Stages

The audience in a theatre with an arena stage surrounds the playing area, hence its other name: theatre in the round. Many people prize the closeness of actors and audiences in arena staging, an intimacy especially well suited to many plays in the modern repertory.

With neither a proscenium arch nor a back wall to mask movements, all property and scenic shifts and all actors' entrances must be done either in blackout or in full view of the audience. Perhaps for this reason, arena stages tend to avoid elaborate scenic effects in favor of close attention to the details of costumes, properties, and acting.

Although less common than either proscenium or thrust stages, arena stages exist throughout the country, most notably at the Arena Stage, Washington, D.C., and the original Alley Theatre, Houston, Texas.

FIGURE 6.3
Alley Theatre
Audience members use the alley stage to find their seats on either side of the central acting alley. Here, the stage is set with scenery at either end for a production of *Black Watch* at St. Ann's Warehouse in Brooklyn, New York.

Other Configurations

Sometimes from choice and sometimes from necessity, acting companies take their performances to audiences instead of having audiences come to them. For such performances, a wide assortment of spatial arrangements must be found or created.

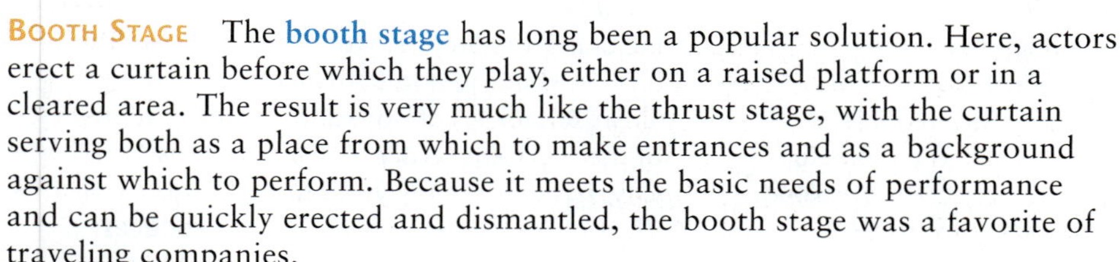

Booth Stage The **booth stage** has long been a popular solution. Here, actors erect a curtain before which they play, either on a raised platform or in a cleared area. The result is very much like the thrust stage, with the curtain serving both as a place from which to make entrances and as a background against which to perform. Because it meets the basic needs of performance and can be quickly erected and dismantled, the booth stage was a favorite of traveling companies.

Alley Stage **Alley stages** place the audience on two sides, with the actors performing between them, and often with scenic units at each end. In some countries, such arrangements are found in regular theatres; in the United States, however, they are used mostly by actors who find it necessary to perform in school gymnasiums.

Finally, only the imagination limits the space in which actors perform for audiences. In the United States, we have records of theatre taking place in streets, parks, factories, and even elevators—again, an index of the great diversity of our theatre.

Spotlight

Pilbrow's design for The Steppenwolf Theatre Company's Upstairs Theatre (right), the smaller of the two Steppenwolf theatres, is quite spare and steeply raked. His design for Chicago Shakespeare Theatre's Courtyard Theatre is ornate, with horseshoe-shaped seating that surrounds a thrust playing area.

Richard Pilbrow

Richard Pilbrow, one of the world's leading theatre consultants, is a leader in the movement to reestablish the intimacy in large performance spaces. Starting as a stage manager in the 1950s, he became a pioneer of modern stage lighting in Britain; his designs have been seen in major cities worldwide. Pilbrow was the first British designer to design lighting for a Broadway musical, *Zorba*, in 1968.

Founder of the successful Theatre Projects Consultants, Pilbrow has consulted on some of the most significant theatre projects in the world. He served as theatre consultant on the Walt Disney Concert Hall in Los Angeles designed by architect Frank Gehry. Opened in 2003, the Walt Disney Concert Hall seats 2,265, but, with Pilbrow's close wrap-around seating design, the theatre is recognized for its excellent acoustics and intimacy.

The physical space of a theatre influences the audience experience. To sit in the early morning light of an amphitheater in Greece watching Sophocles' *Antigone* would have been a different experience from jostling among the groundlings in Shakespeare's Globe just before *The Merry Wives of Windsor*. Both of these historical theatres would be different from today's theatres, if in no other way than that the audience today is usually sitting in a darkened space while the actors perform under controlled, variable-colored lighting.

Pilbrow and his company have influenced the design or redesign of many recent theatres, including the Steppenwolf and Goodman theatres in Chicago and the National Theatre of Great Britain in London, and the restoration of the New Amsterdam Theatre in New York City, home for many years to the stage musical *The Lion King*. Meanwhile Pilbrow produces shows in London and still designs lighting and projections for productions all over the world.

THEATRICAL VENUES IN THE UNITED STATES

Theatre now touches most cities throughout the country. Although its diversity makes classification difficult, we can divide American theatre first into professional and amateur (each with several subcategories). Because some theatres resist these categories, we have a third group: theatres for special audiences.

PROFESSIONAL THEATRE

The definition of **professional theatre** is very complex, but the bottom line is that people who work in professional theatre get paid adequately (not a token amount). Professional theatre artists almost always belong to unions that specify when and how they can work and for how much. No matter where union theatre artists work, their professionalism is governed and guarded by union contract. They can practice their craft at professional for-profit or not-for-profit regional theatres across the United States.

Broadway

Broadway is the term used to describe a small area in New York City where forty theatres with at least five hundred seats each are the remainder of what was once America's center of glamour, glitz, and theatrical legend. Of the forty theatres, five are owned and managed by not-for-profit professional theatre companies; the other thirty-five are commercial venues for rent. Only productions in these theatres are eligible for Broadway's prestigious Tony Awards.

Broadway connotes professional theatre at its best, whether for profit or not: elaborate settings, rich costumes, distinguished stars, polished performances, and sophisticated musicals and plays. A testament to Broadway's authority in theatrical matters is that many other theatres, both amateur and professional, strive to imitate it, and in marketing use the Broadway brand name whether warranted or not. From across the country (and much of the world), people flock to Broadway theatres to experience New York. They expect theatre written by the best-known playwrights, music by America's leading composers, performances by the best actors, and productions designed by the best artists available, for which they are willing to pay—in 2010—as much as $137.50 for an orchestra seat for a musical.

Although New Yorkers also attend the commercial Broadway theatre in large numbers, tourists make up a sizable part of its audiences. Broadway audiences comprise mostly affluent American citizens, a social group that tends to be middle-class or above, white, mature, and somewhat conservative in taste and politics. Commercial Broadway producers reported that in the 2006–2007 season, the average family income of Broadway theatregoers was $98,900. (The median income for all U.S. families in 2006 was $48,201.)

Broadway's Costs Much of Broadway's appeal, and many of its problems, stem from money. The cost of producing a show climbs each year as does the average price of theatre tickets, increasing faster than the general rate of inflation. The 2008 stage musical *Billy Elliot*, for example, based on a popular movie, was budgeted at about $18 million from start-up to opening night. Such costs have continued to climb for several reasons: As real estate prices in Manhattan soar, so do the costs of renting theatre space. Personnel costs rise with the demands of the unions. Costs of the goods and services needed to open a show—lumber and metal for scenery, fabrics for costumes, advertising in newspapers and on television—have increased at an alarming rate. Money is also needed to keep a show running once it has opened. Costs are now so high that even a fairly modest show must run months (rather than weeks) in order to recapture its original investment.

Huge costs have encouraged a "hit-or-flop" syndrome—a commercial Broadway with no place for the modest success. A hit can make big money; a flop can lose millions overnight. Not-for-profit professional theatres off and on Broadway, by comparison, can thrive as modest successes because their costs are significantly lower.

FIGURE 6.4

Discount Tickets

Discount ticket outlets are in many major cities in the United States and in much of western Europe. Shown here, a TKTS outlet in Times Square (left), and discount booths in Las Vegas (top right) and Paris.

Easing Broadway Ticket Costs Broadway theatres, both for-profit and not-for-profit, have tried to ease the costs of tickets. For example, three low-priced ticket sources, TKTS booths in Times Square, South Street Seaport in lower Manhattan, and downtown Brooklyn all sell tickets for Broadway and Off-Broadway shows not sold to capacity, mostly at half price, on the day of performance. In mid-2009, for example, two-thirds of Broadway productions were available at significant discount through the three TKTS outlets.

Other sources for discounted Broadway tickets include such Internet sites as Playbill.com and BroadwayBox.com. Tickets for many productions that are not sellouts can be bought online in advance from these sites at a discount of about 35 percent. With a Playbill.com printout coupon, for example, a theatregoer can buy discount tickets in advance at the box office at no additional cost; if a ticket service were used, service fees would be added to the price of the ticket.

The Road

Many communities regularly import recent Broadway hits by booking the touring theatrical companies (**road shows**) that each year crisscross the country. These commercial tours seldom use the original Broadway cast, but they do use professionals and can even recoup the losses of a Broadway flop. Because road companies travel with complete sets and costumes, they are usually able to offer polished performances of recent hits to audiences who would otherwise be unable to see them. Business is best for big-name musicals, good for plays with well-known stars, and risky for everything else, although certain kinds of shows that may never see Broadway (e.g., family-friendly productions) have found a niche on the **road**. Many road shows are produced by the Broadway League, the trade organization of Broadway producers, and thus are unionized. Other shows are sometimes nonunion.

Off-Broadway

The name **Off-Broadway** derived from the location of its theatres, which were once away from the Broadway theatre district; they are now all over Manhattan. Off-Broadway houses are now contractually defined by their limited capacity (100 to no more than 499 seats) and by their lower-than-Broadway salaries.

The goals of Off-Broadway differ from those of Broadway. Off-Broadway often seeks to serve as a showcase for new talents: Untried artists can work; established artists can experiment with new techniques; new playwrights can find production.

Although Off-Broadway continues to offer employment to actors, directors, and playwrights (producing three or more shows for every one of Broadway's), its production costs have risen and, with them, its need to succeed at the box office. As risk has become less practical, Off-Broadway has become a rather less expensive version of Broadway, for which it sometimes serves as a tryout space. Productions that succeed Off-Broadway may move to Broadway, often with the same casts, directors, and designers, but with larger budgets.

Lower ticket prices Off-Broadway attract a more diverse audience and therefore allow a somewhat more varied repertory. In addition to small musicals and comedies, Off-Broadway produces some serious works and is now home to most new serious plays. For about half what it costs to see Broadway shows, Off-Broadway fare includes revivals from the classical repertory of plays, small musicals, and original plays.

Off-Off-Broadway

As Off-Broadway moved closer to Broadway—in practice, if not in location—some artists felt the need for an alternative theatre where authors, directors, and actors could work closely together to produce plays in an artistic, rather than a commercial, environment. Thus, Off-Off-Broadway appeared in the late 1950s as a place dedicated to the process of creating art and exploring the possibilities of the theatre. It did not want to become a tryout space for Broadway or to succumb to Broadway's or Off-Broadway's commercialism.

Productions feature imaginative but seldom elaborate sets and costumes. Although the casts and designers in such spaces are not necessarily union members and are seldom paid even their expenses, they continue to work, exploring the limits of a vision that is often socially, politically, or artistically alien to current American values. Ticket prices even lower than Off-Broadway's encourage attendance, and the excitement caused by unknown plays and artists draws adventurous patrons to coffeehouses, lofts, cellars, churches, and small theatres tucked away all over Manhattan and even some of the other New York City boroughs.

Although sometimes amateurish and often controversial, the offerings of Off-Off-Broadway provide a genuine alternative to the commercialism of both Broadway and Off-Broadway. Off-Off-Broadway remains the focus of experimental and political theatre in New York in venues that seat fewer than 99 patrons.

Regional Not-for-Profit Theatres

The vitality of regional professional theatres is one of the most heartening developments in the American theatre. In cities throughout the United States and Canada, professional theatres bring art to their audiences. Unlike the Broadway theatre, these groups are almost always organized as not-for-profit enterprises and so in theory can be more adventurous with play selection, production style, and personnel decisions. They contribute to theatre throughout America by diversifying and enriching its repertory, developing new audiences, training and revitalizing theatrical artists, and providing employment opportunities. Perhaps for these reasons, regional theatres have been called "the conscience of the American theatre."

FIGURE 6.5
Not-for-Profit Regional Theatre

Now one of the oldest not-for-profit theatres in the United States, the Guthrie Theatre was founded in Minneapolis. It recently opened its new three-theatre complex built at a cost of more than $125 million. This distinctive structure features a "bridge to nowhere."

Amanda Ortland/Guthrie Theatre

Regional theatres vary in size and ambition. The best of them offer five major benefits:

1. They provide a forum in which new plays and classics can coexist and provide an alternative to the comedies and musicals that are now the mainstays of Broadway. Some, like the Arena Stage of Washington, D.C., have earned reputations through the excellence of their classical revivals. Others, like the Actors Theatre of Louisville, have been especially successful in sponsoring new plays. Such theatres have reversed the tradition of having plays begin in New York and then trickle down slowly to the rest of the country. Much new drama now appears first around the country. The best of it moves beyond its local area and throughout the country, often ending in New York.
2. They develop new audiences for live theatre. The art of theatre suffers without knowledgeable audiences because theatre artists become complacent, accepting the ordinary or the mediocre rather than demanding the excellent. With the growth of regional not-for-profit professional companies, audiences across the country have come to appreciate live theatre as an art form and a cultural resource.
3. They are a training ground and an energizing center for theatrical artists. Colleges and universities begin the training of many young artists; the professional regional companies introduce young artists to the profession, allowing them to work intensively with experienced ones. Today, many of our best talents in acting, directing, and designing begin their careers at one of these regional companies—and some elect to stay there throughout their careers.
4. They are an important opportunity for the seasoned professional. Commercial theatre can dull an artist's creativity and vitality because its repertory is restricted and because its productions, when successful, can run for years, a numbing experience for an artist. Moreover, the commercial theatre seldom offers those roles from the classical repertory that stretch the actor's craft. For these reasons, the best actors are often anxious to spend

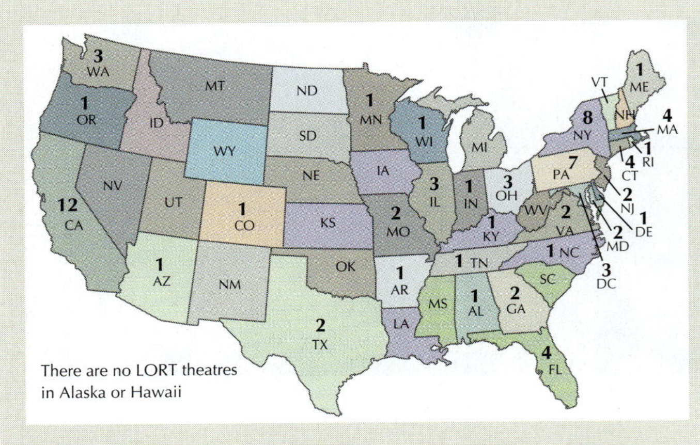

FIGURE 6.6

League of Resident Theatres (LORT)

This select group of 72 not-for-profit professional theatres is among the largest and most prestigious in the United States. As shown, most are on the east and west coasts, but so is most of the population. There are many more not-for-profit professional theatres that are not represented by LORT.

time with a resident theatre, where they can play a wide variety of roles from many of history's best plays. The exchanges between the regional and the New York theatres seem to be raising the standards of the entire profession.

5. They provide more jobs. In New York City, job opportunities are dismal. There are many more professionals than there are jobs. Regional theatres offer an alternative to New York. For several years, more professional actors have been working outside than inside New York; designers, few of whom get more than one show per season in New York, are now shuttling back and forth across the country, providing scenery, lighting, and costumes for professional productions.

Dinner Theatres

Throughout the United States, dinner theatres offer Broadway shows from past seasons, usually musicals, as the mainstay of their repertories. The quality of such companies varies widely. Some use union personnel, and their quality tends to be higher than those that rely on nonprofessionals. The number of dinner theatres is small compared to their heyday in the 1970s. The National Dinner Theatre Association has fewer than twenty-five members, but nonmember dinner theatres probably exist as well.

Restrictions of space and budget cause almost all dinner theatres to simplify the scenery and costumes of the originals in favor of smaller casts, smaller orchestras, and fewer sets, but, like Broadway, most seek to entertain rather than to elevate or instruct their audiences. In addition to the play itself, they add the sociability of drinks and dinner, so that an evening in the theatre is an occasion, not unlike going out for dinner before seeing a show on Broadway.

AMATEUR THEATRE

Amateur theatre is, technically, theatre performed and produced by people who are not paid. The two major kinds of **amateur theatres** in the United States are educational theatres and community theatres.

Educational Theatres

Theatre has a long history in American colleges and universities. Theatre and drama were at first extracurricular, performed at special events, e.g., commencements. They were later included within the curriculum of such departments as classics or English. Drama and theatre became college subjects in their own right only early in the twentieth century, when George Pierce Baker instituted classes in playwriting (and later play production) at Radcliffe College (1903), Harvard (1913), and Yale (1925). By 1914, Carnegie Institute of Technology was offering the first theatre degree. Shortly after World War II, many colleges and universities organized departments of drama (often in combination with speech) and offered, in addition to course work, first undergraduate and, later, graduate degrees.

Although differing in principal emphases, the functions of some educational theatres, especially at the graduate level, now parallel those of many regional professional companies: training future artists, developing new audiences, expanding the theatrical repertory, and providing jobs. Other theatre programs, however, especially at the undergraduate level, have kept their emphasis on liberal arts.

A major goal of academic programs is the education of students in theatre's literature, history, and theory, as well as at least introductory training in acting, directing, playwriting, design, and technical production. Although each program is unique, the general pattern of instruction involves some combination of formal classroom work and public performances of selected plays.

More than two thousand theatre programs exist today. In small cities without resident professional companies, theatre productions at a college or university may be the best or even the only ones for miles around. College and university theatres thus introduce thousands of students to drama and to a variety of staged plays. For many students, these productions are their first brush with live theatre.

Educational theatres usually display a commitment to a wide range of plays and production styles. Alongside standard musicals, comedies, and

Ella Bromblin

FIGURE 6.7

Educational Theatre

Presenting a diverse repertory of plays is part of the educational mission of college and university theatre. Heavily subsidized, and thus not as concerned with box-office success, educational theatres present newer plays along with classics. Shown here is a production of *Journey of the Fifth Horse* (Tisch School of the Arts).

domestic dramas, collegiate seasons are likely to include significant works from the past as well as experimental works. Consequently, audiences for university theatre productions often enjoy more variety than those for community or dinner theatres.

Too, the number of people required to maintain theatre in an academic setting has given the employment potential of the profession a healthy boost. At the college and university level alone, more than ten thousand productions are mounted each year and more than four thousand teachers are employed. When the growing numbers of high school drama classes, elementary programs in creative drama, and producing groups devoted to children's theatre are considered, it becomes clear that the academic complex is a major source of jobs. Indeed, educational theatre, considered at all levels, is probably the largest employer of theatre artists and scholars in the United States.

Community Theatres

Community theatres exist throughout the country, almost always organized as not-for-profit entities. Cities with one or two regional professional companies may have a dozen community theatres. In towns with neither professional nor educational theatre (except, perhaps, the annual high school play), a community group may produce plays in a school, a church, or a civic auditorium, providing entertainment and recreation for both participants and audiences.

Community theatres vary enormously. Some pay none of their participants, drawing directors, actors, and office personnel from volunteers in the community; others pay a skeleton staff—a technical director, box office manager, and artistic director—who work for a governing board of community volunteers. Almost no community theatres pay their actors or stage crew.

In cities and towns without professional companies, community theatres fill the important roles of introducing new audiences to the theatre and of keeping live theatre a part of cultural life. Where professional companies do exist, community theatres serve important recreational needs of people for whom participation in theatre is a greater pleasure than sitting in an audience. In their constant search for volunteers to help with production, such theatres regularly introduce many new people—especially young people—to the world of the theatre. Community theatres are, in fact, the first theatre experience for many people who later enter the profession. Finally, the relatively modest ticket prices of most community theatres bring into their theatres many who might not pay the price of a regional professional company. Some of these newcomers will become lifelong supporters, not only of their local community theatre but also of the regional professional companies and, when in New York, of its commercial theatres.

THEATRES FOR SPECIAL AUDIENCES

Some theatres cannot be categorized according to our earlier scheme, for they have both professional and amateur companies. Such theatres define themselves not by their financial structure but by the specific audiences they aim to serve.

Children's Theatre

Among the most long-lasting of such groups are the children's theatres. Whether an established professional company, a university program, or an amateur group composed of community volunteers, and whether using adult or child actors, a children's theatre aims to produce plays with special appeal to young audiences in order to instill in such audiences a love of the theatre.

The repertory usually consists of plays specially written for kids, using stories and issues of interest to that age group. Their range varies greatly—from imaginative retellings of popular fairy stories, myths, and legends to treatments of contemporary social problems like drugs and divorce. With relatively modest ticket prices and an unusually high commitment to their audiences, children's theatres introduce many young people to the art of the theatre and, from this large group, recruit some as lifelong supporters of all kinds of theatre.

Tim Donahue

Eva-Maris Repolusk

FIGURE 6.8

Theatre for Young Audiences

The New Victory Theatre is the oldest extant theatre building in New York, dating from 1900. It was restored and reopened in 1995 as a not-for-profit theatre dedicated to entertainment for kids and families. Here, La Famiglia Dimitri from Switzerland, a circus-vaudeville troupe, make their American debut at the New Victory.

Political Theatres

In another kind of theatre for special audiences—black theatre, Hispanic theatre, feminist (or women's) theatre, and gay theatre—the goals are openly political. These groups note (correctly) that theatre through the ages has been controlled by middle- or upper-class white males. Although their individual aims vary, political theatre groups share common assumptions:

- The interests of middle-class white males are not everyone's interests.
- Group awareness can be heightened by art. They seek, therefore, a theatre that can illuminate their group's experiences and explore its problems.

These theatres serve their audiences in very different ways. Some favor intense political statements; others avoid polemical works altogether. Many urge a continued separation of their theatres from those of the mainstream; others work to integrate their own art and artists into the commercial theatre as quickly as possible. Some of the theatres produce works with high production values and traditional dramatic texts; others disregard accepted production values and work largely through improvisation. Some seek modest social change; others advocate revolution. Some have budgets of hundreds of thousands of dollars; others have no budget at all. Some charge audiences to attend; others perform in the streets and parks—wherever people congregate—and charge nothing.

Whatever their techniques, these theatres for special audiences strive to offer an alternative to the traditional theatre, which they believe has either demeaned them or ignored them.

KEY TERMS

Check your understanding against this list. Brief definitions are included in the Glossary; persons are page-referenced in the Index.

alley stages 73
amateur theatres 80
apron 71
arena stage 72
balconies 71
booth stage 73
boxes 72
Broadway 75
community theatres 82
educational theatres 81
forestage 71
front of house 71
galleries 71
Off-Broadway 77
Off-Off-Broadway 78
orchestra 71
professional theatre 75
proscenium (theatre, arch) 71
road 77
road show 77
sight lines 72
thrust stage 72
vomitories 72
wings 71

CHAPTER

7

Playwrights

OBJECTIVES

When you have completed this chapter, you should be able to:

- Understand the implications of the words *playwright* and *playwriting*
- Differentiate dramatic dialogue from ordinary language
- Discuss the playwright and the playwright's cultural position
- Explain the playwright's relationships with dramatic and theatrical conventions, with audiences, and with the rehearsal process

THE NATURE OF PLAYWRIGHTS AND PLAYWRITING

We must not misunderstand the nature of the playwright's craft. Playwrights create replicas of human action—not records of it (novels) or responses to it (poems). The complexity of playwriting is suggested by the very language that we use to describe it—*playwright* and *playwriting*. Plays are both *made* and *written*.

Playwright

Wright means "maker." Just as a wheelwright is a maker of wheels and a cartwright is a maker of carts, a playwright is a maker of plays. Because playwrights use words on paper to set down their creations, they seem to be "writing." They are in fact, however, creating and organizing actions, using human-like beings (characters) to do so; they are creating replicas of human actions and then setting forth these replicas in language (writing). It is partly accident that what a playwright does looks like what a novelist or poet does—setting down words on paper. If playwrights had a different set of symbols to work with (like a musician's notes or a choreographer's notations), the differences between playwrights and other writers would be clearer.

Playwriting

Although we refer to a play*wright,* we also talk of *playwriting* and so acknowledge the importance of writing to what a playwright does. Playwrights set forth their replicas of human action in large part by inventing "language" for dramatic "characters" to speak to one another; that is, playwrights write dialogue that actors (pretending to be characters) will speak to one another. Dramatic dialogue, however, is not like ordinary language; it must forward plot, reveal character, and express idea, and in a compressed form. The fact that playwrights write words for actors to say and for audiences to hear means that their language must be more active, more intense, and more selective than either everyday speech or other kinds of fictional speech (novels). Playwrights also "write" nonwords: silences, gestures, rhythms, visual images.

Drama and Literature

This dual nature of playwright and playwriting gives a clue to a quality of drama and dramatists that is sometimes misunderstood. Drama is not primarily literature, and dramatists are not primarily literary artists, although both can be studied as if they were. There is a dimension of literary art in drama, of course, but there are other essential dimensions as well. Many highly respected novelists and poets are quite incapable of writing for the stage (the great Romantic poets Wordsworth and Shelley are examples); such people were fine literary artists, but they were not good theatrical artists. Conversely, the language of many highly regarded playwrights, when analyzed as literature, seems alternately feeble or overblown (e.g., Eugene O'Neill), but when actors speak the lines in the theatre, the effect is powerful and lasting; such playwrights are fine theatrical artists, but they are not good literary artists. Only the rare person is both literary artist and theatre artist in equal measure, Shakespeare being the premiere example.

SOURCES OF PLAYS AND PLAYWRIGHTS

Plays

An idea, an overheard conversation, a need to cry out against an injustice, an urge to break out of self—all these have given rise to plays. This germ may sit in a mind for years before something else urges it into life, or it may bloom at once and become a play written in the heat of the moment. Plays have been written in seven days and plays have been written in seven years. Plays have been partially written and then put away, often forever.

Plays have most often been written by individuals—playwrights. However, they have also been written by two-person teams, the most famous in the United States probably having been George S. Kaufman and Moss Hart (*You Can't Take It with You*). They have also been written by collectives, groups of people either dominated by one individual (who, as in the case of Bertolt Brecht, took most or all of the credit) or functioning as a unit, with individual egos submerged in it. Collectives work best when a shared idea unites the individuals: Collective playwriting has been, for example, practiced by a number of feminist theatres in which the collective is an externalization of an ideal of sisterhood.

Here, we are concerned mostly with individuals. Generally, they write in isolation for this very public art, theatrical performance. Increasingly, however, playwrights may work with actors, both to try new ideas and new scenes and to improvise around ideas, the improvisations then forming the core of the playwright's next step. Or playwrights may work with a director or a producer, not quite in a collaboration but certainly in a creative relationship.

Nonetheless, other than in collective situations, it is the playwright's name that goes on the play, and it is the playwright who sits alone with the blank page or the blank computer screen; it is the playwright who listens to demands for changes once production has started; it is the playwright who makes the changes as the first performance comes perilously near; and it is the playwright who takes the heat if the play fails. Or the credit if it succeeds.

Musicals also have playwrights for the nonmusical script, called "book-writers" or "librettists," the irony of calling any kind of playwright a book-writer not seeming to matter. (The script is "the book"; actors who haven't yet learned lines are "on book," so such playwrights are not really thought of as writing books, but *the* book.)

The librettist is in a different position from the playwright, far more likely to be working on somebody else's idea than an original one of his or her own. It is not story or character, after all, that drives the musical; it is music. As a result, the book must serve the music's needs, creating cues, setting up situations for kinds of music, driving to climaxes that will be musically expressed.

FIGURE 7.1

Playwright as Actor

The seventeenth-century genius Moliere was both a playwright and a gifted actor, playing many of the roles he created, including the protagonist in *The Misanthrope*. Here, a production of that play (in a non-realistic style) at Lehigh University.

Playwrights

FROM THE THEATRE Playwrights frequently come from within the theatre; they are "people of the theatre" who are "theatre-wise." For example, the Roman actor Plautus (see pp. 190) was a playwright who wrote plays for himself and his actors, and the French actor Molière (see pp. 249) was a playwright who created vehicles for himself and his troupe. Shakespeare, only a minor actor, wrote many of his most famous roles for other actors in his company, actors whose special strengths and weaknesses he understood and exploited. Such people of the theatre most often work within the dominant theatrical styles of their day, and they probably dominate the theatrical mainstreams.

FROM OTHER FIELDS Playwrights may start out as something else—not as actors or directors, but as something from outside the theatre altogether. These are not people of the theatre; they are not theatre-wise. Indeed, these newcomers, uninitiated in the current conventions of the theatre, may write in new and refreshing ways and so exert a strong appeal for those bored with current practices. Margaret Edson, for example, was a kindergarten teacher in Atlanta when her prize-winning play *Wit* was first produced in 1995 at the South Coast Repertory Theatre in California.

New plays can benefit from the newcomer's gift of ignorance; that is, newcomers may not follow the plays of the mainstream theatre in form, style, length, subject matter, or language. Plays by such newcomers may rarely find commercial production, but they are often welcomed in the avant-garde, where they are considered experimental. Then, if their appeal lasts, they may form the basis of a new kind of theatre. Indeed, much of the vitality of new movements in theatre of any age comes from the entry of people from entirely outside the theatre who write a play or plays that are unwittingly innovative.

THE INSIDER PLAYWRIGHT Social insiders can make successful playwrights, but usually when they write about a limited or minority culture instead of the mainstream. Black, gay, and feminist playwrights, for example, have written from a position (perhaps constructed) as insiders in the black, gay, and feminist cultures, outsiders in the social mainstream. This kind of insider playwright became more common in the United States in the 1960s. Since then, many such playwrights have worked in political theatre (p. 84), the tendency being for the minority-culture playwright to dramatize the problems of that minority in opposition to the mainstream, and thus to make it visible to the mainstream.

A Case in Point Tony Kushner's *Angels in America* opened on Broadway in the early 1990s after earlier productions in Los Angeles. One of the outstanding dramas of the late twentieth century, it was a controversial play that located itself in the heart of the culture. Its principal subjects included homosexual life, only recently real to most Americans; AIDS, an epidemic little more than a decade old when the play was written; love and personal loyalty; and, through the real historical figure Roy Cohn, political and moral corruption. The character of Cohn, a homosexual homophobe and an assistant to the notorious Senator McCarthy, opened the play to resonances far beyond what it would otherwise have achieved; so, too, did the brilliant concept of the angels of the title.

They, and their lair in heaven, gave the play a religious dimension and a level of spectacle that lifted it far above most dramas of the nineties.

Written in a contemporary idiom, the play was the resonant, meaningful work of a playwright who "wrote what he knew" but metamorphosed his experiences into a penetrating look at America at the end of the twentieth century, and at the situation of some ordinary Americans at the turn of the twenty-first—powerless, alienated from government and God alike, comforted by personal relationships, getting along on grit and humor and luck. It was funny and unsettling and startling and visually splendid, and it put the theatre itself back at the center of the culture, at least for a little while.

THE PLAYWRIGHT'S CAREER

Once a playwright gets started and has some productions, however, the way forward isn't necessarily either clear or easy, as some real-life careers show:

- Edward Albee had his first plays produced when he was 20, in Europe and then in the United States. By 24, his short plays dominated Off-Broadway; when he was 26, *Who's Afraid of Virginia Woolf?* had a Broadway production and was an immediate success. In the years since, he has been on or Off-Broadway many times and has been awarded three Pulitzer Prizes, a Kennedy Center Lifetime Achievement Award, and a National Medal of Arts, but he has also had periods of relative neglect. In his seventies, he is still writing and still seeing new plays produced.
- Charles Gordone was a professional actor who had worked on his play *No Place to Be Somebody* for years before it was finally produced Off-Broadway when he was 44. It won the first Pulitzer Prize ever awarded an African-American playwright and made Gordone instantly—but temporarily—famous. The critic Walter Kerr called him "the most astonishing new American playwright to come along since Edward Albee." In the more than two decades that

remained of his life, he had other careers as actor, teacher, and cowboy poet, but he never again had a new play produced in a major venue.

- Megan Terry's first plays were performed in a small theatre in Seattle in her early twenties, but at about age 30 she began a long-term association with the Open Theatre in New York. *Viet Rock* was both famous and notorious in the 1960s, a rock musical that came from the Open Theatre's collaborative and transformational style. Terry was hailed as an early feminist playwright for *Calm Down Mother* and *Approaching Simone,* the latter winning an Obie. When she was 43, Terry left New York (the Open Theatre had disbanded) and joined the Omaha Magic Theatre as resident playwright. She has written and co-written many plays produced there as well as working as the theatre's photographer. With more than forty plays published and produced around the world, a recipient of many important awards, Terry in her sixties remains a productive playwright who chooses to work outside the commercial theatre.

All three of these playwrights were "successful," but in very different ways and at different ages. None had a straight-line career from first effort to major

Ella Bromblin

FIGURE 7.2

Supporting New Plays

Cantile was developed and first performed at Tisch School of the Arts in New York. In addition to such educational theatres, not-for-profit theatres across the country develop new plays. *Doubt* was first produced at the not-for-profit Manhattan Theatre Club, then moved to Broadway. The play later became a film starring Meryl Streep.

achievement, or a straight-line career of hits thereafter. All displayed great talent. All received both extravagant praise and harsh rejection. Taken together, they pose a question: What is a successful playwrighting career?

TRAINING PLAYWRIGHTS

Unlike actors, directors, and designers, playwrights do not, as a rule, go through structured periods of formal training. To be sure, there are playwriting programs in American universities, but their record of producing playwrights who write plays of recognized quality cannot compare with their records in acting, directing, and design. Courses in playwriting often familiarize theatre students with the problems of the playwright and give an enriching new slant on other areas of theatre work; advanced degrees in playwriting are frequently combined with scholarly work in such a way that playwriting becomes an adjunct of critical study. Playwriting as an academic discipline, however, suffers from the same problems as creative writing in general, and when it seems to produce results it is because the same factors are at work: teachers who are themselves artists and who teach as much by example as by precept; constant encouragement of creativity itself, so that the student is surrounded by other writers and playwrights; and strong professional links with agents, producers, and publishers, so that entry into the mainstream is helped.

Many rules have been laid down for playwrights. They have seldom proved to be permanent—or to be rules. Rather, playwrights are well advised to follow some old maxims:

- Write what you know.
- Write for your own time.
- Write action, not speeches.
- Write for actors, not readers.
- Be passionate, not timid; truthful, not nice.

It often helps, too, to be selfish and ruthless. Writers work in solitude and with many obstacles; personal relationships sometimes suffer.

If, on the other hand, the playwright is in it only for the money, all bets are off, and he or she is wise to play it safe, aim for the middle, listen to marketing research, and imitate whatever made money most recently.

FROM PAGE TO STAGE: PROFESSIONAL ISSUES

Writing the Play

Plays begin as a great variety of things: a story overheard, a chance remark, a note jotted down on a slip of paper. Plays may set out to retell a legend or myth; they may treat a bit of history or a slice of daily life; they may be adapted from a novel or a ballad; they may be an imagined, onstage symbol or gesture. Moving forward from that genesis is part of the playwright's talent, and it is one of the elements that separates playwrights from wannabees.

Lots of people have ideas for plays. The problem is turning them into scripts. For many, the thought of writing a full-length play is a stopper, as formidable as the idea of writing a 400-page book. And true, full-length plays rarely get written quickly or easily; they demand the commitment of months, at least.

How do you leap from the genesis to the play—to character, dialogue, action—to all those pages? In part, the answer lies in the concepts of dramatic theory (see pp. 60–62 and 170), not because most playwrights deliberately apply dramatic theory but because they must work in terms of certain dramatic elements, whether or not they call them by the same names: above all, character, language (dialogue), and action. Idea, too, may be the genesis of a play and may dominate conscious thinking during much of the creative process, but "How do I dramatize the idea?" is an unproductive first question for a playwright to ask because plays are about human action, not ideas.

After the Genesis What happens, then, after the genesis—after the inspiring observation or accident or thought? The playwright tries to move forward. The urge to make a play is there; it is conscious. It drives the imagination—both conscious and unconscious thought. Certain paths are opened for such thought by the nature of the genesis:

- If the genesis is a story that will also be the play's story (as in Greek tragedy, for example), the next step is character: What kind of people are doing these things?

FIGURE 7.3

Genesis of a Play

Plays come from all sorts of beginnings—personal experience, memory, an overheard conversation, a famous event. *The Civil War*, performed here at Virginia Commonwealth University, was rooted in history.

- If the genesis is a person or the playwright's self (character), then the next step may be language (a burst of statements of character) or action, but, inevitably, action has to come early because dramatic character is character in action.
- If the genesis is an idea—outrage at an injustice, satirical amusement at a subject, a thought (e.g., "Revenge is easy to talk about but hard to do")—then the next step is probably character but may be story, a chain of incidents that embody and illustrate the idea.
- If the genesis is language—an overheard remark, a single great line—then the next step is probably character: Who says it and why?
- If the genesis is a situation ("Two guys and a girl are trapped in a stalled elevator, see—"), then the next step might be some dialogue but has to be an action: What do they do, not what do they say?
- If the genesis is history and a real person, then the playwright is already bound by some incidents, probably some meaning, and perhaps even some language (famous quotations, letters, and so on); the next step is probably story—trying to make a fictional beginning, middle, and end of a real life.

The Development Playwriting is an act of the imagination. It is neither entirely rational nor entirely conscious, but certain things will take shape:

- Situation—rough ideas of setting, social level, relationships, important aspects of the play's world: politics, religion, conditions of threat
- Tone—comic or serious or satirical or mixed
- Plot—not merely the story, but the ordering of the incidents as they relate to character, action, and idea
- Form—whether the play is to be long or short, in quick scenes or long acts, in a single piece or three or five

Other matters include rhythm, pace, rising and falling action, and climax, as well as, in certain kinds of drama, "big moments" and surefire act endings. The seasoned playwright, who has worked a lot with actors and may have certain actors already in mind, may also write consciously to give actable depth to character and dialogue for those actors.

Dialogue Much of this work will be externalized as **dialogue**. Playwrights must try to become masters of spoken language, both by hearing it and by creating it. The language of a play carries a huge burden: not only the meaning of the words but also character and tempo and the externalization of much of the action. As well, each character should have unique speech patterns and vocabulary; ideally, each character could be recognized by language alone.

Dialogue can take on a life of its own and lead away from what the playwright sets out to do in a scene. Character may lead this digression, but so can idea, or the interplay of characters-in-action may simply be too tempting. Playwrights can welcome a certain amount of such digression, but they have to cut it off if it threatens the progression of the play itself. Other theatrical concepts are useful here, whether or not the playwright uses the same terms: through line,

Spotlight

In *Crumbs From the Table of Joy,* Lynn Nottage creates the story of Ernestine, a bewildered 17-year-old-girl, on the brink of maturity in 1950 Brooklyn. Nottage's dialogue was especially praised. Here a production by Theatre South Carolina.

Lynn Nottage: A Good Playwright

Born in Brooklyn, Lynn Nottage wrote her first play at the age of six. She knows that her urge to be a playwright came from stories heard in childhood. "I think a lot about the question of why I write," she said. "I think for me the journey begins downstairs at the kitchen table of my house.... To come home from school, and my grandmother would be sitting at the table, and my mother would be sitting at the table. The woman from across the street would be sitting at the table. And they all had stories to tell. They were nurses, teachers; they were activists; they were artists. And I think that is where I got all of my inspiration as a writer."

Nottage's plays center on the history of powerlessness of African-American women. "I think the African-American woman's voice is important because it is part of the American voice," Nottage told an interviewer. "But you would not know that by looking at TV or films.... [M]y mission as a writer is to say, 'I do exist. My mother existed, and my grandmother existed, and my great-grandmother existed, and they had stories that are rich, complicated, funny, that are beautiful and essential.' "

Nottage earned a BA from Brown University and an MFA from the Yale School of Drama. She spent four years as national press officer with Amnesty International "writing press releases, op-eds, and speeches" before devoting her efforts to the theatre.

Nottage's first produced play, a ten-minute one-act, won the Heideman Prize at the Humana Festival of Louisville's Actors Theatre. Nottage went on to receive a Guggenheim Fellowship and a MacArthur Fellows Grant, commonly called the "genius" grant. Her plays have been produced by most of the leading not-for-profit theatres in the United State and other countries. Her 2008 play *Ruined* received the Pulitzer Prize in drama and a handful of other important prizes.

Loosely inspired by Bertolt Brecht's *Mother Courage and her Children, Ruined* takes place in a brothel in today's war-torn Democratic Republic of the Congo. Mama Nadi makes her living selling liquor and pimping her girls to soldiers from all sides. Her cardinal rule is not to take sides in an African civil war. "Survival is the only art I recognize," she says. Mama Nadi embodies the relationship of Western governments to Africa's destruction: She accepts profit if she can find it, but she does nothing to stop the ruin of people and societies.

"A play exists as a literary form," Nottage believes, "until the first moment you sit down in a rehearsal room and allow a group of actors to read it. Then it becomes a dramatic form. During the rehearsal process, you make discoveries because there are things that work beautifully on a page as literature but have no dramatic life."

motivation, objective (pp. 110–112). Working with actors on such a scene will help: Seasoned actors show unease or confusion when motivations go off on a tangent. This can be particularly true when the playwright has let dialogue, especially dialogue about idea, go off on its own.

Finishing a Draft As plays take shape, playwrights may show them to other people—lovers, acquaintances, theatre professionals. When a draft is finished, some playwrights set to work again with a director or a producer or with actors. However it goes, the play is not finished until it is on a stage in front of an audience.

Practicalities Playwrights always have to strike a balance between their own imaginations and the realities of the theatres in which they work. Plays must, among other things, provide a framework for other theatrical arts, especially acting and design, and so plays are circumscribed by both theatrical and dramatic conventions. These matters, and the technical means of accomplishing them, are things that playwriting courses can teach or the playwright can learn in the theatre itself as apprentice or actor.

Audiences "The drama's laws / The drama's patrons give," wrote Samuel Johnson in the eighteenth century. He meant, of course, that audiences, by their attendance and their responses, decide what traits plays ought to have and which plays are good or bad. Audiences, rather than critics or theorists, establish the "laws" of drama.

The remark illustrates the uneasy relationship between the playwright and the audience, for, to the playwright, the audience is a fickle monster that can make the artist either rich and loved or humiliated and poor.

FIGURE 7.4
Playwrights Horizons
For more than thirty-five years, Playwrights Horizons in New York has supported the development of new American plays and playwrights. It is one of the most rewarding theatre venues in New York for adventurous audiences.

Getting the Play Produced

In recent years, the number of theatres in which new plays can be produced in the United States and Canada has increased—notably, the regional not-for-profits and those based in New York. In addition, such organizations as the National Playwright's Conference of the O'Neill Theatre Center give first productions to a wide spectrum of scripts, many of which are later produced elsewhere. New York, however, remains the goal of most playwrights. There are two reasons: money and status. Broadway royalties are far higher than anywhere else, and Broadway production is subject to the best reviewing and is the most prestigious.

Plays are not produced at any of these theatres by accident. Nor are many new plays that attract widespread attention (except at an institution such as the O'Neill Center) scripts that come out of nowhere. Most are submitted to regional theatres or Broadway or Off-Broadway producers by agents. Far less often, a play may reach a producer by way of an actor or a director. In any case, the playwright's first high hurdle is finding that first production, whatever the medium used to reach a producing organization.

Working with the Play in Rehearsal

Producers have readers who read scripts and make comments. When a script is accepted for production, it already has an accompanying list of such comments as well as the producer's own views; added to these will be the ideas of the director when one is chosen. Each principal actor will add ideas, and each of these people—producer, director, actors—may have still other ideas that have come from friends, spouses, lovers, and relatives.

Changes in a script, however, are rarely simple; a Broadway playwright said some years ago that altering a play is like taking bricks out of a wall: For every one that is taken out, half a dozen others have to be put back. At times, the playwright wonders what it was about the play that ever caused people to want to do it, because they have asked for so many changes that nothing seems to be left of the original.

Tim Donahue

FIGURE 7.5

Paying the Playwright

Marsha Norman's 1983 play *'night, Mother*, a Pulitzer Prize winner, has been revived continuously in the United States and Europe, earning her a steady stream of royalties. This production in Madrid was in 2007.

Paying the Playwright

Standard Broadway contracts give the playwright a percentage of the theatre's weekly gross, a percentage that climbs as the gross climbs past certain plateaus. On a hit, these figures can be impressive—thousands of dollars a week. On a modest success, they can be a thousand a week or less. On a flop, nothing. There is, of course, the significant additional income of film and television sales—and, perhaps most important, there is the secondary income of amateur and stock production.

Amateur rights are handled mostly by two organizations, the Dramatists Play Service and Samuel French, Incorporated. They collect royalties on productions by amateurs (community, school, and university theatres) for the life of the play's copyright—since the Copyright Law of 1977, the author's life plus fifty years. Although the royalty on a single performance of a play is small, the collective royalty per year on a play that is popular with the nation's several thousand community and college theatres can be large, and even plays that fail on Broadway can become staples of amateur theatre and go on providing income for decades.

Summing Up

Playwriting is a difficult craft that requires special talent, and it is made far more difficult by the conditions under which plays must find production. Many potential playwrights now move to television and film, and there is some question whether—despite grants, theatres, and organizations that encourage new plays—playwrights will continue to decline in number until the theatre itself recovers its vigor. Relatively few people make a living as playwrights. The same can be said, however, of actors, directors, and designers.

WHAT IS GOOD PLAYWRITING?

Good playwriting is playwriting that produces good theatre. Exactly what makes a play good is the subject of continuing dispute, even among theatre scholars, but some of the traits of such plays have already been suggested in Chapters 3 and 4. The questions at the ends of these chapters can offer a beginning glimpse of what makes for good playwriting.

The great German theorist and playwright Goethe suggested another set of questions to help assess the worth of a play and playwright: (1) What did the author set out to do? (2) Did he or she do it? (3) Was it worth doing? These questions are useful inasmuch as they remind us that a playwright might exhibit great technical skill (he or she set out to do something and did it well) yet still produce an inconsequential play (it wasn't worth doing). Great plays, finally, must do more than entertain, although they must do that at a minimum.

KEY TERMS

Check your understanding against this list. Brief definitions are included in the Glossary; persons are page-referenced in the Index.

copyright 97
dialogue 93
royalties 97
wright 86

CHAPTER

8

Actors

OBJECTIVES

When you have completed this chapter, you should be able to:

- Explain the paradox of the actor
- Explain the relationship between actor and character and between character and real person
- Explain the goals of rehearsal
- Understand the actor's vocabulary
- Explain how an actor creates a role
- Discuss the possibilities of acting as a profession

THE NATURE OF ACTING

Actors stand at the center of the theatre. Without them there is nothing—an empty building, a hollow space. Directors cannot direct or designers design without actors; the playwright can create only works to be read like novels. The actor alone can make theatre without the help of other artists.

The accomplished actor is also a good performer; a superior performer, however, may not be a very good actor. Some kinds of theatre put a higher premium on performing than on acting; circus high-wire work, for example, requires great performers and has no use for actors. Musical comedy, on the other hand, requires both acting and performing, for the ability to "sell" a song requires performing of a high level. In short, the performer plays to the audience; the actor plays the character for the audience.

FIGURE 8.1
The Heart of the Theatre
Only the actor can make theatre without other support. Here, Lily Tomlin does her classic characters in a one-person show without aid of costumes or props.

Accomplished and experienced actors respect the etiquette of their profession, an etiquette that includes being:

- prompt: They arrive for rehearsals on time, alert, and ready to work.
- prepared: They bring to rehearsals whatever homework on the play has been requested.
- constructive, not destructive: They don't make comments about other actors, don't break out of character while another actor is working, and don't indicate in any way that another actor's experiment with a character is dumb.
- respectful: They talk to the director about problems, not to other actors or to the costume designer or to the playwright.
- aware: They know the theatre's past and its literature.

Artistically flexible actors know that only through remarkable efforts of concentration is progress made.

Two Approaches to Acting: Inspiration versus Technique

Our own age is one whose theatrical heritage is primarily a "natural" one, at least in the realistic theatre. The actor's ability to create a sense of emotional truth is much prized. There are at least two ways of reaching this goal, relying on inspiration and developing technique.

Modern American actors sometimes speak disparagingly of an actor who is "technical," meaning one who builds character out of careful, conscious use of body and voice—rehearsed inflections and carefully chosen poses and gestures. Their belief is that "technical" actors work mechanically and so fail to bring imagination and life to their work. The technical actor is seen as "full of tricks."

FIGURE 8.2

The Paradox of the Actor

Every age has its own idea of what seems "natural" or "real," including these Romantic illustrations that look decidedly unreal to us. Yet actors using these gestures were, just like modern actors, experiencing the paradox of the actor—to find images of the natural and the real through a process that is unnatural and unreal.

At the other extreme is the "inspirational" actor's approach to emotional truth. Although carefully rehearsed, the inspirational actor's characterization is not assembled from external behaviors but is created through application of mental and emotional techniques that supposedly work to reach the actor's emotional and mental center and then somehow push outward into onstage movement and vocalization. In theory, the character created by the inspirational actor will be more "natural" because it rises from inner sources that also give us music and poetry. To the inspirational actor, her approach is fresh and her creation original.

Must actors choose how they will work? Must it be one approach or the other? Actually, there is a continuum that links these extremes. Most actors probably use a combination of the technical and the inspirational approaches.

Being and Pretending: A Paradox of the Theatre and the Actor

To reach emotional truth, it has been said, the actor must be the character; on the contrary, another point of view insists, the actor must always stand aloof from the character and pretend. If an actor were really to be the character, how would she control onstage behavior? What would keep the actor from becoming inaudible at times? What would keep the actor playing Othello from actually killing the actor who plays Desdemona? What would cause the actor to modulate the voice, control the tempo of a performance, listen to other actors? And, contrarily, if the actor always pretends, what will she be but a lifeless imitation of humanity? How will the actor keep the speeches from sounding like empty nonsense? How will gestures be anything but graceful hand waving?

Courtesy Rep Stage: Stan Barouh

FIGURE 8.3
Inspiration and Technique
Seeing only the finished performance by a gifted actor, it is usually impossible to tell whether inspiration or technique was employed to hone the character for performance. Here, a production of *Trumbo: Red, White and Blacklisted.*

Because the actor is at the center of the theatre, this paradox is the paradox of the theatre itself: To be convincing, one must lie. The actor both is and pretends, exploiting both technique and inspiration. It is never enough for the actor to be satisfied that a sigh or a smile is perfectly truthful; the sigh or smile must also have the carrying power and the communicative value to be perfectly truthful to the audience.

This concept of theatrical truth was first described by the French theorist Denis Diderot (1713–1784). He used the expression "the paradox of the actor" as the title for an essay on acting in which he tried to capture what seems to be an essential contradiction in the actor's art: To appear natural, the actor must be artificial. Or, said another way, successful acting is making the audience believe that the falseness onstage is true.

The Actor and the Character

In the literary sense, character is a dramatic construct that represents human personality and that expresses itself through action. The effectiveness of a character depends on how well it fits into and effects plot. This idea, derived from Aristotle, has an important implication for the actor: Character is defined on the basis of its function within the artistic whole, the play, and not merely on the basis of how well it imitates a human being. Therefore, a character in a specific play may be a convincing imitation of a human being in its superficial attributes—the character may talk like a human being and may have preferences in clothes and food and entertainment like a human being—and yet it may be a "bad" or "ineffective" character in that it makes no important contribution to the action of the play. An actor who concentrates on mannerisms of the character and fails to grasp and act on the character's function as contributor to the action will fail.

For the actor, character means something like "the imitation of a human being as it expresses itself through the words and the decisions created by the author, in relation to the other characters in the play and their decisions and words." The actor's character exists on the stage (only) and has no life off the stage; the actor's character exists in an artificial time scheme that is quite different from the time scheme of real life.

In short, the actor is a person; the character is a construct. For the character to seem to be a person during the two or three hours of performance, actors must use their consciousness, their instruments, and their imaginations.

TRAINING ACTORS

Although there are supposedly actors who are "born," and although there have been young children without training who were deeply talented actors, it is a fact of theatrical life that all actors must train long and hard and must refresh that training throughout their careers. There was a time when would-be actors "came up through the ranks" as apprentices, moving from small roles in minor companies to larger roles and more important theatres, gaining experience along the way. They learned by observing, taking hints and techniques from experienced actors. Nowadays, the apprentice system of actor training has been mostly superseded by formal training, either in a college or in one or more private studios.

Actor training does not refer to one specific kind of study or to a set period of time. There are a number of effective actor-training systems. The most influential in the United States and Canada are those based on the ideas of Konstantin Stanislavski. Other systems have very different foundations, such as the psychological theory of transactional analysis or the theory of games and improvisations. Different as these are, they are helpful in varying degrees to different actors. No one system is best for everybody. The important thing about these systems is that they organize the work of the actor's consciousness, instrument (body and voice), and imagination. Without a workable system, the would-be actor makes progress only randomly, repeating mistakes and often making bad habits worse.

No matter what the system, actor training almost always involves at least these three characteristics:

- Analyzing the script
- Training the actor's instrument
- Training the actor's imagination

Spotlight

Here, Meryl Streep accepts the Screen Actor's Guild Award for Outstanding Performance by a Female Actor in a Leading Role, for *Doubt*. She has been honored more than any other living actress. © Lucy Nicholson/Reuters/CORBIS. All Rights Reserved.

Meryl Streep: A Good Actor

Meryl Streep embodies the best qualities of good acting and the good actor. Streep's versatility is obvious: In the last few years she has played leading roles in *Mamma Mia!* and *Doubt* (both acclaimed film performances) and *Mother Courage and Her Children* on the stage. Such a variety of roles on stage and screen demonstrate that she is not merely hiding behind a series of well-written parts.

She has earned a shelfful of acting awards for her work onstage and in movies and television. She has been nominated for an Oscar fourteen times, winning twice for best actress.

Meryl Streep was well trained. As a youngster, she studied opera. At Vassar College, she studied acting as a drama major. In 1975, she graduated with an MFA degree in acting from Yale University's School of Drama, whose actor training was firmly based on the ideas of Stanislavski as interpreted in America (see pp. 110–112). Sense memory, imagination exercises, vocal production, and improvisation were also part of the Yale curriculum.

Known for her meticulous and painstaking preparation for each role, Meryl Streep is regarded by her fellow actors as a perfectionist in her craft. In preparation for John Patrick Shanley's *Doubt*, Streep visited the author's first-grade teacher (then seventy years old) to observe her speech patterns because Shanley had told her that this teacher was the model for Sister Aloysius, the character Streep played. Streep joked that "I wanted to sound like I was from the neighborhood." In *Music of the Heart*, another film, she learned to play the violin by practicing six hours a day for eight weeks.

Clearly, Streep has the creativity, imagination, discipline, and stamina that mark any fine actor.

Analyzing the Script

The dramatic script is the foundation of the actor's work. Imagination and instrument are the means through which the script is embodied. Training in script analysis has three principal goals:

Understanding the Entire Drama On the first reading, the actor will be making judgments and sorting out impressions. The actor will read the script as a "notation" for a performance: The potential for production will be grasped, at least in general. An awareness of the play's totality will take shape. Of particular importance to the actor on first reading will be the style of the play, its main impact on its audience, and its overall shape. Under style, the actor will understand the degree of abstraction of the script; the kind of language, whether poetic or mundane; and the historical period. The impact will be comic or serious and will be expressed most importantly through language or action, idea or spectacle. The shape will describe the play's gross structure and its overall rhythms, whether it builds slowly or quickly to crises, whether it relaxes gradually from them or drops abruptly. This first contact with the totality of the play will also indicate what demands it will put on its actors—the special requirements of their instruments and the relative degree of intensity of the emotions to be embodied, among others.

UNDERSTANDING THE PLACE OF THE CHARACTER IN THE WHOLE DRAMA The actor is trained to ask, How does my character contribute to the whole?

Dramatic action means change; when a character is offstage, changes are taking place, and when the character returns, those changes must be noted and accommodated. The actor balances two lines of development: the character's and the play's.

UNDERSTANDING THE DETAILS THAT COMPRISE THE CHARACTER A deeper understanding of the play and the character's part in it emerges from repeated readings, as does a detailed sense of just what the character is. The actor may keep a notebook about the character, including those things discussed under the character section in Chapter 3, "How to Read a Play," especially action and decision, with character traits as they appear in the stage directions, the character's own speeches, and the speeches of others. All must be evaluated in terms of the production and should be discussed with the director and the other actors. For example, one character says to another that she shows "facial contortions" and her voice goes up "two octaves." The actor playing the character described must know whether these things are true (that is, whether the other character's description is accurate) and then work out when and where to use these traits.

It is essential for actors, as for all theatre makers, to look at the play in terms of its theatricality, that is, of those things discussed in Chapters 3 and 4. Such a breakdown gives them a grasp of the play's entirety and of its potential to be effective in performance. It should not, however, dictate character. Grasping a play's idea, for example, must never suggest to the actor the reason for the character's existence, nor should the actor worry about how to "play the idea," or, worse yet, how to be the idea. The actor who says something like "In this play, I represent goodness" simply has not done the proper homework. Except in pure allegory, characters do not represent ideas; they represent persons (who may embody or apply certain ideas).

In the same way, script analysis should help the actor to avoid moral value judgments. Characters in a play are not "good" or "bad" to themselves. Few real persons say, "I am a villain." The actor does not, then, play a villain; the actor plays the representation of a person whose actions may be judged, after the fact, as villainous—by others.

Put most simply, training in script analysis is training to read. It is training to understand what is on the page—not what might have been put on the page but was not, and not what the actor might prefer to find on the page. Script analysis deals with a limited amount of information and tries to squeeze every drop from it; it neither invents nor guesses. Most of all, it requires that the actor read every word and understand it in clear detail; from that clarity and that detail will come an understanding of the script that can be returned to again and again when acting problems arise.

Training the Instrument

"Stage movement" and "voice production for the stage" sound like (and are) titles of academic courses. They suggest that the subject matter can be learned and that then, like familiarity with Shakespeare's plays or a knowledge of calculus, they can be forgotten or assimilated. In actuality, the training of the **instrument**—the actor's body and voice—is a lifelong process.

The Body The actor's body need not be heavily muscled, but it should be flexible, strong, and responsive. The actor does not train as an athlete does (one set of muscles would be developed at the expense of others); instead, the goal is resistance to fatigue, quick responsiveness, and adaptive ability (that is, the ability to imitate other kinds of posture and movement or to adapt movement to, for example, aged posture and movement or the posture and movement of a body much heavier).

Many people who want to learn to act are so tense that they are quite literally unable to act, to "do." Physical tension causes sudden, random, or pathological movement (shaking, trembling) and dangerous misuse of the vocal mechanism. Tense actors may think of themselves as intense and not tense; they see themselves as "really into" a role, when the teacher or the audience sees nervous, confusing, and uncontrolled movement.

Relaxation exercises cover a broad range from disciplines as different as modern dance and yoga. All are intended to cause the consciousness to let go of the body, to return it to its natural state of receptiveness and awareness, and to make the body itself supple and loose.

The actor also learns additional aspects of how the body functions.

Centering. Many disciplines, among them Eastern meditative religions and some schools of modern dance, emphasize exercises that focus on a bodily center—that is, a core of balance and physical alignment, a place from which all movement and energy seem to spring. This idea of a center concerns both the body (balance, weight, and placement) and the voice (breathing and sound making). In yoga, the abdomen below the diaphragm is such a center; in some modern dance, the center is slightly above the pelvis.

Centering leads the beginning actor away from the mistaken idea that the physical self is located in the head and the face, that the voice is located in the mouth and the throat, and that the physical relationship to the rest of the world is located, through gravity, in the feet; rather, the actor finds the center somewhere near the crossing point of an X of arms and legs—a center of gravity, a center of balance, a center of diaphragmatic breathing.

Craig Schwartz

FIGURE 8.4

Concentration

The actors must focus their concentration on the here and now, absorbing character, given circumstances, through line, and an understanding of the entire drama. Here, an actor in *Bloody Bloody Andrew Jackson* at Center Theatre Group seems completely concentrated on what is happening.

Body Language and Nonverbal Communication. We all express our emotional states and our basic psychic orientations through body language. The actor learns to move the physical center to match that of the character. The actor also learns how all of us communicate without words, through such simple gestures as the waving of a hand ("hello" or "come here" or "no thank you") to complex statements of posture and gesture that say things completely different from the words that pass our lips. Such training takes two forms: study of the subject (much of it still in the fields of psychology and anthropology) and application to the actor's body.

- **Rhythmic movement,** including ballroom dancing, simple modern dance, disco dancing, and the like to help the actor to move to an external rhythm.
- **Period movement and use of properties,** including historically accurate and theatrically effective use of fans, canes, swords, shawls—the list is long.
- **Movement in costume,** including theatrically effective movement and gesture in wigs, capes, hoopskirts, boots—again, the list is long.
- **Movement onstage,** including adjustments to the stage space and audience sight lines. Traditional interior settings do not have walls that meet at the same angles as rooms, so stage furniture in such settings is rarely angled as real furniture is. As a result, "crosses" (movements from one point onstage to another) take unreal routes. On thrust and arena stages, the actor learns to play to all of the audience, to adapt posture and movement so that each section of the audience is treated fairly. Too, the actor must learn ways of bending, sitting, and standing that are appropriate to the stage in that they are not awkward or unintentionally comical.

The Voice The human voice is a product of controlled muscular work and chamber resonance (head and chest). Its shaping and control are not simple. Nonetheless, we make sounds and shape them all the time—only to find that our everyday sounds are inadequate for the theatre because they cannot be heard, they cannot be understood, or they are unpleasant. Unlearning and relearning are necessary for most actors.

The actor trains the vocal mechanism for maximum control of every word that is uttered, as well as for the production of sounds that are not words. He or she also seeks training and does exercises in breath control, relaxation of the vocal apparatus, dexterity, resonance, and such technical matters as dialects and accents.

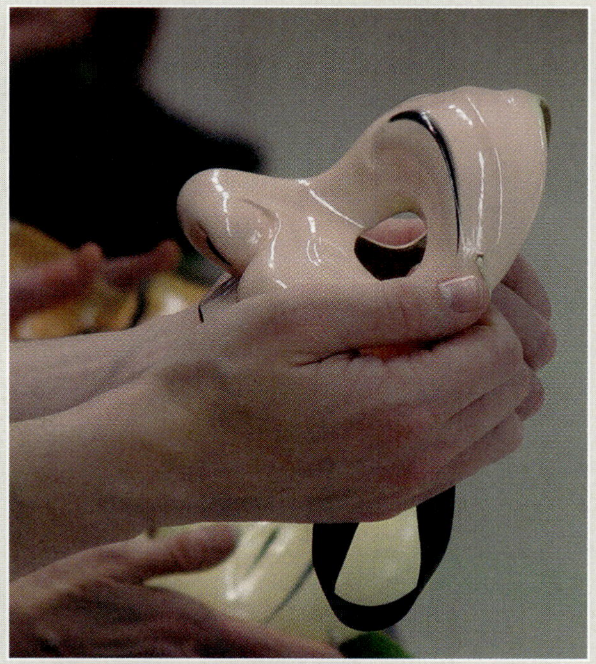

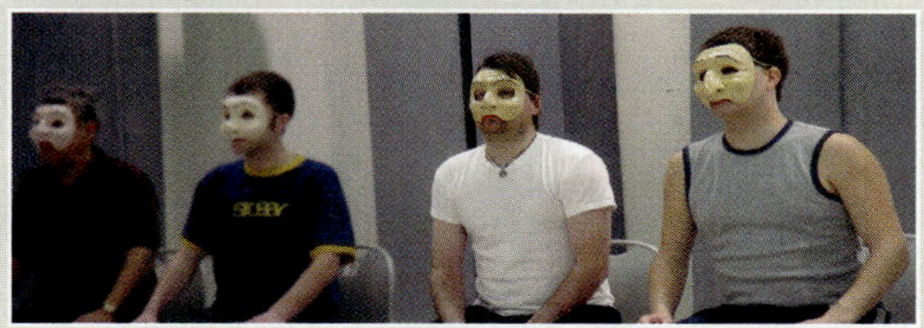

FIGURE 8.5
Mask Work
Transformation of physical identity is often taught with mask training. The masks have a "character," but the actor can't use his face to express the moment, so it must be expressed through the body. Here, an acting class at Wayne State University.

Training the Imagination

The word *training* may be inaccurate. Actors go through a process in a training atmosphere and are encouraged to discover their imaginations. Whether the imagination itself can be trained remains open to question, and many psychological data suggest that what we have called imagination is a capacity of the brain and the mental-emotional self that is always at work but that rarely surfaces. Still, if one can teach the rational brain mathematics, perhaps one can teach the nonrational brain imagination. Most certainly, actors can try to encourage the nonrational brain to speak up and make itself heard.

PLAY Dramas are "plays"; actors are "players." Yet beginners are often anything but playful. A terrible seriousness rules the work. To counter this tendency, they learn how to play, both to play games and to approach the creative act joyously. Many theatre games are versions of children's games or of adult "parlor" games that are noncompetitive fun.

CREATIVE EXERCISES In the belief that all people have imaginations and are creative, teachers devise exercises to free actors from both embarrassment and inhibition.

Image Exercises. The creative mind probably works, at least a good deal of the time, in images rather than in words (although many words are themselves images). Image exercises encourage the actor to grasp the mental pictures the brain offers. For example, simple character creation around pictures, objects, or sounds can be beneficial. An actor is given an object and told to perform a related character for the group: A knife is set out; the actor bends forward, walks with difficulty, the body held to protect its center greedily. From "knife," the actor went to "sharp," sharp in business, a miser, then added the element of "a cutting wind."

Visualization. Group exercises build a scene, each member contributing details and working to see the scene. Such an exercise is useful in touching the actor's sense of creativity, in sharpening concentration and sense of detail, and in preparing for those times in rehearsal and performance when the actor must "see" for the audience.

Sense Memory. Like group storytelling, individual recounting of the picture around a memory encourages a sense of detail and of sense memory. As many senses as possible are incorporated. Such **sense memories** need not come from childhood; they can come from the day before, even moments before. The purpose

Craig Schwartz

FIGURE 8.6

Physical Training

Actor training includes work on strength and flexibility. Here, that training is put to the test in a highly physical scene from *The School of Night*, a new play produced at the Center Theatre Group in Los Angeles.

is to cause actors to capture a sensory moment in all its fullness and, through both remembering it and recounting it, to cause them to be able to create such sensory reality around moments that come not from memory but from the theatre.

Improvisation. No single word and no single tool has been more used and misused in the last several decades than **improvisation**. Improvisation—the creation of quasi-theatrical characters or scenes or plays without the givens of drama—has been used to create theatre (without a playwright), to enlighten an actor about a character, to structure theatre games, and to teach aspects of acting. As a tool for training the imagination, it is an application of the techniques already mastered. In a sense, it is the basis of some of the other techniques; having an actor create a character around an image is such a use of improvisation. It can be used to apply the imagination, to stimulate it, or to supply raw materials not within the actor's experience. (That is, an improvisation focused on a frightening event might help the actor who has never experienced true fear.) To be effective as a training technique, improvisation is kept simple and is carefully focused by the instructor.

The Question of Talent Well-trained actors can achieve impressive levels of success. They use their flexible voice and agile body, their intellectual skills, their developed imagination to embody their roles. Beyond that, is there such a thing as

Craig Schwartz

FIGURE 8.7

Imagination

Actors must train their imaginations. Here, the central characters in the musical *9 to 5* imagine a moment in their lives with a little help from an imagined illegal stimulant.

talent? Talent, we may be able to say, is the ability of the consciousness to inspire in the imagination a set of actions and sounds that the instrument can express to an audience as theatrical character.

Acting Systems

Ideas originated or articulated by Konstantin Stanislavski, modified by the American Method and subsequent theories, continue to dominate the work of most American actors.

THE AMERICAN STANISLAVSKI SYSTEM In this approach, the actor is trained to analyze character to discover:

1. **Given Circumstances.** These are the undeniable givens that the actor must accept: age, sex, state of health, social status, educational level, and so on. Often **given circumstances** are contained within the script, either in stage directions or in dialogue; sometimes they must be deduced or even invented. (How old is Hamlet? Was he a good scholar at the university? Is he physically strong or weak?)
2. **Motivation.** Realistic theatre believes in a world of connectedness and cause. All human actions in such a world are caused or motivated. To play a character in such a world, the actor looks for the **motivation** behind each action. Some teachers have their students make notebooks for each character with a column in which a motivation can be noted after each line or gesture. It is important that the student actor understand that, in this system, all behavior is motivated—every word, every movement, every inflection. All action results from choice.
3. **Objective.** Like motivation, the **objective** is part of a system of causality. It is the goal toward which an action strives. Motivation leads to action; action tries to lead to objective.
4. **Superobjective.** "Life goal" might be an equivalent of the **superobjective** if a dramatic character were a real person. The superobjective includes all objectives pursued by a character and excludes all improperly defined objectives. For example, we might say that Hamlet's superobjective is "to set the world right again"; his objective in the first scene with his father's ghost might be "to listen to this creature from Hell and put it to rest" (thus setting the world right by quieting the ghosts in it). In this case, the objective and the superobjective agree. If, however, the superobjective was defined as "to take my father's place in the world," and the objective in the ghost scene was defined as "to listen to the ghost out of love for my father," the two would have to be brought into sympathy. By defining the superobjective, the actor is able to check on the validity of all the character's objectives.

Both the objective and the superobjective must be active. We have expressed them here as infinitives—"to set," "to listen"—but the actor does better to express them in active terms beginning with "I want," so that their strength and vitality are clearly visible. This "I want" is sometimes called the **through line** of the role.

In developing his system of acting, Stanislavski was interested both in actor training and in the problems of performance. His work cannot be viewed as merely a study of how the actor prepares; rather, it is also a prescription for the continuing refreshment of the performing actor. His system allows the actor to create what has been called the "illusion of the first time" again and again. Put most simply, this means that the actor is able to capture the freshness and immediacy of the "first time" (for both the character and the audience) by going back each time to the mental and emotional roots of the truthfulness of the performance. This process is possible only if performance is grounded in truth discovered during rehearsal—or, in some cases, during performance itself.

Continued performance for the trained actor, then, is not merely a matter of repeating rehearsed sounds and gestures night after night; it is a matter of returning to or discovering internally satisfying truths (motivations and objectives) and satisfyingly effective externalizations of them. Such an approach may not be perfect, but it is far better than the repeated performance that grows tired with repetition and that leaves the actor disliking both the performance and the audience because of boredom.

Craig Schwartz

FIGURE 8.8

Movement

Period costumes present a challenge to actors. They must wear them with ease and move in such a way that the garments seem to be clothes rather than costumes. Here, a moment from *The School of Night* at Center Theatre Group suggests that these actors live in their clothing.

Audience response to performance sometimes suggests at what points a performance is effective or poor, and the actor works at correcting errors as the performance period continues. Thus, the creation of a character must seem completed by opening night, and yet it is never truly finished.

Beyond Stanislavski: Acting in a Postmodern Theatre Although Stanislavski's ideas still dominate actor training in the United States, they may be under challenge, especially outside the commercial theatre. Plays different from those associated with modern realism often require quite different approaches by the actor. Today's new plays and new views of theatre—especially those that are highly experimental—may lead to a different sort of training for the actor.

Many recent plays are not organized by cause and effect; they do not assume a world of causality or connectedness, achieving their unity instead through ideas, perhaps, or mood or visual images. Actors in such plays might, therefore, be expected to place less emphasis on issues like motivation, superobjective, and through line and more, perhaps, on matters of vocal and physical flexibility, symbolism, and aesthetics.

Many recent plays present multiple levels of reality, with irony and parody often important. Actors preparing for such plays may be asked (and indeed have been asked by the German theorist Bertolt Brecht—see pp. 279–280) not only to play the role but also to comment on the role at the same time. Such a request seems to mean that actors must engage the audience in the role while, at the same time, requiring the audience always to recollect that they are watching a role being acted and not a life being lived—the double audience response described in Chapter 2.

One technique for accomplishing this dual process has been costume manipulation and cross-gender casting: The audience may watch a female actor, cast in a male role, put on and take off her costume (and so her role); in this way, the actor can both play and comment on the role and at the same time reveal the social construction of gender within the play and a society.

Separating the voice and the body of the actor is another such technique: The audience hears an actor's prerecorded voice over loudspeakers while seeing the actor moving and, perhaps, hearing him speak.

Many new plays deny the actor a single role or a stable character, the point of these plays often being that human beings themselves lack stable identities. In such plays, actors play multiple roles (including those of animals or inanimate objects) or many characters, and they do so without the changes in costume or makeup that have historically suggested such changes. Called **transformations** (see p. 90, the Open Theatre), such rapidly shifting roles would seem to place a greater premium on vocal and physical dexterity and imagination than on truthful inner work or a strong through line.

AUDITION, REHEARSAL, AND PERFORMANCE

Actor training goes on long after actors get on the stage. Most actors continue to work on their instruments throughout their careers, and many return to professional workshops to refresh and sharpen their inner work. After the initial period of actor training, however—college, sometimes graduate school, an independent studio or teacher—the actor begins to look for roles and, having found one, begins the work of building and performing a character. Each step in the process has its special conditions, and for the professional actor these steps will be repeated again and again throughout his or her life.

Audition

Most actors get roles through **auditions** ("tryouts"). Stars are the exception; sometimes productions are built around them, instead.

Most auditions are done for the director. Usually, the stage manager is there as well, along with someone representing the producer, if there is one. Somebody is there, as well, to read with the actor if a scene with another character is being read. (Usually, the stage manager does this.) At many auditions, actors are expected to bring prepared monologues.

The most important things an actor can show in an audition are basic abilities and the capacity to work creatively with the director and other actors. One of the director's problems in auditions is to try to sort out the creative actors from

FIGURE 8.9

Discovering the Production

Actors, along with other creative and technical support people, meet for presentation of sets and costumes. Here, the designer presents a model of the set and demonstrates how scene changes will be made.

the "radio actors"—those who have the knack of reading well on sight but who lack the ability to create. Therefore, actors are often asked to improvise as part of auditions and to work with other people. Cleverness in a first reading is not necessarily an advantage. What may count more is the capacity to work creatively and interpersonally.

Rehearsal

The actor will undoubtedly arrive at the first rehearsal with many questions. One of the functions of rehearsal is to answer those questions and to turn the answers into performance.

Actors often work very slowly in rehearsal. An outsider coming into a rehearsal after, let us say, two weeks of work might well be dismayed by the apparent lack of progress. Actors may still be reading some lines in flat voices, and, except for bursts of excitement, the play may seem dull and lifeless. This situation is, in part, intentional. Many actors "hold back" until they are sure things are right. They do not want to waste energy on a temporary solution to a character problem. Temporary solutions have a way of becoming permanent: Other actors become accustomed to hearing certain lines delivered in certain ways and to seeing certain movements and gestures; they begin to adapt their own characters to them. Instead, many find it productive to withhold commitment for a good part of the rehearsal period.

Experimenting The actor experiments. Some of this experimenting is done away from rehearsals; homework takes up a lot of the actor's time. Much of it takes place in rehearsals. Again and again, an actor will say, "May I try something?" Or the director will say, "Try it my way." *Try* is the important word—*experiment, test.* The good actor has to be willing to try things that may seem wrong, absurd, or embarrassing.

Most important, the rehearsal period is a time for building with other actors. Actors use the word *give* a lot: "You're not giving me enough to react to," or "Will it help you if I give you more to play against?" Such giving (and taking) symbolizes the group creation of most performance.

At some point during rehearsals, the creative and lucky actor may have a "breakthrough." This is the moment when the character snaps into focus. Motivations and actions that have been talked about and worked on for weeks suddenly become clear and coherent. The breakthrough may be partly a psychological trick, but its reality for the actor is important: The creative imagination has made the necessary connections and has given usable instructions to the instrument. The character is formed.

Creative Problem Solving The rehearsal period, then, is not merely a time of learning lines and repeating movement. It is a time of creative problem solving, one in which the solving of one problem often results in the discovery of a new one. It is a time that requires give and take, patience, physical stamina, and determination. It frays nerves and wearies bodies. The intensity of the

Craig Schwartz

FIGURE 8.10
Illusion of the First Time
These actors repeat their performances dozens of times, yet they must be fresh and immediate at each performance. This eye contact, for example, must continue throughout the performances. Here, a moment from *The School of Night* at Center Theatre Group in Los Angeles.

work may cause personal problems. Nonetheless, many professional actors love rehearsal more than performance because of its creativity.

Performance

Performance causes emotional and physical changes associated with stress. Some change, of course, is helpful; it gets the actor "up" so that energy is at a peak, ready for the concentrated expenditure that rehearsal has made possible. Too much stress, however, cripples the actor. Stage fright and psychosomatic voice loss are very real problems for some. Ideally, good training and effective rehearsal will have turned the actor away from the root cause of stress (dependence on outside approval of the performance); when this does not happen, the actor may have to return to relaxation work or find therapeutic help.

Opening nights raise energy levels because of stress and excitement. As a result, second nights are often dispirited and dull. The wise actor expects this pattern. Again, preparation is a help—complete understanding of the role and of the total performance, creative rehearsal work, and open lines between consciousness and imagination. Before the second and subsequent performances, the prepared actor reviews all character work, goes over notes, reaffirms motivations and objectives. The good actor does not say, "Well, we got through the opening; the rest will take care of itself."

Once in performance in an extended run, actors continue to be aware of a three-pronged responsibility: to themselves, to the other actors, and to the audience. Those responsibilities cannot end with the reading of the reviews.

WHAT IS GOOD ACTING?

Understanding the art of the actor depends, first, on the ability to separate the actor from the role. An attractive or well-written role can obscure the actor's lack of imagination; a poorly written role can hide the actor's excellence; an unsympathetic role can make the actor seem unsympathetic. By learning to read and see plays, we learn to distinguish the character from the actor, and then to see what kind of material the actor had to cope with. For example:

- Good acting has detail and "texture" (variety and human truth), but it is not merely a collection of details; it has what one artist calls a "center," another a "through line"—a common bond tying all details together and making the whole greater than the sum of its parts.
- Good acting has the capacity to surprise. Its truth is recognizable, but it goes beyond imitation to revelation.

Good acting, then, has technical proficiency, truth, a through line, and creativity; bad acting calls attention to itself, lacks technical control, dissolves into mere details because of its lack of a through line, and never surprises with its creation. A good actor possesses creativity, concentration, determination, stamina, access to the imagination, playfulness, the ability to cope with rejection, nonrational thinking, and detailed emotional memory.

KEY TERMS

Check your understanding against this list. Brief definitions are included in the Glossary; persons are page-referenced in the Index.

auditions 113
given circumstances (of characters) 110
improvisation 109
instrument 105
motivation 110
objective 110
sense memories (awareness) 108
superobjective 110
through line 111
transformations 112

CHAPTER

9

Directors

OBJECTIVES

When you have completed this chapter, you should be able to:

- Describe the major tasks of a director, noting which are mostly artistic and which mostly managerial
- Differentiate the worshipful from the heretical director and discuss strengths and weaknesses of both approaches
- Describe the purpose and process of production meetings
- Describe the director's work with actors
- Explain the director's use of space
- Define the art of the director

There have always been theatre people who exercised a strong, central influence on productions, but *directing*, in the sense that the word is now used, is a phenomenon of the late nineteenth century and has continued into the twenty-first. Despite the relatively late appearance of directors, they are now the dominant figures in theatrical production.

THE NATURE OF DIRECTING

When directors came into being, the responsibility for many tasks formerly done by several people, or not done at all, was vested in one person—the director. Directors came into being to unify, to bind all elements of a performance together into a cohesive whole—of both interpretation and presentation. Interpretation here means that the actors and designers all understand the play in the same way and agree on the nature of the intended audience. Presentation here means all the elements that the audience will see and hear—text, actors, scenery, properties, costumes, lighting, and sound. All must fit together, be of one piece, and be appropriate for the intended audience.

To be sure, the degree to which directors unify, make pictures and illusion, and organize and manage depends in part on their situation. For example, in commercial theatres like Broadway's, overall artistic vision and production control may rest with a producer rather than a director, and many routine details of rehearsal and performance may devolve to a stage manager instead of remaining with the director. On the other hand, in high schools and small community theatres, these tasks often fall to the director, so that he or she must personally supervise (or even execute) almost every aspect of a production. No matter the producing circumstance, however, the director is the undisputed head of the team.

FIGURE 9.1

The Director's Responsibilities

The modern director is both artist and executive. The work begins at play selection and ends after (sometimes long after) the first performance. Many tasks go forward simultaneously, ending and beginning at different times.

A Director's Responsibilities

The director's acknowledged responsibilities are spread over at least seven major areas.

- Selecting or approving the play (including work with a playwright on an original script)
- Interpreting the play (analyzing and researching the playscript)
- Creating and communicating the production (scenery, costumes, lighting, sound)
- Developing a ground plan
- Casting and coaching actors
- Staging (including blocking, orchestrating voices, and setting tempos)
- Planning, coordinating, rehearsing, and polishing the production

This list suggests that a director's responsibilities are not only artistic but also managerial. However, these responsibilities are not discrete and separable.

A Director's Traits

This wide range of responsibilities requires a person of many abilities. Effective directors must master these traits:

- Directors need skills in organization in order to plan, coordinate, and schedule. Such skills include an ability to put ideas in order and to combine them with the ideas of other people, as well as the ability to order rehearsals, schedules, and budgets.
- Directors need abilities in making decisions, including the clearheadedness to define problems and see the conditions under which they must be solved (including limitations of time, budget, and available talent).
- Directors need sensitive interpersonal skills to coax performances from actors and to work effectively with all other members of the production team, inspiring each whenever possible, working creatively with them on group solutions to complicated problems, and imposing solutions only when absolutely necessary.
- Directors must have artistic vision and talent, which, although hard to define, are absolutely essential for successful productions.
- Directors need both stamina and concentration if they are to exercise their talent and carry out their many responsibilities.

Directors have to be both artists and managers in almost all of their work, and they are unique among theatre professionals precisely because of this unusual combination of traits. Within the same person, then, the artist proposes and the manager disposes, sometimes at widely different times and sometimes simultaneously.

A Director's View of Text

What is the director's responsibility to the dramatic text? Is it the director's job to put the play on the stage with utmost fidelity, or is it the director's job to create a theatrical event to which the script is merely a contributing part? Can the director cut lines or scenes, transpose scenes, alter characters? Can the director "improve" the play, or must it be treated as a sacred object? Directors vary widely in the way

Courtesy Rep Stage: Stan Barouh

FIGURE 9.2

Text-Centered Directing

The "Worshipful Director" respects the playwright's text. Here, a production of Shaw's *The Doctor's Dilemma* seems to respect the author's realistic setting, period, and costumes. Note, too, the line of the turntable on the stage floor that suggests there are other locales.

they answer such questions. Their views range from veneration of the text by the Worshipful Director to near indifference by the Heretical Director; the play is seen as a holy object on the one hand, as a merely useful artifact on the other.

The Worshipful Director's Approach This directorial approach is playwright-centered. The worshipful director believes that nothing should stand in the way of the script as the playwright wrote it.

The Worshipful Director Argues:

The play is the only permanent art object in performance; it is a work of art in its own right, to be treated with respect and love. Because it has stood the test of time, it has intrinsic value. By examining it, we can know its creator's intentions—what meanings the playwright meant to convey, what experiences the audience was meant to have, what theatrical values were being celebrated. The playwright is a literary artist and a thinker, and the playwright's work is the foundation of theatrical art. It is the director's job to mount the playwright's work as faithfully and correctly as humanly possible.

Quirky modern interpretations are suspect, however: To show Hamlet as a homosexual in love with Rosencrantz or Guildenstern would be absurd and wrong because we know that such a relationship would never have been included in the tragic view that Shakespeare held.

FIGURE 9.3
Director-Centered Directing
Here, a run-through in rehearsal clothes but with setting of Ibsen's *Hedda Gabler* in Barcelona. Note the strikingly modern set—leather sectional seating, chrome verticals, and glass partitions. This director obviously ignored Ibsen's 1890 stage directions and changed the play's given circumstances.

> The director's job is not primarily to create theatre; it is to cause the play to create theatre. The difference is crucial. The director says quite properly, 'I must allow the play to speak for itself and not get in the way.' To do otherwise is to betray the play, and I will not do it even if the 'betrayal' is great theatre.

The text-centered director, then, will often stage a production without cuts, with male roles played by males, with no attention given to ethnic diversity in casting. The playwright's given circumstances are scrupulously followed: sets, costumes, and props will reflect the author's dictates. By choice, the hand of the text-centered director is seldom discernible.

The Heretical Director's Approach This approach is director-centered rather than text-centered; it puts the director on a par with the playwright.

The Heretical Director Argues:

> Interpreting the text means making a theatrical entity of it for an audience—not 'finding its meaning' or 'doing it correctly.' There is no single interpretation of a

play that is correct. There are only interpretations that are right for a given set of performers under a given set of conditions for a given audience.

How, then, can a director judge the rightness of the production? The director does not, any more than a painter judges the rightness of a painting. The director's final criterion is the satisfaction of an overall goal: Is it good theatre? Fidelity to some 'authorized' or time-honored view of the play is not, simply in and of itself, a good thing. It is foolish to say that the director did the play wrong unless what the director did was to make bad or dull theatre. The director has to be faithful to a vision, not to tradition or academic scholarship or propriety; only when that vision fails can the director be said to be wrong.

Does this mean, then, that the director has no responsibility to the 'meaning' of the play? Yes, in the sense that the director's responsibility is to the meaning of the performance, of which the play is only a part. Are we, then, to have gay Hamlets? Yes, if such interpretations are necessary to make the plays into effective theatre and if they are entirely consistent within their productions. It is impossible to know what somebody else's intentions were; an intention that was dynamite in 1600 may be as dull as dishwater in 2010.

The heretical director believes, then, that the author's script is only the starting point for a new theatre experience. The playwright's words are among the least important features of the director-centered production. There may be textual interpolations from other sources; the playwright's text may be cut and rearranged; there may be cross-gender or color-blind casting; there may be striking visual images that seem to have little to do with the text. In short, the director-centered approach sees the director as a co-creator of the production. This approach to directing aligns with postmodernism.

The extremes of the heretical director's views can lead to results that many people find offensive or meaningless; on the other hand, those views can also lead to innovative and exciting productions.

A Continuum Both sorts of directors take a risk: The heretical director takes the chance of being ridiculous, the worshipful director of being vapid. At their best, however, both can create productions that thrill audiences, the one with revelations of familiar material, the other with a brilliant rendition of the strong points of the classic.

The heretical and worshipful directors seem to be at the extremes of a continuum. The vast majority of directors in this century tend to approach productions more centrally. That is, they unobtrusively blend elements of both directorial approaches.

THE DIRECTOR AT WORK

The following seven steps are those that all directors take whether or not they are aware that they are taking them. Not all directors will necessarily approach each step in the same order, but the process presented here is an orderly one that can lead to a successful production.

Selecting the Play

Directors in community, school, and university theatres most often select the plays they direct; in professional theatre, directors at least approve the scripts (if they are staff directors at a regional theatre, say) or find themselves matched to a play by a commercial producer. Directors choose to do plays because the plays excite them; idea and spectacle are probably the most common elements to prompt directorial interest. Experienced directors also have acquired the ability to study the script in depth before accepting an assignment. Once the play has been selected or approved, the task of interpretation begins.

Interpreting the Play

The work of interpretation is an open-ended process that is based on analysis and research, some of which was described in Chapters 3 and 4.

Assessing Potentials and Challenges In early readings, the director usually has both positive and negative thoughts about the play and its audience impact. Two lists could be made, one of potentials (strengthens) and one of challenges (weaknesses). These two lists taken together would show how the director's ideas were forming. Just as artists in any form are inspired by obstacles, so the director is inspired by a script's problems. Let us suppose that the director is considering Ibsen's *A Doll's House,* a realistic nineteenth-century play (see Spotlight on page 276). The play is a classic of its kind and so has established merit; on the other hand, it is also old enough to seem dated to a modern audience in language and some plot devices. Therefore, after early readings, the director could list some strengths and weaknesses:

Potentials	Challenges
Strong subject matter	Creaky structure—melodramatic
Excellent central character	Dated language
Great third-act climax	Some "serious" stuff now "funny"
Good potential for probing Victorian attitudes	Soliloquies, set speeches very hard to make convincing today

Analyzing the Text No matter what the orientation toward the text, the director must now work to analyze it: take it apart, reduce it to its smallest components, "understand" it. Here, "to understand" means to allow the director to stage it. (Sometimes the director will be aided in this task by a dramaturg.) This job of analysis has many aspects, which are often explored simultaneously, both before and during rehearsals.

As a beginning, the director will want to ask and answer the kinds of questions suggested in Chapters 3 and 4. But the director's analysis will be much more detailed. Each decision about the play must be measured against an idea of how the anticipated audience will react. In thinking about audience, the

FIGURE 9.4
Mood
Scenery, color, lighting, costume, and fog set the mood for the Nevada Conservatory Theatre at University of Nevada, Las Vegas production of *Macbeth*.

director will explore many of the issues raised in Chapter 2, but again in considerably more detail. To see the differences between a director's analysis and the more general analyses offered elsewhere, we can look briefly at five representative areas.

Tone, Mood, and Key. Funny/serious, cheerful/sad, light/heavy—the possibilities are many and must be identified for each act, each scene, and each line, as well as for the entire play. Neither laughter nor powerful emotion belongs unchangeably to every line of a script. Even when the proper tone is found for the play, the lines alone will not deliver that tone to an audience. For example, laugh lines must be carefully set up and "pointed," with both business (small activities performed by actors) and timing; moments that have potential for powerful emotion must be mined by the director, working with the actors.

Of particular interest in this aspect of interpretation is mood, the emotional "feel" that determines tempo and pictorial composition, and key (as in "high key" and "low key"), the degree to which effects are played against one another or against a norm for contrast. High-key scenes may even go to chiaroscuro ("light/dark") effects that use the darkest darks and the lightest lights, as in dramatic painting.

The Six Parts. The director must study the play, perhaps using Aristotle's six parts (see Chapter 3), to find which parts are most important and which can be used most creatively to serve the play. Spectacle (including lighting, costume, the pictures created by the actors' movement, and scenery) and sound (including music, sound effects, and language) are often parts the director can manipulate and can bring to the play as "extras" that the playwright has not included. Character, idea, and story, on the other hand, are usually integral to the script itself, although subject to considerable interpretation and "bending" by director and actors. Many directors annotate their scripts in great detail for these three parts, some marking every line of dialogue for its contribution to character, idea, or story. Such annotations give the director both an overall sense of the play's thrust and specific instances of that thrust at work.

An analysis of these elements of the play is critical. A part misunderstood at this stage can mean that a moment or even an important thread through the entire play is lost in performance. To miss a major emphasis can mean a failed production. For example, a play that depends heavily on the beauty and intricacy of its language spoken in performance (sound) will usually suffer if directed to emphasize story or character, with the language overlooked or ignored (a not infrequent problem in productions of Shakespeare's plays). A play of character, if directed for its story, often has incomprehensible spots and long stretches during which nothing seems to happen. Therefore, the director must not only pick the

FIGURE 9.5
Environment
The author and director of *Metamorphoses* incorporated a reflecting pool as the physical and emotional center of the play. Later directors must discover how to integrate this unusual environment with the acting to create evocative images. Here, a production at Virginia Commonwealth University.

part or parts that she can give theatrical life but must also pick the part or parts that the script gives theatrical life. Such choices mean knowing which part(s) is most important, where in the play each has its heights and depths, and how the director will give theatrical excitement to each.

Action and Progression. Performance is active and most plays have progressive actions; that is, they occur through time (audience time and their own time), and they must seem to increase in intensity as time passes—that is, as the audience is led from playwright's preparation through complication to crisis and resolution. When an audience enjoys a performance, whether a period comedy or a serious contemporary play, its responses might be compared to a parabola: They start at a low point, rise higher and higher as time passes, and usually fall off after the climax. The director wisely structures the performance to serve this perceptual structure (or another equally satisfying one). In short, the director cannot allow a performance to become static.

It is not enough, then, to find the important elements and to know where the script emphasizes them. The director must now discover how each element grows in interest as the performance progresses. The word *progression* must be used again and again: What is this character's progression? What is the progression of the story? Is there progression in the spectacle?

If the progression is missed, the audience will become confused or bored.

Environment. As the actor determines given circumstances, the director determines environment: place, time of day, historical period. Much is given in the script; if it is given only in the stage directions, the director may choose to ignore it. Classic plays often have no stage directions at all.

Questions of tone, mood, and key also influence the director's thinking about **environment**. There are excellent reasons for putting a murder mystery in a country house on a stormy night, just as there are excellent reasons for putting a brittle comedy in a bright, handsome city apartment. The director thinks not only of the rightness of the environment for the characters (e.g., if they are rich they should have a rich environment, if Russians they should have something Russian, and so on) but also of the rightness for the indefinable subtleties of mood: the laziness of a warm day, the tension of an electrical storm, the depressing gloom of an ancient palace.

Communicating Decisions The director holds production meetings with designers and technicians to consider budget, designs, shifting of scenery, time for costume changes, location of offstage storage space, and many other matters. As decisions are made, each designer provides the director with a detailed plan in the most appropriate form: color renderings and fabric swatches for costumes; ground plans, scale drawings, renderings, and models for sets; light plots with gel colors for lights. The sound designer (when one exists) may work with an annotated script and lists of sounds (music, sound effects). These renderings, plans, and other materials represent the culmination of the designers' work with the director: detailed, readable plans for a total production, all in harmony with one another and with the director's interpretation of the text.

Creating the Production

Through her early attempts at assessment and analysis, the director develops strong ideas about the production of the play. These ideas will probably be modified and deepened as the director works with the play, but it is the director's interpretation that leads to the creation of a springboard that will shape the whole, guiding the rehearsals and the work of both designers and actors.

Finding a Springboard The director needs a **springboard**, a taking-off place from which to make a creative leap. The terms *concept* and *directorial image* are also used, but concept implies rational thought, and image implies picture making, and the director's process at this stage may be neither rational nor pictorial. Perhaps a directorial springboard can be seen as a combination of concept and image.

Spotlight

Lloyd asked that the women in *Mary Stuart* be costumed in period dress, albeit with a theatrical flair. The male characters, however, were to be dressed in nondescript modern-day business suits to suggest that they were "eternal bureaucrats." The play, written in 1800, returned to Broadway in 2009 after an absence of about forty years. Joan Marcus Photography.

Phyllida Lloyd: A Good Director

Phyllida Lloyd is a British director whose successful career certifies that she is expert at analyzing scripts and solving the problems they present. Her productions are consistently characterized by superb acting and technical polish. In Britain, she has directed classics and revivals of modern classics, new plays, and opera. In the United States, she is best known for two financially and aesthetically successful productions that could hardly be more different: *Mamma Mia!* and *Mary Stuart*.

The most widely known is the musical *Mamma Mia!* based on the hit songs of the Swedish group ABBA. More than thirty million people have seen the stage show. Lloyd also directed the 2008 movie, her second film. Starring Meryl Streep and Pierce Brosnan, the movie matched the stage musical's huge success.

"A great deal of the success of *Mamma Mia!* has been due to the audience recognizing themselves on stage or screen," said Lloyd in the *New York Times*. "It also seemed normal to us that you could be thoroughly silly one moment and deadly serious the next. . . ."

Lloyd's production of Friedrich Schiller's 1800 play *Mary Stuart* in a new translation played the small Donmar Warehouse, transferred to a commercial run in London in 2005, and played Broadway in 2009. The play presents the final days of Mary Queen of Scots as she battles with Queen Elizabeth I for England's throne. Mary is imprisoned as Elizabeth ponders whether and how to execute Mary. Schiller imagined the two rival queens' meeting, staged by Lloyd in a rainstorm. Lloyd capitalized on the play's sense of history and language, sober in tone and theme.

Lloyd said, "Aside from the gender issue, the play deals with the ethics of government—what price homeland security, how to take a potentially unpopular decision and still remain in favour with your electorate. It also portrays two women being 'managed' by a group of seemingly eternal bureaucrats. . . . [The two women are not] able to live their lives like the men around them without jeopardy or reproach.

"I have been very lucky and I think it all goes back to state subsidy for the arts. I gained my training and confidence and credentials in the not-for-profit world and in England that does not mean on the fringe of things. It means right at the centre. It is that experience of handling big projects, big groups of people if you like that led to a commercial musical and then to Hollywood. In the UK there are however—just as in the States—less women directing huge budget musicals, running big institutions and obviously directing anything but lower budget movies—which says something about how when the economic stakes get high girls are seen as a greater risk."

Stan Barouh

FIGURE 9.6
Springboard
The director's springboard for *Trumbo: Red, White and Blacklisted* at Rep Stage led him to use signs and projections on the back wall.

Certainly, very few directors begin their creative work with a reasoned, easily stated idea. On the contrary, many directors begin with a seemingly random, sometimes conflicting medley of ideas, impressions, and half-formed thoughts whose connections may still be hidden. It is then the director's task—and the exercise of a special talent—to sort all these out and to find their connections and to see which can be given theatrical life and which cannot. Therefore, much of the director's preliminary work is a sorting out of raw materials from a whirlwind of impressions.

Agreeing on Interpretation and Presentation Directors are rarely designers, but they know the practical needs and the aesthetic values of both play and production. When feasible, meetings between the director and the designers begin months before rehearsals; practicality may dictate, however, that they come only weeks or even days before casting.

At early production meetings among director and designers, matters of budgets, schedules, and working methods are discussed. Then, once the director has set out her interpretation and approach, the director and the designers work together to translate that interpretation into the presentation—the stuff of theatre. They come to share a vision of mood and decide how best to express it through the visual potency of lighting, set, and costume; they know that inconsistency of mood leads to a severe weakening of the performance. They work to ensure that all elements of the production fit together. The director also works with the designers to achieve progression in the designs to support the progression in the play.

Developing a Ground Plan

The **ground plan** is a "map" of the playing area for a scene, with doors, furniture, walls, and other details indicated to scale (often one-quarter inch to a foot). In a realistic interior, the director can almost design the acting space by simply setting down several directorial needs in detail:

- The number and location of entrances and exits
- The number and location of seating elements
- The number and location of objects that will motivate behavior and movement (for example, stoves and refrigerators, fireplaces, closets, and bookcases)
- Visibility (Can actors be seen in important moments?)
- Special requirements of the script (For instance, is a trap door needed?)

These requirements may be determined by directors before they meet with their designers. Some directors even give their set designer a ground plan, complete except for small matters of dimension. Others might remain open until the designer has created a ground plan around a more general statement of needs.

In the nonrealistic play, or sometimes in the realistic play with exterior scenes, directors may have less rigorous requirements. Still, for variety, mood, and emphasis, the director will probably specify:

- Differences in level (platforms, staircases, balconies)
- Separation of playing areas
- The location of seating elements (benches, low walls, swings, and so on).

As well, other design elements may be suggested or required by the director; for example, the size and shape of the space where a crowd is used, or where a sense of the isolation of a single figure is wanted, or where a feeling of cramped oppression is sought. Special effects may require special space.

Once ground plans are established, they become the basis for all staging. Drawn to scale, they can be used with scale cutouts of furniture and actors to plan staging. They are also the basis for the three-dimensional model that the designer usually provides.

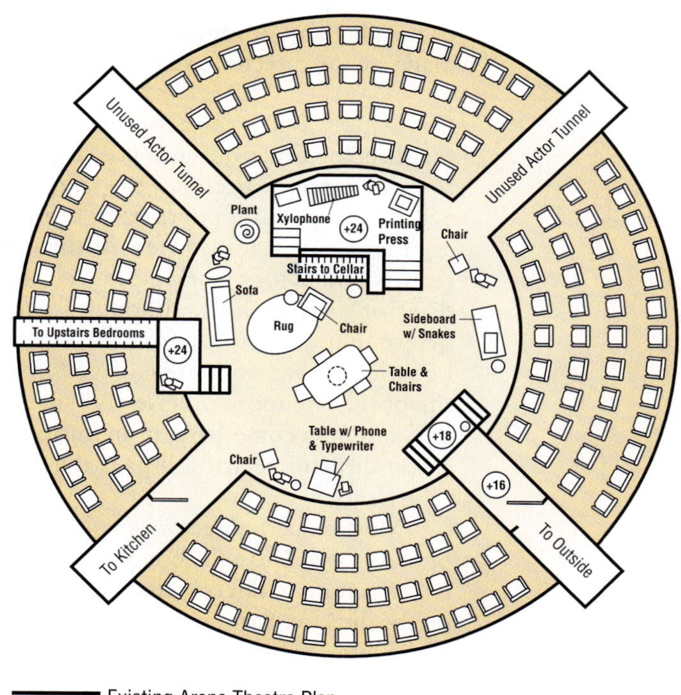

FIGURE 9.7

The Ground Plan

This map of the playing space shows all of the major scenic elements. Ground plans become the basis for staging the entire production. Here, the ground plan for an arena production of *You can't Take It With You*.

Casting and Coaching Actors

The producer or director puts out a casting call and schedules auditions or tryouts. In New York, much casting is done through agents, casting directors, and private contacts. In university and community theatres, almost the opposite situation holds true, because maximum participation is wanted and thus closed or private auditions are educationally suspect. In repertory theatres, of course, in which the company members are under contract, the director must work rather differently to make the contracted company and the plays mesh, and casting and play selection influence each other.

CASTING Casting is of enormous importance in the success of a production as it depends on finding the right actors for the right roles, always a balancing act between the real and the ideal. Although several actors in a cast—whether in professional, educational, or community productions—may be ideal for their parts, other casting decisions may well be a compromise. Even in the plushest professional situations, actor availability, salary requirements, or billing demands can thwart the best intentions.

One twentieth-century director maintained that casting is 80 percent of a play's interpretation—the right actor will enhance the director's interpretation of the play and production, but the wrong actor will undermine the decisions made by the director and designers.

COACHING When the actor and director work in a productive collaboration, the director functions as a coach who advises, inspires, and encourages the actor. The director becomes the sounding board and the artistic conscience of the actor—mentor and interpreter, bringing to the actor's work another dimension, another voice, another view of the whole play and all the characters. Most directors and actors work quite well together. Credit for much of this goes to the director's social skills, although some of it must go to the patience and determination of the actor. The most potent factor may be, in the end, the knowledge that both are engaged in a creative enterprise whose success benefits both. The more precise and sure the director can be, the better. Precision and sureness come from preparation, and so the basis of the most productive actor–director relationships is the director's own work in advance of rehearsals.

Most modern directors involve themselves closely in their actors' creation of their roles. The influence of Stanislavski, in particular, has led to collaboration between actor and director that has developed, in some cases, into a great dependency on the director. Particularly in educational and community theatres, great trust is put in the director by the actors, and many interpretations are virtually handed down entire from director to actor.

Staging the Production

Staging is one of the director's most important responsibilities. No matter how much the actors and even the director are devoted to inner truth and to characterization, the time comes when the director must shape the actors' moves and timing and must give careful attention to movement, picture making, and rhythm. This process of putting the play on its feet is also called **blocking**.

It is in the very nature of theatre that the visual details of the stage have significance, and the director must make that significance jibe with interpretation. Significance is the crux of the matter. We live in a world in which movement and visual arrangement signify: They mean something.

Modern staging pays meticulous attention to picturization and composition as a way of signaling to the audience important aspects of the play and its production. These silent aspects of staging were probably not seen before the mid-nineteenth century, except in special cases. Much of what is taught about directing today is devoted to these matters.

PICTURIZATION Picturization is the storytelling aspect of staging. It's about revealing character, emotion, and motive through movement, body language, and the actor's small activities (e.g., drying dishes).

Movement. As actors are aware of and exploit "body language," so the director is aware of and uses "movement language." Stage movement is often more abundant than real-life movement. In a real situation, people often sit for a very long time to talk, for example, whereas on a stage characters in the same situation will be seen to stand, walk, change chairs, and move a good deal. Partly, this abundance of movement results from the physical distance of the audience—small movements of eyes and facial muscles do not carry the length of a theatre. Partly, it results from the director's need for variety, for punctuation of action and lines, for the symbolic values of movement itself, and for the changing symbolic values of picturization.

Stage movement is based partly on the received wisdom of the movement implied by such statements as "Face up to it," "She turned her back on it," "He rose to the occasion." Too, it serves to get characters into positions with which we have

Jason Ayers

FIGURE 9.8

Picturization

The director places these two characters quite far apart in Theatre South Carolina's *The Violet Hour*. Perhaps the inspiration was "there is a gulf that neither can bridge." Later, as this second moment suggests, they have crossed the "bridge."

Stan Barouh

FIGURE 9.9
Movement
This jarring, violent moment in Rep Stage's *A Lie of The Mind*, combined with the actress's expression, cements an important step in the play's progression.

similar associations: "at the center of things," "way off in the blue," "out in left field." The director is concerned with direction, speed, and amount of movement. Direction reveals both motivation and human interaction; speed shows strength of desire or strength of involvement (impassioned haste, for example, or ambling indifference); amount is perhaps most useful for contrast (a character making a very long movement after several short ones or in contrast with the small moves of several other characters).

Movement patterns have a symbolic value much like that of individual movements and can be derived from the same figures of speech: "twisting him around her finger," "winding her in," "going in circles," "following like sheep," "on patrol," and many others suggest patterns for characters or groups. They are used, of course, to underscore a pattern already perceived in the play or the scene.

Visual Symbolism. The exploitation of the stage's potential for displaying pictures is not entirely limited to the proscenium theatre but has its greatest use there. With the return of thrust and arena stages, however, this framing became impossible, and audiences were located on three or all four sides of the stage, so that each segment of the audience saw a different picture. Thus, only certain aspects of picture making have universal application, and of these the most important by far is visual symbolism.

Stage Relationships. Puns and traditional sayings give us a clue to how another kind of visual symbolism works—and also suggest to us how the mind of the director works as it creates visual images of the sort that communicate to us in dreams. "Caught in the middle," "one up on him," and "odd man out" all suggest arrangements of actors. The additional use of symbolic properties or set pieces—a fireplace, associated with the idea of home ("hearth and family"), for example—gives still greater force to the picture. Thus, a character who "moves in" on the hearth of a setting while also moving physically between a husband and wife ("coming between them") and sitting in the husband's armchair ("taking his place") has told the audience a complicated story without saying a word.

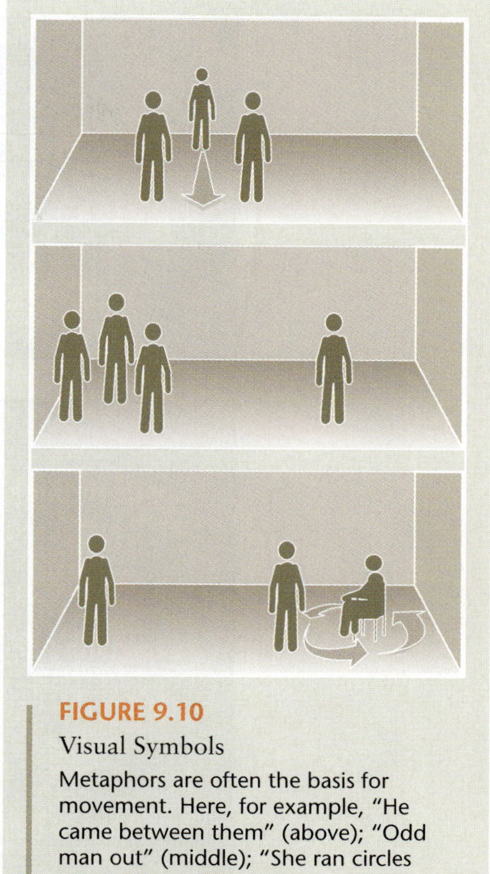

FIGURE 9.10
Visual Symbols
Metaphors are often the basis for movement. Here, for example, "He came between them" (above); "Odd man out" (middle); "She ran circles around him" (below).

COMPOSITION Composition is the technical aspect of blocking that leads the audience to see clearly what the director believes is important.

Visual Aesthetics. Most stage pictures are well composed, or good to look at, but directors are often careful to study the production with an eye to improving the aesthetic quality of the scenes. They try to eliminate obvious visual flaws: straight lines, lines parallel to the stage front, evenly spaced figures like bottles on a supermarket shelf. They look for **balance**, so that the stage does not seem heavy with actors on one side, light on the other. Composition is, finally, an irrational matter and a highly subjective one; directors who concern themselves with it in depth learn much from the other visual arts, especially traditional painting.

Focus. A stage is a visually busy place, with many things to look at; therefore, the audience's eyes must be directed through composition to the important point at each moment. A number of devices achieve **focus**:

- **Framing**: in a doorway, between other actors, and so on
- **Isolating**: one character against a crowd, one character on a higher or lower level
- **Elevating**: standing while others sit, or the reverse, or getting on a higher level
- **Enlarging**: with costume, properties, or the mass of a piece of furniture
- **Illuminating**: in a pool of light or with a brighter costume
- **Pointing**: putting the focal character at the intersection of "pointers"—pointing arms, swords, eyes, and so on

Focus is largely a mechanical matter, but it is an important one that affects both movement and picture making.

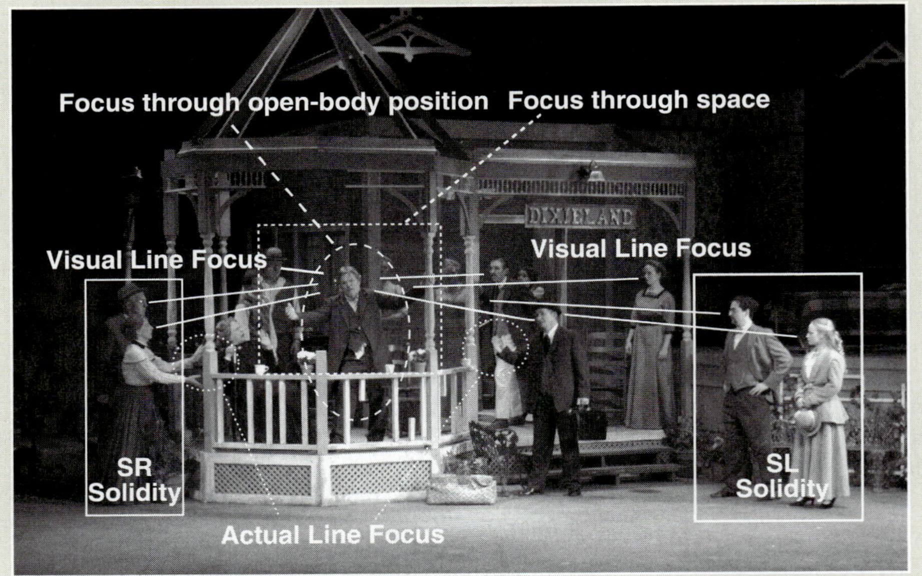

FIGURE 9.11
Focus
The lower diagrammed photo makes evident the composition of a moment from *Look Homeward, Angel* at Theatre South Carolina.

Mood. Mood is established most readily with lighting and sound and with the behavior of the characters. However, certain visual effects of character arrangement contribute, as well: horizontals, perhaps, for a quiet, resigned scene; looming verticals and skewed lines for a suspense melodrama.

Mood values are subjective and irrational, however, and hard to describe. In reality, what the director remains watchful for are clashes of mood, when movement and visual symbols conflict with other mood establishers.

RHYTHM Rhythm is the result of repetition at regular intervals. The elements of rhythm in the theatre are those things that regularly mark the passage of time: scenes, movements, speeches, words. For the director, rhythm includes tempo and timing, both aspects of progression. The director is concerned, then, not only with the interpretation of character and the visual signals of interpretation but also with the rate(s) at which things happen.

We have seen that speed of movement is important to movement's meaning. Now we can say that it is also important to intensity and rhythm. We associate quickness with urgency, slowness with relaxation; change in speed is most important of all. We might compare this phenomenon with the beating of a heart: Once the normal heartbeat (base rhythm) is established, any change becomes significant. The director establishes the base rhythm with the opening scenes of the play and then creates variations on it, and the shortening of the time between moves, between lines, and between entrances and exits becomes a rhythmic acceleration that gives the audience the same feeling of increased intensity as would a quickening of the pulse.

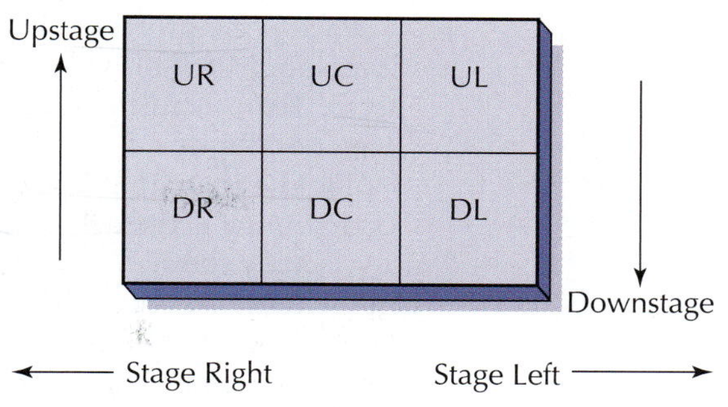

FIGURE 9.12

Proscenium Stage Areas

"Up" and "Down" are away from or toward the front of the stage, dating from the era when the stage sloped from back to front; "Left" and "Right" are from the actor's point of view when facing the audience.

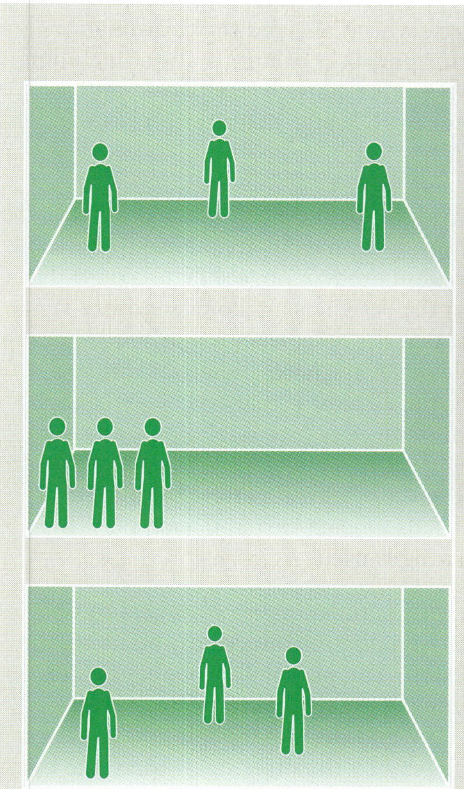

FIGURE 9.13

Composition and Balance

In the schematics, a realistic director would reject the top and middle because one is too balanced, the other not balanced enough. The bottom looks realistically uncontrived but is balanced. A nonrealistic director might prefer the top or middle. While crowded with actors, note how the director of *Floyd Collins* (right) uses placement and lighting to create focus. Produced at the Nevada Conservatory Theatre at UNLV.

Pace is the professional's term for "tempo," but it is not a matter of mechanical tempo. Much of what is meant by pace is, in fact, emotional intensity and energy. Tempo must grow naturally out of understanding and rehearsal of a scene, not out of a directorial decision to force things along.

Timing is complicated and difficult, something felt rather than thought out. Comic timing is the delivery of the laugh-getter—a line or a piece of business—after exactly the right preparation and at just that moment when it will most satisfy the tension created by a pause before it; it also describes the actor's awareness of the timing that has produced previous laughs and of how each builds on those before. The timing of serious plays is rather different and depends far more on the setting of (usually) slow rhythms from which either a quickening tempo will increase tension or a slowing will enhance a feeling of doom.

Planning, Coordinating, Rehearsing, and Polishing

In a commercial Broadway production, many managerial functions are performed by the producer or the producer's office. In community and school theatres, the director performs most or all of them: Scheduling, budgeting, personnel selection, research, and some aspects of public relations all fall to the director's lot.

Scheduling includes the overall flow of production work from inception to performance, including production meetings, rehearsals, and the coordination of design and technical schedules, at least for purposes of information (including costume fittings for actors, clearing of the stage for construction work, and so on). These schedules are kept by the director or the stage manager on such an easily read form as an oversized calendar.

The Director as Liaison Throughout the work of the production, the director is the person who ensures that all members of the production team are pulling in the same direction, working together to ensure a successful production (see Figure 9.14). He or she makes sure that the actors know what the designers are doing, and vice versa, that actors go promptly for costume fittings, that the designers provide needed drawings to the technical staff, and on and on. He or she mediates disagreements and serves as final arbiter of differences. In short, the director is that crucial person who is most responsible for realizing the potential of theatre.

Rehearsing and Polishing Every director has a rehearsal pattern, and every pattern has to be adaptable to the special needs of each cast and each play. In general, however, a structure like the following is used.

First Rehearsal: The Read-Through. The cast gathers, many strangers to one another. The director plays the role of host, making introductions, breaking the ice, moving these individuals toward cohesion. The play will probably be discussed at some length, the director explaining general ideas and the overall direction; the designers may be asked to show and discuss models and sketches. Certain practical matters are got out of the way by the director or the stage manager (the signing of necessary forms, the resolving of individual schedule conflicts, and so on).

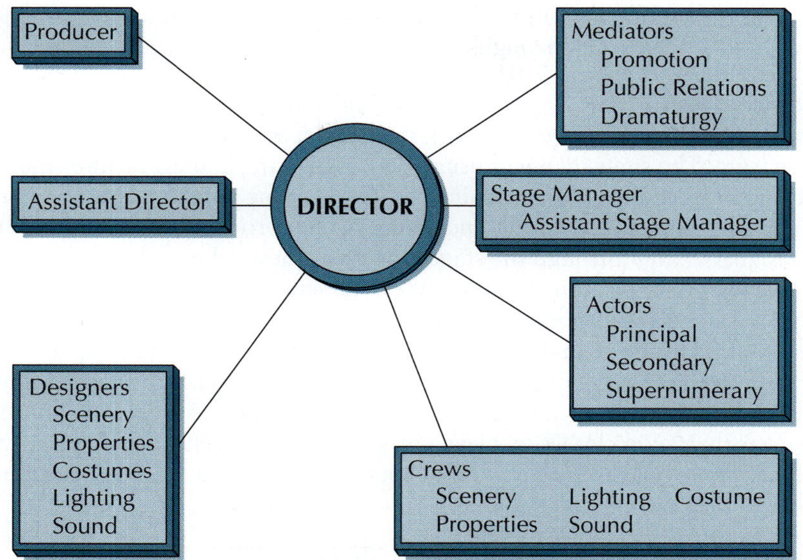

FIGURE 9.14

The Director as Liaison

The director is at the center of a network of people working for the success of the production.

Then the play is read, either by the entire cast or by the director or the playwright. Some directors interrupt this first reading often, even on every line, to explain and define; others like to proceed without interruption so that the actors can hear one another. Either way, once the books are open and the lines are read, the rehearsal period is truly under way. Because the cast is not yet up and "on their feet" during the read-throughs, this period is often called **table work**.

Rehearsal by Units. Rehearsing entire acts is often not the way to do detailed work, and so the acts are further broken down into **French scenes** (between the entrance and the exit of a major character) or scenes (between curtains or blackouts), and then further into **beats** or units (between the initiation and the end of an objective). These short elements are numbered in such a way that, for example, all the appearances of a major character can be called by listing a series of numbers, for example, 12, 13, 15, 17, meaning scenes 2, 3, 5, and 7 of the first act. By scheduling detailed rehearsals this way, the director often avoids keeping actors waiting. This same number system can be used to call scenes that need extra rehearsal.

As a general pattern, it can be said that many directors move from the general rehearsal of early readings into increasingly detailed rehearsals of smaller and smaller units, and then into rehearsals of much longer sections when the units are put back together.

Run-Throughs. A **run-through** is a rehearsal of an entire act or an entire play; it gives the director (and the actors) insight into the large movements and progressions of the play. After run-throughs, the director will probably return to rehearsal of certain small units in order to polish them, but, as performance nears, more and more run-throughs are held.

Technical and Dress Rehearsals. **Technical rehearsals**, the integration of lights, costumes, sound, and scenery into the performance, are devoted to any or all of these elements. The stage manager usually takes over the management of the script and the cues in preparation for running the show during performance. The director makes decisions affecting the look and sounds of the production and conveys them to the designers, often through the stage manager. These rehearsals are devoted almost exclusively to polishing, making the production look and sound its best.

Dress rehearsals incorporate costumes into the other technical elements, and final dress rehearsals are virtually performances. Nothing is now left to chance: Actors must be in place for every entrance well in advance of their cues; properties must be in place, with no rehearsal substitutes tolerated; costumes must seem as natural to the actors as their own clothes (achieved by giving them, weeks earlier, rehearsal costumes that approximate the actual costume); every scene shift and light cue must be smooth, timed as the director wants it.

Opening. Once the show is open, for the director the journey is over. To be sure, polishing rehearsals may be called even after opening night, or full rehearsals if the play is a new one that has gone into previews (full performances with

FIGURE 9.15

Focus

This moment from the University of Pennsylvania's production of *Pentecost* uses several techniques to throw focus to the person high in the setting: Characters point guns, everyone downstage is looking up at the character, and lighting highlights the focal character. This moment, too, took hours of technical and dress rehearsals to incorporate the finished set, costumes, lighting, and sound into a finished production.

audiences but in advance of the official opening) and needs fixing. As a rule, though, when the play officially opens, it belongs to the actors and the stage manager, and the director is a vestige of another era in its life.

TRAINING DIRECTORS

There is no one pathway that leads to becoming a director. Many of today's directors began as actors, choreographers, stage managers, or even designers. Some of today's directors have come from fields entirely outside theatre; others have pursued graduate work in theatre, specifically as directors.

Probably today's directors in the professional and commercial theatres have somewhat more varied backgrounds than do those within the educational theatre, most of whom have a graduate degree in theatre. Most professional directors (but not most academic directors) belong to the Society of Stage Directors and Choreographers.

Directors of whatever background and training, however, are expected to have a body of knowledge and skills. For this reason, theatre accrediting programs do not recognize undergraduate majors or degrees in directing, only graduate ones. For people who want to pursue graduate work in directing, there are two usual pathways: a master of fine arts (MFA) degree in directing or a PhD in theatre history, criticism, or literature, with supervised opportunities in directing.

Because of the complexity of the director's responsibilities, it is difficult to know exactly how to train someone to be a director. Directing, like any artistic practice, has changed since its beginnings. Directing will doubtless change again in the future, but we cannot say with certainty how; for now, the director's training must remain wide-ranging and flexible.

Given the complexity of their task and the training needed, directors might be thought to be in short supply. In fact, however, the market for directors, in both educational and professional venues, is glutted. Unemployment rates are at least as high for directors as for actors. Perhaps this situation is less surprising when we remember that the director is at the center of a network of people working for the success of the production. For every one director there are many actors, designers, and technicians required: It takes a large pyramid of people to support the one figure at its top.

WHAT IS GOOD DIRECTING?

To understand directing, we must be able to assess what the director has brought to the play and what the play offered the director as strengths and weaknesses. Our evaluation of the direction, then, will depend on answers to such questions as:

- How well did the director analyze and interpret the script?
- How well did the director solve the problems presented?

It is important to separate the production being studied from the play being studied. The production is not necessarily bad because it fails to stage the "playwright's intentions," nor is it necessarily good because it either stages the playwright's intentions precisely or turns them upside down. As we have een, different kinds of directors take different approaches; we must try to understand the approach and then evaluate it for what it is.

- Good directing is seen in an internally consistent, exciting production. It deals with the play's problems and exploits the play's strengths in terms of the director's approach.
- Good directing shows most of all in the work of the actors. If the actors are good and are working in a theatrically compelling whole, the director has laid a good foundation. If the actors have not been unified, if they seem to hang in space when not speaking, if they perform mechanically, if they lack motivation at any point, if they do not perform with one another, they have been poorly directed.
- Good directing has technical polish—smooth cues, precise timing, and a perfect blending of all elements—that radiates "authority," the artists' confidence in their work.
- Good directing creates compelling pictures and movement, but only when they expand the work of actors and playwright, never when they contradict—and never when they exist for their own sake.
- Good directing sets the performance tempo without giving it mechanical speed; there is no sense of too fast or too slow, but rather the organic tempo of a living entity.
- Good directing combines all elements into a whole; there is no sense of good ideas left over or of things unfinished. Everything belongs; everything is carried to its proper full development; nothing is overdone.

The good director, then, understands the play and takes a consistent approach to it, bringing the actors to life in a complete production. The bad director does not fully understand the play, often failing to ask detailed questions; does not coach the actors or coaches them only incompletely, or directs them mechanically in postures, positions, and movements dictated by a mechanical notion of visual symbolism and visual beauty; achieves not tempo but clockwork timing; and leaves ideas undeveloped and elements unassimilated.

KEY TERMS

Check your understanding against this list. Brief definitions are included in the Glossary; persons are page-referenced in the Index.

balance 133
beats (unit) 137
blocking 130
casting 129
composition 131
dress rehearsals 138
environment (of the play) 126
focus 133
French scenes 137
ground plan 128
pace 136
picturization 131
rhythm 134
run-through 137
springboard 126
staging 130
table work 137
technical rehearsals 138
timing 136

CHAPTER 10

Designers and Technicians

OBJECTIVES

When you have completed this chapter, you should be able to:

- Explain how mood, abstraction, historical period, and socioeconomic circumstances affect design
- Enumerate the major responsibilities of each designer—scenery, lights, sound, costumes—and of the technical director

FIGURE 10.1
Before Designers
This French theatre from the 1600s shows a stage with a stock setting of houses in perspective. Carpenters and painters were undoubtedly used; however, that the setting was designed is questionable.

Sitting in the modern theatre, we sometimes take the presence of scenery so much for granted that it is easy to forget that theatre does not have its roots in either spectacular effects or localizing settings. We have become acculturated to the presence of physical environments that so closely suit the mood and meanings of each play that we may lose sight of the fact that the theatre for a long period used little more than the theatre space itself as environment, and that for centuries after that it was satisfied with stock settings that could do for many plays: a room in a palace, a garden, a forest. We live in a period of magnificent settings and superb designers; however, stage design has not always been considered fundamental to theatre or its performance.

Much the same thing is true of costume designers, although it seems likely that their art (extended to include the making of masks) is a very old one, whereas the sound designer is a recent innovation. Creators of lighting effects may be said to go back to the Renaissance, but the art of stage lighting came into its own when a controllable means of illumination was invented: gaslight (about 1830).

Actors, directors, and playwrights work with life as their material. Theatre designers, however, work with the environment of human life, and their materials are the materials of our world: light and shadow, fabric and color, wood and canvas, plastic and metal and paint. Because of their materials, designers are far more influenced by technology than are actors, playwrights, or directors. This dependence explains the role of another theatre professional, the technical director. Advances in technology inevitably change the way in which theatre designers practice their art, and, in the case of both light and sound, technology virtually created those arts. Recently, computers have changed the way in which designers make their designs. Therefore, theatre designers stand in both the world of the artist and the world of the technician, and they must be expert in both.

THE NATURE OF DESIGN

Because the designers derive their materials and their subjects from the real world, their art is the creation of worlds on the stage. These worlds are sometimes imitations of the real world, sometimes not; in either case, they use familiar materials, but often in unfamiliar ways. The scenic and costume designers know that their products will be seen under colored light and so will

Courtesy NyghtFalcon

FIGURE 10.2

Serve the Play

The physical design must serve the meaning and mood of the play as well as aid in staging the story. Here, in a production of *The Caretaker* at Triad Stage, the setting is a junk-filled attic that suggests menace.

look different on the stage from the way they look in sunlight; the lighting designer knows that the audience must see the actors, no matter what the demands of mood, color, and emphasis, and that the surfaces being lit are different from the things they imitate; the sound designer may be asked to create sounds that never existed in life or to amplify and distort real sounds to match the needs of an unreal world.

The World of the Play

The world the designers create is the world of the play, which is not at all the same thing as a literal copy of the real world. Each designer goes about his or her task differently in creating that world, but they all share a common goal: to create an environment within which the actors can create convincing life. This goal means that the designers must work as a team and that they must work in concert with the director so that a compatible world is created by all of them.

Tone and Mood

Designers pay close attention to the differences between comic and serious drama, but these two categories are simply not enough. Every play is its own category and must be approached through the range of tones it contains: lightheartedness in several early scenes and great seriousness in a last act; both the romantic quality of a protagonist and the fragility of another major character; both funny gags and the real sadness of a central character's dilemma. And they must express these subtleties in the settings, costumes, lights, and sounds that are required by the scripts.

Level of Abstraction

The designers are faced with a wide spectrum of possibilities, from literal realism to fantasy to almost pure abstraction. At one extreme, for example, could be the setting for an American tragedy, for which the decision might be made to create a literal replica of a house in New England down to the last detail of the patterns in the wallpaper. At the other extreme might be one of the "space stage" settings of the 1920s—abstract constructions of stairs, ramps, and levels. In costuming, we might find real clothes, purchased in stores and dyed to look sweaty and dirty; at the other extreme, we might find costumes that use elastic fabric, extensions of limbs, and various kinds of padding to change the outline of the human body.

Bayreuther Festspiele, Jochen Quast\AP Wide World Photos

FIGURE 10.3

Mood

Composition and lighting create this striking moment for Richard Wagner's opera *Die Walküre* at the Bayreuther Festspiele in Bayreuth, Germany.

In part, the decision about how abstract the designs will be comes from the designers' and director's interpretation of the script; in part, it comes from a decision about how much the abstraction or literalism of the play itself will be emphasized. In a realistic play, for example, the decision to create literal settings and costumes is not an inevitable one; with equal justification, the designers might decide to create a mere suggestion of a house. In the same way, the designers of a play of Shakespeare's may decide that an abstract setting is inappropriate and may go to quite literal, realistic settings.

Historical Period

The shifting of classical plays from one period to another has become common. Designers are confronted constantly with plays that do not have contemporary settings, costumes, and sound. The look and the "feel" of other periods become important aspects of design.

The lighting designer is also affected by historical period, when, for example, ideas about the direction and quantity of light and the quality of shadow come from paintings and engravings of another period. In setting and costume, some of the implications of historical period are obvious; the kinds of problems they raise are most often handled by careful research by the designers. Sound, too, can be affected if period music is used or if certain kinds of sounds are called for—a trumpet flourish or the sound of *Hamlet*'s "peal of ordnance."

Historical period contains a trap for the designers in the perceptions and knowledge of the audience: The designers must consider not only what things looked like in the period but also what the audience *thinks* they looked like. What we know of the 1920s, for example, is conditioned by what we have seen in cartoons, old movies, and magazines—but did all women really bob their hair, and did all men really wear knickers and high collars? In the Elizabethan period, did all houses have plaster-and-timber fronts, and did all men wear puffed-out breeches and hose? Did warriors in the tenth century wear plate armor? Or, to reverse the calendar, will all people in the distant future wear tight-fitting clothes of unisex design?

And there is still another trap: contemporary fashion. Audiences are greatly influenced by their own ideas of beauty. As a result, a hairstyle that is supposed to be of 1600 and that was designed in 1930 will often look more like a 1930 hairstyle than a 1600 one; or, to take a familiar example from the movies, cowboy hats in the movies of the 1940s looked far more like a 1940s idea of what was becoming to men than they ever looked like the actual headgear of westerners of the frontier period.

Designers must therefore think of several things at once when confronted with historical period. It is not enough to go to a book and copy literally what is there.

Geographical Place

Like historical period, geography greatly influences design, unless the decision is made to abandon it altogether (that is, to be abstract instead of literal). The whitewashed houses of the Greek islands are different in color, texture, and scale from the adobes of Mexico or the balconied houses of New Orleans; the traditional clothes of Scotland, Morocco, and Scandinavia are distinct; the light in Alaska and Texas is very different. Sound and light are quite different outdoors from in. Even at considerable levels of abstraction, differences in geography inform some design decisions.

Socioeconomic Circumstances

Wealth and social class influence clothes, furniture, and environment in many places and periods and, therefore, their imitation on the stage. As with the other considerations, a decision may be made to ignore such matters, but a decision must be made. The matter itself cannot be ignored. And the more realistic the play, the more important these considerations become.

Historical period greatly complicates social and economic matters. As with other historical elements, audiences may have general or inaccurate ideas about what constituted the look of wealth or position or power or poverty in a distant era. What, for example, did a wealthy merchant wear in the seventeenth century that a noble did not? What furniture did the noble own that the merchant did not? What separated serf from artisan in the Middle Ages?

Aesthetic Effect

Put most simply, every designer hopes that the designs will have beauty. That beauty is a variable should be clear—the romantic loveliness of a magic forest cannot be compared with a construction of gleaming metal bars and white plastic plates—but that every designer aims at a goal of aesthetic pleasure seems true. Intentional ugliness may occasionally be aimed at, but even then we are tempted to say that the result is beautiful because its ugliness is artfully arrived at.

Composition and balance enter into aesthetic consideration, just as they enter into the considerations of the director. Teamwork is again essential, as setting, costumes, and lights are inevitably seen by the audience as a whole. Thus, unity is also an aesthetic aim, one achieved through a constant sharing of ideas by all the designers.

DESIGNERS AT WORK

Although many of their decisions are reached together at production meetings, the designers do most of their work in solitude or with the technicians who execute their designs—the scene designer with the technical director and builders and painters, the costume designer with cutters and sewers, and so on. At this stage of their work, each specializes and proceeds separately.

The Scene Designer

It is the scene designer's job to create a performing space for the actors and a physical environment for the play's action. The result is the setting, which normally has the added function of supplying the audience with clues about the play's locale.

Other important issues and questions for the scene designer are:

- **Number of settings** Can the entire play be played in one set, or must different sets be designed and changed for each scene, or can some sort of unit set serve for all scenes?
- **Shape and size of the stage** Will the audience surround it or look at it through a proscenium arch? If it is small, how can it be kept from seeming cramped? Will the actors play within the setting or in front of it?
- **Sight lines of the theatre** What peculiarities of the theatre's architecture demand that the settings be built in special shapes so that every member of the audience can see?
- **Means of shifting the scenery** Is there overhead rigging so that scenery can be "flown," or is there an elevator stage or a turntable stage for bringing new settings in mechanically?
- **Materials from which the scenery will be built** Is it better to use traditional flats of wood and canvas, or will built-up details of wood or plastic be better, or will such special materials as poured polyurethane foam or corrugated cardboard or metal pipe be better?
- **Special effects that make special scenic demands** Are there vast outdoor scenes in a proscenium theatre that require large painted drops, or will such unusual events in the play as earthquakes or explosions require special solutions?
- **Decision to imitate historical scenery that creates special requirements** For example, if a seventeenth-century play is to be done with Italianate scenery (pp. 237–239), what will the effects be?

FIGURE 10.4

Communicating the Design

The world onstage is the result of a rigorous design process. The challenge is to select just the right elements to include. Here, the finished design by Jim Hunter of *Amy's View* for Florida Repertory Theatre.

FIGURE 10.5
Sketches
Every scene design starts with a blank sheet of paper. Here, early pencil sketches for *Amy's View*. The created world must not only serve the story, ideas, and mood of the script but also assist the director and actors in staging the play.

- **Demands of budget and schedule** These matters may influence the designer before any designs are made, although preliminary doodles and sketches might attempt to catch the "feel" of the play before any practical matters are dealt with. These early impressions will spring from early readings of the play, and they will eventually be incorporated in some form into the renderings (detailed colored drawings) of the settings that the designer gives the director. Together, they will have worked out the ground plan of each setting, and the ground plan will form the basis of both renderings and three-dimensional models. If the renderings are acceptable, the designer will proceed to elevations and scale drawings of all scenic pieces, and these, with all instructions for building and painting, will go to the production's technical director.

PROPERTIES In addition, the scene designer is normally in charge of the design or selection of all properties, the things used by the actors that are not part of the scenery (furniture, flags, hangings, and so on), as well as such "hand props" as swords, cigarette cases, guns, and letters. When such things must be designed, as in a period play, the designer creates, and the technical staff executes; when they are acquired from outside sources, the designer haunts stores and antique shops and pores over catalogs of all sorts. In plays done with minimal scenery, as in arena staging, the properties take on added importance, and their design and selection must be carried out with the greatest care. A festival such as the one in Stratford, Ontario, has special shops devoted to property making.

Computer-Assisted Design (CAD)

The computer has changed the ways in which many designers work, replacing the pencil with a mouse and paper with a screen. Everything from sketching to coloring is possible with new, powerful programs that cut through such time-consuming jobs as lettering.

Computer-assisted design (CAD), as this process is known, has familiar applications for home use that can be seen at any software store: programs for planning rooms or whole houses, gardens, or small buildings. Architectural CAD programs used in theatre work in the same way; with such a program networked by an entire design staff, the savings in time and work more than make up for the expense. Lighting designers also use such theatre-specific programs as Light Write and Vectorworks Spotlight.

CAD has made older drafting tools—compasses, T-squares, triangles—almost obsolete. It allows the designer to sketch in a simulation of pencil, if that's what is wanted, and then to turn that sketch into an elevation or a three-dimensional picture. Directors can be "walked through" computer mock-ups of several design ideas. Set designers can then use the computer to take the agreed-upon idea to a rendering in any of several styles, from simulated watercolor to bright photorealism, and from there to scale elevations, detailed plans with dimensions, and final renderings from which full-size scenic painting can be done. Directors can be shown simulations of a setting from many points of view.

CAD is not magic, however. As designer Michael Franklin-White has said, "The computer is a remarkable tool. It is changing the way we design, draft, and render. But you still have to draw in order to visualize your ideas. Learn

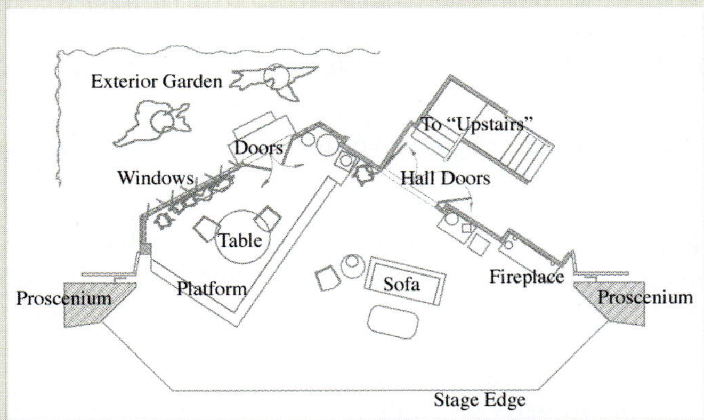

FIGURE 10.6

The Final Ground Plan

Here, a simplified version of the final ground plan for *Amy's View*, a scale drawing that shows the placement of levels, stairs, walls, entrances, furniture, props, and masking. Compare the ground plan (top) to the production photograph in Figure 10.4 and the computer model (below).

when to use the computer, and also when not to. Like pencil and paper, CAD is a tool, a great saver of time and tedium but no replacement for creativity.

The Technical Director

Broadway productions have large technical staffs, and they contract out such jobs as scene construction and painting. Small community theatres may have only a single technician to do almost everything. In all kinds of theatres, however, a person exists to oversee the execution of designs and to organize and manage the technical production and its relationship with the theatre. This person is the **technical director**.

The technical director is responsible for the theatre building around the playing area and behind whatever barrier separates audience from backstage. The job is a tangle of details and responsibilities. The technical director

- knows the theatre building thoroughly and coordinates its maintenance with the building's owner.
- sees that an ample stock of cables, nails, paint, and a thousand other things are kept on hand.
- sees to the upkeep of tools, from pencils to table saws.
- has oversight of backstage scheduling.
- knows what scenery and properties are in storage and maintains their inventories.

In short, the technical director has a huge responsibility and a day-to-day schedule that can be crushing without the most careful planning (and an even temper).

In university theatres, the technical director usually attends meetings at which plays are first selected; even at this earliest stage, his or her advice will be needed to determine whether a potential play is too demanding for the theatre's physical capabilities. Later, the technical director takes part in all production meetings, advising director and designer on the practicability of ideas and the likelihood of deadlines. Throughout, the technical director is responsible for setting and meeting scenic and property schedules. (Lighting may fall within his or her responsibility, as well; costumes generally do not.) On top of all this, in educational theatre the technical director does a great deal of the actual work of construction and painting, as well as instructing students working on the production.

The Costume Designer

The costume designer clothes both the character and the actor, creating dress in which the character is "right" and the actor is both physically comfortable and artistically pleased. This double responsibility makes the costumer's a difficult job. It is never enough to sew up something that copies a historically accurate garment; that garment must be made for a character, and it must be made for an actor. The actor must be able to move and speak and should also feel led or pushed by the costume to a closer affinity with the character and the world of

FIGURE 10.7

Costume Design

Costume designers have to consider both the actor and the character. Here, designs by Nic Ularu for *Star Messengers*, produced by Talking Band at LaMaMa in New York City.

the play. Generally, actors want costumes to be becoming to them personally, and costumers need tact in dealing with people who feel that their legs or their noses or their bosoms are not being flattered.

In designing for the character, the costumer must keep firmly in mind the given circumstances of the character, such as age, sex, state of health, and social class, as well as the focal importance of the character in key scenes (should it form part of a crowd or stand out?), and most important of all, those elements of character that would express themselves through clothes. Is the character cheerful or somber? Simple or complex? Showy or timid? Majestic or mousy?

Other important matters include:

- **Silhouette** The silhouette is the mass and outline of the costume as worn.
- **The costume in motion** Does it have potential for swirl or billow or drape or curve as it moves? Does it change with movement? Will it encourage, even inspire, the actor to move more dynamically? What aspects of it—fringe, a scarf, coattails, a cape, a shawl—can be added or augmented to enhance motion?
- **Fabric texture and draping** Does the play suggest the roughness of burlap and canvas or the smoothness of silk? What is wanted—fabrics that will drape in beautiful folds, like velour, silk, or jersey, or fabrics that will hang straight and heavily?
- **Fabric pattern** Does the costume call for allover, small, repeated patterns, very large designs on the fabric, or none at all?
- **Enhancement or suppression of body lines** Does the production call for the pelvic V of the Elizabethan waist, or the pushed-up bosom of the French

Empire, the pronounced sexuality of the medieval codpiece, or the body-disguising toga? For the individual actor, are there characteristics like narrow shoulders, skinny calves, or long necks that must be disguised?

- **Special effects** Some productions will require animal or bird costumes or fantasy creatures.

In addition, the costumer must consult with both scene and lighting designers to make sure that the costumes will look as they are designed to look under stage light and against the settings. Practical considerations like budget and deadlines are, of course, always important.

The costumer's designs are usually presented as color renderings, normally with swatches of the actual materials attached, and with detailed notations indicated for the costume shop supervisor. From these, patterns are made, when needed; the costumer selects the fabrics and usually oversees their cutting and the construction of the costumes themselves. Most theatre companies of any size keep a stock of costumes from which some pieces can be pulled for certain productions, thus saving time and money. Costume support areas of any size usually include, besides the stock, fitting rooms, cutting tables, sewing machines and sewing spaces, and tubs for washing and dyeing.

The Lighting Designer

When stages were lighted by candles, attempts to control the light were crude and seldom successful. In those days, the lighting designer's work was largely confined to special effects, such as fire. With the introduction of a controllable light source, however, and with the demand in the nineteenth century for more and more realistic imitations of phenomena like sunrise and moonlight, the designer's task became more challenging. The possibilities of stage lighting expanded from simple imitation of natural effects, and lighting became a design element as important and as potent as scenery itself.

The possible uses of theatre light are enormous. Through manipulation of intensity and direction, for example, a designer can change the apparent shape of an onstage object. Through manipulation of intensity and color, the lighting designer can influence the audience's sense of mood and tone. Also through manipulation of direction and color, the designer can create a world utterly unlike the one in which the audience lives, with light coming from fantastic angles and falling in colors never seen in nature.

Modern equipment has made theatre lighting more flexible than early designers ever dreamed. Small, easily aimed instruments (lighting units) and complex electronic controls, often with computerized memories, have made possible a subtlety in stage lighting that was unknown even thirty years ago.

Color, Direction, and Intensity The lighting designer works with three fundamentals: color, direction, and intensity of light. These are partly interdependent because of the nature of the light source, usually an incandescent filament. Color is changed physically by the placement of a transparent colored medium (usually called a gel) in the beam of light. Direction is a function of the location of the lighting instruments, of which hundreds may be used in a contemporary production. Each instrument is plugged into an electric circuit either individually or with a few others to illuminate the same scene. The location of instruments is rarely changed during performance, and so designers are limited by the number of instruments and the number of electrical circuits available to them. Light intensity is controlled by changes in the electrical current supplied to the instrument; this process is called dimming and is done by computer control.

Light Plot The lighting designer's plan is called a light plot (see Figure 10.8). It shows the location and direction of each instrument, as well as what kind of instrument is to be set at each location—usually either a floodlight (soft-edged and

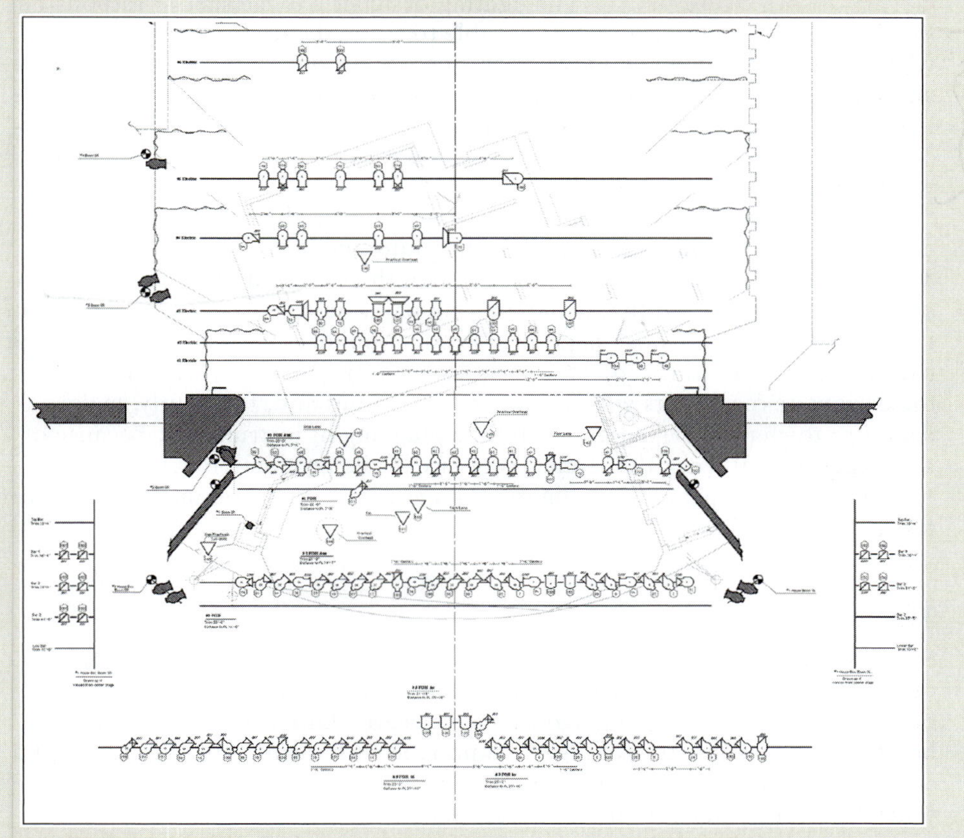

FIGURE 10.8
The Light Plot
A light plot is a scale map showing the exact location and type of each fixture used in a production.

wide-beamed) or a **spotlight** (hard-edged and narrow-beamed). The locations chosen are over and around the playing area, so that light falls on the actors for visibility, sculpting, mood, or time of day. Current practice also includes the use of **scrolling color changers** (devices that can automatically change the color on any standard lighting fixture from one to another) and fully **automated fixtures** (long used in popular music concerts, these high-end remote focusing and special-effect fixtures are now affordable for more and more theatres). In addition, such subsidiary instruments as **striplights** (rows of simple lights without lenses), **footlights** (at floor level along the front of many proscenium stages), and **follow spots** (spotlights that an operator can swivel so that their bright beam can constantly illuminate a moving performer) are sometimes used.

The lighting designer is usually responsible for projected scenery or projected shadows, clouds, and similar effects.

Effects on All Other Areas The lighting designer has the special responsibility of making everyone else's work visible to the audience. Light determines what the audience will see. Light creates depth, for one thing, and it can make an actor's eyes seem to sink into deep sockets or vanish in a bland, flat mask. Light gives or takes color, and it can make costume colors glow with vibrancy or fade into dirty gray. Light is selective, and it can show the audience precisely what is to be seen.

In making the other artists' work visible to the audience, the lighting designer has to consider all three elements: intensity, direction, and color. There are no hard-and-fast rules here; rather, there is need for a manipulation and an experimentation that is like putting paint on canvas. Although much of the lighting designer's work is done in production meetings and at the drawing board, much more of it is done in technical rehearsals, when, with the director, the designer experiments with colors and intensities and, frequently, makes decisions to change the locations and the plugging of instruments. Because of this experimental work that comes very late in the production period (often only days before opening), the lighting designer's work is crammed into a short time, and he or she works then at great intensity.

The Sound Designer

Sound became a theatre art with good stereo equipment and related amplification, blending, and tuning equipment. To be sure, sound was used in theatres before that time, and as long ago as Shakespeare's Globe Theatre, someone had to be responsible for rolling the cannonballs that simulated thunder, but a sound that could be shaped dimensionally and controlled in pure, correct tones was not possible until very recently.

Expertise and equipment have become so sophisticated that the work of the sound designer is now as important and creative as that of the lighting designer. Once limited to concepts of "sound effects" and "background music," the sound designer can now assist in creating the world of the play just as the lighting designer can affect mood and theme.

TRAINING DESIGNERS

Because theatre designers create environments and use materials of the real world to make their art, they must be trained not only as artists but also as artisans. Theatre designers, therefore, study at least two different sorts of subjects: the artistic and the technical; some designers also need another sort of information, the historical, to prepare for their role as theatre designers.

Although some theatre designers (especially in eastern Europe) customarily design all aspects of a production, most in the United States specialize in one area: scenery, properties, costumes, lighting, or sound. All need certain kinds of basic information. For example, all need proficiency in dramatic analysis. Most need to learn about color, line, mass, composition, balance, and other basic elements of design, and most need to master basic techniques of drawing and rendering and use of CAD programs. They require some understanding of visual communication (that is, how people are likely to interpret certain colors, shapes, lines, and proportions). Finally, because every play presents a unique problem in design, all designers need skills in basic research methods that will allow them to pursue the design of any play independently.

FIGURE 10.9
Design Union
Highly selective, United Scenic Artists, Local 829 (USA) represents designers and artists in the entertainment industry. Jurisdiction includes Broadway, Off-Broadway, most major theatres nationwide, and some areas of film and television production in New York City.

Beyond such basic, shared areas of study are others specific to each area, because the technical skills needed by each designer vary considerably. For example, scene designers and technical directors often study basic construction and (occasionally) carpentry; scene designers will usually take courses in scene painting as well. With the arrival of new metals and plastics came a need for training in welding and form making. These designers will also often study engineering to discover how the aesthetic requirements of a design can be safely built and safely used. Costume designers usually study basic sewing, pattern making, drafting, and draping, as well as some specialized areas like millinery. Lighting and sound designers take courses in electricity, electronics, and instrumentation. Most designers now are expected to be proficient in computers.

Because of the importance of plays from the past, training in scenery, property, and costume design (less often in lighting and sound design) usually includes quite a bit of history. Scene designers, for example, need to know the history of architecture and furniture. Costume designers need to know the history of fashion, textiles, and accessories (jewelry, wigs, etc.). The history of visual painting often suggests not only the techniques of painters in each age that designers might want to use to capture the "look" of the age but also the telling details of design—fabrics, jewelry, upholstery, and so on. Sound designers, especially, often want courses in the history of music.

In other periods, training in design came primarily through an apprentice system, in which a beginner worked with a more experienced artist until attaining an acceptable level of craft. Now, however, proficiency in design and technical theatre usually comes from pursuing a graduate degree (especially the master of fine arts [MFA]) in theatre at a university. The job market in design and technical theatre remains strong (unlike that in acting, playwriting, or directing), in part

Spotlight

Thanks to the pioneering work of George Izenour, light-board operators are able to see the stage as they control the lighting. Here, two technicians from the University of Texas at Austin work the lights for a production of *Romeo and Juliet.*

George Izenour

Early electric stage lighting was often operated by a team of two to five technicians in the basement of a theatre, each pulling an array of mechanical handles or turning dials to control the lighting. Their only communications with the stage were cue lights going on and off, telling them when to execute a cue. Later, they had headsets and could hear a stage manager call cues, but they could not see the stage and so could not see the effects of their efforts.

Yale professor of theatre George Izenour introduced the first electronically controlled dimmer for theatrical use in 1948. Developed from early vacuum-tube technology and crude by today's standards, the thyratron-tube dimmer that Izenour applied to theatre was a large and noisy device, but it allowed an operator to control the dimming of the stage lighting remotely. Izenour's system thus allowed lighting operators to move to the wings (offstage behind the proscenium) or to the back of the auditorium, gaining a view of the stage while remotely controlling the thyratron-tube dimmers in the basement. Although Izenour's thyratron-tube dimmer was quickly replaced with solid-state dimmers, his breakthrough was radical—a key element in the birth of modern stage lighting.

Izenour started his theoretical work on the electronic dimmer at Wittenberg College, where he had received a graduate degree in physics (and, as an undergraduate, had acted in plays). After graduation, he gained additional engineering experience in antisubmarine warfare technology during World War II. He later experimented with the mechanical, synchronized movement of scenery as well as with advanced techniques of stage lighting. Izenour was also an historian of theatre structures and an early scientific theatre acoustician. A pioneering consultant on new theatre buildings, he specialized in multiple-use spaces for the performing arts. After Izenour's death in 2007 at age 93, his firm, George C. Izenour Associates, continued to work in theatre design and consultancy.

Today, stage lighting is usually controlled from computers located at the rear of the auditorium with a clear view of the whole stage. (The dimmers are still located elsewhere to muffle their noise.) When the operator can see the stage, adding and adjusting lighting during the production can be more precise and more artistic. Because theatrical lighting can be complex, cues need to be coordinated with what the actors are doing. Computerized control allows a lighting change to extend over many minutes smoothly in ways that a human operator on a knob or switch cannot duplicate. A stage picture can go seamlessly from day to night with computer lighting controls, taking twenty minutes if desired. Communication among director, lighting designer, stage manager, and actors is enhanced when all can see the stage. George Izenour's pioneering work made these changes possible.

because the need for such people far exceeds the number of them well trained in these fields; university training usually leads to steady work in either the professional or educational theatre.

WHAT IS GOOD DESIGN?

Good design is good art. But it is created in terms of the production, and it is created within the context of other artists' decisions. Knowing what is the product of a designer and what of a director can often be difficult, however, and, especially in our director-dominated theatre, assessing each designer's work is sometimes challenging.

Good design, above all, serves the actor—giving the actor good spaces in which to act, clothing the actor, illuminating the actor.

Good design serves the production. It does not necessarily serve the "playwright's intentions"; interpretation may have greatly changed this production from those intentions. Obvious changes may have been made—in historical period, geographical location, social class—along with less obvious ones (genre, mood, style); the play may even have become the framework, in this production, for an idea the very opposite of the original intention. In serving the production, good design meshes with other elements and does not call attention to itself.

FIGURE 10.10
What Is Good Design?
Good design serves a production's goals and helps to create an effective world for the play. Here, a costume by Lisa Martin-Stuart for the Aquila Theatre Company's production of *The Comedy of Errors.*

Good design, when possible, is dynamic, not static: It has the capacity to change as the performance progresses. Such change is clearest in costumes and lighting, less so in scenery, when the number of sets is limited. A set that makes a powerful statement right off the bat and never goes beyond it for the entire performance may be a bad set.

Good design is not redundant. It does not merely "state the theme." It has its own complexity.

Good design has detail and texture (variety within the whole): Light is not merely a bland wash of light; a costume is not merely a wide stretch of draped and sewn fabric; a setting is not merely a painted surface.

Good design has technical finish. Designers must design within the technical limitations of their theatres so that everything the audience sees is technically well done. Often, designers oversee the technical work or approve it; nothing second-rate should pass their eyes.

Good design is daring: It tries new technologies, avoids old solutions, and chances failure.

Summing Up

The good designer, then, is one who creates effective works of visual art that serve the actor, that are right for the performance, that are richly textured and dynamic, and that can be perfectly finished by the technical capabilities of the theatre. The bad designer is one who ignores the actor; who creates ugly or uninteresting things; who designs for a predetermined idea of the play, not for this production; who creates statically; who ignores the capabilities of the technical facilities and allows shoddy work to go on the stage.

KEY TERMS

Check your understanding against this list. Brief definitions are included in the Glossary; persons are page-referenced in the Index.

automated fixtures 154
computer-assisted design (CAD) 148
dimming 153
floodlight 153
follow spots 154
footlights 154
gel 153
light plot 153
properties 148
renderings 148
scrolling color changers 154
silhouette 151
spotlight 154
striplights 154
technical director 150

PART

III

THEATRE OF OTHER TIMES AND PLACES

Theatre History

THEATRE: PRESENT AND PAST

We study theatre's past in part to understand how theatre relates to the larger culture—how forces for change work in theatre and beyond it. We also study theatre's history to discover how we differ from (and how we resemble) the peoples and practices of other times and places. Finally, we study theatre's history to enhance our experiences of today's theatre, both as audience members and as theatre practitioners.

Theatre history, however, is no more free of fads, hidden agendas, and unstated assumptions than any other kind of history. In the United States, it has been heavily tilted toward American subjects, and then toward British and European ones; it has remained fairly indifferent to those of Asia and Africa.

The growing globalism at the beginning of the twenty-first century, however, argues for widening our vision to include other cultures. This book continues to emphasize Western traditions because they have dominated North American culture, but we have treated major theatres and dramas of Africa and the East as well, pointing to interconnections when they exist and explaining conventions that differ from those with which we are most familiar.

As you read what follows, then, you should notice where emphases have been put and where omissions have occurred. You should ask yourself why these are as they are, remembering that in history of all sorts, a lack of evidence in one area and an oversupply in another greatly affects how much appears on the page. The modern period, for example—especially since the invention of photography and cheap printing—has so much information about itself that we have a hard time limiting it. Remember, too, that time is a quirky editor—through accident, war, intentional erasure, and neglect, it loses masses of information that would be thought vital if we could have it. Remember, too, the old adage of historians: It is the winners who write history. And remember, finally, that until quite recently, most people went unrepresented in history, including theatre history, which took as its subject people very like the ones who wrote the history: educated, male, close to the center of power, white, often affluent.

It has been said that art validates the center of power. No more important understanding can come from the study of theatre's past than to learn how theatre art and sociopolitical power come together and drift apart, validating and then becoming invisible to each other. To understand that relationship is to understand how theatre history is history.

THE SWEEP OF THEATRE HISTORY

"Looking into history is like shining a flashlight into a cave," one historian has said. "You can't see the whole cave, but as you play the flashlight around, a hidden shape is revealed."

Our light shines mostly on western Europe and the United States, the cultures most directly relevant to us. We do from time to time, however, flick the beam to other traditions long enough to illuminate major theatrical traditions unfolding there, showing that other sophisticated traditions existed—and still exist—alongside our own. Within the Western tradition, three major shapes can be seen, and we have organized our history around them (see Figure III.1).

Part IIIA Façade Stages: The First Thousand Years (534 BCE–c. 550 CE)

The earliest confirmed records of theatre are those of Athens, Greece, in the fifth century before the common era (BCE). Greece was then at the western edge of several highly developed civilizations, most notably those in China, Persia, and Egypt. Athens created a rich theatrical tradition with two kinds of formal drama: tragedy and comedy; actors playing in front of neutral backgrounds in outdoor spaces with audiences curved in front of them; a performance style that included music, dancing, and masks; and the world's first and still-important work of dramatic theory,

Façade Stage

FIGURE III.1

Façade Stage

The Roman theatre at Sabratha, Libya, built around 200 CE, where actors played on a façade stage.

Aristotle's *Poetics*. When Alexander the Great unified Greece and took his armies eastward in the 330s BCE, he carried this theatre as far as modern Afghanistan and northern India. Although no direct connection can be proved, India developed its own Sanskrit drama and dramatic theory soon thereafter.

After Alexander, both political and cultural power in the Mediterranean moved westward from Greece to Rome. The Romans built unified theatre structures as far north as Britain and around most of the Mediterranean fringe, including North Africa.

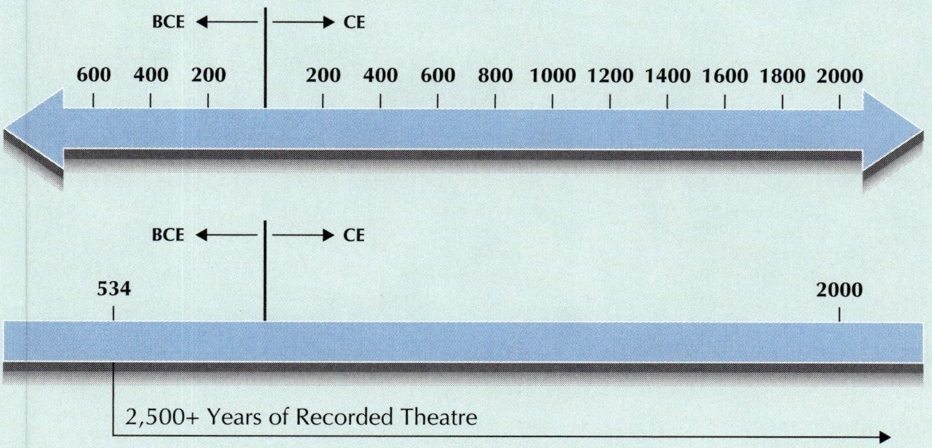

FIGURE III.2

Timelines

The timeline shows that theatre has a history of more than twenty-five hundred years, compared with film's one hundred and ten and television's sixty.

Rome had an important written comedy and a less important tragedy, both based on Greek models. But after the first century BCE its dominant form was mime, which left no dramatic theory or scripts of any quality but was hugely popular. When the Roman Empire split in two in the fourth century of the common era (CE), the eastern part, centered in Constantinople (modern Istanbul), flourished; the western empire declined and after the sixth century CE existed only in name. Theatre continued in the east, with mime a popular form throughout the vast eastern empire, stretching even to southern Russia. Theatre seems to have almost disappeared in the west. The first part of our history ends here.

Part IIIB Emblem, Environment, and Simultaneity: The Next 700 Years (c. 950–c. 1650)

Theatre—or at least records of theatre—did not surface again in western Europe until the late tenth century CE. Then, "Latin music drama," a sung drama performed in Benedictine monastic churches as a part of the liturgy, appeared in England; a Christianized version of Roman comedies, perhaps staged, perhaps not, appeared in Germany. These two kinds of drama were soon joined by other religious and secular theatres throughout Europe. In whatever venue, the medieval plays shared a staging that put the performance in existing (found) spaces, with symbolic distance, acting, and costumes. By the fourteenth century, secular plays and professional actors began to appear; by the sixteenth, they had overwhelmed the earlier religious dramas. In

Tim Donahue

FIGURE III.3

Found Spaces

A single day's performance in a patio captures an audience of people passing by during Suzan-Lori Parks's *365 Days / 365 Plays* project. Found spaces are anywhere that actors and audiences can gather to witness a performance.

Thrust Stage

FIGURE III.4

Thrust Stage

The outdoor Adams Theatre at the Utah Shakespearean Festival has a stage with the audience seated on three sides.

Photo by Karl Hugh. Copyright Utah Shakespearean Festival 2008.

Japan during the same period, an entirely unrelated form, *Noh,* was appearing; based in Zen Buddhism, it was mystical, symbolic, and austere.

In the late sixteenth century, a professional, secular theatre replaced the religious theatre. In England and Spain, medieval theatrical conventions (generalized playing area and symbolic structures) persisted, but they now appeared in freestanding theatres rather than found spaces. Spanish and English public theatres, including Shakespeare's Globe, were partly open overhead, and both featured an elevated stage that thrust into the audience and, through doors at its back, opened to a part of the structure that housed dressing rooms and stage machinery. Theatres of great spectacle rose in the east about the same time—in Japan, *Kabuki,* which used the world's first rotating stage; in China, early precursors of Beijing opera. Both used stunning costumes, makeup, masks, and movement. With the end of England's and Spain's Golden Ages, the second part ends.

Part IIIC Illusionism: From c. 1550 to the Present

Indoor theatres with a stage at one end became more common, and new staging conventions developed in Italy, conventions that moved theatre away from emblem and toward illusion. In Europe, an age of great scenic display and great scenic designers and inventors began in the middle of the seventeenth century (earlier in Italy). It was matched by great, sometimes pyrotechnic acting. Theatres got bigger as cities grew, and performances attracted new audiences drawn by the spectacle.

With the coming of railroads in the mid-1800s, entire productions could travel, multiplying the potential audience and making theatre the most popular entertainment in European and American cultures.

Proscenium Stage

FIGURE III.5

Proscenium Theatre

The Théâtre Antoine in Paris has a large proscenium opening filled in this photograph with a painted curtain.

After 1850, forward-looking artists moved the style of acting, scenery, and plays toward Realism, the mirroring of surface reality. Such plays demanded, and such audiences seemed to want, smaller theatres again, with both acting and scenic area entirely behind a proscenium, through which the audience looked at the performance as through a picture frame. Realism spawned immediate reactions, all of which changed but failed to replace Realism as the dominant form.

The increasing westernization of the world had profound effects on world theatre. As European colonialism swept through Africa and Asia, Western drama and theatre came along with it, with major effects: Realistic dramas and illusionistic staging began to be produced in their colonies, the dramatic and theatrical conventions of their own traditional dramas were adapted to fit a Western aesthetic more closely, and dramas such as *Noh* and *Kabuki* came to be viewed and treated as museum pieces.

Spotlight

Study Alert

Students should continue to use the Web site supported by the authors of *The Enjoyment of Theatre:* www.theatrestudyguides.com. It contains sample true/false questions (along with correct answers), study tips, and practice essay questions to answer or think about. There is a study guide for each of the eleven chapters devoted to theatre history and the survey of global theatre.

Two additional meta-sites may be useful: www.theatrehistory.com and www.artslynx.org/theatre/history.htm. The authors believe these sites are generally reliable.

The Internet is an amazing tool and can help uncover considerable information, but it has drawbacks and limits. Anyone with a computer and Web access can publish a site without a knowledgeable editor or an expert to review the information presented.

PART

IIIA

FAÇADE STAGES

(534 BCE–c. 550 CE)

The first phase of theatrical and dramatic history for which we have records began in the sixth century BCE and ended around 550 CE, a period of about one thousand years. These thousand years are studied together because they share certain major conventions of performance:

- **A façade stage,** where actors performed in front of a neutral (nonrepresentational) background
- **A relationship with religion,** in which plays were presented as a part of larger, religious celebrations
- **A sense of occasion,** because performances were offered only on special occasions and never often enough to be taken for granted
- **A noncommercial environment,** in which wealthy citizens or the state itself bore the costs as part of the obligations of citizenship
- **A male-only theatre,** in which women participated only as audience

This theatre appeared first in Greece and later, in modified form, in Rome. Roughly contemporary with Roman theatre was a theatre and drama in India, which may or may not have been related to those of the West.

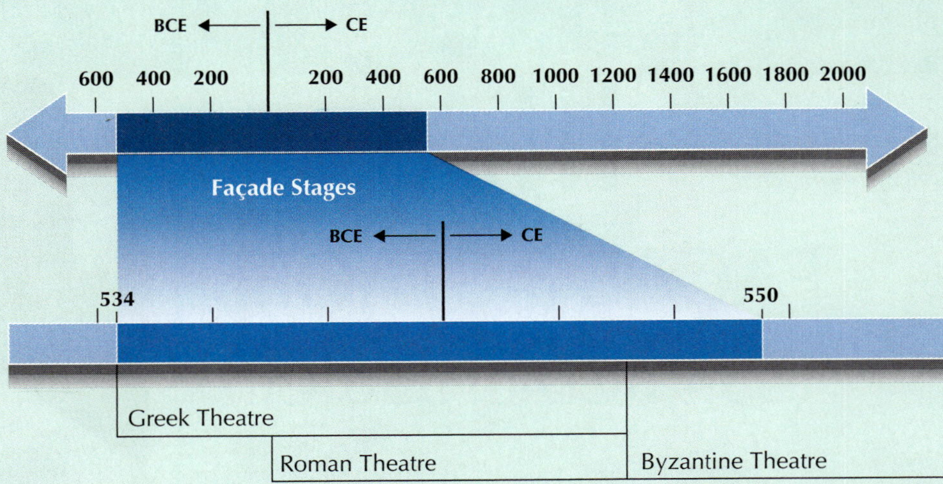

FIGURE IIIA.1
Timeline
Façade stages dominated theatre for its first thousand years. Drama and theatre, first recorded in Athens, Greece, in 534 BCE, appeared in Rome three hundred years later.

CHAPTER

11

The Theatre of Greece

OBJECTIVES

When you have completed this chapter, you should be able to:

- Explain why there are different theories of the origins of theatre and what some of those theories are
- Discuss the relationship between theatre and religion in Greece
- Discuss the role of competition in Greek theatre festivals
- Trace the development of the Greek physical theatres and their plays and playwrights
- Identify the major periods of Greek theatres, with approximate dates
- Explain how a Greek performance would have looked in the principal periods—what masks and costumes were used, what a chorus did, what acting space was used
- Explain important differences between tragic and comic performances and occasions

CONTEXT

The very first records of drama and theatre come from Athens, Greece, and date from the sixth century BCE. Within a hundred years, Athenian drama had reached a peak of excellence seldom equaled since. The result is that, when people speak of Greek theatre today, they are almost certainly referring to the plays and productions of the fifth century BCE in Athens.

Why drama and theatre should have arisen there and not in other civilizations of the time remains a mystery, but the position of Athens in the ancient world offered some advantages.

Greece, a peninsula about half the size of New York state, with its numerous bays, harbors, inlets, and adjacent islands, has one of the longest coastlines in the world. Its geography made it, during the sixth century BCE, the leading merchant of the Mediterranean, a role it took over from the Phoenicians. Exporting pottery, olive oil, wine, and slaves, Greece brought in a variety of items from North Africa and the East, where advanced civilizations were already flourishing in Egypt, China, India, and Persia (today's Iran). In fact, Greece formed the western edge of the then-civilized world and served as a crossroads for trade.

To speak of "Greece," however, is misleading, for there was no unified nation. Rather, on the peninsula were organized individual city-states, each called a *polis* (pl. *poleis*) and each consisting of a town and its surrounding countryside. Each polis issued its own coinage, raised its own armies, and so on. Although several were important (e.g., Corinth, Sparta, Thebes), by the fifth century BCE (400s), Athens had emerged as both cultural leader and trading giant, with its own outposts in Italy, Sicily, France, and Spain. As the word *outposts* suggests, western Europe was at the time a cultural backwater. And Athens itself was a small city by modern standards—100,000 people, about the size of Utica, New York.

By the fifth century BCE, the golden age of Athenian theatre and drama, Athens had already established the world's first democracy, providing a model for the participation of citizens in the decisions and policies of government. The polis had become so central in their lives that a later philosopher defined *man* as "a political animal," that is, as one who lives in a polis. Part of being political was being social—people who could, lived in the town, even though they might have a farm in outlying lands. Under Pericles, its great fifth-century BCE ruler, Athens created statues and buildings, arts and philosophies whose excellence made them important in European culture for more than two thousand years. By then as well, Athens had developed an alphabet that included both vowels and consonants, becoming the first in history to represent speech both systematically and consistently.

Athenians took great pride in their civic accomplishments. To celebrate its culture, facilitate the exchange of goods, and pay tribute to various gods, Athens sponsored a number of public festivals each year. At three of these festivals, each devoted to the god Dionysus, the earliest recorded theatre and drama appeared. Why did this new art arise? Why did it take the form it did? Why was Athens, rather than Egypt, Persia, China, or India, the birthplace of drama?

THEORIES OF THE ORIGINS OF THEATRE

There is almost no written evidence from which to draw information about the origins of Greek drama. The exception is Aristotle's *Poetics*. There are, however, several theories about how theatre began.

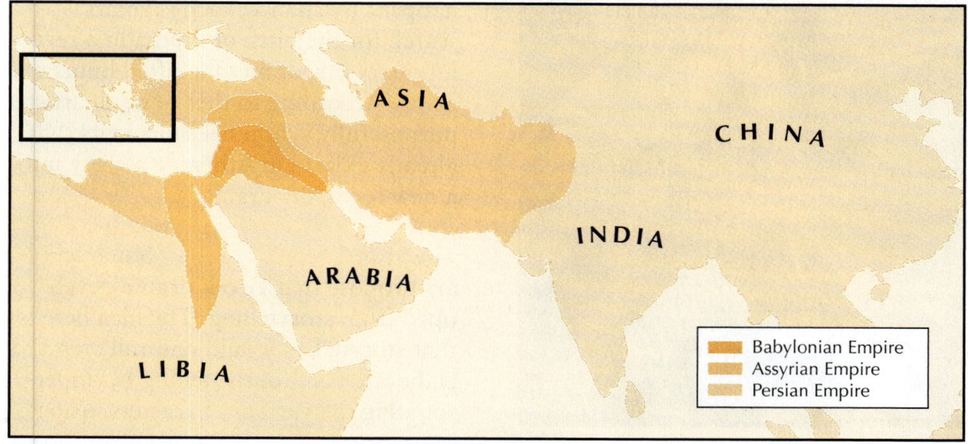

FIGURE 11.1

The Civilized World

By the fifth century BCE (400s), Greek city-states (above) influenced much of the Mediterranean, including some outposts on the Italian peninsula. But Greece was at the far western reaches of the civilized world, with older cultures well established in China, India, and much of today's Middle East (below).

Aristotle and the *Poetics*

The earliest account is Aristotle's *Poetics,* written about two hundred years after the fact. He claimed, in Chapter 4, that "tragedy was produced by the authors of the dithyrambs, and comedy from [the authors] of the phallic songs." Dithyrambs were choral odes (poems performed by a chorus). Phallic songs were rites celebrating male sexual potency, but their precise nature is unknown. Because Aristotle was writing about two hundred years after the first recorded theatre performance, we have no idea where he got his information. In the absence of certainty, several theories have arisen to explain how and why drama came into being. These theories have relied on evidence drawn from fields such as anthropology and linguistics and from contemporaneous artworks, especially vase paintings.

Guthrie Theatre

FIGURE 11.2

Aeschylus's *The Agamemnon*

The Guthrie Theatre produced a somewhat condensed Oresteia trilogy as *The House of Atrerus.* The masks, designed by Tanya Moiseiwitch, leave the mouth uncovered so the actor's articulation would not be muffled. The production, directed by Tyrone Guthrie, toured Los Angeles and New York, among other cities.

The Ritual Theory Probably the most fashionable, but not necessarily the most correct, view of the origin of theatre is the ritual theory, which proposes that Greek drama evolved from early religious rituals devoted to the god Dionysus.

The Great Man Theory Some scholars propose that the appearance of tragedy and comedy arose as creative acts of human genius. Arguing that art neither evolves like a biological organism nor happens by chance, such scholars search for the birth of drama in a revolutionary invention of a gifted human being. According to this view, an artist purposefully synthesized elements that already existed in Athenian society into a new form, the drama.

The Storytelling Theory Some scholars propose that Greek drama developed from storytelling. The idea here is that storytellers would naturally tend to elaborate parts of the telling by impersonating the various characters, using appropriate voice and movement. From here, it seems a short step to having several people become involved in telling the story; from this telling, it is thought, drama and theatre arose.

The Dance Theory Other theorists suggest that movement rather than speech was at the core of drama.

The idea here is that dancers first imitated the physical behavior of animals and humans. When dancers costumed themselves in appropriate skins and garments, they came to impersonate the animals and humans. When several dancers joined together in impersonation and then embroidered this performance with sounds and words, drama was born (the argument goes).

In fact, no one knows the origin of Greek drama. The argument over origins is often an argument over the nature of theatre itself. To anthropologists, who look on theatre as a kind of performance closely related to impersonations as different as the Mandan Buffalo Dance, the Iroquois False Face Society, and the Egyptian "Passion Play," the essence of theatre is ritual, and so they tend to favor the ritual theory. To artists who look at world theatre and see a form rich in human meaning and almost indescribable in complexity, only an artist's creation can explain its beginnings, and so they favor the great man theory. For those who believe drama began with the actor, the storyteller theory works best; for those who find the essence of Greek drama in its chorus, the dance theory seems most persuasive.

TRAITS OF GREEK THEATRE

During the preceding discussion, we have encountered three important traits of Greek theatre, traits that may seem odd when compared to current theatrical conventions.

- **Greek Theatre Was Closely Associated with Greek Religion.** A form of polytheism ("many gods"), Greek religion was both private (a part of daily life and centered in the home) and public, expressing itself at a number of major festivals, each devoted to a specific god.

- **Greek Theatre Was Performed Only on Special Occasions—the Festivals.** During its golden age, drama appeared only in Athens and at only three festivals of Dionysus: the City (or Great) Dionysia, the Rural Dionysia, and the Lenaia. An altar was a permanent fixture of the performance space.

- **Greek Theatre Was Choral.** In addition to actors, the performance of Greek drama required a **chorus**, a group of men who dressed alike, who were masked alike, and who moved, sang, and spoke together most of the time. The chorus affected Greek drama in important ways. Its costumes, songs, and dances added much spectacle to the performance. Because the chorus danced as it spoke, chanted, and sang, its rhythms indicated, both visually and orally, the changing moods within the play. Perhaps most important of all, the chorus—like the actors—participated directly in the action, providing information, making discoveries, deciding, and doing.

  The chorus also influenced a number of theatrical practices. Because the chorus usually came into the performing space soon after the play opened and remained there until the end, its presence had to be considered in both the physical layout of the theatre and the action of the drama. It required a space large enough to move about in. Its presence had to be justified and its loyalties made clear whenever characters shared secrets. Because the vocal and visual power of the chorus was great, the actors undoubtedly adjusted their style of performance so as not to be overwhelmed by the impact of the chorus.

To these three traits, we need to add two others, which also differ markedly from modern practice:

- **Greek Theatre Was Competitive.** Dramatists competed for awards in writing, and actors competed for awards in performing. To ensure fairness in the competition, various rules governed who competed, who judged, and who won.

  Plays were produced by the city-state in cooperation with selected wealthy citizens. (Women were not considered citizens.) At the **Great Dionysia**, three tragic writers (always male) competed each year for the prize. To compete, each submitted three tragedies and one **satyr play** (a short comic piece that followed the tragedies and occasionally burlesqued them). One day was set aside for the work of each tragic author; therefore, each year nine tragedies and three satyr plays were presented at the Great Dionysia. At the Lenaia, only four tragedies competed each year, each by a different playwright. At both festivals, five comic playwrights (always male) competed for a prize, and a single day was set aside for this competition.

- **Greek Theatre Was Subsidized.** How the competitors were selected is unknown, but, once chosen, each author was matched with a wealthy citizen-sponsor, who was then responsible for meeting the costs incurred by the chorus. These citizen-sponsors could have a major effect on the outcome of the contests. Legends tell us that *Oedipus Rex* lost its competition because of a sponsor too stingy to fund a suitable production, but that Aeschylus's *Euminides* had costumes and masks so spectacular and frightening that pregnant women miscarried when they first saw the chorus, the result of the lavish support of its sponsor.

Jason Ayers

FIGURE 11.3
A Chorus
This chorus for a modern production of *The Agamemnon* at the University of South Carolina wore similar costumes and masks as a means of presenting the chorus as if it were a single entity in the production.

PLAYS AND PLAYWRIGHTS

Of the thousands of plays written for the Greek theatre, only forty-six survive complete, although many fragments have also come down to us. Most plays come from fifth century BCE Athens and from four authors: Aeschylus (seven), Sophocles (seven), Euripides (eighteen), and

Aristophanes (eleven). From these four authors came some of the world's greatest plays—plays that are still performed for their powerful effects on audiences, plays that have provided other playwrights (from William Shakespeare and Jean Racine to Eugene O'Neill and Wole Soyinka) with stories, and plays that have given their names to underlying patterns of human behavior ("Oedipus complex," "Promethean struggle"). A fifth name—Thespis—is important, although such a person may never have existed.

Thespis

The semilegendary Thespis supposedly wrote tragedies using only one actor and a chorus. Although none of Thespis's works survived, they probably were based on the intensification of a single event rather than the development of a story, because stories require that changes occur. With only one actor and a chorus, the opportunity to introduce new information into a scene (and thus introduce change into a situation) was severely limited. The continual disappearance of either the actor or the chorus to fetch new information would obviously have been awkward and was thus necessarily curtailed.

Aeschylus

Aeschylus probably introduced a second actor, thereby permitting change to occur within the play. Although a second actor would also allow conflict between two characters, Aeschylus still tended to depict a solitary hero, one isolated and facing a cosmic horror brought about by forces beyond his control. With such a grand tragic conception, Aeschylus required great scope, and so he often wrote trilogies, three plays on a single subject that were intended for performance on the same day. One of his trilogies, the *Oresteia* (458 BCE) (comprising the *Agamemnon,* the *Choëphoroe,* and the *Eumenides*), has survived intact along with several single plays. All display characteristics for which Aeschylus is admired: heroic and austere characters, simple but powerful plots, lofty diction. His general tone is well summarized by an ancient commentator: "While one finds many different types of artistic treatment in Aeschylus, one looks in vain for those sentiments that draw tears."

Sophocles

Sophocles was credited with adding the third actor and with changing practices in scenic painting and costuming. Less interested than Aeschylus in portraying solitary heroes confronting the universal order, Sophocles wrote plays that explored the place of humans within that order. The tragedy of Sophocles' heroes typically erupts from decisions made and actions taken based on imperfect knowledge or conflicting claims. Various aspects of the hero's character combine with unusual circumstances to bring about a disaster caused not by wickedness or foolishness but merely by humanness. For Sophocles, to be human was to be potentially a hero of tragedy.

Spotlight

Oedipus
Blind prophet Tiresias confronts doomed King Oedipus in *Oedipus*, a new version of Sophocles' play by Ellen McLaughlin at The Guthrie Theatre in 2005.
Photo by T. Charles Erickson.

Sophocles' *Oedipus the King*, 427 BCE

Part of a group of three plays often referred to as the "Theban plays," *Oedipus the King* is considered one of the greatest dramas ever written. The other two plays in this Theban cycle are *Antigone* and *Oedipus at Colonus*. (The three were not written as a trilogy). Sophocles is believed to have written more than one hundred plays, but only seven have survived. *Oedipus* was much admired by Aristotle, who used examples from this play to illustrate his description of Greek tragedy.

The Story of the Play

Oedipus, king of Thebes, is appealed to by the people (the chorus) to save them from the plague that grips the city. Oedipus has already sent his brother-in-law, Creon, to the oracle at Delphi for a solution; Creon returns and announces that the oracle says that the city must banish the murderer of the former king, Laius. Oedipus vows to "reveal the truth" and save the city.

He calls the blind seer Tiresias to him and asks his advice. Tiresias is evasive and then, pressured, says, "It is you." Angered, Oedipus turns on Tiresias, saying that he and Creon are plotting against him. The old seer warns Oedipus of one who is "his children's brother and father, his wife's son, his mother's husband."

Oedipus rages again against Creon. His wife, Jocasta, widow of the former king, Laius, tells him of another old prophecy: Laius would be murdered by his own child. When she describes Laius, Oedipus is shaken and demands to see the one survivor of the killing of Laius. He tells of his own long-ago visit to Delphi and a prophecy that he would kill his father and sleep with his mother, which caused him to flee Corinth, his childhood home. He recounts the later killing of a stranger at a crossroads.

A messenger from Corinth comes with news that Polybus, the king of Corinth and Oedipus's supposed father, is dead. Oedipus is not to grieve, however—Polybus was not, the messenger says, Oedipus's real father; rather, the messenger as a young man got the infant Oedipus from a shepherd; the baby's ankles were pierced—hence the name Oedipus, "swollenfoot."

Jocasta, suddenly frightened, begs Oedipus to give up his quest for the truth. An old man, the survivor of the attack on Laius, is dragged in. He was the shepherd who gave the infant Oedipus to the messenger; now, hounded by Oedipus, he says that the infant was to have been abandoned in the wild because he was the child of Laius and Jocasta, and there was a prophecy that he would kill his own father, but the shepherd gave him to the messenger to take away, instead.

Oedipus sees the truth: He is the source of the plague, the murderer of his father, the husband of his mother. Jocasta kills herself.

Oedipus blinds himself with the pins in Jocasta's jewels. He begs to be driven from the city.

The role of the chorus in Sophocles' plays remained important but not so central as in Aeschylus's. Conversely, the individual characters in Sophocles tended to be more complex, to display more individual traits, and to make more decisions. The result is that in Sophoclean tragedy, the actors, not the chorus, control the rhythm of the plays. Unlike Aeschylus, Sophocles did not need a trilogy to contain his tragedies; his plays stood alone. Of the more than one hundred attributed to him, seven have survived. Of these, *Oedipus Rex* (c. 427 BCE) is recognized by most critics as among the finest tragedies ever written.

Euripides

Euripides was never very popular during his lifetime but came to be highly regarded after his death. Growing up at a time when Athens was embarking on policies of imperialism and expansionism, Euripides became a pacifist and a political gadfly. Although the populace viewed him with considerable distrust, the intellectual elite apparently admired him. It is reported, for example, that Socrates, one of the wisest men of the age, came to the theatre only to see the tragedies of Euripides and that Sophocles dressed his chorus in black on learning of the death of Euripides.

In comparison with the plays of Aeschylus and Sophocles, those of Euripides are less exalted and more realistic. His characters seem less grand and more human; their problems are less cosmic and more mundane. Euripides tended to examine human relationships and to question the wisdom of social actions: the purpose of war, the status of women, the reasons for human cruelty. *Medea* (431 BCE) is an example.

In keeping with Euripides' iconoclastic outlook came changes in dramatic technique. Replacing the philosophical probings common in the plays of Aeschylus and Sophocles, Euripides substituted rapid reversals, intrigues, chase scenes, and romantic and sentimental incidents of the sort later associated with plays called *melodramas*. (Euripides is said by some to be the father of melodrama.) He further reduced the role of the chorus, until sometimes it was little more than an interruption of the play's action. As the role of the chorus declined and the subjects became more personal, the language became less poetic and more conversational. Many of the changes that Euripides introduced into Greek tragedy, although denounced in his own time, became standard dramatic practice during the Hellenistic period.

Aristophanes and Old Comedy

Comedy was introduced into the Great Dionysia in 486 BCE, fifty years after tragedy. It seems never to have been comfortable there, perhaps because the festival was an international showcase for Athenian culture and thus often visited by foreign dignitaries. The real home of comedy was the winter festival, the Lenaia, where a contest for comedy was established in 442 BCE. At both festivals, an entire day was set aside for competition among the comic playwrights, five of whom competed.

FIGURE 11.4
Oedipus the King
Modern productions of classic plays sometimes take nontraditional approaches. This Nevada Conservatory Theatre adaptation presented in Las Vegas was retitled *Oyedipo*.

Of the twelve extant Greek comedies, all but one are by Aristophanes; therefore, information about comedy during the classical period necessarily comes from these plays. It is possible, of course, that Aristophanes was atypical, and so the conclusions drawn from his works may be incorrect.

Although no two plays are exactly alike, surviving examples suggest a set structure for old comedy (the political comedy of the classical period):

- Division into two parts separated by a direct address by the chorus or choral leader to the audience, breaking the dramatic illusion
- A first part consisting of a prologue, during which an outrageous idea is introduced, and then a debate as to whether the idea should be adopted, ending with a decision to put this "happy idea" into action (In Aristophanes' *The Birds* (414 BCE), for example, the happy idea is to build a city in the sky.)
- A second part made up of funny episodes and choral songs showing the happy idea at work

The happy idea is the heart of old comedy: It is outrageous and usually fantastic, and it contains social or political satire. In *The Birds,* building the city in the sky is an attempt to get away from the mess on earth. The happy idea also enables the spectacular costuming and behavior of the chorus, which often gives the play its name (the birds found in the sky).

THEATRE BUILDINGS AND PRACTICES

Although almost all extant Greek plays date from the fifth century BCE, most of the extant Greek theatre buildings date from later periods—sometimes much later periods. The result is unsettling: For the time when we know about theatre buildings and production practices, we know almost nothing about plays; conversely, for the time when we know the plays, we know almost nothing about the theatre buildings.

In Greek, *theatre* meant "seeing-place" or "spectacle-place." Athens' first theatre was apparently in the market, but it soon moved to the outskirts of town. There, the Theatre of Dionysus, Athens' first important theatre, was situated on a hillside, where the audience sat, with a circular playing area (the **orchestra**) at its base; a path or road separated audience and playing area and provided entrances (*parodoi*). This arrangement—hillside, orchestra, *parodoi*—was fundamental to all Greek theatres (see Figure 11.8). In many theatres of the time, however, the orchestra was rectangular rather than circular, an arrangement that would make sense inasmuch as tragic choruses (unlike the dithyrambic chorus) displayed themselves in ranks and files rather than in circles.

FIGURE 11.5
Old Comedy Made New
Lysistrata's sexual humor and antiwar theme have made it popular with modern audiences. Here is a modern-dress adaptation in contemporary language at the Theatre South Carolina.

By the middle of the fifth century, a scene house (***skene***, "tent" or "booth") had been added at the edge of the orchestra opposite the audience. Its original layout is unknown, but it probably had two or three openings and was first needed as a changing room for the actors, only later becoming a kind of setting. It may first have been cloth (a tent) but was certainly wood in short order, becoming stone only centuries later. Whether wood or stone, it provided background and acoustical support and allows us to call the Athenian theatre a **façade stage**—a conventional form in which actors perform in front of a non representational, often architectural, façade, with the audience arcing to three or fewer sides.

Important reminder: Because the fifth-century theatre was wood (rather than stone), it was impermanent, and so architectural examples of this theatre have not come down to us. The stone theatres whose pictures appear in many books are from later years, the periods for which we have no plays.

Audience

The outdoor theatre put the audience at the mercy of the weather; certainly, individuals must have used cushions, sunshades, umbrellas, and so forth. The Athenian hillside, with its wooden benches, could hold about fourteen thousand, and the audience was as visible as the actors in the natural sunlight. Theatre was apparently open to all, including women and slaves, but the exact social makeup of the audience is unknown. Records suggest that it could be unruly.

Acting

The first victor in the Athenian tragic contest is supposed to have been Thespis, who also acted in his play (c. 534 BCE)—hence *thespian* for actor. Acting, like

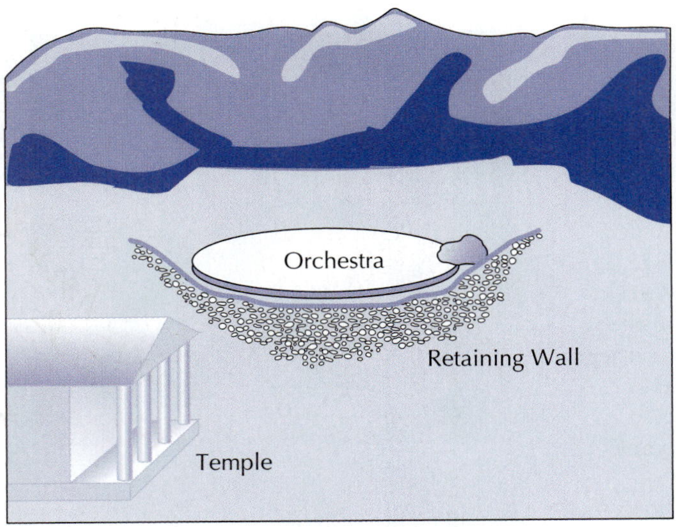

FIGURE 11.6
Theatre of the 400s BCE
A conjectural reconstruction of the early Theatre of Dionysus, showing audience area, orchestra, rock outcropping, and temple.

playwriting, remained a competitive activity during the classical period, and rules governed its practice. For example, all actors were male. Apparently no more than three *speaking* actors were allowed in the tragedies and five in the comedies, although any number of extras might be used. Because the leading actor, or **protagonist**, was the only one competing for the prize, he was assigned to the playwright by lot, so that chance rather than politics decided who got the best roles. The second and third actors were probably chosen by the playwright and the protagonist in consultation. With only three actors, doubling of roles was required, for the plays themselves often had eight or more characters. If the protagonist had an exceedingly demanding role, like the title role in *Oedipus Rex,* he might play only one character, but the second and third actors were expected to play two or more secondary roles. Doubling, the use of masks, and the use of only male actors suggest that the style of Greek acting was more formal than realistic; that is, although the acting was true and believable *on its own terms,* its resemblance to real life was of considerably less importance than its fidelity to the dramatic action. Given the size of the audience, the physical arrangement of the theatre, and the style of acting, it should be no surprise that vocal power and agility were the actor's most prized assets. Actors, like sponsors and chorus members, performed as part of their civic duties. They were not paid professionals.

Settings and Machinery

The *skene* was the essential setting. We do not know whether its appearance was changed to suggest different locations; that is, we don't know whether there was scenery in our sense of that word. We do know that some sort of **flat** (two- dimensional surface for painting) existed, but we do not know how it was used, or where.

We do know that two machines provided special effects:

- The **eccyclema** was a movable platform capable of being rolled or rotated out of the *skene* to reveal the result of an offstage action. In Aeschylus's *Agamemnon,* for example, the body of the murdered Agamemnon is "revealed" (rolled out?), and in the *Eumenides,* the Furies (avenging goddesses) seem to have entered first while asleep (rolled into view?).

- The mechane was some sort of crane that allowed people and things to "fly" in and out. In Aristophanes' *The Clouds,* the character Socrates hangs over the performing space during some of his dialogue, and in Euripides' *Medea,* Medea flies away to escape her pursuers. In fact, Euripides so often has gods fly down to sort out the characters' problems at the end of his tragedies that a too-obviously-contrived ending of a play came to be called (in Latin) a *deus ex machina* ("god from the machine").

Properties were numerous, and we hear of altars, tombs, biers, chariots, staffs, and swords being used in tragedy. Comedies often required furniture, food, clubs, and so on.

FIGURE 11.7

Outdoor Theatre

Outdoor theatres are not limited to the Greek era; they are found around the world. Here, the ancient Theatre of Dionysus at the foot of the Acropolis in Athens as it appears today (top). *The Lost Colony,* an outdoor drama in North Carolina, has been drawing summer tourists for more than seventy years.

Costumes and Masks

Because in Greek theatre one actor played several roles, costumes and masks were exceedingly important—they enabled audiences to identify quickly and certainly which character in the play the actor was impersonating. The mask and the costume, in a sense, were the signs of character. A different principle governed the chorus, whose goal was to make its individual members appear to be a group, and so choral costumes and masks were similar. Although historians once argued for "a tragic costume" for tragic characters, most now agree that some version of normal Athenian dress seems likelier. In tragedy, such dress was perhaps more elegant than normal, and in comedy it was certainly altered to make it laughable—ill-fitting, exaggerated, and so on—but the basic look was recognizable.

From references in plays, we know that a costume's appearance allowed audience members to know a character's traits:

- **ethnicity** (references are made to some dressed as Greeks and to others dressed as foreigners)
- **gender** (males and females are identified as such at a distance)
- **social role** (military heroes, servants, shepherds, and so on were visually identifiable)

FIGURE 11.8
The Theatre at Epidaurus
By the middle of the fifth century BCE, the Athenian theatre had a wooden stage house (*skene*) with roof and doors (number uncertain). By the beginning of the fourth century, the seating area was connected to the skene by two arches, seen here. It is believed that the audience entered through these archways, as did the chorus at the plays' beginning. A well-preserved example of these Greek theatres is Epidaurus, seen here with a setting for Aristophanes' *The Knights.*

In the case of comedy, the costume for certain male characters featured a stuffed, oversized penis (phallus). The color of costumes was also a sign: Reference is made to black for characters in mourning and yellow for an especially effeminate male character, to cite only two examples.

All performers, both actors and chorus members, wore masks. They were full-face, and they carried their own hairstyle and, of course, their own set facial expression. During the fifth century BCE, the masks looked natural in tragedy, although in comedy they could distort features to provoke laughter. Again, masks for actors aimed for individuality and quick recognition of character, whereas choral masks stressed resemblance, membership in a group. Occasionally, comic masks resembled the faces of living people, a fact we glean from an account of Socrates, who, from his seat in the audience, stood up and turned so that others could see that the mask worn by the actor in a comedy mimicked his own face.

THE END OF ATHENS' GOLDEN AGE

At the end of the fifth century BCE, Athens lost its premiere position among the Greek poleis. First it was defeated by Sparta, a militaristic state with few aspirations to high culture. With Spartan influence came some sort of censorship, which had the immediate effect of toning down the political satire of Greek old comedies and substituting comedy with a less biting tone (called **middle comedy**). Then, near the end of the fourth century BCE (300s), Alexander the Great overran all the Greek poleis and folded them into a single, centralized government. He then conquered many of the advanced civilizations that abutted him, lands south through Egypt and east as far as India and modern Afghanistan and Pakistan. Founding Alexandria (Egypt) as his capital, he ruled one of the world's great empires in a brief age now called the **Hellenistic period**. As Alexander and his armies conquered lands, they exported Greek culture to them.

The culture of Hellenistic Greece, however, differed from that of Athens. The individuality of the various poleis declined, replaced by a cosmopolitan culture centered in Egypt. Gone were Athenian democracy, its great drama, and the centrality of its gods. The trend was toward a common government, common civilization, and common religion. The empire's center of gravity shifted away from the Greek peninsula, which now rested on the westernmost edge of Alexander's holdings, and toward the east, where different religious and philosophical systems were already highly developed. Towns and then cities grew up, as trade competed with agriculture for attention. Within a hundred years, the Hellenistic world had more than four hundred cities with populations over 200,000, that is, twice the size of Athens during its golden age (fifth century BCE).

Greek drama changed. Plays began to be performed throughout Greek lands, not merely at Athens, and they were now performed on special military and civic occasions as well as during Dionysian festivals. Satyr plays disappeared. Tragedy declined in popularity; such tragedies as were written apparently modeled themselves on Euripides' plays, with a reduced emphasis on the chorus and an increased emphasis on sensation, realism, and melodrama. (Only fragments of such tragedies exist today.) Tragedies from the fifth century BCE continued to be revived,

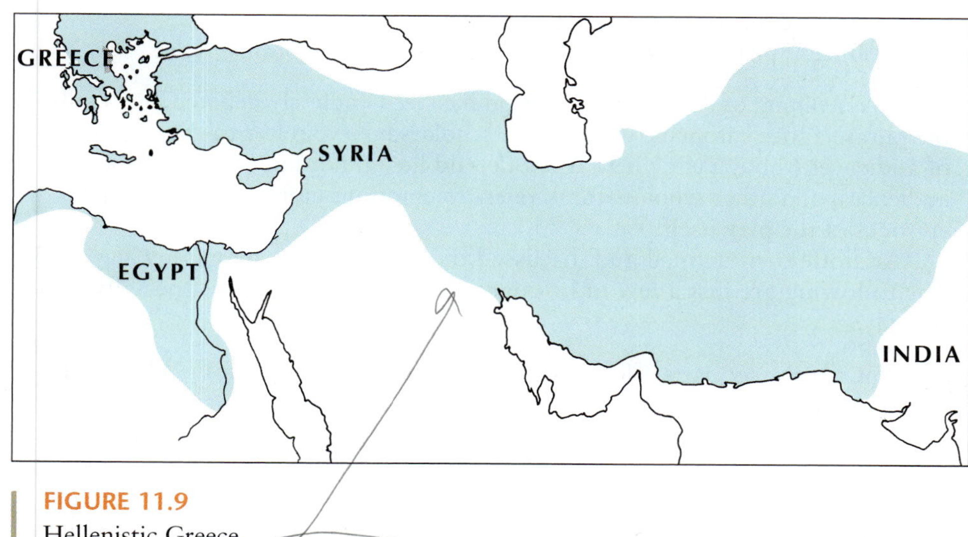

FIGURE 11.9

Hellenistic Greece

The conquests of Alexander the Great in the 300s BCE extended Greek influence but led to a shift of power away from Athens. Theatres began to be built throughout Greek lands, and acting became professionalized.

however, attesting to their power to move audiences. Comedy remained popular, but it abandoned both its political bite and its formal structure. New comedy, as Hellenistic comedy is now called, told domestic tales of middle-class life structured as a series of episodes interrupted by incidental choral songs. New comedies took as their subjects such things as love, money, and family, often including intrigues involving long-lost children and happy reunitings. Although there are many fragments, only one complete new comedy remains, *The Grumbler* by Menander.

Although actors remained exclusively male, they became professionalized, organizing themselves into a performing guild called the Artists of Dionysus. From changes in the plays (and also in theatre buildings, costuming conventions, and masks), we can infer that acting style changed, becoming grander, showier, and more formal in tragedy, and probably less boisterous, more restrained, and more representational in comedy.

Aristotle and the *Poetics*

Of far greater consequence than the drama itself during these years was Aristotle's theory of drama, the *Poetics,* written very early in the Hellenistic period, probably in response to the philosopher Plato's condemnation of theatre. Providing a theoretical definition of the form tragedy (his theory treated neither comedy nor mixed forms), Aristotle set the boundaries for the next two thousand years of dramatic theory, with the following major points about tragedy:

- Imitates "action that is serious, complete, and of a certain magnitude"
- Takes "the form of action, not narrative"
- Produces "pity and fear and the catharsis of such emotions"

The meaning of Aristotle's definition has been endlessly debated, especially the phrase about catharsis, which some scholars believe refers to the response of audiences (though elsewhere Aristotle said he did not intend to talk about audiences) and other scholars think refers to emotions embedded within the episodes of the play itself.

Aristotle then defined and discussed the six parts of a play (see Chapter 3). The following are just a few of his many comments on drama, especially tragedy:

- **Plot.** Of the six parts, plot was the most important to Aristotle. He therefore discussed it in the most detail, considering its *wholeness* (having a beginning, a middle, and an end, connected by causality); its *unity* (so that if any part is removed, the whole is disturbed); its *materials* (suffering, discovery, and reversal); and its *form* (complication and dénouement).
- **Character.** He argued that the best tragic protagonist is one who causes his own downfall through some great tragic error (*hamartia*).
- **Language.** The play's language should be both clear and interesting.
- **Spectacle.** Spectacle is the business of the stage machinist rather than the poet.

Because the *Poetics* is so packed with ideas and its translation is so difficult, its meaning has been debated for two thousand years. Certainly, it remains the base from which most discussions of dramatic theory must proceed, through either acceptance or rejection of its primary tenets.

The Hellenistic Period and Its Theatres

Theatre buildings also changed. Great stone theatres sprang up both on the Greek peninsula and on conquered lands (especially modern Turkey), and they tended to share common features:

- A two-storied *skene*
- A long, narrow, high stage attached to the *skene,* usually with steps or ramps at the ends but sometimes with entrances and exits only through the *skene*. Its use is unclear.
- An orchestra, as before, but now of uncertain use.

Unfortunately, we do not know how plays were staged in Hellenistic theatres. Were actors on stage? in the orchestra? some combination of the two? Where was the chorus?

Costumes and masks also changed, and they changed in similar directions. Those in tragedy tended toward greater size and grandeur. Unlike masks of the golden age, the masks of tragedy during the Hellenistic period are the familiar masks of cliché, having a high headdress (***onkos***) as well as exaggerated, often distorted, eyes and mouths. Footwear for tragedy may have featured a high platform boot, called a ***cothurnus,*** rather than the soft slipper of former days. Such changes enlarged the physical appearance of the

FIGURE 11.10
Hellenistic Theatre Buildings
Stone remains of several Hellenistic theatres have led scholars to speculate that a typical Hellenistic theatre looked something like the reconstruction shown here.

FIGURE 11.11
Hellenistic Masks
Tradition suggests that this bas-relief shows the comic playwright Menander. The masks seem fairly late and may be comic.

actor and brought him greater focus, suggesting an altered acting style. Comic masks ranged from somewhat lifelike to quite outrageous, matching the types of characters that began to repeat in comedies of the period.

Truth be told, drama and theatre from the Hellenistic period would not be important except for three things:

- The promulgation of Aristotelian theory
- The mistaken assumption that these buildings and practices represented the buildings and practices of fifth-century BCE Athens
- The strong influences of these plays, buildings, and practices on Roman theatre and possibly on Indian theatre as well

Before leaving Greece, we should note that there existed alongside these state-supported festival theatres another kind of performance, the **mime**. Very little is known about it except that it seems to have been popular and perhaps slightly disreputable. Its troupes included women, its actors apparently often played barefoot, and mime troupes were not allowed to perform as part of the festivals (probably explaining why so little evidence about them has come down to us).

After Alexander died, his Hellenistic empire soon collapsed, with various pieces of it drifting into other rising centers of power. By a hundred years before the common era, Greece had fallen within the sphere of a spreading Roman influence as the center of civilization shifted west. From this time, Hellenistic theatrical trends continued but were altered to bring them more in line with Roman practice. Not only were Roman theatres built on Greek lands, but Hellenistic theatres also began to be remodeled to make them look

FIGURE 11.12
Greek Mime
This detail based on a vase painting may show a dramatic scene from mime as played in Greek outposts on the Italian peninsula. The appearance of comic nudity, including the oddly shaped bodies and phalli of many male comic figures, may have been achieved through tights and padding.

more like Roman theatres, producing hybrids that we now call Graeco-Roman theatres (the age itself is sometimes referred to as the **Graeco-Roman period**). Although records show that theatre performances persisted in Greece, the center of influence—and with it the theatre—had clearly shifted west, to Rome itself.

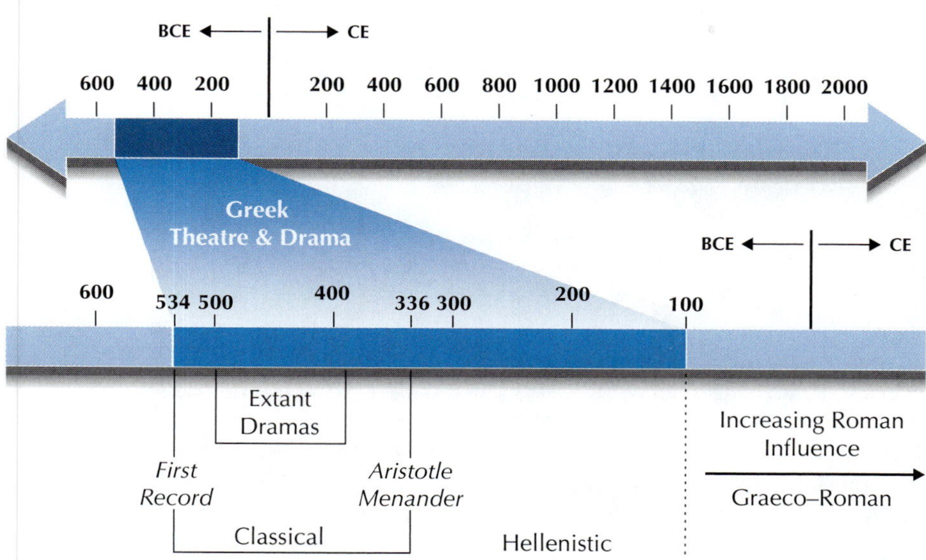

FIGURE 11.13

Timeline

Although Greek theatre's first records date from the sixth century BCE, its golden age was the fifth century (400s) BCE. The later Hellenistic period (300s to 200s) saw the building of stone theatres and the theorizing of Aristotle. After c. 100 BCE, influence shifted increasingly from Greece to Rome.

KEY TERMS

Check your understanding against this list. Brief definitions are included in the Glossary; persons are page-referenced in the Index.

chorus 171
cothurnus 183
eccyclema 178
façade stage 177
flat 178
Graeco-Roman period 185
Great Dionysia 172
Hellenistic period 181
mechane 179
middle comedy 180
mime 184
new comedy 182
old comedy 176
onkos 183
orchestra 177
protagonist 178
satyr play 172
skene 177

CHAPTER

12

The Theatre of Rome

OBJECTIVES

When you have completed this chapter, you should be able to:

- Discuss the relationship between theatre and religion in Rome
- Trace the development of Roman physical theatres and their plays and playwrights
- Identify the major periods of Roman theatres, with approximate dates
- Explain how a Roman performance would have looked in the principal periods—what masks and costumes were used, what acting space was used
- Explain the important differences between the plays of Plautus and Terence and those of Seneca
- Explain the importance of Vitruvius and Horace

CONTEXT

Greek culture had penetrated parts of the Italian peninsula even before the golden age of Athenian drama, when Rome was only one small town among many. The people of the Italian peninsula were mostly self-sufficient herders and farmers, who early established a republican form of government. Having relatively little interest in arts, literature, and philosophy, they excelled instead in practical activities, becoming superb agriculturalists, soldiers, engineers, builders, and rhetoricians. Their religion was polytheistic, with most Roman gods having clear Greek equivalents. (Bacchus corresponded to Dionysus, for example.) They also had a gift for adapting useful ideas from other cultures, whose practices they modified to suit Roman tastes and needs.

While Alexander the Great was building his Greek empire, a distinctly Roman culture began to coalesce. First, Rome unified much of the Italian peninsula and then, having built a navy, began to expand to other lands around the Mediterranean Sea, which was soon thought of as the "Roman Lake." By the third century BCE, Rome was a leading Mediterranean power. When Alexander's Hellenistic empire began to break apart, Rome moved to fill the void left in the west.

FIGURE 12.1

Map

During Athens' golden age (400s BCE), Rome was simply one small city among many on Italy's peninsula, less important than the Etruscans to the north and the Greeks to the south. During Greece's Hellenistic period, however, a distinctly Roman culture emerged in Italy; it overtook the Greek culture by the start of the common era.

It was in this republican Rome that theatre and drama appeared in 240 BCE. Regrettably, the same major problem haunts the study of Roman theatre as of Greek: For the periods when we know most about plays (BCE), we know least about theatres because they were built of wood and have not lasted; conversely, when we know most about theatres (CE), we know almost nothing about plays.

ROMAN FESTIVALS AND THEATRE OF THE REPUBLIC

Roman dramatic and theatrical practices mostly reproduced those of Hellenistic Greece (see pp. 183–185) but were modified by earlier Italian traditions of performance. Roman festivals, called ***ludi***, differed from Greek festivals mostly by having activities such as acrobatics and ropedancing compete directly with plays for public attention. At first, there was a single play, but the number of plays grew steadily over time.

Drama

No Roman tragedy that was meant to be performed survives. Fragments suggest, however, that they resembled Hellenistic tragedy (see p. 181). Some presented upper-class Greeks (in which actors wore Greek costume); others told of upper-class Romans (in Roman attire). Seneca wrote nine tragedies that survive, but scholars believe they were not intended for performance. Tragedy was never very popular in Rome, perhaps because as a people the Romans lacked deep interest in philosophy and ethics, the usual emphasis in Athenian tragedy.

Comedy was far more popular and, like tragedy, divided into two types: that written about Greeks (this time middle or lower class, and so costumed) and that about Romans (ditto). In addition to many titles and fragments, twenty-seven complete comedies survive, all by two authors: Plautus and Terence, both of whom wrote during the second century BCE (100s) and about the Athenian middle class. Both drew heavily from Greek new comedy for their stories and approach. *Neither used a chorus*. Despite these strong similarities, the two authors are very different in other ways and so suggest quite a range within Roman comedy.

Plautus, the older of the two authors, was an actor as well as a playwright. Of the more than one hundred works credited to Plautus, twenty-one have survived, a tribute to his popularity. Probably his experiences as an actor accounted for the theatrical (as opposed to literary) qualities of his comedies. Plautine comedies are noted for:

- Loosely linked episodes
- Many visual gags and verbal wordplay
- Characters who are ludicrous in appearance as well as behavior
- Direct address to the audience, breaking dramatic illusion

Among his many plays, *The Braggart Warrior, The Menaechmi, Pot of Gold,* and *Amphitryon* have been copied by Shakespeare, Molière, and others.

The more refined comedies were written by Terence. His plays were more elegant than Plautus's but also less robust and free. They were more thoughtful but less fun. Terence's comedies had:

- Plots that often combined two or more of the Greek comedies into a single, highly complicated dramatic action

FIGURE 12.2

Roman Mimes

The word *mime* refers to both a kind of performance and the actors who performed it. Mimes did not normally wear masks. Roman mime performances became more popular than other forms of theatre by the Christian era. The grotesque figure with the knife has a face that suggests a genetic defect and is typical of some of the cruelty of later mime performance.

- Prologues that were unusual because Terence argued matters of dramatic theory, encouraged audiences to behave politely, and defended himself from the attacks of critics
- Carefully contrived actions that seemed to proceed by cause and effect, thus avoiding the episodic quality of Plautus's comedies
- Characters that appeared more normal and human than Plautus's and thus more sympathetic

It may help to distinguish Terence from Plautus to know that, although Plautus is occasionally performed even today, Terence almost never is. And Terence, not Plautus, was used in schools during the Middle Ages as a way to teach the Latin language and proper Latin usage.

Although comedy had always been more popular than tragedy in Rome, its popularity waned within fifty years of Terence's death. Therefore, by the time the first stone theatre was built (55 BCE), the great period of Roman tragedy and comedy was over.

Theatre Buildings, Scenery, Costumes, and Masks

Roman theatres, like Greek theatres, were façade stages. As far as we can tell, their basic arrangement remained scene house, aisleways, and orchestra. Assuming that Rome's early wooden theatres resembled its later stone ones, Roman theatres differed from Hellenistic theatres in several ways:

- They stood on level ground (rather than hillsides), with built-up,stadium-style seating.
- Their orchestras were half-circles, rather than full circles or rectangles.
- Their long, deep stages were closed at both ends by the building itself, which jutted out.
- They used a front curtain, the first to do so.

FIGURE 12.3
Theatre of Marcellus
This was one of the first permanent (stone) theatres built in Rome (c. 17 BCE). This engraving from the late 1700s shows much of what then remained of the theatre. The site still exists and is a popular tourist attraction.

As in Greece, the façade of Roman theatres served as background. In tragedy, the doors of the façade represented separate entrances to a palace or other public building, with the stage floor representing the ground in front of the building. In comedy, the doors were entrances to separate houses, with the stage representing a street running in front of them. There were ***periaktoi***, machines that could be rotated to reveal painted scenes. Records tell of two *periaktoi*, one

Spotlight

At least seven of Plautus's plays were incorporated into the musical *A Funny Thing Happened on the Way to the Forum*, including the play *Miles Gloriosus* or "The Braggart Soldier." Here the braggart soldier character in Virginia Commonwealth University's production of *A Funny Thing....*

Plautus's *The Menaechmi*

Written by Plautus (c. 254–c. 184 BCE), *The Menaechmi* is probably the most often revived Roman comedy. It has also served as a source for other works, most notably Shakespeare's *Comedy of Errors* and two American musicals, *The Boys from Syracuse* and *A Funny Thing Happened on the Way to the Forum* (which drew material from other Plautine comedies as well). The play's appeal probably comes from its farcical story, strong visual gags, and such familiar comic characters as the wily servant who outsmarts his master; the parasite, a Roman equivalent of today's rock-star groupie; the courtesan, a cross between a high-class call girl and a mistress; and the nagging wife.

The Story of the Play

A businessman from Syracuse takes Menaechmus, one of his identical twin sons, on a business trip, where the youngster disappears in a crowd. After a fruitless search, the father returns home alone, where, griefstricken, he dies, and the grandfather renames the remaining twin Menaechmus in honor of the lost brother. When this second Meneachmus grows up, he leaves with a servant to search for his long-lost twin. This information is revealed in a prologue before the action begins.

After years of searching, Menaechmus 2 arrrives in the city of Epidamnus, where Menaechmus 1 has been living with a wealthy but quarrelsome wife. Following yet another argument with his wife, Menaechmus 1 storms out of the house, stealing a dress to give to his mistress, Erotium. Menaechmus 1 gives his present, orders a feast, and then leaves with his parasite to attend to business. Thus is the stage set for dual confusions.

Erotium, seeing Menaechmus 2, insists that he sit down and eat a feast that she has prepared (for Menaechmus 1); when Menaechmus 2 has eaten, she asks him to take a bracelet (an earlier gift from Menaechmus 1) to a jeweler. He's happy to oblige. Meanwhile, the parasite, having become separated from Menaechmus 1, returns and sees Menaechmus 2 leaving the feast with the bracelet. Angry at Menaechmus for eating without him, he tells the wife about the gifts to Erotium, so that when Menaechmus 1 returns, he finds that his wife is in a tizzy and his mistress has locked him out of her house. He leaves just as Menaechmus 2 returns, carrying the dress and bracelet. He encounters the angry wife, who first attacks him and then decides he's crazy, ties him up, and carts him off to a doctor. Menaechmus 2, of course, has no idea what's going on: He's had a splendid free meal and tried to do a favor in return, only to be assaulted and called crazy.

The mistaken identities are finally sorted out by Menaechmus 2's servant, who thus earns his freedom. Menaechmus 1 announces that he will sell everything he owns (including his wife) and return with his brother to Syracuse.

near each end of the stage. Because they could not possibly have hidden the whole façade, they must have served simply to inform the audience of location, not to portray any place in a realistic way. Although these early wooden theatres were temporary, they could be quite spectacular, according to ancient accounts.

As in Greece, all actors of comedy and tragedy wore masks, and the masks resembled those of Hellenistic Greece, with high *onkos* and distorted eyes and mouth for tragedy, and a range from somewhat realistic to comically distorted for comedy. The conventions of costuming were also rooted in Hellenistic conventions (see p. 181), with actors wearing a version of either Greek or Roman dress (depending on the kind of tragedy or comedy).

Audiences

Theatres of the *ludi* were free and open to all, and probably somewhere between ten and fifteen thousand people attended. Great care was taken to ensure the comfort of audiences, with wide and numerous aisles allowing for ease of entering and exiting the space.

THE EMPIRE AND THE END OF ROMAN DRAMA

About a hundred years before the beginning of the common era, Rome's republican government gave way to an imperial one, and soon thereafter it confronted the growing challenge of a new religion, Christianity, that had arisen in one of its own territories. Whereas Rome was perfectly happy to accommodate this new god (it had routinely adopted the gods of any culture with which it came into contact), Christians refused to allow their god to be assimilated into the Roman pantheon. Indeed, they insisted that their god alone should be worshipped, a rigidity unwelcome in a culture whose religion depended more on traditions than passions.

FIGURE 12.4

Roman Comedy

Although a few comedies of Plautus are still produced, Roman comedy is most popular today as adapted by Molière, Shakespeare, and American musical theatre. Here, *A Funny Thing Happened on the Way to the Forum*, as produced by Virginia Commonwealth University.

Within three hundred years, the Roman Empire had spread as far north as England, through parts of Africa and the Middle East, and as far east as Syria. Christianity had spread with it. This expanding empire traded widely, importing luxury items from the East and exporting mass-produced, useful articles. The sprawling empire encouraged more roads, better water management, a strong civil service, and a permanent military class. Travel, encouraged by both war and trade, promoted a kind of cosmopoli-tanism. Despite their growth, Romans still did not define themselves through their art, literature, or philosophy. Instead, they concentrated on increasing personal comforts (through elegant homes, public baths, entertainments) and continued to demonstrate their superiority in practical matters. For example, they wrote how-to manuals.

Three Important Texts

Two how-to manuals, both written near the turn into the common era, are of special importance to theatre and drama, because, when they were rediscovered during the Renaissance (c. 1400s), their advice on how to build theatres and write plays was put into practice.

VITRUVIUS The Roman architect Vitruvius wrote a ten-volume work, *De Architectura,* on how to lay out a city. As a part of this larger work, he set down guidelines for building both theatres and the scenery to go in them. Without illustrations and with often ambiguous descriptions, the books were easily—and badly—misinterpreted by Renaissance designers, but their influence was enormous.

HORACE The Roman poet Horace described how to write good plays in his *Ars Poetica,* a work that was to exert even more influence during the Renaissance than did Aristotle's *Poetics,* which it superficially resembles. Unlike Aristotle's work, a philosophical inquiry into the nature of the form of tragedy, Horace's is a practical guidebook aimed at people who want to write plays. As such, it is considerably more prescriptive than Aristotle's work, suggesting such things as:

- The importance of keeping comedy and tragedy separate
- The need to have a unity of time and of place as a way of achieving unity of action
- The need for drama to teach as well as please

Ars Poetica had no immediate influence on Roman practice. Its importance, like Vitruvius's, comes from its powerful influence much later on Renaissance theory and drama.

SENECA The third important text is really a set of texts. Although Roman tragedy and comedy were not played in public theatres by the 100s, dramatic readings were apparently given at banquets in private homes. Ten such literary tragedies have come down to us, nine by Seneca, who wrote them just after the turn of the common era. The importance of Seneca's tragedies rests neither on their literary excellence nor on their position among contemporary Roman audiences, but on their monumental effect on later writers, who discovered, translated, and copied them (see pp. 233–234), probably because they were both linguistically and physically more accessible than the earlier Greek tragedies.

Seneca's plays display five characteristics assumed to be typical of Greek Hellenistic tragedy:

- A chorus that is not well integrated into the action, and so the (usually four) choral odes (songs) serve to divide the plays into five parts
- Protagonists that are often driven by a single dominant passion that causes their downfall
- Minor characters that include messengers, confidants, and ghosts
- Language that emphasizes rhetorical and stylistic figures, including extended descriptive and declamatory passages, pithy statements about the human condition (*sententiae*), and elaborately balanced exchanges of dialogue
- Spectacular scenes of violence and gore

Although Seneca's plays are now rarely performed, they are important, like the writings of Vitruvius and Horace, because of their influence on Renaissance writers, who rediscovered tragedy through Seneca and tried to follow what he did in writing their own tragedies.

Theatre Buildings

Despite these three important written sources, theatre buildings rather than texts dominated the empire. In the common era, Rome built great stone theatres, first on the Italian peninsula and then throughout its empire (remains are still visible in Lybia and Turkey, for example). Although the basic pattern of scene house,

FIGURE 12.5
The Roman Theatre at Sabrata, Lybia
This restored Roman theatre in North Africa features the traditional three story highly decorated façade of columns. Note that the stage is connected and thus unified with the seating area.

aisleways, and orchestra remained, stone theatres were probably more ornate than earlier wooden ones. Now used by audiences rather than choruses, the aisles separating the scene house from the orchestra were covered, causing the buildings to form a single architectural unit, rather than two (as in Greek theatres). The façades were decorated with such details as statuary, niches, and columns. A roof extended over part of the stage, both protecting the elaborate façades and improving acoustics. Audience comfort remained a high priority, with awnings sometimes protecting audiences from sun and rain and, in at least one theatre, a primitive air conditioning system consisting of large fans blowing over ice brought down from mountaintops.

Theatrical Entertainments

Into these theatres came new theatrical entertainments that replaced comedy and tragedy. An indigenous rural Italian farce, called Atellan farce after the region in which it originated and featuring four grotesquely masked characters, was popular for a while. **Pantomime**, a solo dance performed by a nonspeaking performer (wearing a mask with a closed mouth), could be comic but was more often serious. It filled the void left by tragedy.

Most popular of all, however, was **mime**, which may have come from Greece, for Greek mime (the word refers both to the form and the performers) had a long history, although it was never performed at Greek festivals. In Greece, mime seemed unimportant, but Roman mime became so popular during the empire that it drove all other forms of theatre from the stage.

FIGURE 12.6
Roman Stone Theatres
Well-engineered and constructed, many Roman stone theatres still exist; some have been reconstructed for performance. Here, Verdi's opera *Aida* at the summer opera festival in the nine thousand-seat Théâtre Antique in Orange, France.

Several traits of mime make it important:

- Mime included women as performers, the only theatrical entertainment in Greece or Rome to do so.
- Performers in the mime did not usually wear masks, so their faces were both noticeable and important. Indeed, mime performers were often successful because of their looks: the very handsome or beautiful and the extraordinarily grotesque or ugly.

Mimes could be either comic or serious, simple or spectacular, but, whatever their form, they usually dealt with contemporary life. They became both Rome's most popular and its most notorious theatrical entertainment during the empire (in both east and west). Some female mime actors set fashions in clothes and behavior; one (Theodora) married an emperor; some became the equivalent of movie stars. Despite this popularity, few complete mime scripts have been passed down to us; the assumption is that they, perhaps like sitcom scripts, were thought (by those who kept libraries) to have no lasting value.

Christian Opposition to Theatre

Christianity's opposition to theatre was not to Roman comedies or tragedies, which it had not seen and did not know. The opposition was to mime. Because some mimes included real sex and violence as part of the performance and because many of them mocked Christianity, Christian writers and believers demanded—unsuccessfully—the outlawing of theatre. Mime was not alone in its excesses; equally popular were chariot racing, gladiatorial contests, animal fights, and sea battles in which violence and death were also expected and applauded. Although these entertainments took place in special buildings such as **amphitheatres** (e.g., Rome's Colosseum) and *circuses* (the Circus Maximus), theatres were occasionally appropriated for such events, reinforcing the arguments of those who wanted to ban theatre. That mime had to compete directly with these other kinds of performance probably explains its occasional rawness. That mime replaced comedy and tragedy in Rome's public theatres surely offers hints about Romans and their culture. The antipathy between theatre and the church, which dates from the early Roman Empire, finds echoes still today.

THE BREAKUP OF THE EMPIRE

By the early 300s CE, the Roman Empire had become too large and unwieldy to rule effectively. It was therefore broken into two administrative units, with the western unit claiming Rome as its capital and the eastern unit being ruled from Constantinople, a new city built by the Emperor Constantine. Constantine moved to this new capital, taking much of the population of Rome with him, thus tilting the empire's center of gravity far to the east. The result was a shift in power and cultural influence. Constantinople grew more powerful and turned eastward. Rome, now a much smaller city, once again found itself on the western fringe of the civilized world.

By the middle of the sixth century (500s), the western empire was disintegrating, its system of roads and waterways crumbling, its trade sporadic, and its security

FIGURE 12.7

Roman Entertainments

During the Roman Empire, elaborate entertainments with animal fights, chariot races, and even naval battles became popular and drove traditional theatre from the center of cultural life. The bottom image is of the Colosseum in Rome as it appeared in the 1750s when this etching was made.

destroyed. Whatever unity remained in western Europe came mostly from the Christian church through a network of churches and religious houses bound through the pope in Rome, but the center of the western empire had fallen.

THE EASTERN (BYZANTINE) EMPIRE AND THEATRE

Constantinople and the eastern empire, on the other hand, flourished. Considering themselves Romans, the citizens for a time continued to speak Latin, to enjoy chariot races and theatre, and to trade with such Italian satellites as Ravenna, but increasingly trade was with countries to the east. The eastern Romans adopted Greek for official documents, however; established a Christianity (now called Orthodox) that was tied more closely to the government than to the pope; and gradually easternized, some say "orientalized," their culture. Later called *Byzantine* (after the early town of Byzantium, which Constantinople had replaced), this empire had a thriving trade, a successful military, and a highly developed culture that included theatre.

Constantinople never entirely lost contact with the west; it continued to send gifts, receive envoys, and marry its leading families with those of the west. Still, its major interests lay increasingly to the east. This rich Byzantine culture persisted for almost another thousand years. Weakened by one of the western crusades in the thirteenth century (1200s), the eastern Roman Empire was finally overwhelmed by Muslim Turks in the fifteenth century (1400s), just as the former western empire was beginning to recuperate and enter its great Renaissance.

Byzantine theatre is not well known in today's western world, for a couple of reasons. The languages in which its records appear are not those in which most western scholars are competent, and many of the records were, until the late 1980s, inaccessible because they were held behind the so-called Iron Curtain. With the fall of the Soviet Union and the political realignment of Russia and the United States, however, more information is now becoming available. The scholarship suggests that Byzantine theatre included:

- The continuation of mime
- An interest in Greek tragedy (which may have been literary only)
- The exportation of performances and an idea of performance to Asia Minor and what is now Ukraine

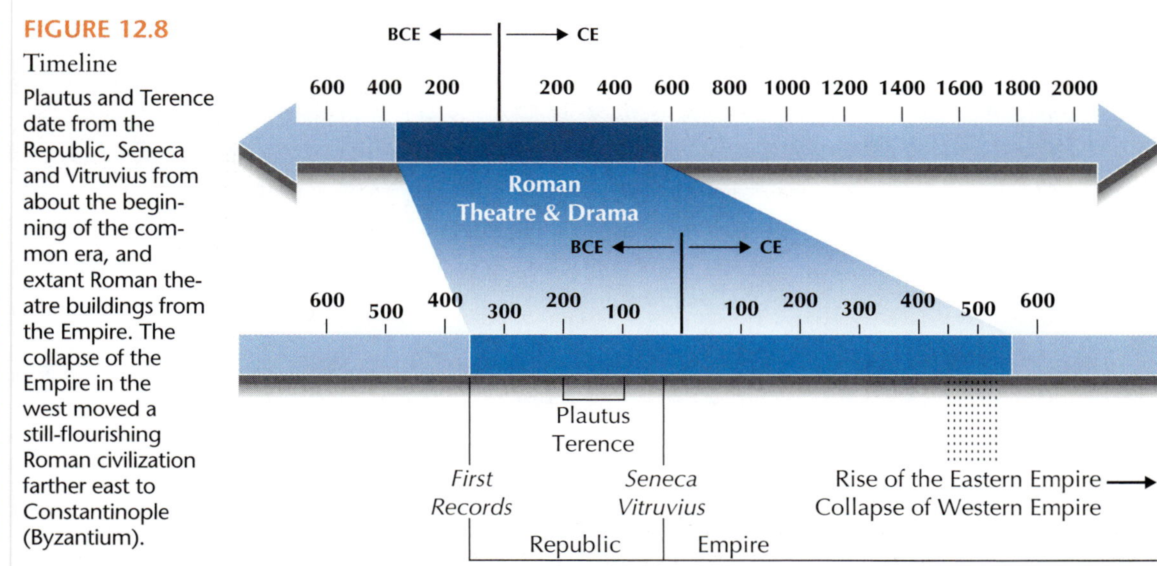

FIGURE 12.8

Timeline

Plautus and Terence date from the Republic, Seneca and Vitruvius from about the beginning of the common era, and extant Roman theatre buildings from the Empire. The collapse of the Empire in the west moved a still-flourishing Roman civilization farther east to Constantinople (Byzantium).

Just as Roman theatre of the west left a legacy for the Renaissance in western Europe, so, too, may have Byzantine theatre. There are tantalizing hints that Byzantine theatre may have influenced both Italian popular theatre and the medieval theatre of Europe.

The Roman Empire—east and west—was thus unparalleled among great civilizations because it remained intact so long, although its final iterations would scarcely have been recognized by the Italians who first created it.

KEY TERMS

Check your understanding against this list. Brief definitions are included in the Glossary; persons are page-referenced in the Index.

amphitheatres 195
ludi 187
mime 194
pantomime 194
periaktoi 189

PART

IIIB

EMBLEM, ENVIRONMENT, AND SIMULTANEITY

(c. 950–c. 1650)

The second phase of theatrical and dramatic history began in the tenth century and ended about 1650 (approximately two hundred years earlier in Italy). Theatres during these six hundred years shared several important theatrical conventions and so can be usefully studied together. Their major shared traits are:

- The communication of meaning through **emblems**, shorthand embodiments of richer content (a flag standing for a country, a crown for a king)
- The use of existing environments for performance
- A staging convention of simultaneous settings in which several locations are presented simultaneously to the audience
- Complicated plays with numerous characters, many lines of action, and elastic time and place
- A mostly male theatre, in which women participated only as audience

Over the last two centuries of this period, rapid change led to overlap between this period and a new one then coming into being. This overlap was possible because of social and economic stratification into a court theatre, a popular theatre, and an embryonic professional and commercial theatre.

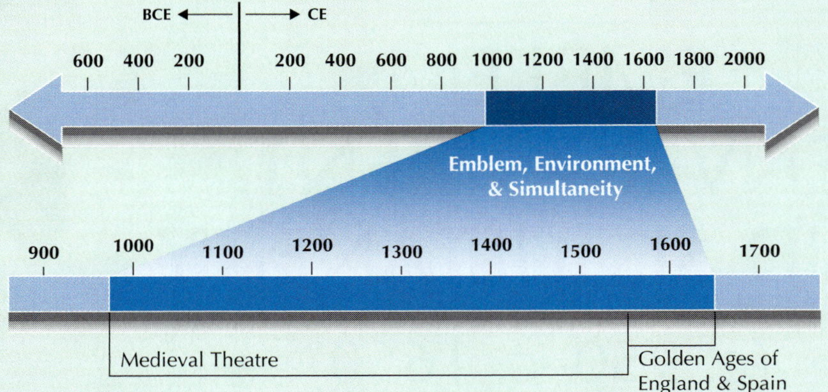

FIGURE IIIB.1
After the fall of the western Roman Empire (c. 550 CE), organized theatre disappeared from Europe until the end of the tenth century, when it reappeared using different conventions. These conventions were, in turn, replaced after about 1650.

CHAPTER 13

Theatre in the Middle Ages

OBJECTIVES

When you have completed this chapter, you should be able to:

- Explain how and when a new kind of theatre came into being several hundred years after the fall of Rome in the West
- Discuss how the medieval theatre was part of its culture
- Trace the changes in medieval theatre from its beginnings to its end
- Describe the physical types of medieval theatres, and discuss how the various theatres were funded and organized

CONTEXT

Even after the 500s, Constantinople continued as a center of trade and civilization. Increasingly "Orientalized" and bureaucratized, the Byzantine Empire had a highly developed culture, one focused on luxury and one that looked east rather than west for its markets and goods. Arts and entertainments, including theatre, flourished there through most of the period, not ending until the 1450s.

Western Europe, on the other hand, was in increasing disarray after the fourth century, and, after its collapse in the sixth century, Rome had no political successor. Some city-states of the Italian peninsula avoided the general decline by maintaining strong trading connections with Constantinople or other cultures. Western Europe, however, continued to crumble as various forces that had before served to unify Europe weakened or disintegrated. The Roman system of roads and waterways fell into disrepair, and transportation and communication became at first troubled and at last almost impossible. Laws were ignored and order broke down, replaced by the rule of force. Bands of pirates and brigands grew wealthy and influential enough to challenge rulers. Without the support of a government, the monetary system failed, and barter, with all its cumbersome trappings, became the basis of trade. Out of this disarray emerged a different kind of Europe, one with different languages, traditions, and cultures—one that was fragmented and local, lacking a center of the sort Rome had provided.

The prevailing social organization was feudal, in which the social base was not the town but the manor, a self-contained agricultural unit that could offer

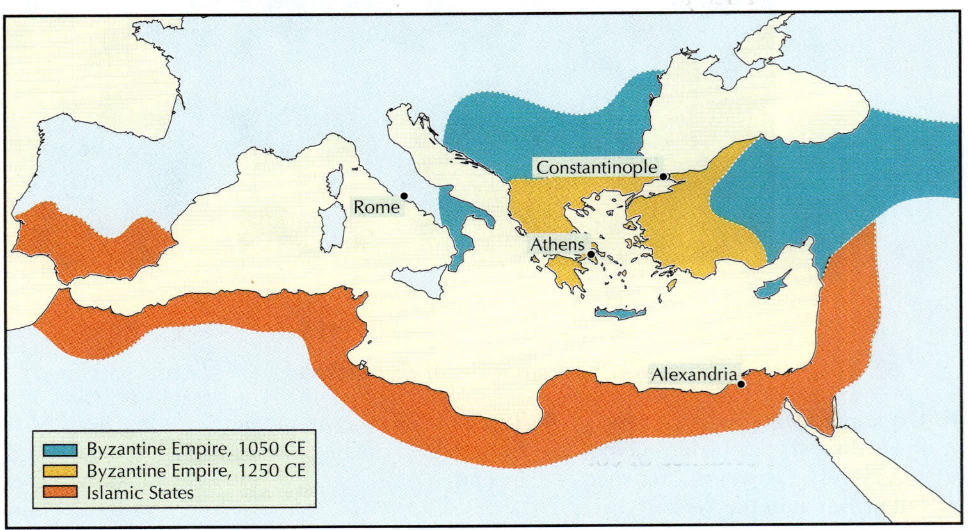

FIGURE 13.1

The Byzantine Empire

While western Europe was in disarray, the eastern Roman Empire, centered in Constantinople (Byzantium), flourished and traded with both Europe and the Far East. After the seventh century CE, the influence of newly Islamic states of the Middle East and North Africa grew, spilling over into Spain.

security to those within it. On the manor, each serf owed absolute allegiance to the lord. Serfs worked the land and maintained the manor in return for protection by the lord, who would fight to maintain safety for those within. Just as serfs owed allegiance to their lord, lesser lords owed allegiance to more powerful ones, who could call on them to raise armies. Travel among manors was irregular, a fact that worked against unity within Europe.

The Christian church, on the other hand, was a weak unifying force because its services were conducted in Latin, its pope led the whole church, and its priests and especially its monks occasionally traveled. Like social organization, church organization was hierarchical, with priests reporting to bishops, bishops to archbishops, archbishops to cardinals, and, finally, cardinals to the pope. This hierarchy ensured an orderly governance in an otherwise chaotic world, and its teachings gave it a substantial base of power.

The power hierarchies of both feudalism and Christianity were essentially pyramidal, with one (male) person at the top, relatively few (male) persons immediately under him, and so on, until at the base of each pyramid were the peasants, that great mass of people who tilled the land and provided all those above them with the necessities and amenities of life. The two pyramids interlocked when church leaders were drawn from the noble classes; the peasants provided goods and services for both church lords and secular lords.

The life of the medieval peasant was one of work, ignorance, and want; that of people above the peasant varied. Because earlier historians saw this extended period as a lower one between two higher ones (Rome and the Renaissance—the "rebirth"), they called this the Middle Ages or the medieval (middle) period.

EARLY MEDIEVAL DRAMA AND THEATRE

For many years, historians believed that no theatre or drama outlived the collapse of Rome, but it is now certain that theatre continued in the Byzantine Empire and that remnants of professional performers traveled about in Italy, France, and Germany. Scattered references to *mimi, histriones,* and *ioculatores* (all words to describe actors) surface periodically in Western medieval accounts, but the degree to which such performers performed actual plays, as distinct from such variety entertainments as juggling, tumbling, dancing, and rope tricks, is not known. If theatre (as distinct from performance) existed at all, it was feeble.

Two almost simultaneous events toward the end of the tenth century marked the reentry of theatre into western Europe. The first, the plays of Hroswitha, offer incontrovertible evidence of continuity with Roman drama; the second, the liturgical manual of Ethelwold, shows the Christian church staging a small play as part of a worship service.

Hroswitha and Ethelwold

A religious leader (and noblewoman), Hroswitha was attached to the Benedictine monastery near Gandersheim (in modern Germany) and linked to a court that had ties to Constantinople. She wrote seven plays (c. 950), the first still-extant dramas since the early days of the Roman Empire. Based on the comedies of Terence, Hroswitha's plays sought to celebrate "the laudable chastity of holy maidens" and *may* have been performed at court and at the monastery. Hroswitha is important on three counts:

- As the first known female playwright
- As the first known post-Roman playwright
- As proof of an intellectual continuity from Rome to the Middle Ages

For reasons not entirely clear (but perhaps related to the fact that men have written most histories), Hroswitha's contributions have been largely overshadowed by a different strand of theatre, one that also emerged in the tenth century and also at a Benedictine monastery.

Ethelwold, Bishop of Winchester, England, issued in 975 the *Regularis Concordia,* a monastic guidebook, which, among other things, described in detail how one part of an Easter service was to be performed. For about a hundred years before Ethelwold, the church had been decorating and elaborating various of its practices. Music, calendar, vestments, art, architecture, and **liturgy** (rites, public worship) had all changed in the direction of greater embellishment. One sort of liturgical embellishment was the **trope** (an interpolation into an existing text). One Easter trope was sung by the choir antiphonally and began, "*Quem quaeritis in sepulchro, o christocole.*" Translated into English, the trope read in its entirety:

> Whom seek ye in the tomb, O Christians?
> Jesus of Nazareth, the crucified, O heavenly beings.
> He is not here, he is risen as he foretold;
> Go and announce that he is risen from the tomb.

It was this trope to which staging directions were added in Ethelwold's *Regularis Concordia.* Ethelwold's text (less so Hroswitha's) reveals three conventions that operated in medieval theatre. Medieval staging was:

- **Simultaneous** That is, several different locations were present in the performing space at the same time, hence **simultaneous staging**. Such an arrangement meant conceptualizing two different kinds of space: small scenic structures that served to locate the specific places (called **mansions**) and a neutral, generalized playing space (called **platea**) (see Figure 13.2).

- **Emblematic** That is, meanings from the performance reached the audience through costumes and properties that were signs or symbols whose meanings communicated easily. Among mansions, for example, an animal mouth signified hell and a revolving globe stood for heaven.

- **Environmental** That is, performed in available spaces rather than in structures specially built and set aside for the purpose.

Hroswitha's plays had no immediate successors, but from the tenth through much of the sixteenth century, many dramas such as ***Quem Quaeritis*** were performed inside monastic and later cathedral churches as a part of the liturgy (and so are also called *liturgical drama*). Such plays were chanted or sung (rather than spoken) and were given in the language of the church (Latin), and so are called **Latin music drama**. They were acted by clergy, choirboys, monks, and occasionally traveling scholars and schoolboys (and, sometimes, nuns); the actors, then, were almost always male (except in convents).

From the very short *Quem Quaeritis*, Latin music drama blossomed into many plays of varying lengths and varying degrees of complexity. The subjects of most such plays were biblical, usually drawn from events surrounding Christmas and Easter: the visit of the three Marys to the tomb, the travel of the Magi, Herod's wrath. Other Latin music dramas, however, depicted such diverse stories as the life of the Virgin Mary, the raising of Lazarus, and Daniel in the lion's den. Almost all were serious, but at festivals like the Feast of Fools and the Feast of the Boy Bishops, the usual dignity was abandoned and in its place was substituted considerable tomfoolery. Latin music dramas continued to be performed in churches well into the sixteenth century, overlapping other types by hundreds of years.

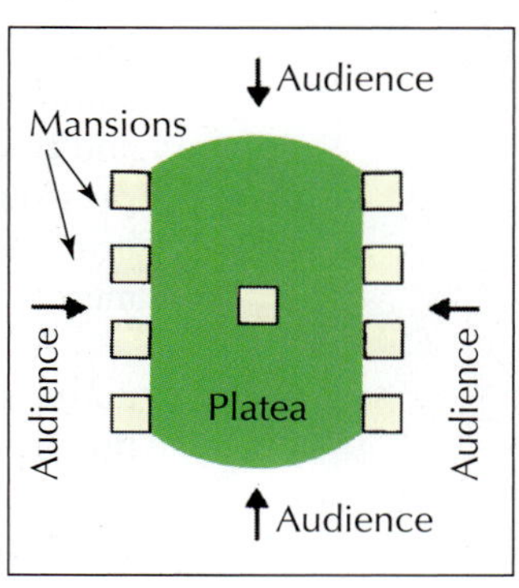

FIGURE 13.2
Simultaneous Staging
Medieval staging used two kinds of spaces: generalized playing space (a platea) and specific locations (mansions), which appeared simultaneously in or around the platea.

Plays performed in the church were produced by the church. Actors were churchmen (except in convents, where churchwomen performed). Costumes were based on church vestments, rich with meaning. Although early audiences consisted only of those residing in the monasteries or convents, when the plays began to be performed in cathedral churches as well as monastic ones, general audiences attended.

MEDIEVAL CULTURE AND THEATRE, c. 1200–1550

Several shifts within medieval culture began to coalesce by 1200. Population increased rapidly. Towns grew up around monasteries and manors to provide goods and services, serving as centers of trade. Increased trade encouraged the development of still more towns; many now located where goods that had been shipped by water (the preferred method) were transferred to land (roads were still terrible). The names Ox*ford* and Cam*bridge* reflect this origin. Trade expanded again when a series of crusades against Muslims and others (including inhabitants of Constantinople) prompted new shipbuilding, opened new sea routes, and established new trading ports and new markets, an expansion aided by improved sea manuals and the discovery of the compass.

Commercial theory changed. Early medieval theory was grounded in theology: Usury was condemned, merchants were supposed to work for the benefit of society, and profit was considered a kind of parasitism. No more. Merchants began to form monopolies, and maximum profit rather than just price became the goal. Modern commercial structures (e.g., banking, partnerships) emerged. Because merchants and tradespeople lived outside the feudal system, they gradually undermined it by providing refuge for serfs seeking to escape their lords. Towns sponsored fairs to bring people from great distances and so facilitate trade. Thus, towns and commerce competed directly with manors and agriculture for social leadership.

At about the same time, the domination of the church and its monopoly on matters of faith began to erode, with Martin Luther later posing the most direct threat (1521). The separation of religion from everyday life was under way.

With the decline of feudalism and the authority of the church, and with the emergence of towns and nationalism, the era was metamorphosing into a new kind of culture: That is, after about 1200, western Europe was in a transition between medieval culture and a new one that would coalesce by 1550 (one hundred or so years earlier in Italy)—the Renaissance.

Religious Drama outside the Church

After about 1200, medieval drama reflected these cultural shifts in several ways. In addition to Latin music drama, which continued to be performed in churches, new kinds of religious drama appeared. These dramas differed from Latin music drama in several ways:

- They were performed outdoors rather than inside churches.
- They were spoken rather than chanted or sung.
- They were in the vernacular (e.g., French, English, German) rather than in Latin.
- Laymen, rather than priests and clerics, served as actors.
- The stories and themes, no longer limited to liturgical sources, became more far-ranging.
- The performances tended to cluster in the spring and summer months, especially around the new Feast of Corpus Christi, rather than spreading throughout the church year, as before. They became known as **Corpus Christi plays**.

Of these changes, the most significant was the shift from a universal language (Latin) to the various national tongues, for with this shift came an end to an international drama and the beginning of several national dramas, a trend important to the future of both theatre and drama.

The plays remained decidedly religious, if not always scriptural. In general, they dealt with:

- Events in the life of Christ (e.g., *The Second Shepherd's Play*) and stories from the Old Testament (e.g., *Noah*)—plays often called *mysteries* or **mystery plays**.
- The lives of saints, both historical and legendary, called *miracles* or **miracle plays**
- Didactic allegories, often about the struggle for salvation (e.g., *Everyman*)—so-called *moralities* or **morality plays**

Although the plays differed in subject matter and form, they shared several characteristics. First, they aimed to teach or to reinforce belief in church doctrine. Second, they were formulated as melodramas or divine comedies—that is, the ethical system of the play was clear: Good was rewarded, evil punished. Third, the driving force for the action was God and His plan rather than the decisions or actions of the dramatic agents. To a modern reader, the plays often appear episodic, with their actions unmotivated, their sequences of time and place inexplicable, and their mixture of the comic and the serious unnerving.

In fact, their traits expressed the medieval view. The plays presented the lure and strength of sin, the power and compassion of God, and the punishment awaiting the unrepentant sinner. They called for all people to repent, to confess, and to atone for their sins.

Because history was God's great lesson to humankind, the drama that expressed His plan was nothing less than the entirety of human history, from creation to doomsday. Any combination of events, any juxtaposition of characters, and any elasticity of time or place that would illuminate God's plan and make it more accessible and compelling was suitable drama. The great dramas of the 1400s and 1500s that showed this history are called **cycle plays**, or **cosmic dramas**, and some took days, even weeks, to play from beginning to end.

Why such dramas came to be done outside the church building has been endlessly debated. Some thought the plays had been forced out of the church because of abuses such as those at the Feast of Fools. Others argued that the plays' appearance outdoors merely reflected the changing needs of the plays and their audiences for more space and freedom. More likely is the increasing power of towns, which fastened on plays and other public shows as expressions of their

Jane Hatcher, York Mystery Plays Archive, The National Centre for Early Music, Walmgate, York Y01 9TL UK

FIGURE 13.3

Medieval Plays in Modern Production

Since 1951, the York mystery plays have been produced in York, England. Currently, the plays are produced by The National Centre for Early Music at St. Margaret's Church in York. Performances are staged both at single locations and on pageant wagons, like the *Noah and the Flood* shown here.

new status. Whatever the reason for the development, records of religious plays given outside of churches appear by 1200 and are common by 1350, when relatively abundant accounts describe a civic and religious theatre of magnificent proportions throughout most of western Europe.

Staging Religious Plays outside the Church

Although churches continued to produce Latin music dramas throughout the period, other religious plays had different producing arrangements. Sometimes town officials took charge; sometimes special committees did the job. Sometimes

In *Everyman,* the character names have two meanings, one identifying a person in the play and one symbolic. Here, Everyman (left) and Death, in Hugo von Hofmansthal's version of *Everyman* produced in Salzburg.
©Leonhard Foeger/Reuters/Corbis

Anonymous, *Everyman*, c. 1490

Everyman, a popular morality play rediscovered in 1900 after a lapse of more than 400 years, is simply structured: Everyman is called by Death to the next world. Everyman then searches for a friend to accompany him on this journey. All but one forsake him. Each character is a personification of an abstract quality rather than a fully realized character—Knowledge, Beauty, Strength, and so on. Thus the character names have two meanings, one identifying a person in the play and one symbolic. The play's structure is a string of episodes rather than a causally organized progression of incidents. *Everyman* is the most often produced of all the medieval plays.

The Story of the Play

God sends Death to summon Everyman, who must bring a "sure reckoning." When Death gives the message to Everyman, saying he must "go a long journey," Everyman cries that he is not ready; he begs for time; he tries to bribe Death, who tells him he must make the journey and should find what friends will go with him.

Everyman asks various friends—Fellowship, Kindred and Cousin, Goods—to go with him, and they agree until they learn what the destination is; then they depart.

Good Deeds speaks "from the ground." He cannot go because he is too weak to walk, but he calls his sister, Knowledge, who says, "Everyman, I will go with thee and be thy guide."

Knowledge takes him to Confession; after confessing, Everyman whips himself as a penance, and Good Deeds is able to rise and walk.

Knowledge gives Everyman a "garment of sorrow" to wear instead of his worldly clothes. She tells him to call his Five Wits, his Beauty, his Strength, and his Discretion. Everyman receives the sacrament and then journeys to his grave, where Beauty refuses to enter with him; then Strength, then Discretion, then Five Wits desert him, but Good Deeds remains at the graveside. They pray, and then Everyman goes into his grave alone.

An angel appears, saying his reckoning is "crystal-clear," and a Doctor (learned man) gives a short speech to explain the play.

labor and religious organizations (**guilds** or **confraternities**) assumed responsibility, often under the town's protection.

Guilds were frequently called on to produce a single play in a group, sometimes on the basis of particular skills or association with the play's subject: Noah plays, which required a real (perhaps half-size) ship, went well with shipbuilding, for example. Because of both financial investment and tradition, plays tended to stay with the same guild for many years. As the plays and processions showed the wealth of the town, so the play and its properties showed the wealth of the guild.

Roles in the plays were open to all male members of the community (in France, occasionally, women might perform) and were generally performed without compensation. As in any primarily amateur operation, the quality of the performances varied considerably, and it was probably in an attempt to upgrade the general level of acting that many cities hired professional "property players" to take the leading roles (after c. 1450) and to instruct the others. Although these few actors were paid, they were not looked down on as socially undesirable, as were professional actors in secular plays.

We have no textbooks of medieval acting. We believe that it was, like the costumes, emblematic. It probably depended on reducing the character to large, symbolic strokes, without "inner" work or "psychology." We do not know how amateurs handled the problem of being heard and understood outdoors. Some pictures of the period show prompters or directors, book in hand, standing among the actors; this professional may literally have been cueing gestures and turns of voice.

Some plays and some roles suggest a tradition of satirical or comic playing, with caricature an established technique. The traveling actors of the countryside probably emphasized low comedy and certainly passed on techniques and traditions that would flourish later with Shakespeare's clowns.

The staging of religious plays outside the church took two major forms, still within the conventions of emblem, environment, and simultaneity:

- Fixed staging, which occurred throughout Europe, except in parts of Spain and England
- Movable staging, which was used most often in parts of Spain and England

In fixed staging, mansions (or **scaffolds**) were set up, usually outdoors, in whatever spaces were available (e.g., courtyards of noble houses, town squares, the remains of Roman amphitheatres). Depending on the space, the mansions were arranged in circles, straight lines, or rectangles, and the *platea* and the audience area were established accordingly. Although the individual arrangements varied, heaven and hell (ordinarily the most ornate mansions) were customarily set at opposite poles.

In movable staging, **pageants** (**pageant wagons**) allowed the audience to scatter along a processional route while the plays were brought to them and performed in sequence, much like a parade with floats. Each play, then, was performed several times. A likely pattern was for the first play (e.g., creation) to be presented at dawn at the first station; when it moved to the second station to perform, the second play (e.g., the fall of man) was presented at the first station. For most of the day, several plays were performing at once. The word *pageant* is important in a discussion of movable staging because it was used to describe the play itself, the spectacle of the plays in performance, and also the vehicle on which the presentation was staged.

The enormous complexity of some late medieval dramas also required specialists to oversee the production and to serve as the medieval counterpart of the modern producer. Because special effects in the dramas were so extraordinary, some men, called **masters of secrets**, became specialists in their construction and workings, which included:

- **Flying** Angels flew about; Lucifer raised Christ; souls rose from limbo into heaven on doomsday; devils and fire-spitting monsters sallied forth from hell and back again; platforms made to resemble clouds (**glories**) bore choruses of heavenly beings aloft.
- **Traps** Appearances, disappearances, and substitutions were popular, as when Lot's wife was turned into a pillar of salt and tigers were transformed into sheep.
- **Fire** Hell belched smoke and flames (in 1496 at Seurre, an actor playing Satan was severely burned when his costume caught fire), and buildings ignited on cue.

Costumes were primary carriers of meaning within the convention we have called emblematic: They indicated, symbolically and clearly, the nature of the wearers. At its most sophisticated, this convention became a rich source of both meaning and spectacle: In a parade of the seven deadly sins, Pride was dressed entirely in peacock feathers (the feather's "eye" symbolizing the love of display and self-admiration); a costume recorded for a late morality play had symbols of coinage embroidered all over it. In the guild-produced plays, large sums were spent on such costumes, which were then used year after year. Masks were rare, probably being restricted to devils.

Audiences for these great outdoor performances of the towns comprised a broad spectrum, from local religious figures to town officials to ordinary citizens. The audience was not universal, however, because a fee was usually charged, and so some of the population was most likely excluded. The well-to-do paid extra to sit in stands or special scaffolds or, when pageant wagons were used, in the windows of selected houses. Those who paid the least stood to watch the plays. Those who paid nothing may have been able to see the processions, if not the plays.

Secular Drama

At about the same time that religious dramas appeared outside the church, the first records of secular dramas appear. Secular drama may have been an outgrowth of outdoor religious drama, or it may have developed quite independently, growing out of traditions from early pagan performances. When the great

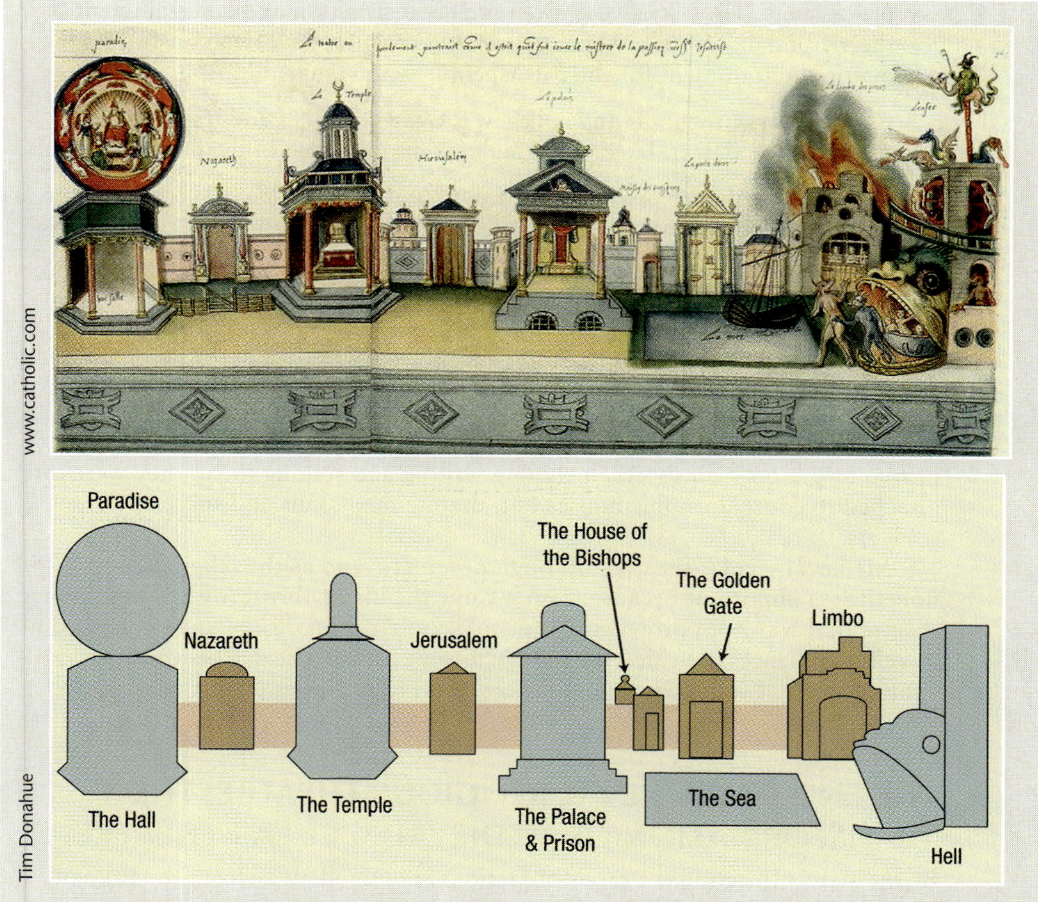

www.catholic.com

Tim Donahue

FIGURE 13.4

Fixed and Moveable Staging

Most fixed performances on the European continent took place in open spaces like city squares or the remains of Roman arenas; indoors, they took place in religious or public buildings. Mansions remained fixed throughout such performances (top illustration and key). In some parts of England and Spain, on the other hand, mansion-like structures were set on wagons that traveled through a city, taking the plays to fixed positions where audience seating (sometimes quite elaborate, seldom free) was set up for the privileged; everybody else stood. (See Figure 13.3).

religious plays were at their zenith, this secular tradition was moving tentatively toward maturity. Several principal venues of secular drama existed:

- **Street Pageants and Entries** Towns staged street pageants and entries in connection with various special occasions, often during the visit of an important dignitary. As a part of these events, plays were combined with elaborate processions. The plays were given for the instruction and entertainment of the visiting dignitaries, whose procession through the town constituted the major entertainment for the townspeople who watched it.

- **Roman Plays** In schools and colleges, Roman comedies and tragedies were studied, copied, translated, and emulated during much of the fifteenth century.
- **Farces** For ordinary people in the towns and countryside, farces poked fun at all manner of domestic tribulations, particularly infidelity and cuckoldry.
- **Morality Plays** In many instances, secular morality plays featured classical gods and heroes rather than Christian virtues and vices, and occasionally morality plays were drawn into the religious battles of the Reformation: For example, anti-Catholic moralities costumed devils as Catholic prelates and Christian figures as Protestant ministers; anti-Protestant moralities did just the reverse.

Toward the end of the period (after c. 1450), a class of professionals appeared to put on such shows, including writing and staging them; they were often attached to courts or noble houses but, despite their skills and success, were servants.

Medieval secular theatre, although never as grand as the religious, was nonetheless important because from it came the major thrust toward developing a theatre that was both professional (people could earn their living at it) and commercial (audiences provided the money to support it). Theatre became a kind of commodity that some people (audiences) paid to see other people (artists) do.

THE END OF MEDIEVAL RELIGIOUS THEATRE: THE TRANSFORMATION OF MEDIEVAL SECULAR THEATRE

By the sixteenth century, a series of factions splintered away from the Roman Church; this religious Reformation quickly became political as rulers and nations found reasons to break from Rome or stay with it. The religious theatre was a visible annoyance to both Protestant and Catholic authorities, offending the one with doctrines already rejected, offending the other with doctrines better kept in church, at least until things quieted down. Worse, zealots on both sides were writing morality plays that cast their opponents as devils. In place after place, religious plays were therefore outlawed by both Protestants and Catholics: Paris, 1548; England, 1558; the Council of Trent, 1545–1563.

The end of medieval religious drama was quick. It had reached its height only shortly before it was banned. Much of the best and most elaborate medieval religious theatre came between 1500 and 1550.

Medieval theatre in the West, however, left important legacies: its conventions of acting, staging, and playwriting and its highly developed technology of special effects. These practices grounded a newly emerging northern Renaissance theatre, whose flowering in England and Spain produced their golden ages. The early professionals who had worked in the late medieval theatre were the forebears of a great upsurge of professionalism visible after about 1550. And most significant of

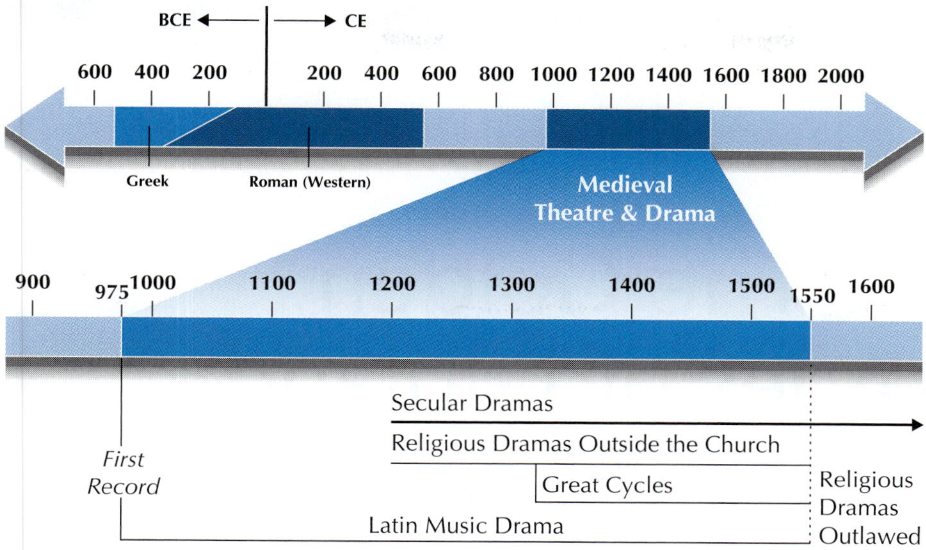

FIGURE 13.5
Timeline
So far as we know, medieval theatre and drama appeared in the late 900s as a sung Latin playlet in England and as imitations of Terence in Germany by a cloistered woman (Hroswitha), possibly influenced by Byzantine culture. By the end of medieval theatre in the mid-1550s, there were great civic cycles, moralities, miracles, and a range of secular performances.

all, when churches and towns ceased to produce theatre, theatre became a commercial venture. Regular performances in capital cities replaced occasional performances in small cities and towns; permanent theatre structures replaced the streets or town commons; and professional actors replaced amateurs. Commercial theatre replaced communal theatre just as surely as towns and trading replaced manors and feudalism.

KEY TERMS

Check your understanding against this list. Brief definitions are included in the Glossary; persons are page-referenced in the Index.

CHAPTER

14

The Golden Ages of England and Spain

OBJECTIVES

When you have completed this chapter, you should be able to:

- Discuss major traits associated with the Renaissance
- List the principal kinds of drama, important playwrights, and plays from the age of Shakespeare and the Spanish Golden Age
- Distinguish between public and private theatres
- Describe the major staging conventions of Shakespeare's theatre and compare them (that is, note similarities and differences) with medieval conventions
- Compare the physical theatres of Shakespeare and the Spanish Golden Age
- Compare the role of women in the theatres of Shakespeare and Spain
- Explain the importance of masques in English theatre history

CONTEXT

Italy, perhaps because still weakly tied to Constantinople by tradition and trade or perhaps because once the heart of an empire, made the transition from a feudal society to a modern, commercial one earlier than the rest of western Europe. Indeed, by 1300 in Italy, new ideas, social organizations, attitudes, and discoveries had begun to peek through the medieval order. For the next two hundred years, these new ideas gradually took hold and spread throughout western Europe, heralding the arrival of the **Renaissance** ("rebirth"). (See Chapter 15.)

Once under way, the Renaissance unfolded throughout western Europe, but it did so at different rates and with different effects:

- Italy and southern Europe embraced Renaissance ideas earlier and developed somewhat differently from England, Spain, and northern Europe, at least for a while. But even within the Renaissance of northern Europe, stark differences were visible.
- Spain and England, both strong naval powers and vigorous traders, were early rivals. Spain, importing gold from its Central and South American colonies, pulled money to its profligate central government and clung to Roman Catholicism and absolute monarchy. England, on the other hand, developed a strong merchant class, broke with Rome, and moved toward constitutional monarchy.

By c. 1550 (when medieval religious drama ended), the Renaissance had already revolutionized many former attitudes and practices throughout western Europe, though it had done so on different timetables and with different effects. Regardless of date or location, however, several traits distinguish this new Renaissance culture from the medieval culture preceding it.

Humanism

People of the early Middle Ages had supposed that the temporal world would be destroyed, that the unrighteous would be purged, and that the righteous would be transported to a world of bliss. In the Renaissance, however, new secular and temporal interests joined earlier divine and eternal ones. A love of God and His ways, long the basis of human behavior, was joined by a newfound admiration for humankind, whose worth, intelligence, and beauty began to be celebrated. This new concern for people and their earthly lives was called **humanism**.

Secularism

At about the same time, the older theology, a complete system based on divine revelation, gave way to competing philosophical systems that stressed **secularism** (that is, they advocated ethical conduct as an end in itself rather than as a prerequisite to heaven, and they argued for logical systems of thought independent of divine revelation). In science, an earth-centered astronomy was challenged by a sun-centered universe in which human beings were relegated to life on a relatively minor planet, no longer at the center of creation.

Rare Books, University of South Carolina Libraries

FIGURE 14.1

London before the Great Fire of 1666

This engraving shows London sometime before the Great Fire of 1666. On the north side of the Thames, the original St. Paul's Cathedral dominates the city. On the south side are several tall buildings with flags, probably theatres or bear-baiting areas.

Reformation

Within the church, demands for reform led to breaks with Rome: Some Christians (such as Martin Luther) protested against the church at Rome and launched what came to be called the *Reformation.*

In sum, although God, His Church, and His theology remained a central fact of human life in the Renaissance, they were no longer absolute and unquestioned. Humanism and secularism were competing with them for acceptance. But the emergence of new ideas and attitudes was only part of the phenomenon. Vital, too, were factors that encouraged the widespread dissemination of the new spirit, factors such as the growth of trade and the arrival of the printing press.

The World Widens

By the Renaissance, exploration and discovery had increased commercial areas far beyond the Mediterranean and close-in Atlantic. Marco Polo had opened Asia, Columbus had opened the Americas, and a series of West African ports hopscotching to the Cape of Good Hope opened a feasible sea route to India. Improved navigation aids and some road improvements joined with new postal systems to improve both transportation and communication. (For example, a trip of seventy-five miles that took eight days in 1500 took only six by 1600.) New organizations arose for raising capital (e.g., joint stock companies) and insuring against catastrophic loss (e.g., associations among merchants). Wholesalers and middlemen transformed the nature of trade and took their share of the growing profits.

The Fall of Constantinople

Along with goods, trade led to the exchange of ideas. At the center of most of the various trade routes of the fourteenth century were the city-states of Italy, which soon became centers of a commerce in ideas, skills, and products. When Constantinople fell to the Turks in 1453, many scholars and artists came to Italy and with them came plays and treatises from ancient Greece and Rome, rescued from endangered libraries. Their study and interpretation began almost at once.

The Printing Press

The introduction of the Gutenberg printing press to Italy at about the same time allowed the rapid reproduction of documents arriving from the East as well as of the interpretations and imitations of these documents. Certainly, the printing press allowed a veritable explosion of accessible information, so much so that, by 1500, numerous academies in the city-states of Italy were devoted to the study and production of Roman plays. Shortly thereafter, Italians began writing their own plays in imitation of the Roman models.

The Arts

Patronage of the arts during the Renaissance was a major and acknowledged source of prestige, and, because the nobles' courts engaged in rivalries over which was to become the cultural center, painters, musicians, sculptors, architects, and writers flourished.

Such changes in viewpoint and technology predictably brought changes in theatre and drama. Theatres in both England and Spain, although influenced by Renaissance ideas, also built on secular staging conventions of the late Middle Ages. Both produced glorious dramas and robust public theatres soon after the end of medieval religious drama (c. 1550). By 1600, both were enjoying their Golden Ages of theatre and drama, with new freestanding theatres, professional players, paying audiences, and expansive plays of great complexity.

THE RENAISSANCE IN THE NORTH: THE AGE OF SHAKESPEARE

The reign of Elizabeth I (1558–1603) brought greatness to England. With her ascent to the throne, the nation achieved the political and religious stability that permitted its arts and literature to thrive. When, in an attempt to mute religious controversies, the government outlawed religious drama, it opened the way for the rapid development of a secular tradition of plays and playgoing. When the queen finally agreed to the execution of Mary Stuart, her chief rival for the throne and the center of Catholic assaults on the church and throne, Elizabeth's political situation was secured, and the domination of Anglican Protestants within the Church of England was affirmed. The English navy defeated the Spanish Armada in 1588 and established itself as ruler of the seas and leader among the trading nations. England, for the first time in generations, was at peace at home and abroad and was filled with a national confidence and a lust for life seldom paralleled in history.

Physical Theatre

In 1576, two commercial theatres opened in London, one an outdoor (or "public") theatre and the other an indoor (or "private") theatre. Therefore, when Shakespeare arrived in London about fifteen years later, these two sorts

FIGURE 14.2
Public Theatre
The Swan drawing is a rare piece of visual evidence for an Elizabethan public theatre: It shows a theatre open to the sky, with a roofed structure pierced by doors, and an audience on three sides of a raised stage that is thrust out from the structure. Scholars disagree on the value of the drawing as evidence for actual practices of the time, although its overall sense of such a theatre agrees with much of what we know from theatre contracts, stage directions, and the Spanish theatre.

of theatre were well established, and he wrote for and acted in both. Although their precise appearance cannot be known, their general features are well established.

Public Theatres Outdoor, **public theatres** (of which nine were built between 1576 and 1642) consisted of a round or polygonal, roofed, multileveled auditorium that surrounded an open **yard**, into which jutted a platform raised to a height of four to six feet. The entire yard (or **pit**) and part of the stage platform were unroofed. The audience, probably numbering as many as 2,500, surrounded the playing area on three sides, some standing in the pit and others seated in the **galleries** or the still more exclusive **lords' rooms**.

The actors worked on a raised stage and apparently awaited cues and changed costumes in a **tiring house**, located at the rear of the platform. Covering part of the stage was a roof (the **heavens**) supported by columns resting on the stage and apparently decorated on its underside with pictures of stars, planets, and signs of the zodiac. Gods and properties flew in from the heavens.

The stage floor was pierced with **traps**, through which characters could appear and disappear. Connecting the tiring house with the stage were at least two doors, which often represented widely divergent locations (as, for example, when one led to the fields of France and the other to the shores of England). Atop the tiring house, a flag flew on days of performance, and at a level just below, in an area called the **hut**, were probably housed the various pieces of equipment and machinery needed for special effects. A **musicians' gallery** was apparently located just below the hut, at the third level above the stage.

Other points are less certain. The plays clearly required two playing levels, an upper and a lower, and some sort of **discovery space**, a place where objects and characters could be hidden from view and discovered at the appropriate time. Because the available evidence will not permit the issues to be resolved, ideas about the appearance of Shakespeare's playhouse must remain tentative.

Private Theatres About the indoor **private theatres** even less is known. They were roofed, smaller, and therefore more expensive to attend than the public playhouses. Despite their name, they were open to anyone caring to pay.

Initially, the private theatres attracted the most fashionable audiences of London, who came to see erudite plays performed by troupes of boy actors. As the popularity of children's troupes waned, the adult troupes that performed in the public theatres in the summer took over the private houses for their winter performances. The fact is significant because it indicates that the arrangement of the stage spaces in the theatres was probably similar.

FIGURE 14.3

Private Elizabethan and Jacobean Theatre

The Blackfriars Playhouse at the American Shakespeare Center in Staunton, Virginia. This modern and speculative reconstruction of the Blackfriars indoor theatre is based on documents from the period, none of them visual. Note the two audience galleries that go around three sides of the theatre (the original structure had three galleries). The modern audience area is not darkened during these performances, and the audience sits on benches, as probably did the original audiences. Compare it to the Swan drawing (Figure 14.2) and the theatre shown in the Spotlight. Courtesy of the American Shakespeare Center. Photo by Tommy Thompson

Audience

Audiences for the public theatres were like medieval audiences, but more urbanized and probably more sophisticated. They did not include the poor or the very rich. Audiences were sometimes rowdy, easily distracted, and they were probably heavily male. A good portion of the audience was educated enough to get jokes and learned allusions; most of them were fascinated by language, and so sat rapt through long soliloquies and much lyric poetry.

Private theatres supposedly attracted a more discerning and probably a more affluent audience. They sat indoors, were warmer in winter, less bothered by rain and slush. Probably mostly male, they were self-aware as embodiments of the "new."

Production Practices

Both the physical arrangement of Elizabethan theatres and the medieval features of the plays argue against the use of elaborate scenery. In the theatre, there were few places to hide scenery and no way of moving it on and off stage readily, and the action moved from place to place quickly, with little or no break. Small properties were therefore important, and we find stage directions for the use of ladders, chairs and tables, tapestries, a freestanding arbor, and so on. The underlying conventions were clearly medieval, with a chair representing a throne room, for example, and an arbor for a garden. The onstage columns and the two doors also sometimes represented specific locations, thus resembling medieval mansions. On the other hand, such things as "a view of Rome" appeared on lists of properties, and so perhaps some locations were illustrated in paintings. Most of the stage platform worked like a medieval *platea,* serving alternately as a bedroom, a throne room, and a rampart in quick succession.

Costuming was probably more important than scenery to spectacle. Contemporary accounts mention rich fabrics in many colors. Again, the basic convention was medieval, undoubtedly emblematic, with real Elizabethan dress the basic look. Nonetheless, other periods, countries, and races were signified by individual costume pieces—a turban, a Roman breastplate—but historical accuracy was unknown.

Most actors wore contemporary dress, some of it the castoffs of patrons or wealthy friends. Actors mostly supplied their own costumes, and building up a stock would have been important to an actor; however, unusual characters—devils, angels, allegorical figures, Turks, savages—would have called for help from the theatre company. This was a society emerging from medieval ignorance of the great world, and the theatre was one place where sophisticated London saw its new knowledge in three living dimensions.

Masks were used rarely, and then only for specific reasons; they were no longer a major convention of theatre.

Actors and Acting

A royal official, the Master of the Revels, licensed acting companies. The license protected actors from harsh medieval laws against players ("rogues and vagabonds"). Actors in the London troupes were further protected by nominal servant status in noble households: Servants "belonged" to a household and found a medieval (feudal) shelter there. Despite this status, a few actors became wealthy. Shakespeare was able to retire as a gentleman.

The troupes themselves were organized as self-governing units—**sharing companies**—whose members shared expenses, profits, and responsibilities for production. A very few members owned a part of the theatre building itself; these were called **householders**. The most valuable members of the company held a whole share in the costumes, properties, and other company possessions; lesser members owned only half or quarter shares, with their influence and income reduced accordingly. In addition, each company hired some actors and stagehands (**hirelings**), who worked for a salary rather than for a share of the profits.

The precise style of acting is unclear, but vocal power and flexibility were prized. Plays of the period offered ample opportunity to display breath control and verbal dexterity in the monologues, soliloquies, complicated figures of speech, and symmetrical and extended phrases. On the other hand, oratorical and rhetorical techniques did not seem to overpower the actors' search for naturalness. Contemporary accounts, including lines from Shakespeare's *Hamlet,* speak of an acting style capable of moving actors and audiences alike. The goal was apparently a convincing representation of a character in action performed by an actor with a well-tuned vocal instrument.

Because all actors were male, the roles of women were taken by men or young boys, many of whom were apprenticed to leading actors in the troupe. Among the actors, most specialized in certain kinds of roles (e.g., clowns, women, or heroes), and some were widely admired in Shakespeare's day: Richard Tarleton as a clown, Richard Burbage as a tragedian.

By the time Shakespeare arrived in London about 1590, then, his was a proud and growing nation whose power wanted to be celebrated. In place in the capital was an English secular theatre with permanent buildings, professional actors, and a legitimacy based on its own identification with capital and court.

Courtesy of the University of Texas at Austin, Department of Theatre and Dance

FIGURE 14.4

Shakespeare's Reach

Macbeth is one of Shakespeare's most often staged tragedies. Actors, directors, and designers have been attracted to the scope and challenges of the play, which has also been adapted to opera, film, and television. Here, the witches with Macbeth in a production by the University of Texas at Austin.

Plays and Playwrights

Adding to the general well-being of the nation was the vigor of the court, the schools, and the universities, where scholars were remaking Italian humanism and classical documents with an eye to English needs and preferences. In particular, some university students (the University Wits) were applying classical scholarship to the English public stage and laying the foundations for the vigorous theatre to come. These University Wits brought the erudition of humanistic scholarship to the English stage.

Thomas Kyd and Christopher Marlowe, in particular, broke new ground in tragedy. Both adapted techniques from Seneca. Marlowe created a "mighty line" of sonorous blank verse, the tragedy *Doctor Faustus*, and the history play *Edward the Second*. Kyd is remembered for his revenge play *The Spanish Tragedy*.

SHAKESPEARE (1564–1616) Born in 1564 in provincial Stratford-upon-Avon, a day's journey from London, Shakespeare was a middle-class boy who grew up as the nation moved from medieval to Renaissance culture. Not university educated, Shakespeare nonetheless received the solid basics of village schools: Latin, the classics, the foundation of writing style. His early life appears to have included acquaintance with powerful local families; his father, although a tradesman, was a man of position in the town.

Shakespeare married a local woman but did not stay long in his hometown. By his midtwenties, he had gone to London to take up the perilous profession of acting, putting his father's trade behind him. He took with him, however, the rural England and the English characters of his youth, which would inform his plays and his poetry for his entire life.

Between 1590 and 1613, a period now acknowledged as the greatest age of English drama, Shakespeare wrote thirty-eight plays, which for convenience are customarily divided into three types:

Butler University Theatre

FIGURE 14.5
Two Noble Kinsmen
This play is generally accepted as a collaboration in 1613 between Shakespeare and John Fletcher. It was first presented at the private (indoor) Blackfriars Theatre.

- **History plays** (those treating English history). *Henry IV* (Parts 1 and 2), *Henry V, Henry VI* (Parts 1, 2, and 3), *Henry VIII, Richard II,* and *Richard III*
- **Tragedies.** *Romeo and Juliet, Julius Caesar, Hamlet, King Lear, Othello, Macbeth,* and *Antony and Cleopatra*
- **Comedies.** Ranging from popular romantic works, like *Love's Labor's Lost, As You Like It, Twelfth Night, Much Ado about Nothing,* and *A Midsummer Night's Dream,* to the darker tragicomedies, like *All's Well That Ends Well* and *Measure for Measure*

Shakespeare's plays and those of his contemporaries in England (and Spain) shared more ideas and techniques of playwriting with the Middle Ages than with Greece and Rome. Six important traits of golden age plays (including those of Shakespeare) are:

- **An Early Point of Attack** Plays begin near the beginning of the story, with the result that the audience sees the story develop onstage rather than learning about it secondhand through messengers or reporters.
- **Several Lines of Action ("Subplots")** Early in the plays, the various lines appear to be separate and independent, but as the play moves toward its resolution, the several lines gradually merge so that, by the play's end, the unity of the various lines is evident.
- **A Large Number and Variety of Incidents** The mixing of tears and laughter is not uncommon, nor is the close juxtaposition of tender scenes of love with brawling scenes of confrontation.
- **Free Use of Time and Place** Action unfolds across several months or years and in several locales.
- **A Large Number and Variety of Characters** Casts of thirty are common, and among the characters can be found kings and gravediggers, pedants and clowns, old people and youths, city dwellers and rustics, rich people and poor ones.
- **A Varied Language** Within the same play are found lyric passages, elegant figures of speech, ribald slang, witty aphorisms, and pedestrian prose, all carefully chosen to enhance the play's dramatic action.

The art of Shakespeare and his contemporaries was an expansive one that filled a large dramatic canvas with portraits of a wide cross section of humanity engaged in acts ranging from the heroic to the mundane. The texture of the plays is rich, detailed, and allusive. With Shakespeare's death in 1616 came a decline in the quality, if not the quantity, of drama. Although many playwrights were esteemed in their own day, none has achieved the modern admiration accorded Shakespeare. The golden age of English theatre was already in decline after 1616.

Pistolesi, Andrea\Andrea Pistolesi

FIGURE 14.6
The New Globe Theatre in London
Completed in the late 1990s, the structure seeks to replicate the Globe, the outdoor theatre where many of Shakespeare's plays were first staged. The New Globe is located on the south bank of the Thames close to the site of the original. The modern theatre holds 1,880, five hundred of whom stand in the pit.

Court Masques and New Conventions: Inigo Jones

Not all theatre was done in public and private playhouses. By invitation only, some individuals formed a courtly audience for plays and spectacles staged in royal and noble houses. Although both Henry VIII (Elizabeth's father) and Elizabeth had supported theatrical entertainments, it was the Stuart kings who followed them, James I and Charles I, who perfected splendid court **masques**.

Stuart masques were allegorical stories designed to compliment a particular individual or occasion. Their texts were little more than pretexts for elaborate scenic displays and lavish costumes. Although the major roles and all of the comic or villainous characters were played by professionals, the courtiers themselves performed the heart of the masques, three spectacular dances. Great sums of money ensured the splendor of the entertainments; one such masque cost a staggering 21,000 pounds at a time when the average *annual* wage for a skilled worker was about 25 pounds.

Although many leading dramatists wrote masques, Ben Jonson was the most significant. Annoyed that the text assumed such a clearly secondary position to the scenery, Jonson stopped writing masques in 1631.

The star of the masques was not the playwright but the scenic designer, Inigo Jones. An Englishman by birth, Jones studied in Italy, where he learned the newest techniques of stage painting, rigging, and design. He introduced many of these into the English court when, in 1605, he staged his first masque for James I. *By the end of his career, Jones had introduced into the English courts* (but *not* into the theatres) *all the major elements of Italianate staging then developed* (see p. 237).

Stuart masques, then, have a significance that exceeds the number of persons who saw them:

- First, they were using Italianate systems of staging during the first half of the seventeenth century, at a time when the English public and private theatres still relied on scenic practices that were essentially medieval.
- Second, the close association of the masques with the monarchy, added to their expense, were major factors in the closing of theatres when a shift in power occurred.

THE CLOSING OF ENGLISH THEATRES

In 1642, a civil war broke out. It pitted those in favor of monarchy, courtiers, and an Anglican Church that echoed Roman Catholicism against (to oversimplify the many contentious issues to the point of caricature) those who favored Parliament, merchants, and a much simplified Anglicanism. The parliamentarians under Oliver Cromwell won, deposed the king, seized power, and closed the theatres (in part because they had been so closely associated with the monarchy). Music, however, was not banned, and so a writer of masques named William Davenant produced operas, staging them using the Italianate system. Thus were Italianate conventions of staging introduced to the English public, having by then been used at court for almost forty years.

With the closing of the theatres in 1642, an English secular theatre based loosely on medieval conventions closed as well. When English theatres reopened in 1660, England adopted the Italianate conventions already in use on the Continent.

Old Dominion University: Scene Design and photo by Anita Tripathi Easterling

FIGURE 14.7

Spanish Golden Age Drama in Modern Production

A modern interpretation of Calderon de la Barca's *La Vida es Sueno (Life Is a Dream)*, probably written before 1636.

THE SPANISH GOLDEN AGE

During the Middle Ages, Spain's theatre had paralleled England's in important ways. Its medieval dramas had included Latin music drama, religious plays, comedies and farces, school and university plays, and even court interludes. Their staging conventions were similar; both used movable more often than fixed staging. During the transitional period

Spotlight

A conjectural drawing of the Corral del Principe, thought to be typical of Spanish Theatres of the Golden Age. The reconstruction by John J. Allen, reprinted with permission of the University Press of Florida.

Spanish Theatre: The Corral del Principe

In the early 1580s, two new theatres were built in Madrid to replace those that had existed since the 1560s. One, the Corral del Principe, became the city's dominant theatre for more than a century. Both were owned by a religious confraternity to raise money for its hospitals; the theatres also got some needed legitimacy.

Corral—the word for the open space among several houses—became the synonym for a permanent theatre. It was the Spanish solution to the problem of creating an enclosed space where audiences could be controlled and made to pay a fee to enter. Inside the rectangle enclosed by the houses, builders put up at one end a stage only twenty-eight feet wide (the size of a modern livingroom) and twenty-five feet deep. It was raised above the *patio* (pit), the cheapest area (standing room behind, benches in front), which was only the width of the stage and about fifty feet long. Along its sides ran a raised level of boxes or loges, preferred and more expensive seating. Opposite the stage at the end of the patio were more boxes and, above them, a separate seating area for women with its own entrance from the street. From the back of the women's gallery to the back wall of the stage and from side to side, this was an intimate theater—the size of the in-bounds area of a modern basketball court.

Like other corrales, the Principe also used windows in the houses on each side, behind which were high-end boxes—rooms, really—owned and controlled by the house-owner. Their privacy apparently attracted upper-class women, and the women's gallery above the patio may have become a middle- and lower-class area like the patio itself and as rambunctious.

The stage was roofed. Part of the patio could be covered with an awning, although this seems to have been for sun, not rain.

At the back of the stage was a two-level area that could be curtained; there seem also to have been doors there and on the sides. The stage floor was trapped, and overhead was fairly sophisticated flying machinery. Live music was common, but it is unlikely that either musicians or audience members sat on the small stage.

Scenery in the Corral del Principe was selective but sometimes complex: fountains, trees, a ship's mast and rigging (presumably for the actors to climb), the castles (superstructures) of a Moorish and a Christian ship. Costumes by the first third of the seventeenth century were often expensive and showy, although with only emblematic historical accuracy (turbans for Moors, togas for Romans) and mostly contemporary clothes.

The Corral del Principe may be taken as typical of Spanish theatres of the Golden Age. It was small, rather medieval in its arrangements, and often rowdy, but some of the greatest of the world's plays were first performed there.

from the Middle Ages to the Golden Age, small troupes of professional players toured until permanent theatres were built in Madrid in the early 1580s.

The public theatres of Spain, like the English theatres, remained essentially medieval. The earliest permanent public theatres, the Corral del Cruz and the Corral del Principe, were both outdoor theatres with thrust stages. Audiences stood in a central yard or sat in galleries and boxes on three sides of the stage. The stages, whose backgrounds were pierced with entrances, were partially roofed (held up by two columns), were served by traps and flying machines, and featured both a discovery space and a secondary acting area above the stage. Conventions of scenery, costume, and playwriting also resembled those of England. As in England, the Spanish court theatres used the newer, Italian conventions. (See p. 237.)

The location of Spanish theatres, each of which was typically set up in the yard at the center of a block of houses, was a telling difference between English and Spanish theatres. An awning stretched over a part of the yard as protection against the elements. Audiences not only stood or sat in covered benches along the side of this yard or in galleries or boxes opposite the stage, but they also could rent spaces in the windows of adjoining houses.

Women as Audience and as Actors

The Spanish theatre's acceptance of women was significantly different from the English, at the same time more permissive and more restrictive. It allowed women to act after the mid-1580s but put women audience members in a separate gallery with its own entrance—guarded—from the street. Many women went there masked, perhaps to avoid being recognized.

Legal permission for women to act was also shaky. Attempts were made to rescind the permission to act as early as 1587; in 1589, churchmen made a determined push to remove them and replace them with boys—so long as the boys wore no makeup. The governing council thought that the risk of boys in makeup was greater than the risk of women and so said the women could stay. Spanish actresses, however, like actresses in many countries, were long considered immoral and a threat to men.

Summing Up

The Golden Age theatres of England and Spain mixed medieval conventions with new practices. Both cultures maintained essentially medieval conventions of drama and theatre (except at their courts, where Italian conventions prevailed), but with one important difference: Both could now boast a sophisticated secular drama performed by professional actors in theatres built specifically to house them. In a major departure from medieval theatrical practice, theatre had become professional rather than communal.

Plays and Playwrights

Spain's Golden Age, however, was noted not for its theatrical practices but for its plays. During this one hundred years, Spanish playwrights wrote thousands of plays. Like medieval and contemporaneous

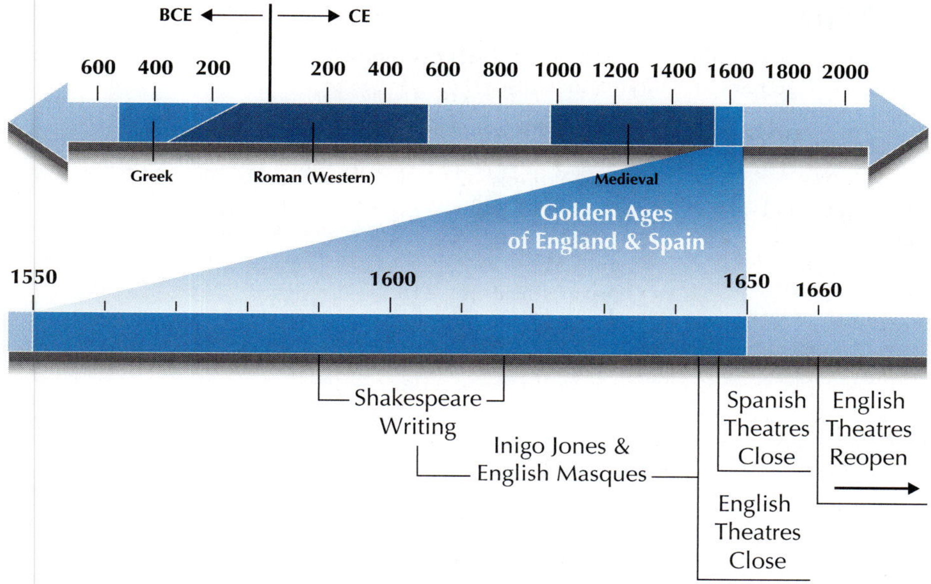

FIGURE 14.8

Timeline

The Golden Ages of England and Spain overlapped the final years of medieval theatre, beginning roughly in 1550 (when religious drama ended) and ending about 1650, when both theatres were closed for political reasons. When English theatres reopened in 1660, they were physically different and almost immediately used female actors.

English plays, they featured a welter of characters and events, spanned many times and places, and mixed laughter and tears. Secular tragicomedies, plays on religious subjects, cloak-and-sword plays, and farces were all popular.

The earliest important playwright, Lope de Rueda, specialized in farces and religious plays. Another, Lope de Vega, may have originated the cape-and-sword plays, swashbucklers that subsequently influenced both English and French dramatists. The author of more than five hundred works, Lope de Vega is now best known for his play *Fuenteovejuna.* The most respected Spanish playwright of the Golden Age, however, was Pedro Calderon de la Barca, whose *Life Is a Dream* (see Figure 14.7) epitomized the poetry and intellect of his best works. Calderon stopped writing for the stage about 1640; the theatres were closed shortly thereafter for royal mourning (1644–1649). When they reopened, the Golden Age had passed, although the public theatres remained in use into the eighteenth century.

KEY TERMS

Check your understanding against this list. Brief definitions are included in the Glossary; persons are page-referenced in the Index.

court theatres 226
discovery space 218
galleries 218
Golden Age (England, Spain) 217
heavens 218
hirelings 220
householders 220
humanism 215
hut 218
lords' rooms 218
masques 223
musicians' gallery 218
pit 218
private theatres 218
public theatres 218
Renaissance 215
secularism 215
sharing companies 220
tiring house 218
traps 218
yard 218

PART

IIIC ILLUSIONISM (c. 1550–c. 1960)

The third phase of theatre's history dates from about 1550 through about 1960. Theatres during these four hundred years shared several important theatrical conventions and so can be grouped for study. Their major shared traits are:

- Theatre buildings with a proscenium arch, which frames the action on stage
- Scenery and costumes that seek to create the illusion of fidelity to life outside the theatre
- A mostly commercial environment
- A mix of men and women
- A stratification of theatre

These new conventions took hold first in Italy and then spread through western Europe and its colonies, where they dominated theatre practice through much of the twentieth century (see Figure IIIC.1).

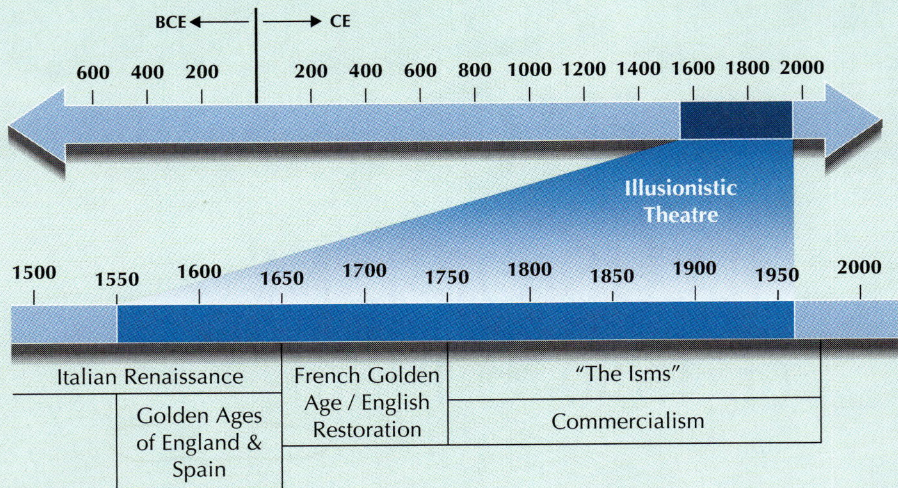

FIGURE IIIC.1

A new set of dramatic and theatrical conventions arose during Italy's Renaissance and soon spread throughout most of western Europe.

CHAPTER

15

The Italian Renaissance

OBJECTIVES

When you have completed this chapter, you should be able to:

- Define and discuss Neoclassicism, Italianate staging, and commedia dell'arte
- Explain how Neoclassicism departed so radically from medieval theatre
- Trace Italianate staging from Vitruvius through Serlio to Torelli
- Discuss the importance of Roman ideas and their interpretation to Renaissance theatres

CONTEXT

The Renaissance in Italy, unlike the same years in England and Spain, revolutionized theatre and drama. In their efforts to recapture the practices of Greece and Rome, Italian artists set theatres in Europe on a new path—a path toward illusionism. Theatre was thereafter to seek an illusion of real life.

Three contributions of the Italians were to have far-reaching effects:

1. The neoclassical ideal in playwriting and criticism
2. The Italianate system of staging and architecture
3. A popular theatre known as commedia dell'arte

MAINSTREAM THEATRE

Theory: Neoclassicism

Neoclassicism literally means "new classicism," but in fact it was based far more heavily on Rome than on Greece. Neoclassicism, as first developed by the Italians and later adopted throughout most of western Europe, rested on five major points:

- Verisimilitude and decorum
- Purity of genres
- The three unities
- The five-act form
- A twofold purpose—to teach and to please

VERISIMILITUDE Central to neoclassical doctrine was a complex concept called verisimilitude—literally, "truth seeming." But the meaning of *verisimilitude* is more involved than its facile definition might suggest, for artists have always aimed to tell the "truth." Thus, the critical problem for a student of Neoclassicism is to understand what "truth" meant to the neoclassicist.

Truth for the neoclassicist resided in the essential, the general, the typical, and the class rather than in the particular, the individual, and the unique. To get at truth, a neoclassical artist had to cut away all that was temporary or accidental in favor of those qualities that were fundamental and unchanging. To be "true" meant to be usually true, generally accurate, typically the case. Such a view of truth placed a premium on classification and categorization, and in verisimilitude truth had a meaning very different from that ascribed to it by our own age's view of the importance of individuality and uniqueness.

Neoclassical truth implied other matters as well. Verisimilitude in drama required the elimination of events that could not reasonably be expected to happen in real life. Although an exception was made when ancient stories or myths incorporating supernatural events were dramatized, even then the dramatist was expected to minimize the importance of such events, perhaps by putting them offstage. Because in real life people generally talk to one another rather than to themselves, monologues and soliloquies were customarily abandoned in favor of dialogue between major characters and their confidants (see p. 37).

Characters in neoclassical drama were expected to embody the traits normally held by members of their group in manners and conduct; that is, they were to behave as was appropriate for their sex, age, social class, and so on. Such characters were said to display **decorum**. Indecorous characters drove the plots of neoclassical plays, for they were the ones who suffered either tragic consequences or comic ridicule.

FIGURE 15.1
Torquato Tasso's *Aminta*
This adaptation of Tasso's 1573 pastoral drama at Butler University Theatre emphasizes the lighthearted nature of the original. Italian plays of the early Renaissance are not often revived.

Finally, because it was believed that God ruled the world in accord with a divine plan and that He was a good God, verisimilitude required that dramatic actions be organized according to moral principles—so that good was rewarded and evil punished. Although in daily life good occasionally went unrewarded and evil unpunished, such observable events were believed to be aberrational and therefore unsuitable subjects for drama.

Purity of Genres Verisimilitude also inspired **purity of genres**, meaning that the two major forms, tragedy and comedy, must not be mixed. The injunction against mixing did not mean merely that funny scenes were improper for tragedy or that unhappy endings were inappropriate for comedy. Both tragedy and comedy were far more rigidly defined than today, and the rule against mixing the forms meant that no element belonging to the one should appear in the other. For example, **tragedy** was supposed to depict people of high station involved in affairs of state; its language was to be elevated and poetic; its endings were to be unhappy. **Comedy**, on the other hand, was supposed to display persons of the lower and middle classes embroiled in domestic difficulties and intrigues. Its language was always to be less elevated, often prosaic, and its endings were to be happy. Purity of genres meant, then, that a prose tragedy or a domestic tragedy could not exist—both were a contradiction in terms. It also meant that kings and queens could not appear in comedies, nor were affairs of state suitable subjects for comedy.

The Three Unities Verisimilitude and interpretations of classical examples created the neoclassical notion of the **three unities**—time, place, and action. Although Aristotle had argued cogently for plays with a unified action, neoclassical theorists were more concerned that their plays unfold within a

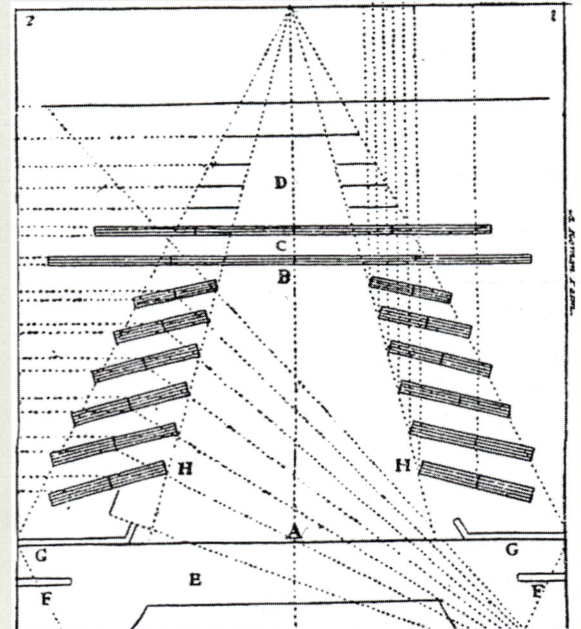

FIGURE 15.2

One-Point Perspective Stage Layout

Behind the Renaissance forestage, a single vanishing point was the apparent meeting place of lines that created an illusion of depth greater than the actual theatre could offer.

reasonable time and a limited place so that verisimilitude would not be strained. No audience would believe, the neoclassical argument went, that months had passed or oceans had been crossed while the audience sat in the same place for a few hours. Theorists varied in the strictness of their requirements for unity (some argued for a single room, others for a single town; some required that the playing time of the drama equal the actual time elapsed, others that no more than twenty-four hours elapse). Most Italian theorists accepted some version of the three unities after about 1570.

The Five-Act Form By then, as well, neoclassicists had adopted the five-act play as standard for drama, a norm probably derived from the theories of Horace and the practices of Seneca (five sections separated by choruses), although neither had used the "act" as a dramatic unit.

A Twofold Purpose—to Teach and to Please The neoclassicists found a justification for drama and theatre in the ability of these to teach morality while entertaining an audience. To teach and to please were defined as the dual purposes of drama, and playwrights took care that their plays did both. The idea of a drama existing only for its own sake or as an expression of an individual artist was not accepted.

By 1600, neoclassical ideals were being accepted in other parts of Europe. They remained dominant for the next two hundred years among educated and courtly audiences. Neoclassicism's propriety and concentration may account for its lack of appeal to many people, who sought more spectacle than the three unities permitted. Thus, despite the acceptance of Neoclassicism as an ideal, its tenets were undercut in a variety of ways—by spectacle, for example.

Physical Theatre: Illusionism

The Italianate theatre and its system of staging, like Neoclassicism itself, developed as a mixture of ideas and techniques from ancient Greece, Rome, and contemporary Italy. Most important from the ancients was the work of Vitruvius (see p. 192).

Vitruvius in the Renaissance Early in Italy's Renaissance, Vitruvius's Roman work on architecture, which had existed only in manuscripts, was printed. By 1500 it was the acknowledged authority in the field, and interpretations and commentaries in Italian followed. Although he had written about architecture and scenery, Vitruvius had provided no illustrations. As a result, the Italians translated him and provided illustrations in terms of their practices, most notably a fascination with *linear perspective*—a means of representing spatial depth (three dimensions) on a two-dimensional surface. On the stage, perspective became a means of representing greater depth than in fact existed.

Perspective Although known to the Romans, perspective, when rediscovered by Italian painters, caused an artistic revolution. Artists worked to master the "new" technique, and spectators hailed its ability to trick the senses. The "vanishing point," to which objects receded away from the viewer, became, in stage design, the key to false, or forced, perspective, through which a stage depth of thirty feet could be made to seem three hundred. On the stage, achieving this sense of depth often meant actually constructing three-dimensional objects (usually buildings) in false perspective. An actor—whose real size could not be changed—would dwarf the upstage buildings if he appeared up there, and so acting took place in front of the scenery.

In 1545 an Italian, Sebastiano Serlio, published *Dell'Architectura,* an interpretation of Vitruvius that dominated theatre architecture and design for the next century. Vitruvius, of course, had described the circular, outdoor Roman theatre. But wealthy Italians wanted plays done indoors in wealthy homes. Therefore, when the first indoor theatres were designed, the task was to adapt Vitruvius to rectangular spaces and to accommodate them to linear perspective.

An early solution was the Teatro Olimpico, which had five onstage doorways (corresponding to Vitruvius's five stage openings), but with a vista in perspective constructed behind each doorway (and each with its own vanishing point).

While the uniqueness of the Teatro Olimpico fascinates scholars, the façade stage with perspective alleys became an anomaly. Instead, the plan of another

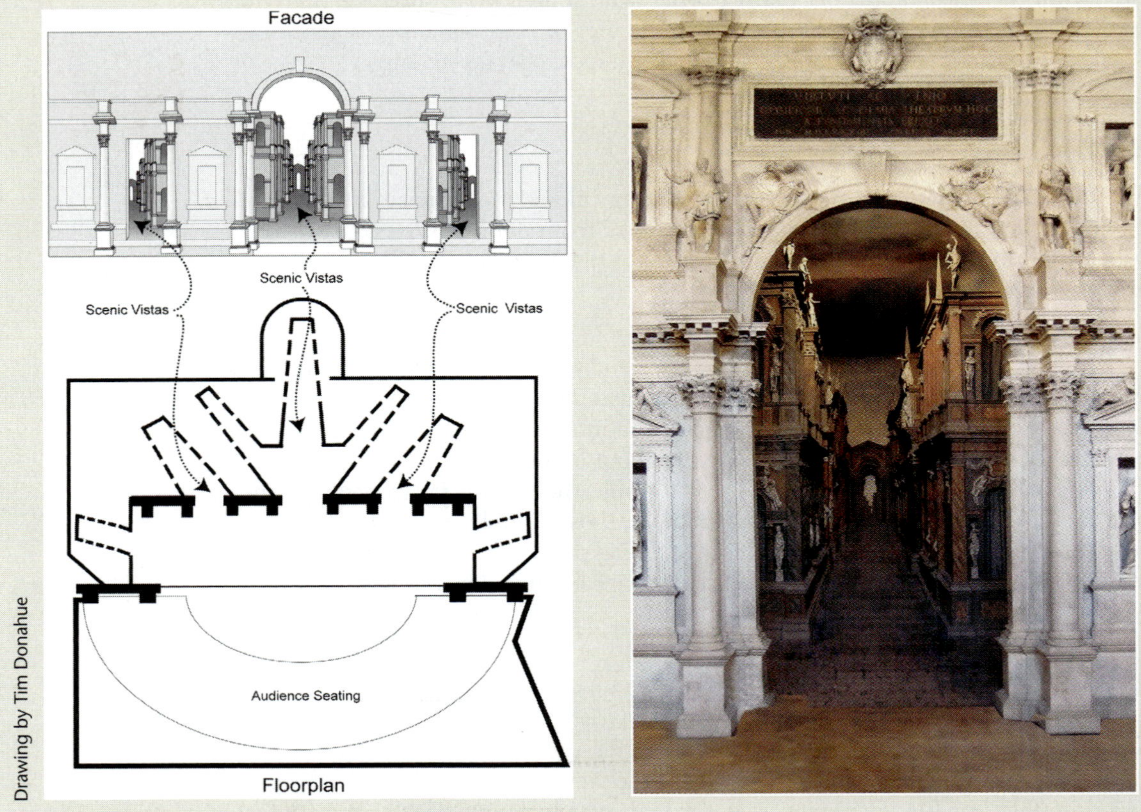

FIGURE 15.3

Teatro Olimpico

The Teatro Olimpico was an early compromise between a Roman façade stage and the Renaissance passion for perspective. Each of five doors framed a three-dimensional vista in false perspective, giving each member of the audience a view down at least one. Actors worked on the stage; they probably used the doorways but did not walk into the false perspective structures: They would have destroyed the illusion, because as the scenery seemed to shrink, the actor would not have done so. Compare the diagram with the picture of the actual space (right). Note the slightly widened semi-circle of the orchestra.

wooden theatre, the Teatro Farnese built in 1618–1619 in Parma, became the model for theatre architects for hundreds of years.

Production Practices: Illusionism

Vitruvius's scanty descriptions of tragic, comic, and satyric scenes became, in Serlio's books, detailed illustrations in false perspective. In the remainder of *Dell' Architectura,* Serlio provided tips on the use of colored lights, fire effects, fanciful costumes, and pasteboard figures in a perspective setting. Serlio's scenography was thus the basis for what we now call **Italianate staging**.

Rare Books and Special Collections, Bowling Green State University

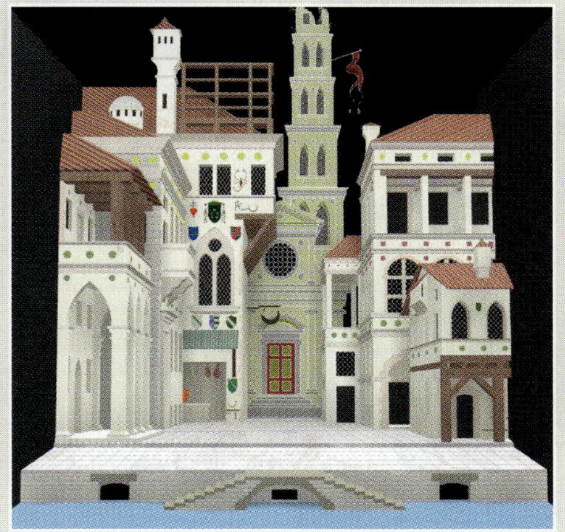

Centre for Advanced Studies in Architecture, University of Bath, UK

FIGURE 15.4

Serlio

Combining Vitruvius's writings on the Roman theatre with the Renaissance interest in perspective, Serlio created his own ideal scenery for tragedy (left), comedy (right), and pastoral (satyric) plays. The Centre for Advanced Studies in Architecture, University of Bath, United Kingdom, created the color rendering of Serlio's comedy scene using computer-assisted design.

Italianate Staging With certain modifications related to place and date, Italianate settings throughout Europe shared the following features during the sixteenth, seventeenth, and early eighteenth centuries:

- Scenery painted in **single-point perspective** (all objects recede to the same vanishing point), as calculated from one seat toward the back of the orchestra (usually the seat of the most important noble or patron).
- Scenery consisting of **wings**, which were paired flats (wooden frames covered with fabric and painted), each pair closer together as they were farther from the audience, so that the lines of the inner edges of the flats receded toward the vanishing point. The setting culminated upstage in a **backdrop** (painted two-dimensional hanging) or a **shutter**, a pair of wings pushed together. Shutters could be opened to reveal even deeper perspective space or pierced to make a *relieve* through which greater depth was glimpsed.
- Scenery placed behind both a proscenium arch and the actors, forming a background rather than an environment to surround them.
- A **raked stage**, slanted upward from front to back to increase the sense of depth. Sometimes only the stage behind the proscenium arch was raked, sometimes the entire stage, causing the actors to climb or descend (hence our terms *upstage* and *downstage*).
- Machinery and rigging hidden overhead by **borders**, framed or unframed fabric painted like sky, clouds, leaves, and so on.

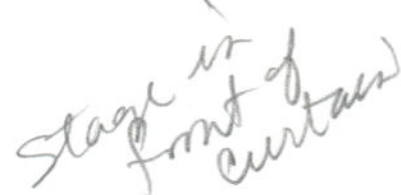

Spotlight

Teatro Farnese

The Teatro Farnese offered a different compromise between a Roman theatre and emerging Italianate architectural conventions. A Roman-style semicircular seating area was shoehorned inside a rectangular building, and the elaborate façade of Roman theatres appeared to the sides of a new proscenium arch.

Teatro Farnese, Parma, Italy

The Farnese theatre shares some of the architectural attributes of the Teatro Olimpico. Both are wooden structures (set inside of a stone building) in which theatres inspired by Roman models were fitted into a large, rectangular room. Much of the architectural detail in both theatres reflects the ornate façades of many Roman theatres.

But there the likenesses diverge radically. The Olimpico, built between 1580 and 1584, housed a façade stage with perspective alleys, while the Farnese, built about thirty-five years later, made a bold leap in theatre architecture by installing a permanent proscenium stage, complete with a mechanism under the stage to change scenery.

The Farnese is the first permanent indoor proscenium-arch theatre. Designed by Giovanni Battista Aleotti and built between 1618 and 1619, the theatre was never much used. It was largely destroyed by an Allied bombing raid during the Second World War. Reconstruction based on drawings and engravings began in 1952 and was completed about a decade later.

Shown below is a model of the horseshoe-shaped seating used in the reconstruction of the theatre; it can seat about three thousand. The flat floor in front of the seats was used for balls or was sometimes flooded for mock naval battles. The proscenium view shows the intricate façade that echoes its Roman antecedent.

Movable Scenery: Torelli Having developed this system, Italian artists set about almost at once to give it movement, to shift scenery, and to allow rapid changes of place. The most effective system was shown in 1645 when Giacomo Torelli astonished audiences with fluid, fast, apparently magical changes. The secret was his **chariot-and-pole system**. Small wheeled wagons ran on tracks under the stage, each with a pole that extended through a slit in the stage high enough to support a flat. The idea was elegant and simple: As the chariots moved, so the flats moved; pulling a chariot toward the center brought a flat into view; pulling the chariot away from the center caused a flat to disappear. With the chariots harnessed by ropes and pulleys to the same winch, stage mechanics could turn one wheel to change an entire setting. Torelli, no stranger to self-promotion, earned the title The Great Wizard by coordinating these changes with special effects (flying, lightning, explosions).

Rare Books, University of South Carolina Libraries

FIGURE 15.5

Special Effects Machines

Renaissance stage designers devised more and more elaborate systems, using ropes and winches, to create visual effects. These inventions, which have their origins in medieval stage machines, were used for centuries. Here, in a nineteenth-century illustration, a ship is made to sway to simulate the effect of waves.

Contradiction in Mainstream Theatre

A contradiction clearly existed between the ideals of theory—the unities of time, place, and action and an avoidance of the supernatural—and the ideals of scenic design, whose artists increasingly emphasized rapid change of place and spectacle. This tension was resolved by keeping an austere style for neoclassical plays while expending creativity and money on operas, ballets, and lavish *intermezzi* (entertainments given between the acts of a neoclassical play)—a way of having cake and eating it at the same time.

By the mid–seventeenth century, Italian opera had become the most popular (and spectacular) form of entertainment in Italy. As it was exported to the rest of Europe, so were its scenic techniques. (In London, remember, Davenant had staged operas after the theatres were closed in 1642; even in English, the word *opera* probably signified as much about scenery as it did about music.)

AN ALTERNATIVE THEATRE: COMMEDIA DELL'ARTE

Neoclassical dramas and elaborately staged operas were primarily the entertainment of the noble, the wealthy, and the educated. Among other classes, another, very different kind of dramatic entertainment flourished in Italy: the **commedia dell'arte** ("professional playing"). Although neither the origins nor the sources of commedia are well understood, its major characteristics were well established by 1550, and Italian troupes were touring western Europe by 1600.

FIGURE 15.6
Commedia dell'Arte
Commedia troupes had both males and females, as well as masked and unmasked stock characters. Starting with a basic scenario or storyline, the performers would improvise much of the entertainment. Shown here, three later French interpretations of commedia dell'arte characters.

Commedia players—both male and female—worked from a basic story outline (**scenario**), within which they improvised much of their dialogue and action. Each actor in the troupe played the same stock character in almost every scenario and therefore wore the same costume and mask, reused the same bits of comic business (***lazzi***), and even repeated some of the same dialogue from scenario to scenario. Most troupes had ten or twelve members; each troupe had one or two sets of young lovers (*innamorati*) and a number of comic "masks" (characters)—Capitano (the captain), Pantalone (the merchant), Dottore (the doctor), and several *zanni* (servants) such as Arlecchino (Harlequin), Brighella, Scaramuccio, and Pulcinello. Male actors outnumbered female. Both mask and costume became traditional for each character (except the lovers, who wore no masks).

Organized as sharing companies, such troupes toured constantly as they tried to scratch out a living without the protection or the financial support of

T. Charles Erickson

FIGURE 15.7

Modern Commedia dell'Arte

This world-premiere production of *The Miracle at Naples* by David Grimm was mounted in 2009 by The Huntington Theatre Company in Boston. It uses the rough-and-tumble conventions of commedia to tell its story of love lost and then found again.

noble houses. Although the influence of commedia extended throughout Europe, its ephemeral nature militated against its leaving a lasting record (especially scripts), although this popular Italian comedy has been revived and imitated in many more recent cultures.

ITALY: ECLIPSE

Despite Italy's unquestioned leadership in dramatic theory and scenic display and in spite of its unique popular comedy, by 1750, except for opera, Italy was no longer a world leader in theatre. Both England and France had outstripped their teacher and attained an international reputation by the end of the seventeenth century, and both achieved a lasting acclaim never given the Italians from whom they drew.

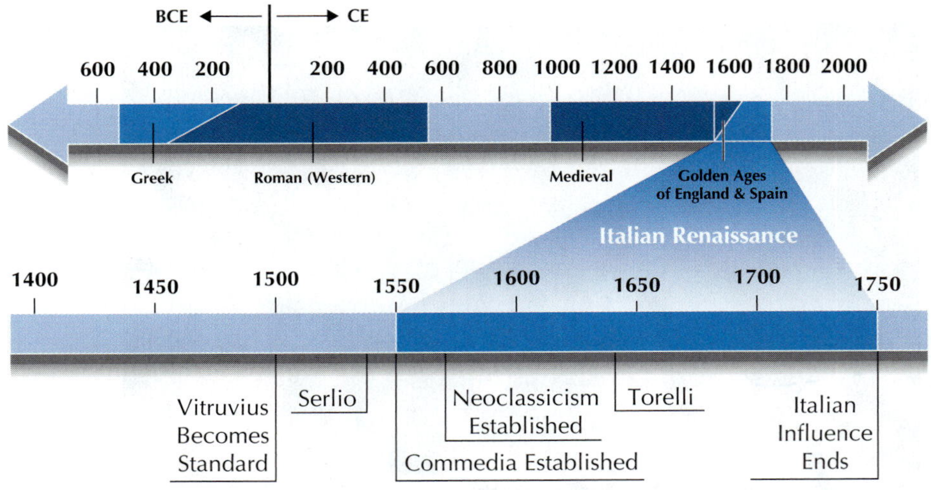

FIGURE 15.8

Timeline

The Italian Renaissance began about a hundred years before the Golden Ages of Spain and England. By c. 1550 (when religious drama was ending in England), Neoclassicism, Italianate staging, and commedia dell'arte were known in Italy. Italianate staging long continued to be important.

KEY TERMS

Check your understanding against this list. Brief definitions are included in the Glossary; persons are page-referenced in the Index.

backdrop 237
borders 237
chariot-and-pole system 238
comedy 233
commedia dell'arte 239
confidants 232
decorum 233
illusionism 232
Italianate staging 236
lazzi 240
Neoclassicism 232
perspective 235
purity of genres 233
raked stage 237
scenario 240
shutter 237
single-point perspective 237
three unities 233
tragedy 233
verisimilitude 232
wings 237

CHAPTER

16

The Triumph and Decline of Neoclassicism

OBJECTIVES

When you have completed this chapter, you should be able to:

- Explain the significance of the production of *Le Cid*
- Discuss the different performances likely to have been seen in the public and the court theatres of France
- Sketch events leading to the formation of the Comédie Française
- Explain how sentimentalism affected French drama and theatre
- Discuss the relationship between French theatre and English Restoration theatre
- Describe the major conventions of English Restoration theatre
- Name major kinds of drama existing during the English Restoration
- Suggest how changes in English law facilitated the beginnings of English-speaking theatre in the American colonies

FRENCH THEATRE

Its Beginnings

The ideas and practices of the Italian Renaissance reached France early, but the politically unstable France had little energy for developing a strong secular theatre. The early steps of French theatre were therefore tentative. Through the early 1600s, its practices remained essentially medieval. Farces performed by traveling actors were the mainstay of a scattered French theatre, and its audiences were famous for their unruliness. At about the time of Shakespeare, the first notable (and extremely prolific) French playwright appeared, Aléxandre Hardy, whose plays resembled those of England's and Spain's Golden Ages (e.g., many characters and sprawling actions). Like those of his contemporaries, Hardy's plays used simultaneous settings and emblematic costumes. Although his audiences were more genteel than those for the earlier farces and included women as well as some people from the court, his theatre was still a pretty rough place.

FIGURE 16.1

French Theatre in the Early 1600s

French theatre remained mostly emblematic and simultaneous, with scenery still scattered rather than gathered in one place.

With increasing political stability, Paris became France's theatrical center. The first professional acting troupe established itself there permanently in 1625. Its theatre was the Hotel de Bourgogne, a space built seventy-five years earlier for the production of religious plays (just as they were being banned). When rival professionals began to settle in Paris, however, they chose indoor tennis courts for their theatres. A theatre converted from a tennis court had a long, narrow auditorium with a small stage at one end, probably with an upper level (as in both London and Madrid) and some sort of "inner stage" below. The resulting theatres were small and intimate, holding six or seven hundred people. Staging conventions remained basically medieval.

Thus, at a time when the English and Spanish theatres were well into their Golden Ages and Italian theatre was revolutionizing theory and scenery, the French theatre was only just establishing itself.

By the 1630s, however, French theatre and its audience were sufficiently important to make them a focus of government interest. Because the French court of the time was closely linked by marriage and

FIGURE 16.2

Italian Influence on French Theatre

By the 1630s, Italian conventions were encroaching on French practice (note the backdrop in single-point perspective and the placement of scenic pieces), but some medieval influence was still visible, as shown in the simultaneous representation of different places stage right and stage left. (from the *Mémoire de Mahelot*, a compilation of sketches by the designer Laurent Mahelot)

policy to Italy, Italian practices became the model for France, in theatre as elsewhere. In theatre, Italian practice meant promoting Neoclassicism and Italianate staging.

Neoclassicism: Corneille and *Le Cid* A number of well-educated men began to write for the theatre. Chief among them was Pierre Corneille, whose play *Le Cid* (1636) marked a turning point. Based on a Spanish play of the Golden Age, *Le Cid* was reshaped by Corneille to bring it closer to neoclassical ideas but not into strict conformity with them: The original six acts were reduced to five; its several years were compressed into a single day; the many locales were squeezed into a single town. Still, the play had a happy ending, and its numerous incidents strained neoclassical verisimilitude. The recently formed French Academy—itself an example of aggressive Neoclassicism, a literary society supported by those in power—praised the elements of *Le Cid* that conformed to the rules but condemned those that strayed. French playwrights, including Corneille, got the message: Critical acclaim (and approval from those in political, financial, and social power) would come from lining up with Neoclassicism. After 1636, Neoclassicism would dominate French drama for more than a hundred years. In 1641 the first Italianate theatre was built in

Paris. Giacomo Torelli (see pp. 238–239) was brought to Paris in 1645 to install a chariot-and-pole system. His productions marked the acceptance of all Italianate scenic practices in Paris: Almost immediately, the tennis court (public) theatres had to adapt or die; they installed some form of Italianate scenery. Thereafter, simple neoclassical settings competed with lavish operas, ballets, and **machine plays**, plays written specifically to exploit the new scenery.

ITALIANATE STAGING: PUBLIC VERSUS COURT THEATRES Italian theory and staging played out differently in France, however. The triumph of Neoclassicism was manifest primarily in the French *public* theatres, where a distinct French style of drama developed, one both austere and terse. The triumph of Italianate staging, on the other hand, found its fullest expression in the *court* theatres, where plays from the public theatres were restaged with ballet interludes, movable scenery, and gorgeous costumes, and where king and courtiers played heroes of romance and mythology in purpose-written entertainments that moved out into parks and gardens, sometimes with mock tournaments and battles. Italianate scenery in the public theatres was more modest but shared the basic visual conventions of the court.

FIGURE 16.3
The Sun King
Lavish court entertainments including theatre flourished under Louis XIV's patronage. Pictured here is a ballet costume worn by Louis XIV as Apollo, The Sun.

The Sun King and the Golden Age

Both the court and the public theatres reached their peak during the reign of Louis XIV, a king who drew power to himself as the sun attracts the planets. Calling himself "The Sun King," Louis XIV declared, "I am the state," and he believed it. Absolute power, ego, and show were summed up in the word *gloire,* which carried over from war into theatre; it also extended to the building of great follies, such as Louis's palace at Versailles, where he surrounded himself with France's nobility. When Versailles opened, the court withdrew from Paris. Louis pursued an aggressive campaign of national self-display, not only through military adventures but also through the arts, including theatre.

Theatres benefited. They got both royal subsidy and royal patronage, but not enough to survive without public support, and so they were sometimes in the position of serving two masters at once. At its best, this theatre offered great variety and superb quality, satisfying an audience that became the most demanding and sophisticated in Europe—and which replaced Italy's as the model for Europe.

In addition to the continuing dominance of Neoclassicism and enthusiasm for Italianate staging, the pinnacle of French theatre meant:

- The emergence of two great playwrights to join Corneille
- The expansion to five permanent professional theatres in Paris, later reduced to three, with strict government control through monopolies

Playwrights

Racine. Although Pierre Corneille continued writing, his fame was eclipsed by that of Jean Racine. Born three years after the first production of *Le Cid,* Racine was educated by Jansenists, a Catholic sect with an overriding preoccupation with sin and guilt, concerns that permeated Racine's major plays. Trained in the classics, Racine based his only comedy, *The Litigants,* on Aristophanes' comedy *The Wasps,* and his most esteemed tragedy, *Phèdre* (*Phaedra*), on Euripides' *Hippolytus.*

Phèdre is a model of Neoclassicism. Because the play's major conflicts occur within the character Phèdre, the neoclassical requirements for unity are easily accommodated; and because Phèdre's passion leads to her downfall, neoclassical commitment to the punishment of evil is satisfied. *Phèdre,* unlike *Le Cid,* is neoclassical through and through, and its achievement in plot, character, and diction placed it among the masterpieces of dramatic literature. France had accomplished what England would not: lasting and popular drama based on neoclassical theory.

Molière. French comedy found its genius in the actor-dramatist Molière. At about the time that theatres were closing in England, Molière was leaving home to join a traveling theatrical troupe in France. By 1660 he was head of the troupe, wrote most of its plays, and had firmly established it as a favorite of Louis XIV. Perhaps the greatest comic writer of all times, Molière used his own experiences as an actor as well as his knowledge of Roman comedy, Italian commedia, and French farce to create comedies that ridiculed social and moral pretentiousness.

Molière's comedy typically depicts characters made ludicrous by their deviations from decorum. Although his dialogue is often clever, verbal elegance and wit for their own sake do not form the core of his plays; instead, the comedies depend heavily on farcical business (such as commedia's *lazzi*) and visual gags. Of his more than twenty plays, the best known are probably *Tartuffe, The Miser,* and *The Imaginary Invalid,* whose leading role Molière was playing when he was stricken. Denied last rites by the church because he was an actor, he was granted Christian burial only through the direct intervention of Louis XIV.

Spotlight

Phèdre is, in keeping with neoclassic doctrine, punished for her evil desires by death; she commits suicide. This production at Butler University is clearly postmodern.

Jean Racine's *Phèdre* (*Phaedra*), 1677

Racine (1639–1699), Corneille, and Molière were the greatest French playwrights of the latter half of the seventeenth century. In Racine's *Phèdre,* based on Euripides' *Hippolytus,* the title character lusts after Hippolytus, her stepson. *Phèdre* is the quintessential neoclassical tragedy, embracing all of the elements of Neoclassicism including a five-act structure written in Alexandrine verse. The play also observes the three unities of time, place, and action. Phèdre is, in keeping with neoclassic doctrine, punished for her evil desires by death.

The Story of the Play

In Troezen, Hippolytus, son of Theseus, the king of Athens, is about to set out to look for his long-absent father; he confesses he is doing so partly to avoid Aricia, whom he loves despite "glorying in his chastity."

Phaedra, Theseus's wife and Hippolytus's stepmother, is said to be "dying in her nurse's arms." She appears—weak, distraught—but the mention of Hippolytus rouses her, clearly causing pain. She confesses to her nurse, Oenone, that she loves him and is dying of that love.

Word comes that Theseus is dead. Phaedra can now confess her love to Hippolytus; however, his thoughts are of Aricia, whom he tells he will support as a claimant to the Athenian throne. Phaedra tells Hippolytus she loves him and begs him to kill her.

However, Theseus suddenly returns; the rumor of his death is wrong. Phaedra is guilt-stricken, horrified, frightened, but her nurse advises her to protect herself by accusing Hippolytus of having tried to seduce her. Given permission by the frantic Phaedra, the nurse then does so; Theseus confronts his son, who refuses, as a matter of honor, to tell his father the truth about Phaedra. Theseus asks Neptune to avenge him on Hippolytus.

Phaedra learns that Hippolytus loves Aricia and rages. Hippolytus and Aricia vow to marry and to flee.

Hippolytus rides off alone in his chariot. A messenger brings the news that Neptune has sent a monster from the ocean that so terrified Hippolytus's horses that they have dragged him to his death.

The nurse drowns herself. Phaedra commits suicide.

THEATRE COMPANIES By 1660 there were five permanent, professional troupes in Paris, including Molière's, a commedia troupe from Italy, and the opera, music, and dance troupe headed by Jean-Baptiste Lully. All were sharing companies and all included women. France had no householders—actors who, in England, owned parts of the theatre building. Only the most talented actors settled in Paris as members of these troupes; the rest still toured.

Spotlight

Molière was an active member of his troupe and acted many key comedic roles. Here he is the title character in *Sganerelle.*

Molière's *Tartuffe*, 1669

Born Jean-Baptist Poquelin (1622–1673), the actor, dramatist, and company manager, took Molière as his stage name. Molière's first great success in Paris was his performance before the young king Louis XIV of *The Doctor in Love,* which he wrote and played the title role in. His strength as a comic actor was quickly recognized. He wrote more than thirty-six plays, many of which, including *Tartuffe*, are regularly staged today.

The Story of the Play

Orgon, a well-to-do bourgeois, has made a religious zealot, Tartuffe, a pampered guest in his house. Orgon is obsessed by Tartuffe—will hear no wrong of him, cannot do enough for him—despite Tartuffe's being despised as a hypocrite by Orgon's brother, Cléante; his wife, Elmire; his son, Damis; and the witty servant, Dorine. Cléante pleads that Orgon use moderation and restraint, but Orgon is unmovable. Orgon tells his daughter, Mariane, that he wants her to marry Tartuffe, but Mariane loves Valère and is disgusted by Tartuffe.

Tartuffe tries to make love to Elmire; he is overheard by Damis, who tries to expose him to Orgon. Tartuffe turns the accusation upside down by saying he is too humble and too pious to defend himself. Orgon turns against his son and throws him out of the house, swearing he will strike him out of his will and make Tartuffe his sole heir. He urges Tartuffe to be with Elmire constantly to show Orgon's faith in him.

Elmire, disgusted, tells Orgon that until then she had passed off men's advances as something a wife dealt with herself, but his actions toward Damis are too much: She will show him the truth about Tartuffe. She hides Orgon under a table and then calls Tartuffe into the room and pretends to welcome his advances. Tartuffe is eager, lustful; he wants "tangible proof" of her feelings. Elmire coughs to get Orgon's attention, but he doesn't come out from under the table. She asks about Tartuffe's piety; he tells her that he can "remove Heaven's scruples" about adultery. She keeps coughing. Finally, unable to get Orgon to come out, she sends Tartuffe to make sure nobody is nearby and then all but pulls Orgon out. He is stunned. Elmire is sarcastic: "What, coming out so soon? Why don't you wait until the climax?"

Orgon, his obsession ended, confronts Tartuffe and tells him to leave the house, but Tartuffe instead orders Orgon and the family out: Tartuffe owns the house through Orgon's deed of gift. Worse, Tartuffe has private papers that Orgon entrusted to him that can ruin Orgon with the government.

A process server arrives, threatening Orgon's arrest. The police follow, but they arrest Tartuffe instead—the king knows the truth of Tartuffe's hypocrisy and is just.

Within fifteen years, however, government control and a tendency toward centralization affected the acting companies. With Molière's death, his troupe was joined with two others to form the Comédie Française, which became France's national theatre. Membership in this sharing company was fixed; therefore, new members could not be elected until others had retired or died. Because of its financial rewards, including a substantial pension for retired members, the list of applicants was long.

The Comédie Française was granted a monopoly on the (legal) performance of tragedies and comedies in Paris. Lully's company held a monopoly on musical entertainments and spectacles. The Italian troupe—after a short banishment for a political indiscretion—got exclusive rights to what came to be called comic operas. Thus, less than a century after the freewheeling days of the first professionals, French theatre was rigidly structured, with three legal troupes that were expected to continue their traditions, not to initiate the new. The result was a highly polished but conservative theatre—and the suppression of competition.

Sentimentalism

As Louis XIV became both more conservative and more religious with advancing age, French culture in general shifted toward conservativism, adopting a set of values now called **Sentimentalism**. According to this view of the world, each individual is basically good. This doctrine contrasted with the previous (neoclassical) view that human existence was a continuing struggle between good and evil. According to the sentimentalist, evil came about through corruption; it was not part of human nature at birth. Sentimentalism thus implied that, although people might not be perfect, they were perfectible. Literature should therefore show virtuous people acting virtuously in their daily lives. Sentimentalism affected both serious dramas and comedies.

Changes in Production Practices Design likewise began to change. Although the basic conventions of costume remained unchanged (contemporary rather than historical), the costumes themselves were prettified and sentimentalized, even in commedia. In scenery, the introduction of **angle perspective** (moving the vanishing point away from the center and toward the side) and of multiple vanishing points not only allowed actors to work closer to the scenery but also increased the number of "perfect" seats in the audience, suggesting the acceptance of more than one perception or "truth."

Changes in Performance Practices Acting, too, grew ever more conservative. The earlier tendency of actors to specialize in certain kinds of roles became gradually more rigid until, by 1750, clearly defined **lines of business** emerged. New actors, both male and female, were hired as **utility players** and gained their experience by playing a great number of small and varied roles. They then declared a specialty in a specific kind of role: a "walking" lady or gentleman (third line); a specialist in low comedy, or "stage eccentric" (second line); a hero or heroine (first line). Once committed to a particular line of business, actors did not stray far from it, regardless of age.

Along with lines of business came a practice known as **possession of parts**, an agreement that an actor who played a role in the company possessed that role for as long as he or she remained in the company. Both practices placed a premium on tradition—and, often, on age—and inhibited innovation.

Acting style depended heavily on vocal power and versatility and on formality and elegance rather than "truth to life." For example, some actors apparently intoned or chanted the poetic and lyrical passages of tragedies, much as the recitative of opera is delivered today, and many actors played for *points*, expecting to receive applause for passages particularly well delivered (in which case, the actor might repeat the passage).

FIGURE 16.4
Angle Perspective
Adding second and third vanishing points and shifting the main vanishing point off center extends the vista behind the actors—and sometimes dwarfed them. As this etching demonstrates, multipoint perspective made the scenic background more interesting.

With no outlet for the talents of the many actors and writers who did not get into the Comédie Française, and with dwindling enthusiasm for Neoclassicism, French men and women began to work in illegal theatres—that is, theatres other than the monopolies. Joining jugglers, dancers, and others who had worked at fairs for centuries, theatrical troupes began to play outside the law, practicing all kinds of tricks to avoid open conflict with the monopolies. From the experiments of these "illegitimate" theatres came a robust alternative to the government theatres—a theatre that was strictly commercial, one supported by a paying audience. Housed in the fairs (it would move to the boulevards in the next century), this theatre aimed to be entertaining and to attract the largest number of spectators possible, their money paying the actors and providing the spectacle.

ENGLISH RESTORATION THEATRE AND BEYOND (1660–c. 1750)

We left the English theatre at the moment when another Stuart king was being restored to the throne (1660), hence the name of the period—the Restoration. During the years the English theatre had been closed, William Davenant had

Jason Ayers

FIGURE 16.5
Molière in Modern Production
Productions of Molière's popular comedies are mounted throughout the modern world. Here a production of *Tartuffe* at Theatre South Carolina.

produced his few "operas," introducing Italianate staging to the English public for the first time. (It had long been in the court, remember.)

With the return of king and court from France, English theatres reopened in 1660. Their model, however, was not the theatre of Shakespeare's London; it was now the theatre of Paris. The English theatre now included at least four French traits:

- Women actors, who quickly assumed all female roles except witches and comic old women, which continued to be played by men (as in Molière's company). The presence of women onstage encouraged, fairly or not, the risqué reputation of Restoration theatre.
- Conventions of Italianate staging
- Newly designed theatre buildings that met the needs of Italianate staging
- New, French-inspired producing arrangements. The king granted two monopoly patents, one to Davenant and another to Thomas Killigrew, thus limiting London to only two "legitimate" theatres. Although often challenged, these patents were reaffirmed through most of the 1700s.

When theatres first reopened in 1660, they used either old theatre buildings that still stood, or they adapted tennis courts, as in France. As new theatres were built, however, they blended Shakespearean and French features. The auditorium was divided into box, pit (now with benches), and gallery. Favored audience members now sat on the stage itself, as in France. The stage comprised both a proscenium arch with a raked stage behind it and a forestage that thrust into the pit. Most scenery was located behind the proscenium arch, where grooves were installed to facilitate scene changes, but most acting took place on the forestage, which was roughly the size of the area behind the proscenium. Early Restoration playhouses were intimate, with as little as thirty feet from forestage to rear boxes.

Staging conventions were Italian by way of France. Wings, borders, and shutters formed stock sets appropriate for comedies, tragedies, and pastorals. For costumes, most actors wore a sumptuous version of contemporary fashion. Acting depended heavily on vocal power and versatility and on formality and elegance rather than "truth to life." Lines of business and possession of parts determined which actors played which roles, contributing in England, as in France, to an increasingly conservative style of acting. Lighting was still by candle, and so audience and actors were equally visible.

Jason Ayers

FIGURE 16.6

English Restoration Theatre

This contemporary production of William Wycherley's *The Country Wife* at Theatre South Carolina incorporates the conventions of the English Restoration stage into its design. There is a deep forestage (reached here by four steps), a proscenium arch (with proscenium doors and stage boxes above them), and scenery in single-point perspective. However, it has to be remembered that Restoration theatres were small and narrow, and the distance from the front of the forestage to the farthest box could be as little as thirty feet.

Restoration Drama

Dramas of the Restoration likewise showed French influence. Plays written during the age of Shakespeare continued to be produced, but they were often adapted to bring them into closer accord with neoclassical theory. Newly written plays differed in both content and form from the Elizabethan. The worlds they embodied were those of a highly artificial, aristocratic society, probably influenced by life at Louis XIV's court, and their dramaturgy more closely reflected continental Neoclassicism than Shakespeare. Most famous today are the Restoration **comedies of manners**, plays whose witty dialogue and sophisticated sexual behavior reflect the highly artificial, mannered, and aristocratic society of the day. The heroes and heroines are "virtuous" if they succeed in capturing a lover or tricking a husband. "Honor" depends not on integrity but on reputation, and "wit," the ability to express ideas in a clever and apt way, is prized above all. The admirable characters in the plays are those who can operate successfully within an intricate social sphere; the foolish and laughable are those whose lack of wit or upbringing denies them access to social elegance. In short, the comedies depict the mores and conventions of a courtly society in which elegance of phrase and the appearance of propriety were more highly prized than morals and sincere feelings. Among the most famous authors of Restoration comedies were William Congreve, whose *The Way of the World* is still produced, and William Wycherley, whose *The Country Wife* can still titillate and amuse.

"Heroic" tragedies presented a conflict between love and duty. In a world far removed from that of the Restoration comedies, tragic heroes were flawless and heroines chaste. The dialogue was based on heroic couplets, two-line units of rhymed iambic pentameter. The idealization and formality of this kind of tragedy made it unusually susceptible to parody, and so burlesques of it soon appeared.

Succumbing to both the onslaught of burlesque and the changing tastes of audiences, heroic tragedies declined in public favor, their place being filled by neoclassical tragedies like John Dryden's *All for Love,* a rewriting of Shakespeare's *Antony and Cleopatra* that brought it closer to the principles of Neoclassicism.

Audiences

Restoration audiences were small (c. 650) and fairly cohesive—young, courtly, and self-confident. Regularly in attendance were royalty and the upper aristocracy, many of them veterans of exile in France with the king. Some women in the audience wore masks, as much to increase their attractions as to hide them. This theatre was a place to be seen as well as to enjoy the plays. Within fifteen years, however, non-courtiers began to take up theatre as a leisure-time activity in ever-larger numbers, causing a shift in audience taste.

Sentimentalism

In England as in France, the eighteenth century brought with it a change of values. Between about 1700 and 1750, society steadily grew more conservative, middle class, moralistic, and sentimental.

The amoral tone of the Restoration comedy of manners became offensive to many, and in its place developed the view that drama should teach morality. At first, the change was merely in the plays' endings: Young lovers philandered and cuckolded throughout four acts of the play but, in the fifth, repented and declared their intention to lead a moral and upright life henceforth.

SENTIMENTAL COMEDY By the 1730s, however, heroes and heroines were becoming embodiments of middle-class values, struggling cheerfully against adversity until, at the end, their courage and persistence were rewarded. Prized especially were characters able to express their insights into human goodness in pithy statements (sentiments). Thus, the label "sentimental hero" implied not only one who embodied virtue but also one whose speech was rich in sentiments. The audiences of the day experienced "a pleasure too exquisite for laughter," and so sentimental comedy dominated English comic drama by the middle of the eighteenth century—a clear break with Neoclassicism.

Serious Plays Heroic and neoclassical tragedy were increasingly replaced by a kind of serious drama, alternately called domestic tragedy and *middle-class tragedy*. George Lillo's *The London Merchant* (1731), for example, was a major break with the neoclassical ideal: A middle-class hero is led astray by love and is ultimately punished. Although the play aimed to teach morality by showing the punishment of evil, it was nonetheless a far cry from strict Neoclassicism because it was written in prose, featured a middle-class hero, and dealt with affairs of the heart and the marketplace rather than affairs of state. None of these more serious plays, however, satisfied the English taste for scenic splendor and spectacular effects.

Minor Forms Opera and a number of so-called minor forms developed to provide outlets for visual display. Native English opera was gradually replaced by spectacular Italian opera, whose popularity soared in the eighteenth century. As well, English pantomimes combined elements of commedia dell'arte, farce, mythology, and contemporary satire with elaborate scenes of spectacle in short afterpieces, that is, short entertainments to be performed after the evening's play. Often, the dialogue was merely an excuse for major scenes of transformation, in which Harlequin, by a wave of his magic wand, changed places and people into new and dazzling locales and characters. Because new scenery was often commissioned for pantomimes, many innovations in the design and execution of settings in England can be credited to pantomime.

Changes in Production and Performance Practices Such changes in drama were accompanied by changes in production and performance practices. As more middle-class people came into the audience, existing theatres were enlarged, and new theatres built larger; within a hundred years, the intimate theatre of the Restoration had been superceded by those seating 1,500 or more. Theatres began to commission painters to provide new settings for some plays (especially those featuring familiar locations), and these painters, adopting new techniques for suggesting depth, made it possible for actors to work closer to scenery than before. Increased emphasis on scenery led to a gradual decrease in the size of the forestage and a need for more space behind the proscenium arch. As a result of these shifts, by 1750 there was little difference in appearance between English and continental theatres.

By the middle of the 1700s, then, English theatres, like French theatres, had adopted the conventions of Italianate staging, neoclassical drama, and formal acting. In both, women were now on stage and in the audience. Both cultures had developed theatrical centers in their capital cities, where their kings maintained monopolies over a strictly limited number of theatres. Actors talented and experienced enough to perform in the monopoly theatres lived good lives; others, however, lived precariously, working in small cities and towns and touring outlying areas.

By the early 1700s, European audiences (including those of a just-developing German theatre) had already begun to tire of the austerity of neoclassical dramas. As audiences became increasingly middle class, sentimentalism and spectacle began to be prized; both found expression in opera, ballet, and new dramatic forms. When monopoly theatres disdained the innovations, commercial theatres sprang up to house them, first at the fairs of London and Paris (hence, **fair theatres**) and later in London's West End and Paris's boulevards. Actors who found themselves squeezed out of the monopoly theatres played there or toured the provinces.

ENGLISH THEATRE IN AMERICA

From among the many English actors who found themselves squeezed out of the London theatre came the beginnings of theatre in the United States. Rather than touring rural England, William and Lewis Hallam chose to assemble a company (mostly families) and sail to a distant English province, an outpost of the New World.

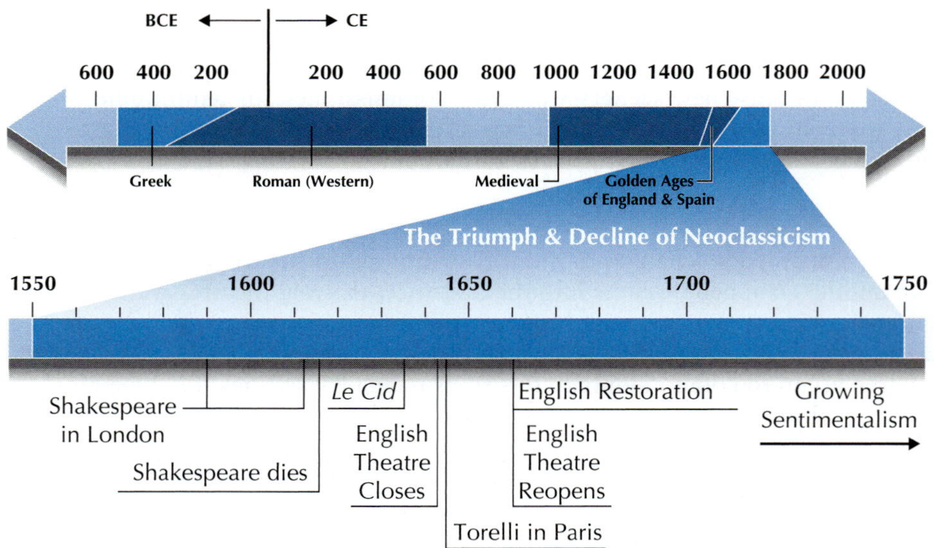

FIGURE 16.7

Timeline

The golden age of French theatre did not begin until those of England, Spain, and Italy were nearing their ends. French theatre, like France itself, came to dominate Europe, influencing English theatrical conventions and bringing them closer to continental practice after 1660.

In 1752 the troupe arrived in Virginia and, after building a theatre, opened with Shakespeare's *The Merchant of Venice.* This group (although reorganized and enlarged after the death of Lewis Hallam and renamed the American Company in recognition of America's break with England) toured the towns of the East Coast with almost no competition until the 1790s. Its repertory, acting styles, and production conventions were English, with appropriate adjustments made for the needs of almost constant touring.

KEY TERMS

Check your understanding against this list. Brief definitions are included in the Glossary; persons are page-referenced in the Index.

afterpieces 255
angle perspective 250
comedy of manners 253
domestic tragedy 255
fair theatres 256
lines of business 250
machine plays 246
pantomimes 255
possession of parts 251
sentimental comedy 255
Sentimentalism 250
utility players 250

CHAPTER

17

Successful Failure

Theatre and Reform, c. 1750 to the 1950s

OBJECTIVES

When you have completed this chapter, you should be able to:

- Describe the split in the Western theatre in the late 1700s
- Explain ways in which Romanticism differed from Neoclassicism
- List several major traits of Romanticism and explain how those traits expressed themselves in theatre and drama
- Sketch the arrangement of audience areas in the theatre before and after Wagner
- Compare (that is, identify similarities and differences in) Romanticism and Realism
- Compare Realism and Naturalism
- Describe changes in acting in the shift from Romanticism to Realism
- List and define briefly the major avant-garde theories and play types from c. 1890s–c. 1950s
- List and describe briefly the major avant-garde theatres and movements from c. 1890s–c. 1950s

CONTEXT

History is filled with contradictions, none, perhaps, greater than those of the theater from the mid-eighteenth century until the mid-twentieth. On the one hand, theatre in Europe and America achieved a popularity never before equalled; on the other, people in those same places tried with increasing energy to reform, restore, improve, or save it. These attempts split both theatre and drama into a commercial strand and a something else that was later called the **avant-garde** ("advance guard"—the term was, significantly, a military one). Because the two strands developed along different, although connected, paths, we are treating them in two chapters; this chapter deals with the avant-garde from the mid-eighteenth to the mid-twentieth centuries. The next chapter deals with the commercial theatre and the ways in which it used avant-garde experiments.

THREE COUNTRIES, TWO EXPERIENCES

Germany

Germany's experience was different from England's and France's. "Germany" was still a hodgepodge of small states, duchies, and principalities linked by little except language. Despite a glorious tradition of music, it had no permanent theatres at the beginning of the 1700s. Such traveling players as there were played idiotic low comedy or blood-and-thunder bombast for (powerless) low-class audiences. In 1725, however, Johann Gottsched (a Neoclassicist and playwright) and Carolina Neuber (head of an acting troupe) introduced the first "serious" German drama and theatre; other permanent theatres quickly sprang up, sixty-five of them by 1800. But they were not located in a central capital that was also a nexus of absolute power; they were spread all over the German cultural area. German theorists and artists were not so much reformers, then, as innovators: They were trying to assert a cultural centrality that German theatre had never known, and they used the language of art and seriousness. They tilted toward English models. (They knew Shakespeare from touring seventeenth-century English companies; Gottsched promoted French ideas, but failed.)

FIGURE 17.1

English Comedy

Richard Brinsley Sheridan's *The School for Scandal* opened at the Theatre Royal in Drury Lane in 1777, a comedy of manners like many of the comedies of the Restoration but with sentimentalism instead of cynicism. Here, a production by the University of Missouri.

England and France

How did the separation of theatre into commercial and avant-garde start in England and France? As we have seen, by the early 1700s the theatre had begun to lose its ties to the old monarchies. At the same time, the audience base started growing, first into the middle and then into the working class, with the result that the theatre's potential audience grew, but not necessarily for the old kind of theatre. England had had its Glorious Revolution in 1688, ending the Restoration period, and thereafter Parliament shared power with a king who ruled less by divine right than by the negotiated consent of the governed. In France, Louis XIV died in 1715 after seventy-two years of first nominal, then actual absolute power, and he was replaced by a corrupt regime that was wiped out by the revolution of 1789. The monopolies that had tied the theatres to power weakened, and in their place came large audiences who had not power but money, which they used to buy entrance to new, "illegitimate," commercial theatres (e.g., of the fairs and boulevards).

By the mid-1700s, theatrical energy was shifting to these commercial theatres, which offered new kinds of plays in spectacular settings, leaving the monopoly theatres to traditional practices and traditional audiences. As a result, theatre flourished, but the more popular it became in its new venues, the farther it got from the old center of power. A series of reformers began to try to steer it back—the subject of this chapter. They usually couched their pleas in terms of art, not of literal connections to central power, often asking for a return to "serious" drama and theatre—a language that now looks like an unconscious recognition of what was really happening.

Reforms

Thus started, in all three countries, the accelerating movement that tried to reconnect theatrical art with power and with the elite that wielded it. Major waves of would-be reform came at the turn of the nineteenth century (Romanticism), in the last quarter of the nineteenth century (Realism), and throughout the first half of the twentieth century (all kinds of *isms*). All had impact on the popular, commercial theatre. All failed. Theatre never recovered its ability to "validate the center of power."

Theatrical innovators—reformers—were often a generation behind these changes. They saw their own declining centrality, but they tried to aim their demands for seriousness and art at a world that was going or already gone. The commercial theatre, however, was happy to sweep up such innovations as pleased its audience.

FIRST WAVE: ROMANTICISM, 1750–1850

Context

What do these things have in common?

- The Declaration of Independence
- *Frankenstein*

- "'Beauty is truth, truth beauty,'–that is all / Ye know on earth, and all ye need to know."
- Art—with a capital *A*
- *The Rights of Man*

There are two answers: First, they fall into the same hundred years and, second, they are expressions of **Romanticism**, a cultural shift so radical that a later observer said that it "destroyed Neoclassicism."

What was Romanticism?

The period from about 1750 to about 1850 was "the world turn'd upside-down." Major political revolutions happened in the Americas and France; the industrial revolution began; demographics changed as population migrated from country to city and across oceans and borders to North America, Australia, and South America. Steam power, mass communications (high-volume printing, cheap newspapers), railroads, and photography came into being. Nations for the first time supported compulsory education. The international slave trade was outlawed by Britain, the ban enforced by its navy.

Out of this turmoil, the cultural and intellectual cluster we call Romanticism came into being.

The Nature of Romanticism: The Beginning of Our World

We now tend to think of Romanticism as a set of theoretical ideas.

It is better to think of it as a set of effects, which were then articulated as theoretical ideas by several people in several countries at more or less the same time, those ideas then becoming causes in their turn. And it is wise to remember that these were political ideas as well as ideas about society, psychology, art, and the nature of the world; that they were only secondarily about the theatre; and that the ideas were not necessarily consistent. One critic much later suggested that we should speak of romanticism*s* (plural), not one Romanticism. Nonetheless, long after the fact we can see five certain common interests:

- **Rebellion.** Romanticisms were revolutionary. In art, Romanticism wanted to overturn Neoclassicism. In politics, equality and the idea of a social contract binding government and governed were Romantic. Socially, early feminism, personal religion, and opposition to slavery were Romantic. Romanticisms hated a status quo that inhibited equality and individualism.
- **Art with a capital *A*.** Creative and intellectual Romantics all but invented the idea of Art as a special activity. The Artist was a special being—a creative genius able to see truths hidden from others.
- **Nature.** Natural feelings were more reliable than reason or authority. Civilization and education corrupted nature. Children, savages, and peasants were uncorrupted, therefore nearer innocence. Nature was a window through which the child and the Artist could see Truth.
- **Anti-industrialism.** Art and beauty were "sublime"; factories were "dark Satanic mills." Cities were unnatural and corrupting. Early industrialists were seen by Romantics as greedy bean counters without souls—the opposite of

the Artist. Industry was ugly (noise, smoke, buildings) and therefore the opposite of Beauty (another way to Truth).

- **Uniqueness.** Truth was also found in the particular, not the general. To establish uniqueness was to establish identity.

People at the time did not necessarily see these five ideas clearly. Political activists saw mostly their own impatience with top-down government; artists saw their own disgust with top-down "rules"; middle-class people saw their own distaste for slavery or slums or dreadful working conditions. Many literate people picked up the jargon of Romantic art—"sublime," "picturesque," "grotesque"—and, insofar as they used it, they were "Romantic," but the spread of the jargon probably had more to do with mass communications than with commitment. And romanticisms created their own opposites: after the French Revolution, the top-down government of Napoleon; after the British ban on the slave trade, the American Civil War.

But the romanticisms have a contemporary feel to them. If you could step back right now into the world of 1740, you would find its culture and its behavior alien, but if you could step back into the world of 1820, you would find some of it familiar—ideas about individualism, freedom of choice, human rights, the environment. To be sure, you'd have to land among the right people—mostly upper middle class and educated—but if you did, you would see why Romanticism is still important: It was the beginning of our world.

Romanticism in the Theatre

The effects on the theatre were significant, if erratic. Romantic theatre artists disdained Neoclassicism *and* frivolous theatre and tried to reform both. They began slowly and unevenly, and they were rejected by conservative theatres, above all the Comédie Française; yet contradictorily, perhaps, it was in the monopoly theatres where the Romantics wanted to see their ideas applied—that, after all, was where the connection with power had been and where the connection to the upper class still was.

Yet where ideas crept in partly unnoticed were the "boulevard" (from their locations in Paris), fair (big public fairs were outside the old laws), and nonmonopoly theatres. The ideas were "in the air"—they had come, after all, from the same causes that let ordinary people see and think in new ways, including in the theatres as audiences. International trade and imperialism, for example, created a knowledge of exotic places, and so they began to show up in plays and settings. The new interest in childhood and primitivism brought children, common people, Native Americans, peasants, and Africans to the stage, both as hot topics for hack playwrights and as real concerns of intellectuals. Plays were set in newly detailed scenery of forests, dungeons, jungles, caves, both because new plays required them and because visual artists were themselves now more interested in nature and detail. The new faith in feelings brought plays that appealed to emotions rather than intellect to audiences already attuned to Sentimentalism, to emotional religious sects, and to new novels about the emotions.

FIGURE 17.2

Size of Romantic Theatres

Buildings got larger after 1750, with the audience in box-pit-and-gallery seating. Here, the English artist Thomas Rowlandson's rendering of Covent Garden Theatre in the early 1800s; the play appears to be Shakespeare's *Henry IV, Part I.*

In England, most of all, then in Germany and America, Shakespeare was elevated to a cultural icon. His plays were performed from London to the California gold fields; they were read aloud in Hamburg drawing rooms and around the fires of the fur-trapping "mountain men." With the Bible, Shakespeare became a binding force of English-language culture that gave it a frame of reference, a common elevated language, and a common rhythm that lasted well into the twentieth century. In France, however, where Neoclassicism persisted longer, Shakespeare was not seen on the stage until an English company brought the plays in the 1830s.

Perhaps the most important outside force acting on the theatre, however, was demographic. Migration and urban growth meant that for the first time a mass audience existed. Industrial employment meant that for the first time large parts of the working class could afford the theatre. These changes affected the size of theatres, which got bigger; the nature of the drama, which got more sensational; and the business organization of the companies, which got more commercial as the old monopolies withered or ossified. (See Chapter 18.)

Romantic Attempts at Reform The most conscious efforts to put Romantic ideas into effect in the theatre came in dramatic theory and drama. Especially in Germany, a distinct body of "serious" Romantic plays was written and is still in the German repertory. A recognizable gap appeared, however, between "important" (serious, literary) plays and popular ones in France and England. Partly, this

FIGURE 17.3
The Inside of the State Theatre, Hamburg, Germany

The rendering of the interior is crude (the people are erratically out of scale), but this theatre in the early 1800s had a pit orchestra; box-pit-and-gallery seating; and a large candelabrum in the audience area. German theatre had developed rapidly in half a century.

was the gap between the old monopolies and the new, mostly commercial theatres; partly it was the gap between self-aware "Art" and what was called hackwork. Over the long haul, Art lost, in good part because it would not see the theatre itself as art; rather, the theatre was a corrupted thing that had to be reformed.

Germany. Romantic drama found its home in Germany. Germany produced a seminal theoretical work, Gotthold Lessing's *Hamburg Dramaturgy* (1770), which rejected French Neoclassicism as a model and recommended instead Shakespeare. Lessing wrote specifically of art and genius, recommended natural language, praised sentimental comedy and domestic tragedy, and argued for heroes who were human beings, not aristocratic or royal titles. He also wrote several plays, including so-called philosophical dramas, the most lasting—as a literary, not a theatrical, work—*Nathan the Wise.*

Hamburg Dramaturgy, and especially its urging of Shakespeare as a model, in turn influenced young German radicals calling themselves the **Storm and Stress** (an in-your-face term of the day, from a play written by one of them), including two who were to become German classics: Johann Wolfgang von Goethe, whose *Faust* is an acknowledged literary, but not theatrical, masterpiece, and whose novel *The Sorrows of Werther* ("spleen, morbid sentimentality, romantic melancholy, and disgust of life," according to one critic) gave Romantics a mythic hero and even a costume; and Friedrich von Schiller, whose commitment to liberty showed in *The Robbers* and *William Tell,* both successes that led to many imitations. The subjects of these plays tell us much about self-aware Romanticism—love and loss, liberty, the fight against despotism, free will and wisdom. So do the kinds of characters—robbers, rebels, lovers, questioners. Perhaps most significant is the form of the plays, whose authors demanded the right to roam freely in time and space (like Shakespeare) and not be limited by "the unities," and their poetry, which was intense, usually unrhymed, and rhythmic—neither everyday speech nor neoclassical artifice.

England. In England, however, attempts to create a serious body of Romantic drama labored too closely in the shadow of Shakespeare, and a false Shakespearism ruined many plays. Too, serious English Romantics refused to meet the needs of the theatre, including pleasing the audience, which they thought was the problem, not the solution. Even when England's great poets tried seriousness in the theatre, they usually failed; Byron did write a tragedy that worked, *Werner,* a lurid tale of revenge and despair, but it barely escaped the trap into which most serious Romantic drama fell—that of mistaking the most extreme moments of Shakespearean tragedy for the tragedy itself. English Romantics who wanted to bring a new seriousness to the theatre were not alone in thus failing to find a dramaturgy to match the emotional expression in which they believed; the resulting plays therefore often lacked internal probability and had long passages of great dullness separating moments of incredible bombast. Romantic language pushed the envelope and sometimes became wild, torrential, overblown—a verbal diarrhea to match the emotional diarrhea of its heroes. Few of these plays have lasted, and no wonder; rather, what has lasted have been Italian operas made from them, in which music supplied the quality that the spoken dramas couldn't.

Joan Marcus Photography

FIGURE 17.4

Schiller's *Mary Stuart*

Friedrich von Schiller's *Mary Stuart* is based on the rivalry between Mary, Queen of Scots, and her cousin, Elizabeth I of England. Originally premiered in 1800, the play's themes of greed and deception can still capture modern audiences. Here, Janet McTeer as the lead in Phyllida Lloyd's 2009 production of *Mary Stuart* at a Broadway theatre. McTeer received the 2009 Drama Desk Award for Best Actress for her work on the production.

France. In Paris, Romantic dramas made it to the boulevard theatres in 1790 but were shut out of the now-hidebound Comédie Française until 1830, when Victor Hugo's self-aware *Hernani* was staged and caused a riot. Hugo won, but it was like mating with a corpse. The Comédie was belatedly revived by the energy of Romanticism, but the movement itself ran out of steam a few years later, so watered down in the popular theatres by that time that storm, stress, and riot fizzled.

Drama had been caught in a contradiction: Serious literary Romantics wanted to create Art for a sensitive, therefore limited, audience; the theatres wanted to bring in the largest possible audience. The extreme artistic position was **closet drama**, plays written to be read, not staged. Neither closet dramas nor bad poetic tragedies could restore the theatre to its neoclassical position.

Romanticism was pretty well over as a movement by the 1840s. It had succeeded in destroying Neoclassicism; it had planted its flag at the Comédie Française; the English monopoly "patents" had died of old age; and German theatre had had what one source calls its Golden Age. Romantic drama had not reformed the theatre, however.

FIGURE 17.5
Romantic Shakespeare
An engraving from about 1775 based on the Hogarth painting of 1745, pictures David Garrick, one of England's greatest actors, in the title role of shakespeare's *Richard III*. The S curve of the body position expresses the emotionalism of the Romantic era.

What persisted was Sentimentalism, which had adapted itself to trivialized Romanticism and which matched Victorian taste, which was middle class, fussy, and "moral." What the Romantics left most conspicuously to the future, however, was the image of the Artist—special, gifted, emotional—and of Art, which entered Victorian culture as a kind of secular religion (so long as it was moral and approved by experts).

An Aftershock: Richard Wagner

Richard Wagner is now known as an opera composer. His influence on modern theatre, however, has been enormous for two innovations: (1) the idea of unity and a unifying artist and (2) a separate, classless audience space.

THE MASTER ARTWORK Wagner had a huge ego and knew he was a genius in the Romantic mold. His concept of a unified theatrical production meant a master artwork conceived and executed by a "master artist" who would run the whole show (ideally, Richard Wagner himself). The idea would go far to establish the director in the modern theatre.

THE SEPARATED AUDIENCE In 1876, Wagner got his own theatre at Bayreuth. It epitomized his ideas: several "nesting" proscenium arches between audience and actors, not just one; a hidden orchestra pit; steam jets between audience and playing area to emphasize a "mystic chasm"—the separation of the master artwork from the audience.

Perhaps more important, Wagner put his audience in the dark and got rid of box, pit, and gallery. Now, the audience sat in a fan-shaped orchestra that was "classless," and every seat had an equally good view of the stage. Called continental seating, the arrangement became standard in the twentieth century.

The effect was in one sense a democratic one, but it had the autocratic effect of putting the entire audience in the same passive surrender to the stage—no catcalls from upper galleries, no bored aristocrats whispering in boxes. It was a top-down theatre space for an art in which the master artist gave and the audience received, both suited culturally to a Germany that had just been unified under the top-down leadership of Otto von Bismarck.

FIGURE 17.6
Wagner the Theoretician
The interior of Wagner's theatre at Bayreuth was an important influence on the future of theatre architecture and audience seating. Wagner eliminated box, pit, and gallery (creating the most common modern audience arrangement) and put the emphasis on the proscenium arches and what went on within them.

SECOND WAVE: REALISM, 1850–1950

The phenomenal popularity of commercial theatres in the nineteenth century did little to satisfy reformers. What they saw was a theatre with a huge audience, doing productions that used the best technology of the day, all of which seemed to them wasted; some saw it as wasted in sheer overproduction; others saw it as wasted on triviality. Again, a call for "seriousness" would come; this time, however, the buzzword would be not Romanticism, but **Realism**.

The idea that art should show real life was hardly new. It was implicit in Renaissance theory, explicit in every portrait or still life. It was explicit in *Hamburg Dramaturgy.* And a literal rendering of life became concrete with the invention of photography (about 1840). In the theatre, local color and scenic detail dated to the eighteenth century, as did the prototype of the **box set**, an imitation of a room with side walls rather than wings; it was common by the end of the Romantic period. In drama, commercial playwrights were writing "problem plays" that seemed to examine real-life issues. Acting was "real" enough by the 1830s that Walt Whitman said that Charlotte Cushman's performance as a woman dying of a severe beating was "too real."

Why, then, a new theatrical radicalism that called itself Realism? Because the pre-Realisms mentioned earlier were inconsistent; because the plays, including "problem plays," were more trendy than serious; because acting was obviously acting, not being; because box sets, with their painted canvas walls, were obviously sets; because the theatre, the radicals said, was all about laying on *stuff* and not getting serious.

The Realists got serious.

By the 1850s, problems of inequality, industrialization, and urbanization were well known and widely discussed. Urban poverty was on the rise and with it urban crime. Fear of political instability (a legacy of Romanticism) led toward repression, which fanned dissatisfaction. For some, it was the best of worlds, but for many, it was the worst; the tension is part of what we mean by the word *Victorian*—the middle- and upper-class ability to maintain awareness of problems while using apparent ignorance as a coping mechanism ("Nice people don't mention such things").

Science was offering new theories that threatened old ideas: Charles Darwin proposed evolution, which left humanity without uniqueness and apparently at the mercy of environment. At century's end, Sigmund Freud proposed the unconscious, which jerked the feet from under good intentions and double standards. One effect of both was to dislodge humankind from the philosophical pedestal on which it had rested since the Middle Ages; another was to displace Romantic ideas, especially their optimism and their faith in Nature as a window on the ideal. Instead, it became "Nature red in tooth and claw." At the same time, "social Darwinism" gave oppressors a response to do-gooders: Social inequity was merely a survival of the fittest.

The impact on serious art, including theatre, was to turn it toward question and challenge of the status quo.

REALISM AND NATURALISM: THREE IMPORTANT LEADERS

Realists—and their more extreme relatives, advocates of **Naturalism**—believed that truth resided in the material objects observable in the physical, external world. They were also objectivists: They believed that truth could be discovered through the application of scientific observation and could be replicated by a series of objective observers, not by Romantic art.

According to the Realists and the Naturalists, the function of art, like that of science, was the betterment of humankind, and the method of the artist should be that of the scientist. Plays should be set in contemporary times and places, for only they could be observed firsthand by the playwright. Because the highest purpose of art was the betterment of humanity, the subject of plays should be contemporary life and its problems.

While sharing with Realists a belief in science as a solver of problems, the Naturalists differed in their definition of what problems most needed attention and in their hope for the future. The Naturalists stressed the problems of the poor

From Oliver Sayler, *The Moscow Art Theatre Series of Plays*

FIGURE 17.7
Realism and Naturalism
Here, Anton Chekhov's *The Three Sisters* at the Moscow Art Theatre in a realistic setting. Compare this image with those of the same play in Figure 17.11.

and tended to be pessimistic about their solution. According to the Naturalists, people were victims, not actors in life. Their destiny was controlled by factors like heredity and environment, over which they had little influence. Because the Naturalists attempted to give the impression that their plays were an actual record of life, the dramas often appeared formless and unstructured, traits that gave rise to the phrase "a slice of life" to describe some Naturalists' plays.

Despite the period's interest in the mass of people, and despite democratizing forces, this was an era of self-defined great men (and a few women). Forceful people—remember Wagner—tried to change the world. The master artist appeared in several guises.

Georg II, Duke of Saxe-Meiningen

One of the earliest creators of realistic staging was Georg II, Duke of Saxe-Meiningen (fl. 1870s–1880s). In some ways, the duke was merely perfecting and popularizing ideals of staging promulgated much earlier; nonetheless, it was he who influenced later Realists.

Saxe-Meiningen objected to many practices of the commercial mainstream because they resulted in productions that lacked unity (internal consistency) and seemed artificial. For the duke and his court theatre, the art of the theatre was the art of providing the illusion of reality; he therefore sought methods of production that would lead to "an intensified reality and [would] give remote events the quality of actuality, of being lived for the first time." To this end, the duke stressed accurate scenery, costumes, and properties; lifelike acting; and unity.

Production Practices The duke believed that all elements of a production required coordination. The setting must be an integral part of the play, and so he encouraged his actors to move *within* the setting rather than merely playing in front of it (as was currently fashionable). If actors were to move within an environment, the scenic details had to be three-dimensional rather than painted, and so actual objects were used in the settings. Simultaneously, the duke strove to provide several levels (e.g., rocks, steps, and platforms) so that the scenic design would not stop abruptly at the stage floor. In these ways, he did much to popularize the use of three-dimensional staging.

Historical accuracy in both scenery and costumes was important. To increase accuracy, he divided each century into thirds and differentiated among various national groups within each period. He used authentic fabrics instead of the cheaper substitutes often seen in commercial theatres of the day.

Acting There were no stars in Saxe-Meiningen's group. Each member of the company was eligible to play any role; and each member, if not cast as a major character, was required to play in crowd scenes, something commercial stars

FIGURE 17.8

Saxe-Meiningen as Director

The new stage Realism—individualized crowd members, varying levels, varied postures and arm positions—is shown in an engraving of the funeral-oration scene in *Julius Caesar.* The Duke of Saxe-Meiningen is said to be the first director, although he had predecessors.

never did. Each actor in a crowd scene was given lines and actions and put into a group led by an experienced actor. Actors were to avoid parallel lines on stage, to make crosses diagonally rather than parallel with the curtain line, to keep one foot off the ground whenever possible (by placing it on a step or by kneeling on one knee), and not to copy his or her neighbor's stance. Actors were told to look at one another rather than the audience, to react to what was said and done onstage, and to behave naturally, even if it meant delivering a line while not facing the audience. Makeup was based on historical portraits. These practices now seem obvious, but in the 1870s they were startling.

Influence Beginning in 1874 (eight years after the duke took over the theatre), the Meiningen company began touring western Europe and Russia. The troupe gave more than 2,800 performances in thirty-six cities. From these performances came its international reputation and its influence.

André Antoine and the Théâtre-Libre

André Antoine, an amateur actor, abhorred the commercial theatres of Paris, disapproved of the way actors were trained at the Paris Conservatoire (France's leading school for actors), objected to the scenic practices of the major theatres, and decried the flimsiness of contemporary popular drama. What was needed, Antoine concluded, was a theatre in which new and controversial plays could get realistic productions. Therefore, when an amateur group to which he belonged balked at producing a new play, Antoine undertook the production himself and, spurred by early success, became the full-time director of his own new theatre in 1887. He named it the Théatre-Libre (Free Theatre) and described it as nothing less than "a machine of war, poised for the conquest of Paris." It was, among other things, an alternative, or avant-garde, theatre. It is worth noting the differences between Antoine and Saxe-Meiningen at this point:

- Antoine was far more interested in new plays.
- Antoine faced tough government censorship.
- Antoine had to make a theatre from scratch.

Plays Although Antoine produced a wide range of plays at the Théâtre-Libre, he seemed most comfortable with plays in the Realistic and Naturalistic styles. Because Antoine organized his theatre as a subscription (members only) house, he was able to bypass threats of censorship. Consequently, he was able to introduce to Parisians a wide range of French and foreign authors whose works were considered too scandalous for production in major theatres.

Production Practices—The "Fourth Wall" Antoine believed with the Naturalists that environment influenced human behavior, so he made his settings as believable and lifelike as possible. He designed a room and then decided which "wall" of the room was to be removed so that the audience could see in. Antoine also used actual three-dimensional objects rather than their painted substitutes. For one play, he brought real sides of beef on his stage; for another, real trees and birds' nests; and for another, a real student's actual room furnishings. The attention he paid to realistic detail and his reliance on actual objects led to his being called by many the father of Naturalistic staging. Jean Julien, a contemporary of Antoine's, seemed to sum up the goal of Antoine: "The front of the stage must be a fourth wall, transparent for the public, opaque for the player."

ACTING Antoine believed that actors should appear to be people, not actors. He wanted his actors to say their lines naturally, just as one might engage in a conversation with friends and, at the same time, to move about the furniture and accessories as in real life. Sincerity and conviction were the qualities he sought, and so he advised his actors to ignore the audience and to speak to one another in conversational tones—in short, to try to *be,* rather than to *act,* the characters in the play. Perhaps for these reasons, Antoine often used amateurs who had not received conventional training for the commercial theatre and who were therefore more receptive to the experimental style of Naturalistic acting.

INFLUENCE The major contributions of Antoine and the Théâtre-Libre were

- To popularize acting techniques leading toward naturalness on stage
- To gain acceptance for scenic practices now known as **fourth-wall** Realism, with all that implies about scenic detail and literal objects
- To introduce a new generation of playwrights (both French and foreign) to the theatregoing public of Paris
- To establish a model for a censor-free theatre

The most significant experimental theatre of its day, the Théâtre-Libre gave rise to a number of similar noncommercial theatres throughout the world. Called the **independent theatre movement**, this blossoming of small theatres in several countries almost simultaneously gave the impetus to, first, an international idealism and then an ultimate acceptance of Realism as the mainstream of the commercial theatre, an acceptance complete by early in the twentieth century.

Realism

Konstantin Stanislavski and the Moscow Art Theatre

When the Meiningen company toured Russia in 1885 and 1890, Konstantin Stanislavski and Vladimir Nemirovich-Danchenko saw it. They decided to establish a new kind of theatre in Moscow whose goals were to remain free of the demands of commercialism, to avoid overemphasis on the scenic elements of production, and to reflect the inner truth of the play. For this theatre, the Moscow Art Theatre established in 1898, Nemirovich-Danchenko was to select the plays and handle the administration, while Stanislavski was to serve as the production director.

ACTING AND DIRECTING By 1917, Stanislavski had developed, from personal experience and observation of others, his major ideas for training actors, ideas that he codified in a series of books that have since been translated into more than twenty languages (the dates are for the American editions): *My Life in Art* (1924), *An Actor Prepares* (1936), *Building a Character* (1949), and *Creating a Role* (1961). Together,

From Oliver Sayler, *The Moscow Art Theatre Series of Plays*

FIGURE 17.9

Stanislavski and the Moscow Art Theatre

Here, Maxim Gorki's *The Lower Depths*, a Naturalistic play set in a flophouse. Stanislavski, center, on the table.

these books represent what has come to be called the Stanislavski "system" of actor training, although Stanislavski himself insisted neither that his was the only way to train actors nor that his methods should be studied and mastered by everyone.

As a director during the early years of the Moscow Art Theatre, Stanislavski worked in a rather autocratic fashion, planning each detail of his actors' vocal inflections, gestures, and movements. But as his interest in the problems of the actor grew, and as his actors became more skillful, he abandoned his dogmatic approach and became an interpreter and helper to the actors. His ideal became for the director and the actors to grow together in their understanding of the play. Only after the group had grasped the psychology of the roles and the complex interrelationships (often a three-month process) did the actors begin to work on the stage.

INFLUENCE What began in 1898 as an experiment in external Realism was by 1906 an experiment in psychological Realism. When the Moscow Art Theatre toured Britain and the United States early in the twentieth century, the word "ensemble" was used again and again to describe the company, which seemed natural and unified, without stars. The Stanislavski ideal had become an established tradition in Russia by the time of the revolution (1917). Because a number of Russians trained in "the system" then left their country and became acting teachers, the ideas of Stanislavski came to London, New York, and then Hollywood.

Plays and Playwrights

Realism in the drama began tentatively and cautiously. Although other writers had presaged Realism, it was the Norwegian Henrik Ibsen who launched Realism as a major artistic movement.

Rita Hoeppner as Hedda Gabler.
Photo: Lenny Cohen.

FIGURE 17.10
Henrik Ibsen
Ibsen's *Hedda Gabler* continues to be one of the most revived plays from this period. Here, *Hedda Gabler* in a contemporary production at North Carolina's Triad Stage.

IBSEN With plays such as *A Doll's House* (1879) and *Hedda Gabler* (1891), Ibsen assumed his controversial role as an attacker of society's values. Structurally, his plays were fairly traditional: They told a story and moved logically from event to event, just as well-made plays had done for years. But their content was shocking: When individuals came into conflict with society, they were no longer assumed to be guilty and society blameless. Indeed, social customs and traditional morality were exposed by Ibsen as a tangle of inconsistencies and irrelevancies. Questions like the proper role of women, the ethics of euthanasia, the morality of business and war, and the economics of religion formed the basis of serious probings into social behavior. Theatrical producers throughout the world who believed that drama should be involved in the social issues of the day applauded the Norwegian dramatist, and soon other artists began to translate, produce, and, later, emulate his plays.

SHAW In England, George Bernard Shaw became one of Ibsen's most vocal and influential supporters. Unlike many realists, Shaw always retained his sense of humor; he almost always wrote comedies (e.g., *Major Barbara* [1905] and *Misalliance* [1910]), and their popularity did much to ensure the final acceptance of Realistic drama in England before the close of World War I.

CHEKHOV Anton Chekhov scored his first success in 1898 when *The Seagull* was produced at the Moscow Art Theatre. Chekhov's plays differed from those of Ibsen and Shaw in their tendency toward poetic expression and symbolism. His manipulation of language, with measured pauses and artful repetitions, produced a sense of reality as well as music and allusion. In some ways, he foretold the Russian Revolution by depicting the isolation of the aristocracy and its inevitable extinction.

Naturalistic Playwrights Émile Zola called for "living characters taken from real life," who spoke everyday language and offered "a material reproduction of life"; he called for playwrights who scientifically analyzed and faithfully reported the social problems of the world with a view to their correction.

Among the most successful playwrights in the Naturalistic style were Gerhart Hauptmann and Maxim Gorky. Hauptmann's *The Weavers* (1892) uses a group protagonist to show the devastation that comes to already impoverished workers when industrialization threatens their way of life. Gorky's *The Lower Depths* (1902), by depicting the seemingly hopeless lives of people living in a flophouse, explores whether religion or political reform offers the best chance for change.

FIGURE 17.11
Anton Chekhov's *The Three Sisters*
In Chekhov's lifetime, the Moscow Art Theatre produced his plays realistically (see Figure 17.7). In this production by Virginia Commonwealth University, the setting is simplified and nonrealistic. The patterned lighting incorporates Impressionism's manipulation of light and shadow for emotive effect.

THIRD WAVE: AVANT-GARDISM, 1890–1950

Although the Realists were themselves innovators, another group reacted against them almost immediately. The split deepened as a trivialized Realism was taken over by the commercial theatre, and Art again dictated that serious people would revolt against both Realism and its commercial adaptation.

But what was wrong with Realism? In essence, the objections to it boiled down to three:

- Realism wasn't *theatrical*. The audience was shut out; a separate world existed beyond the fourth wall, with actors behaving as though the audience wasn't there. It was *too much* like life.
- Realism was dull: The language was mundane, the characters flat, the action—if truly lifelike—boring.
- Third, Realism had to struggle to be significant; if no more was at stake than the fate of one ordinary individual, what was the larger meaning?

These objections to Realism coalesced around a view that Realism was inimical to Art, a view that is one of the bases of the avant-garde ideas called "Modernism" in all the arts. (Significantly, major Realists didn't talk much about Art.) We know Modernism best in painting (Picasso, Cubism) and in

Spotlight

Henrik Ibsen Photo: George T. Tobin, "Henrik Ibsen." The Granger Collection, New York.

Henrik Ibsen's *A Doll's House*, 1879

Ibsen (1808–1906) is often called the father of modern drama. He wrote more than two dozen plays in every major style of the nineteenth century—from Romanticism to symbolism—but his realistic plays like *A Doll's House* are those most often produced today. When he turned exclusively to writing plays in his early forties, he was already an experienced company manager, stage manager, and director.

The Story of the Play

Nora Helmer is a married woman and a mother, but some of her behavior is childlike, and her husband Torvald, a priggish bank manager, treats her as a charming toy (and, implicitly, a sexual toy). When an old friend of Nora's, Mrs. Linde, comes to ask if Torvald can give her a job at the bank, Nora confesses that she is not so childish as she appears: She has "saved Torvald's life" by borrowing money when he was ill to send him to recuperate in Italy. Torvald does not know of the debt, which she has been repaying from her household money, so Torvald thinks she is a spendthrift, as well.

Her creditor is Krogstad, who works at Torvald's bank and is going to be fired; he demands that Nora intercede for him or he will reveal to Torvald not only her borrowing but also the fact that she forged her now-dead father's signature to the note.

Krogstad is fired; his job is to go to Mrs. Linde. He demands again that Nora help him get a better job at the bank; when she cannot, he leaves a letter for Torvald in the letterbox. Nora, recognizing that the truth must come out, believes that Torvald will stand by her, even share the blame; she tells Mrs. Linde that there will be a "miracle." Still, waiting for her husband to find the letter, she becomes more and more frantic and talks of suicide; she dances for her husband a tarentella that becomes wild, manic.

Krogstad and Mrs. Linde meet at Nora's and recognize each other—they are former lovers who now decide to reconcile. Krogstad says he will retrieve the letter, but Mrs. Linde tells him that "this unhappy secret must come out."

After a party, Nora tries to keep Torvald from the letter. Torvald is sexually aroused; he calls her his "most precious possession." He reads the letter and his mood changes: She has "ruined his happiness, threatened his future." They will have to go on living together "for public appearances," but she will not be allowed to raise his children. Nora's "miracle" does not happen.

The maid brings another letter. Torvald reads it and cries, "I am saved!" Krogstad has sent him the forged note to destroy and said he will keep silent.

Nora has become quieter and quieter. Now she sits her husband down at the table and, in a lengthy scene, explains how wronged she has been. "I have been your doll wife, Torvald." Finally, she leaves him and the children—coolly, calmly—telling him that her first duty is to herself. She goes out; Torvald cries out her name, then says that there is still hope—and there is the sound of the house's outer door slamming.

literature (Joyce), but it was also a force in the theatre, where it was believed that the theatre had to be "re-theatricalized," that innovation itself was valuable, and that form or style was as important as content so long as both were *artistic*.

Many modernist attempts followed to retheatricalize the theatre. In one direction, they redefined theatrical space by throwing out the proscenium arch and the picture-frame stage; in another, they threw out the box set and detailed settings, replacing them with varying kinds of stylized or abstract scenery, including settings of ramps, stairs, and levels. Others tried to retheatricalize acting by throwing out "ensemble" and "inner truth" and going for a style that was bigger, more external, more physical and symbolic. None replaced Realism but several modified it.

Reactions against Realism: Four Important *"isms"*

Impressionism (fl. 1890s) was a style that sought to capture fleeting moments of awareness that were believed to constitute the essence of existence. By reproducing these glimpses, art could provide insights into the truth that lay underneath the external world—the opposite of Realism. Probably the playwright who wrote most successfully in the style was Maurice Maeterlinck. In short plays like *The Intruder* (1890), Maeterlinck presented a world far removed from reality. Subjectivity permeates the plays, which are typically moody and mysterious, hinting at a life controlled by unseen and inexplicable forces. The actions seem hazy, distant, out of focus; indeed, in the theatre, the plays were often played behind gauzes (scrims) or clouds of fog, and they moved between patches of light, dark, and shadow. Some of Impressionism's techniques were adopted by Realists like Ibsen (in his later plays), Chekhov, and Tennessee Williams.

Symbolism (fl. 1890s) had two major figures. Adolphe Appia believed that artistic unity was the fundamental goal of theatrical production and that lighting was the element best able to fuse all others into an artistic whole. Like music, light was capable of continual change to reflect shifting

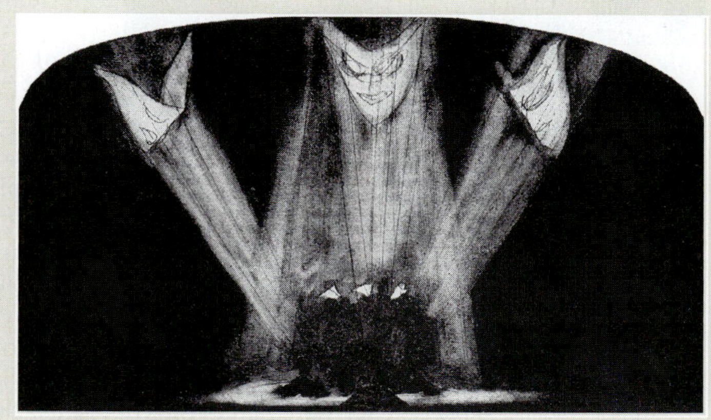

FIGURE 17.12

Shakespeare and Expressionism

This sketch for *Macbeth* (1921) by the American designer Robert Edmond Jones emphasizes the three witches, who hover over the entire production and change shapes as Macbeth moves to his death. Jones was a leader in the New Stagecraft, which was adamantly opposed to stage Realism.

moods and emotions within the play, and light could be orchestrated by variations in its direction, intensity, and color to produce a rhythm to match the dramatic action. Because he found an aesthetic contradiction between the three-dimensional actor and a two-dimensional floor set at right angles to two-dimensional painted scenes, Appia gave the stage floor and scenery mass. He solved the problem in part by devising three-dimensional settings composed of steps, ramps, and platforms, among which the living actor could comfortably move.

Like Appia, Gordon Craig opposed scenic illusion and favored instead a simple visual statement that eliminated inessential details and avoided photographic reproduction. His emphasis was on the manipulation of line and mass to achieve, first, a unity of design and, ultimately, a unity for the total production. Although Craig placed less emphasis on the importance of the actor and the text than Appia, they agreed on the importance of the visual elements of the production. Perhaps it would not be an injustice to designate Appia as the formulator of the theories that Craig later popularized. Appia and Craig influenced the New Stagecraft and then commercial theatrical design.

FIGURE 17.13

Expressionism in Film

The quintessential example of Expressionism is found in the German film *The Cabinet of Doctor Caligari.* Note the nightmarish distortions.

Expressionism (fl. 1910–1930s) usually focused on political and social questions in a stage world close to nightmare. Plays unfolded in a world of bizarre and garish colors, jagged angles, and oddly proportioned objects. Actors moved in mechanical or puppetlike ways and often spoke in disconnected or telegraphic conversations. They bore names of types rather than people: The Mother, The Son, The Cipher. Conventional ideas of time and space collapsed. Ernst Toller, whose best-known work was *Man and the Masses* (1921), was a leading Expressionist.

Expressionism has been influential for three reasons:

- Many of the techniques were adapted and used in film (*The Cabinet of Doctor Caligari*).
- Techniques were adapted by Realistic playwrights, notably Eugene O'Neill and Arthur Miller.
- It was an influence on "epic theatre" (see pp. 279–280).

Constructivism (fl. 1920–1935), the practice of Vsevolod Meyerhold, paralleled that of the German Expressionists. Although early in his career Meyerhold directed experimental works for Stanislavski, during the 1920s he devoted himself to developing a theatrical art suitable for a machine age. He relied on two major techniques: biomechanics and constructivism. **Biomechanics** was a training system and performance style for actors based on an industrial theory of work: They were to be well-trained "machines" for carrying out the assignments given them, and so they needed rigorous physical training in ballet, gymnastics, and circus techniques. Constructivism was a theory of visual art in which scenery did not attempt to represent any particular place but provided a "machine" on which actors could perform. In practice, sets designed for Myerhold were combinations of platforms, steps, ramps, wheels, and trapezes. A goal of both biomechanics and Constructivism was to retheatricalize the theatre.

FIGURE 17.14

The Metamorphosis

If Impressionism resembled a dream, Expressionism resembled a nightmare. Here, in an adaptation of Franz Kafka's short story *The Metamorphosis*, staged by Butler University Theatre, we can see the distortions of a nightmare, although the style seems both constructivist and expressionist.

Brecht and Artaud

Although these styles (*isms*) have influenced today's theatre, the theories and practices of Bertolt Brecht and Antonin Artaud have probably been more influential. These two theorists operated from quite different sets of assumptions about the nature of theatre and the purpose of art, but they shared a disdain for Realism. It may be useful to think of Brecht as developing from Expressionism and Artaud from Impressionism and **Surrealism**. Together, their theories can help account for much experimentation of the 1960s and 1970s.

Bertolt Brecht and Epic Theatre Bertolt Brecht believed that theatre should educate *citizens* (participants in a political system) in how to bring about socially responsible change. He saw theatre as a way of making a controversial topic easier to consider. His commitment to a socially responsive theatre doubtless came,

FIGURE 17.15
Symbolism
Butler University's interpretation of Oscar Wilde's Symbolist play *Salome.* Symbolism was anti-realistic, often erotic, often concerned with pathology.

in part, from his being both Jewish and leftist at a time when Hitler was rising to power in Germany.

Traditional German theatres, whether those of Wagner or Saxe-Meiningen, had sought an illusion that allowed the members of the audience to believe in and identify with the onstage actions. Because Brecht was a Marxist and viewed theatre as an instrument for change, he objected to a theatre that mesmerized its audiences and made them passive. He therefore tried to redefine the relationship between the theatre, its audience, and society. He proposed that if he jarred audiences out of their identification with the action, he would succeed in forcing them to think about what they saw onstage. Brecht sought, therefore, alternately to engage and estrange his audiences, a technique he called *Verfremdungseffekt* (usually translated as the **alienation effect** or, simply, the **A-effect**).

The complex of staging and playwriting used by Brecht came to be called **epic theatre**. "Epic" captured many of the qualities that Brecht prized: the mixing of narrative and dramatic episodes, the telescoping of time and place, and the spanning of years and countries (similar to epic poetry).

Although Brecht was not the first to use either these techniques or the term *epic,* Brecht popularized the term and the practices through his own plays, his theoretical writings (particularly the "Little Organon for the Theatre," 1948), and his productions at the Berliner Ensemble, after 1954 East Germany's most prestigious theatre.

Antonin Artaud and the Theatre of Cruelty Although Antonin Artaud was an actor, director, playwright, poet, and screenwriter, it was as a theorist that he made his greatest impact. *The Theatre and Its Double,* a compilation of Artaud's major essays, was published in France in 1938 but was not translated into English until the late 1950s. Because Artaud believed that important ideas came not from logical reasoning or rational thinking but from intuition, experience, and feelings, he developed his ideas through images and visual metaphors rather than language.

Artaud rejected the primacy of language. He wanted to remove the script from the center of his theatre, for he believed that words and grammar were insufficient carriers of meaning. Truth came instead from spiritual signs whose meaning emerged intuitively and "with enough violence to make useless any translation into logical discursive language." Artaud wished to substitute

Spotlight

Antonin Artaud in a scene from the film *The Passion Of Joan Of Arc.* Photo: Henry Guttmann\Getty Images Inc. Hulton Archive Photos.

Antonin Artaud's *Jet of Blood*

Artaud's *Jet of Blood* is bizarre even by today's standards. With a playing time of less than five minutes, the story (insofar as one exists) unfolds through repetitive, banal dialogue and detailed stage directions that demand startling visual effects, in keeping with Artaud's desire for sight and sound to overpower language in the theatre. *Jet of Blood* with its assault on the senses is a telling example of what would become theatre of cruelty. Young Man and Young Girl begin the play, speaking of love for nine lines. Then comes the first set of stage directions (translation by Ruby Cohn):

> *Silence. There is a noise as if an immense wheel were turning and moving the air. . . . At the same time two Stars are seen colliding and from them fall a series of legs of living flesh with feet, hands, scalps, masks, colonnades, porticos, temples, alembics, falling more and more slowly, as if falling in a vacuum. . . .*

After crying out, "The sky has gone mad," the young man exits with the girl, presumably to have sex. Knight and Wet-Nurse (holding her swollen breasts in her hands) argue about the young couple. They exit and the young man returns, crying out that he has lost the girl. Eight more characters enter. Then more stage directions:

> *At this moment night suddenly falls on stage. The earth quakes. There is furious thunder and zig-zags of lightning in every direction . . . all the characters can be seen running around bumping into each other and falling then getting up and running about like crazy. Then an enormous hand seizes the Bawd by her hair, which bursts into flame and grows huge before our eyes.*
>
> *HUGE VOICE: Bitch, look at your body!*
>
> *The Bawd's body is seen to be absolutely naked and hideous beneath her blouse and skirt which become transparent as glass.*
>
> *BAWD: Leave me alone, God.*
>
> *She bites God in the wrist. An immense spurt of blood lacerates the Stage, and through the biggest flash of lightning the Priest can be seen making the sign of the cross. When the lights go on again all the characters are dead, and their corpses lie all over the ground. Only the Young Man and the Bawd remain. . . . The Bawd falls into the Young Man's arms.*

The now flat-chested wet-nurse returns holding the dead body of the girl, and the young man holds his head in his hands. The wet-nurse lifts her skirt and the young man is transfixed. More stage directions:

> *A multitude of scorpions crawl out from beneath the Wet-Nurse's dress and swarm between her legs. Her vagina swells up, splits. . . . The Young Man and Bawd run off as though lobotomized.*

This next line of the young girl ends the play: "The virgin! Ah that's what he was looking for."

Two questions:

1. How in the world could such a play be staged? (A version of *Jet of Blood* can be seen on YouTube.)
2. Why would theatre and drama scholars spend so much time discussing this play?

FIGURE 17.16
Bertolt Brecht
Although the title in English is *The Good Woman of Setzuan,* Brecht's German title is less gender specific: *The Good Person of Setzuan.* The play includes several decrepit gods and a woman who tries to do good but doesn't necessarily succeed. Brecht despised bourgeois (commercial) theatre and therefore Realism, yet he prized the use of real, already used objects as properties. Everything, he believed, should make a statement.

Jason Ayers

gestures, signs, symbols, rhythms, and sounds. Theatre was intuitive, primitive, magical, and potentially powerful.

Artaud called for a **theatre of cruelty**. To achieve it, he developed a number of techniques seldom used in commercial productions. He wanted to bombard the senses and so experimented with ways of manipulating light and sound. In both, he adopted the abrupt, the discordant, the sudden, the shrill, the garish. Lights changed colors quickly, alternated intensity violently; sound was sudden, often amplified. Scenery was subservient to the other elements of production, with the audience placed in an environment created by actors, lights, sound, and space (Artaud preferred barns and factories to conventional theatres). The actors were encouraged to use their bodies and their voices to provide scenery, sounds, and visual effects and not to be bound by notions of psychological realism and character analysis. Actors were to address the senses of the spectators, not merely their minds.

Artaud's theories, in many forms and with many distortions, were appropriated and applied after 1960 by theatre artists, moviemakers, and especially rock musicians. Whatever one may think of his pronouncements, it is clear that, although long in coming, their acceptance has been widespread.

AVANT-GARDE THEATRES AND MOVEMENTS

The Art Theatre Movement

Reactions to Realism and to commercial theatre came in the form of new kinds of theatres as well as the new kinds of theories and plays just discussed. Just as the

Realists had started the first "independent" theatres, reactions against those very theatres brought about a proliferation of "art" theatres, soon followed by other radical or "experimental" or "little" theatres into the 1960s. Taken as a group, they can be called the avant-garde.

The **art theatre movement** was an after-the-fact term for this very mixed bag, which included these theatres as well as others as different as the Abbey in Dublin, Ireland. The "art" of the art theatres was still partly romantic but existed against the background of a changed culture, that of turn-of-the-century Europe—imperialist, stuffy, class-conscious, money-conscious. It foregrounded a somewhat superficial, sometimes glib, sentimentalized belief in the power of beauty to improve life. That belief was mostly elitist, as were the art theatres.

The art theatre came a bit late to the United States. When it did, it was bound up culturally with several other fashions: the civic pageant, which was also genteel and "artistic"; the first programs in "theatre arts" at colleges and universities; and the New Stagecraft.

The **New Stagecraft** was an avant-garde tendency in stage design that favored simplified, sometimes abstract settings; nonrealism; lighting as a major design com-

FIGURE 17.17

Theatre of Cruelty

Artaud's ideas underlay the theatre of cruelty, especially the production of Peter Weiss's *Marat*/Sade (the short title) as directed by Peter Brook. Its "cruelty" was embodied in both the action and in a threat of assault on the audience by the actors; although fictitious, that threat seemed real enough to break the long-established bond of "safety" for the audience. Here, *Marat/Sade* at the University of South Carolina.

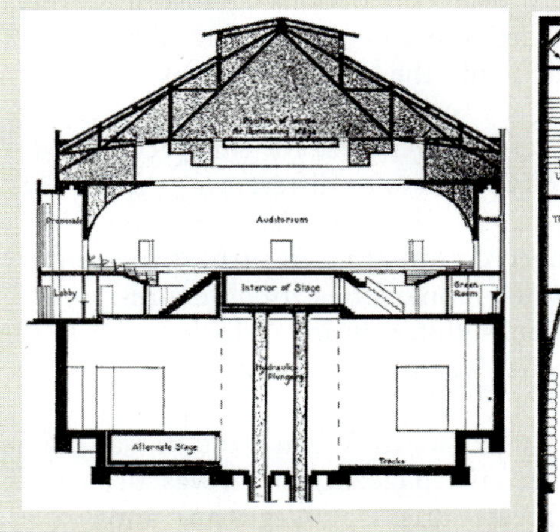

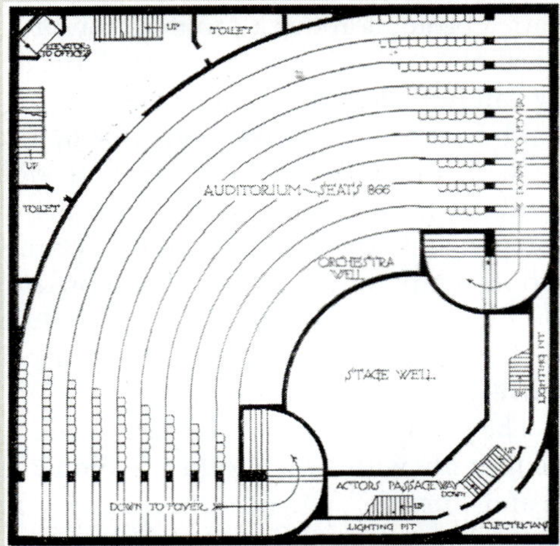

FIGURE 17.18

New Spaces for a New Theatre

Leaders of the New Stagecraft were looking to free American theatre from the realistic, picture-frame staging of the proscenium arch. Norman Bel Geddes here proposed an arena space (left), shown in side view with a full-stage elevator that allowed the entire set to be lowered to the basement for scene shifts. Thrust stages (right), lacking a proscenium arch, placed spectators on three sides of the stage, which jutted out into the audience area.

ponent; and alternatives to the proscenium stage. European in origin and based heavily on the ideas of Appia and Craig, it surfaced in the United States when Sam Hume (a designer who had been working at the Moscow Art Theatre) organized a New Stagecraft exhibition in Boston and New York in 1914–1915. It was, in fact, the future: Designers like Norman Bel Geddes, Robert Edmond Jones, and Lee Simonson made the **New Stagecraft** dominant in American design by 1930.

The first American art theatres arrived more or less with the New Stagecraft; that they soon became known as "little" theatres was significant (that is, they attracted small audiences). The Abbey Theatre's American tour of 1911 seems to have inspired them: The Chicago Little Theatre began in 1912, the Boston Toy Theatre and the Wisconsin Dramatic Society about the same time, and by 1925 there were little theatres "from Maine to California, sophisticated Greenwich Village to the open spaces of Vancouver." Amateur, artistic, and mostly elitist, their most famous example was the Provincetown Players, which had started in a shack in the art colony at Provincetown, Massachusetts, in the summer and moved to New York's Greenwich Village in 1915. The Provincetown Players staged the early plays of Eugene O'Neill and included people as diverse as journalist John Reed and poet Edna St. Vincent Millay; people from it helped found the Theatre Guild (see pp. 308–309).

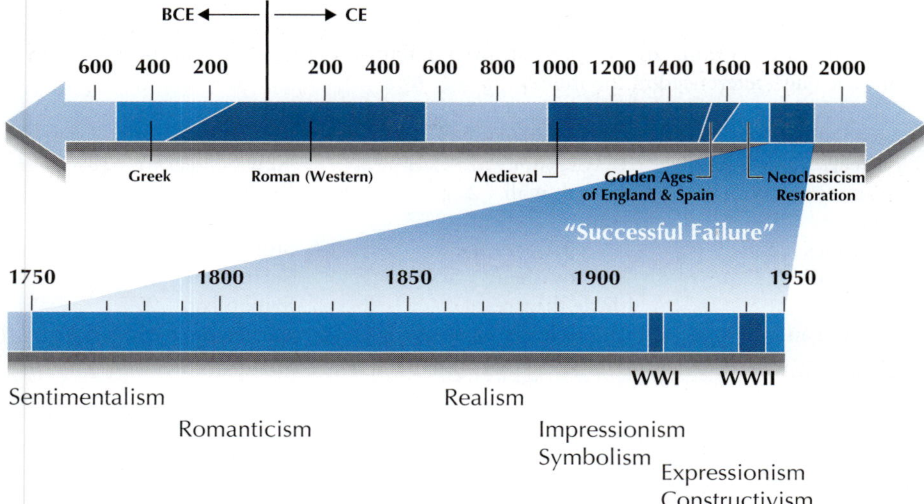

FIGURE 17.19

Timeline—The "*isms*"

Building on the sentimentalism of late Neoclassicism, Romanticism flourished in the early 1800s, giving way to Realism by the late 1800s. Thereafter came a flurry of other "isms," each striving to reposition theatre in its culture.

The **little theatres** became a movement and an influence because they quickly had a voice: Their organ was *Theatre Arts Magazine,* which gave national distribution to their ideas. It described individual theatres and kept readers up on what was going on in Europe and at home. By 1930, however, *Theatre Arts* was turning toward the New York–based commercial theatre for its copy. The little theatres still existed, but many had used up their enthusiasm for art and had become community theatres. Art and Beauty had not proved potent at either paying the bills or solving social problems, and no wonder: They were ideas from before "the War"—World War I—and the cynicism and striving of the 1920s was not congenial to them, nor, in much of the United States, was the provincialism then being lampooned in *The New Yorker.* The Great Depression and the rise of fascism in Europe finished Art and Beauty as ideas with power, not least because those ideas were associated with German culture.

The fading of *Theatre Arts Magazine* marked the death of the little theatre movement but not of avant-gardism in the United States. Much of the same energy went into leftist theatre in the 1930s, but it appeared again after World War II in new forms.

KEY TERMS

Check your understanding against this list. Brief definitions are included in the Glossary; persons are page-referenced in the Index.

alienation effect (A-effect) 280
art theatre movement 283
avant-garde 259
biomechanics 279
box set 267
closet drama 265
Constructivism 279
continental seating 266
epic theatre 280
Expressionism 278
fourth wall 272
Impressionism 277
independent theatre movement 272
little theatre movement 285
master artwork 266
Naturalism 268
New Stagecraft 283
Realism 267
Romanticism 261
Storm and Stress 264
Surrealism 279
Symbolism 277
theatre of cruelty 282

CHAPTER

18

The Rise and Triumph of Commercialism, c. 1750 to the 1950s

OBJECTIVES

When you have completed this chapter, you should be able to:

- Describe the ways in which theatre business reflected changing business practices outside theatre
- List and explain the major traits of melodrama
- Compare romantic and realistic melodrama
- Name some major writers of serious and comic drama from the mid-eighteenth to the mid-twentieth centuries
- Sketch the emergence of American musical theatre and name some of its major plays and practitioners
- Describe the changing theatre buildings and scenic practices during the period
- Trace the major lighting changes during these years

The last chapter covered major attempts to reform the theatre between 1750 and about 1950. This chapter covers exactly the same period but looks at another movement—the rise and triumph of commercialism. Commercialism took place at the same time and showed some of the same characteristics as Romanticism, Realism, and the artistic movements, but without their ideological underpinnings. It came to dominate the theatre, even to be what most people meant by "theatre."

CONTEXT

The years from 1750 to 1950 were the period of commercialization—the triumph of capitalism and the glorification of wealth. "Captains of industry" made fortunes in railroads, steel, oil, textiles, canals, road building, manufacturing, and mass communications. Such fortunes were possible because of industrialization, increasing population, and empire—from the mid-eighteenth century to the mid-twentieth, European nations colonized and then lost South Asia and Africa. New technologies made long-distance transport, mass production, and mass consumption possible. New ideas of business organization and new laws made big business and big fortunes possible, so that Mark Twain called the last decades of the nineteenth century "the Gilded Age."

These same two hundred years saw also the transformation of a large swathe of North America from a sprinkling of French, English, and Spanish colonies to an independent nation that became, after World War II, one of the world's two great powers. Spared the damage from the war that wrecked Europe, the United States became the engine that drove its rebuilding; in the process, the United States became the leader of world capitalism and the commercialization of culture.

The theatre took part in this historical movement. It could not ignore the new working-class audience that poured into cities, or the expanding middle class that occupied new urban developments, or the more distant audiences now reachable by railroad and steamship. Nor could it ignore profits, now possible on a scale never imagined by Shakespeare or Molière. By 1900, American commercial theatre was one of the most successful of all time; therefore, we draw many of our examples from the United States. Many of the trends discussed in this chapter were seen throughout the West.

COMMERCIAL THEATRE

The fully developed **commercial theatre** (i.e., after c. 1860) was one in which profit was the primary goal, with income from ticket sales the principal source. Capitalization came either from individual wealth or from limited companies created for the purpose. The creators of theatre—actors, directors, designers—became salaried employees.

At first glance, it might seem that the theatre had always been commercial, an enterprise to make money by selling tickets. Commercial pressure on theatre, however, was long muted by support from a crown, from aristocrats, from local governments, or from the church. Starting before 1750, however, those subsidies declined and the need to pursue profit increased.

From Actor-Managers to Producers

As these commercial pressures increased, theatres organized themselves differently. Earlier sharing companies that had toured or located in small cities had led perilous lives. When income went down, all the shares went down; collecting capital was difficult; and most sharing companies were lucky if they owned decent costumes, much less scenery or a theatre. To reduce these risks, actors came to prefer salaries to shares, even though this change made them employees rather than part owners. This shift, however, required a changed business organization. In some companies, a leading actor now managed the company (the **actor-manager**), made decisions once made by the group of sharers, and paid the others; in other, somewhat later companies, a director managed (director-managers, ultimately **producers**).

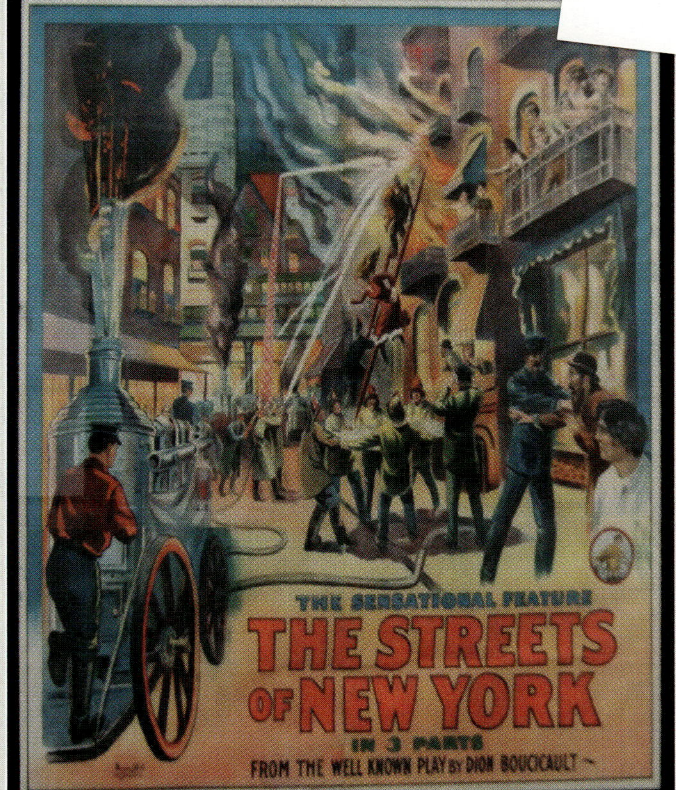

Courtesy of Museum of Modern Art, New York

FIGURE 18.1
Melodrama
This genre dominated the popular theatre of the 1800s and early 1900s and moved seamlessly into movies and then television. Fires were great theatre; so were volcanoes, ships, trains, floods, and disasters of all kinds. Posters such as this for *The Streets of New York* advertised melodramas to the masses.

The Star System

Through the 1700s, theatre companies tended to stay together in one place or in a few places reachable by horse. Changes in technology broke this pattern. By the early 1800s in the United States, for example, actors were playing a circuit of theatres up the Mississippi River from New Orleans, something possible only with steam power. With paved roads and an expanding rail system after the 1840s, national and even international stars could move fairly quickly between cities, where they usually played with resident companies. This **star system** brought William Macready, for example, from London to both U.S. cultural backwaters and Paris, where he introduced Shakespeare to French audiences. However, the star system had the unhappy effect of eroding the quality of the resident actors, who now merely supported the visitor. Stars later began to travel with their own supporting actors and then their own production units; somewhat later still, lesser actors formed combination companies (that is, complete producing units) to travel the nation and the world. Combination companies were common by 1900, and the combination system was then the norm.

The theatre was also affected by the way the rest of society did business. The late nineteenth century saw money and power increasingly concentrated in fewer hands. Monopolies were created as large businesses swallowed small ones, until few rivals remained, marking the age of the robber barons and the great "trusts" in the United States. Bigger business created its own reactions: Working people organized to secure safer conditions, more money, and more power.

Theatrical Syndicate

Theatre was part of all this. Since Shakespeare's day, entrepreneurs had owned theatre buildings; by the 1800s, a businessman might own several theatres in different cities and send companies from one to another, creating a circuit. Toward the end of the nineteenth century, one group in the United States, the Theatrical Syndicate, realized that if they could own all the theatres, they could control all theatre, including ticket pricing and actors' salaries. The syndicate bought buildings, organized the buildings into circuits based on transportation routes, centralized the booking of combination companies in New York (causing actors to have to live there), and created a near-monopoly by the early twentieth century. It effectively ended the tradition of stock or sharing companies. ("Summer stock" was a pale remnant through most of the twentieth century.) Not surprisingly, actors and then other theatrical workers organized. Actors Equity staged its first strike in 1916.

Theatre's increasing commercialization had other consequences. As theatre depended more and more on ticket sales and was managed more and more by businesspeople, profit trumped art, committing the theatre to popular culture because the triumph of profit caused theatre to rely on a mass audience. When, then, movies and later television became the entertainment of choice for that audience, the theatre lost its hold on mass consciousness. By 1950 the theatre was no longer central to either popular or high culture. It existed as a hybrid of the two, essential to neither.

DRAMA IN THE COMMERCIAL THEATRE

Since the mid-eighteenth century, as many as twenty thousand plays have been staged in commercial theatres around the world. Of this number, few have ever been revived. Most of the best plays from the period were first done in subsidized, independent, or art—not commercial—theatres; of the rest, we have to remember that timeliness and subject matter were often more commercially important than quality. This is not to say that plays from the commercial theatre were bad; it is to say that they had their own goals. Above all, commercial plays had to be *accessible*—without signals that would offend a mass audience, including challenge, moral shock, and political innovation (all of which could be found in the plays discussed in Chapter 17).

As will be seen, the dominant dramatic genre of the period was **melodrama**, which was hugely popular but usually trivial; its nineteenth-century type has gone out of fashion and is even found funny now, so it is seldom revived. Comedy has fared better, perhaps because commercial comedy has sometimes not been so closely tied to a moment. Musical theatre, at least as conceived after the mid-twentieth century, has been more durable, and revivals are now staples in London and New York.

FIGURE 18.2
Sentimental Victims
Melodrama thrived on victimization. Here, two stereotypical victims, the mother and the weeping child—in a snowstorm, no less.

Shifts in Drama

Three major cultural changes can be seen as underlying the shifts in drama after 1750.

The Rise of Sentimentality **Sentimentality** is the arousing of feelings out of proportion to their cause—"easy tears." Most often, too, the cause is the situation or type rather than a particular character, calling up a stereotype to which the feelings are already attached—the helpless child, the threatened virgin, the faithful dog. Sentimentality is related to Sentimentalism: Both have strong ideas of good and evil; both believe in love, happiness, and virtue; both use lots of words and overblown language to express themselves. Both emphasize male values that suited the age of commercialism: family, fidelity, loyalty, work, and obedience to superiors. Sentimentalism, however, was a literary idea; sentimentality is a social or personal attitude.

To audiences new to the city, sentimentality was a satisfying response to stereotypes that called up a lost rural life. To the rising middle class, sentimentality allowed for easy tears that cost nothing: A businessman could weep over a hungry child, applaud the happy ending, and then go home and ignore servants who had emigrated from the Irish famine only months before.

Sentimentality became popular with audiences not interested in subtlety. It encouraged identification. It was safe. Usually, it was socially conservative. By contrast, the unsentimental playwright George Bernard Shaw was subtle, alienating (through laughter), unsafe, and socially disruptive. It is no accident that his comedies triumphed by turning sentimentality on its head.

The Shift from the Active to the Acted-On Sentimentalism, unlike earlier drama, was concerned with victims as much as with heroes. Sentimentality found its easiest stereotypes among such victims. The result was a 180-degree turn from heroic drama to what one critic has called "losers' stories." The focus became victimization and the reaction to it instead of heroic effort in the face of opposition—Tennessee Williams's Blanche Dubois, for example (see p. 297). It is worth noting, however, that such victims were usually presented as single cases and were not generalized to cause the audience to think about a real social problem: The rural virgin threatened by the evil young aristocrat was not connected to issues of poverty and exploitation.

The Collapse of Genre With the end of the "rules" of Neoclassicism, the idea of genre started to crumble. Tragedy pretty much ceased to exist except as "closet drama," because the ideas that had defined it had died. Melodrama took its place. Comedy became little more than a play with a happy ending or a funny play with gags. There have, nonetheless, been attempts to revive the old generic distinctions, most of all that of tragedy. Arthur Miller has argued that *Death of a Salesman* is a tragedy, with a common man substituted for the aristocratic tragic hero. Most of all, the question of genre was irrelevant: Midway through the twentieth century, in a mass culture, what was the point of calling up a dramatic theory that hadn't had power for two hundred years?

Kinds of Drama

Shakespeare Revived Romantics revived Shakespeare, finding in his work the breadth and the emotional power they prized. From the 1770s until well after 1900, his plays remained among the most often produced in the world. Playing Shakespeare's tragic roles became the test of an actor. A great Hamlet or a great Juliet was an international star. Lines from the plays were common in everyday speech; the characters were role models: It was Shakespeare, along with the Bible, that gave a changing society connectedness. Attempts to imitate Shakespeare were generally unsuccessful, however; what audiences wanted in new plays was something emotional, prosaic, and spectacular.

Melodrama Melodrama was the most popular dramatic genre of the period. What audiences loved was its exploitation of unquestioned good and evil, with the good always under threat from the evil but triumphing at the end. Almost as important was melodrama's sentimentality. Both the good/evil dichotomy and the sentimentality in which it was enveloped typified a period looking for stability in a time of great change.

That said, what has to be remembered is how enjoyable melodramas were. They were full of energy, whipping from adventure to adventure; they had thrills, emotions, and a good deal of laughter—many of the melodramas were full of comic sequences. Their workmanship was often clumsy, their coincidences transparent, their language overblown—but they gave enormous pleasure.

Music. *Melodrama* means "music drama," a term taken from the widespread use of music within the plays. Melodramas used emotional music (still used in movies and television) to push mood and to announce surprise (loud crash of music) or to build suspense (tense, unsettling music). Music also appeared as **signature music**, the same theme played whenever a certain character entered or left or performed some audience-arousing feat. (The scores later written for silent movies did the same.) A pit orchestra was essential to early melodrama; some melodramas also used vocal songs.

FIGURE 18.3

Stock Types

The villain drove the action of melodrama; the comic man or a natural disaster sometimes frustrated him and saved the hero or heroine for another attempt on them by the villain.

A Simplified Moral Universe. Melodrama presented a simplified moral universe in which good and evil were clear and were embodied by easily recognizable characters. Physical attractiveness typified the hero and heroine (often in love with each other); costume also announced their character types (see, for example, Figure 18.3). Helping the hero was the comic man (and sometimes comic woman), who often saved the hero and frustrated his enemies. It was evil, however, that propelled the action in the person of a villain, also recognizable by costume and physique (older, heavier) and sometimes by social rank—a nobleman or landowner. He initiated the action by threatening the hero or heroine; he or she escaped, often saved by the comic man; and the villain threatened again, and again there was an escape, and so on. The structure was thus episodic, progressing by threat and escape, each more extreme than the last until the final incident, when hero and heroine might move from certain death to happy marriage within minutes. By the end of the romantic period, this action was being played out in three acts rather than the neoclassical five.

Spectacle. Many romantic melodramas also depended on spectacle—fires, explosions, drownings, earthquakes—as threats to the good characters or as obstacles to the villain. Many also featured animals: "equestrian dramas" (horses) and "canine melodramas" (dogs). (Movies such as *Lassie Come Home* and *National Velvet* thus had a long pedigree.) Romantic interest in the sea and the navy during the Napoleonic Wars gave rise to "nautical melodramas." These, and "rustic" (rural) melodramas, "gothic" melodramas (sometimes medieval, often what we would call horror, e.g., *The Vampire*) and others, filled the theatres. After 1850, middle-class theatres increasingly played realistic melodramas, and romantic melodramas increasingly became the fare of the lower-class theatres, but it is important to remember that romantic melodrama persisted right through the period and moved seamlessly into silent movies. The term *Neoromantic* is sometimes used to describe this later use of romantic elements.

FIGURE 18.4

Shakespeare Revived

Here, Ira Aldrich in Shakespeare's *Titus Andronicus.* Although born in the United States, Aldrich had a brilliant career in Europe frequently playing Othello and, in white make up, King Lear, Macbeth, and Shylock.

Realistic Melodrama Realistic melodrama began to appear about 1850. Theoretical Realism would not appear in the avant-garde theatres until the 1870s, but it had precursors that went back to the 1700s. The box set (1830s) was a step toward realistic interiors; photography and improved printing made "real" views of the world familiar. As well, the end of Romanticism and the rise of a practical-minded business class shifted attention from the exotic and the never-never to the familiar and the utilitarian, and particularly to the middle-class drawing room and the issues of money and status (including moral status and "belonging" in society). **Gentlemanly melodrama** became a feature of middle-class theatres. It was less lurid in language and incident than romantic melodrama, its incidents themselves more carefully linked by cause and effect. Less reliant on violent spectacle, it put melodrama into middle-class costume but kept the action of threat and escape—for example, a well-to-do woman threatened with revelation of her shady past—but sometimes extended the single threat and its resolution across the entire play. So common that they became a cliché satirized in Oscar Wilde's *The Importance of Being Earnest* were scenes of the finding of a long-lost child or the reunion of long-separated mothers, brothers, sisters, or children. Such scenes derived from Greek New and Roman comedy; that comic root symbolizes the importance to melodrama of the satisfying ending.

Uncle Tom's Cabin. Most realistic melodramas remained wedded to victims, sentimentality, and social conservatism. Strains of Romanticism persisted in them—big speeches, excessive gestures of self-sacrifice or love. Probably the most important melodrama in the world was *Uncle Tom's Cabin* (first version 1852), based on the novel by Harriet Beecher Stowe. Published before the age of copyright, it was pirated, adapted, and translated without permission wherever there were theatres. The play remained strong through World War I (1914–1918), when more than a dozen companies were still touring it in the United States. Some actors spent their lives touring the play, and *Tomming* was a recognized actors' term. First staged at the pivot between romantic and realistic melodrama, the play included an escape across an ice-clogged river by a runaway slave pursued by dogs; a dead child being carried to heaven by angels; and virtuous Uncle Tom being beaten by the villain, Simon Legree.

Spotlight

A nineteenth century woodcut advertising *Under the Gaslight.*

Augustin Daly's *Under the Gaslight*, 1867

Augustin Daly (1836–1899), playwright, director, critic, and theatrical manager, was one of the most influential figures in American theatre during the last half of the nineteenth century. He wrote or adapted more than ninety plays. *Under the Gaslight* is the quintessential realistic melodrama, a play in five acts in which social status is prominent. The famous railroad scene, in which the comic man is tied to the railroad tracks but rescued by the heroine just before the oncoming locomotive is about to kill him, became a staple in many other realistic melodramas and in many early films.

The Story of the Play

In an upper-class New York drawing room, Laura Courtland, engaged to Ray Stafford, is confronted by the villainous Byke. Laura tells her flighty cousin Pearl to tell Ray the truth that Byke threatens to reveal: Laura is not a real Courtland but an adopted former street child. Ray decides to break off the engagement, writes Laura a letter, then crumples the letter and shoves it into a pocket, saying he loves her. Later, however, at a gathering at swank Delmonico's Restaurant, the letter falls out, and sneering society women read it and banish Laura. This time, Ray fails to stand by her, and she goes, an outcast.

Three months later, Laura is living incognito in a basement with Peachblossom, a street child. Byke and his female accomplice, Old Judas, try to kidnap them but are foiled by Snorkey, a one-armed Civil War veteran who leads Ray to Laura. Ray pleads for a second chance, but Byke and Old Judas return and kidnap the women and then try to get Laura to a New Jersey hideout from a Hudson River pier. Snorkey and a gang of street boys thwart them; Laura is thrown into the river, and Ray dives in after her.

Some time later, at an elegant country house, Ray is now engaged to Pearl. Laura is a reclusive guest, but she flees, still loving Ray. In a nearby woods, Snorkey overhears Byke and Old Judas plotting to murder Laura and rob Pearl. At a railroad, the fleeing Laura is exhausted and arranges to spend the night locked in a signal shed; Snorkey appears, but Byke captures him and puts him, tied, on the railroad track. Laura hacks her way out of the locked shed with an axe and rescues Snorkey just as the train roars by.

Back at the country house, Byke is stealing Pearl's jewels when Laura, Ray, and Snorkey catch him. Byke announces that Pearl, not Laura, is the adopted child thief; Laura is a real Courtland. Peachblossom announces that Old Judas has been killed in an accident. Ray switches his engagement from Pearl back to Laura, and Snorkey is to marry Peachblossom.

Playwrights of Melodrama. Most melodramas, both romantic and realistic, were written by hacks hired by the theatres. Buffalo Bill Cody, for example, toured for years in hack melodramas about the West before he started the Wild West Show. Gentlemanly melodramas, on the other hand, were sometimes written by eminent but now forgotten literary people. An author important to subsequent playwrights was the Irish-American Dion Boucicault, who demanded a percentage of box office receipts instead of a flat fee, thus starting the practice of **royalties**. By 1866, the first international copyright agreement was made, partly because of Boucicault, allowing playwrights to share the spoils of commercialism.

Melodrama After 1900. Melodrama remained a dominant genre into the last third of the twentieth century, although toned down in its excesses of both action and language by Realism. It is still, for example, the genre of soap opera and the suspense thriller, as well as of many plays in which an unquestioned assumption of goodness is threatened by unquestioned badness, with goodness and badness more recently defined not in moral terms but in terms of power—the sensitive loner oppressed by heartless prudery, the AIDS victim oppressed by small-minded fear.

OTHER SERIOUS DRAMA "Great" plays have been rare in commercialism. When important serious plays have been produced in commercial theatres, they often were by playwrights who had made their reputations elsewhere. George Bernard Shaw came out of the independent theatre. Eugene O'Neill, the majority of whose plays were performed at the Provincetown Playhouse and the

FIGURE 18.5

The Most Famous Melodrama in the World

Uncle Tom's Cabin toured the world for generations in various adaptations. Here, it is being played in Paris about 1900. (From *Le Théâtre.*)

Theatre Guild, came late to Broadway. The commercial theatre has generally wanted challenging or "difficult" playwrights to prove that they can win an audience elsewhere before risking money on them.

In the United States, however, two playwrights of real challenge and difficulty appeared in the commercial theatre just before the middle of the twentieth century: Tennessee Williams won the Drama Critics Circle Award for his first major Broadway production, *The Glass Menagerie* (1945), a wistful memory play reminiscent of the impressionists and Chekhov. *A Streetcar Named Desire* (1947) won both the Pulitzer Prize and the Drama Critics Circle Award and established Williams as a major American playwright.

Arthur Miller is, like Williams, a realist of sorts, but whereas Williams's work tended toward the dreamlike and impressionistic, Miller's moved in harsher, more expressionistic ways. *All My Sons* (1947) told of an American businessman who knowingly sold inferior products to the U.S. military in order to turn a profit. In *Death of a Salesman* (1949), realistic scenes are interspersed with scenes remembered by the disordered protagonist, Willy Loman. *Death of a Salesman* won both a Pulitzer Prize and the Drama Critics Circle Award.

COMEDY Perhaps, given the loosening of generic ideas, we ought to speak of "comic plays" rather than "comedy," at least as it used to be understood. "Plays with happy endings" might better define many plays of the period between 1750 and 1950, except that most melodramas had satisfying endings, and so comedy must be understood to include a wide range of plays from farce to nonmelodramas with happy endings and a light tone.

As with serious plays, Shakespeare was a dominant figure. His romantic comedies, with their stellar female roles, offered the nineteenth-century culture female models who were attractive, often witty, virtuous, and ultimately subservient to males—Viola, Rosalind, Isabella, Beatrice, Portia. They became nineteenth-century icons throughout Europe and America.

Sheridan and Goldsmith. Early comic plays, created in either monopoly theatres or theatres in transition to commercialism, partook of the older sentimental comedy but often made gentle fun of Sentimentalism itself. They kept the five-act structure of Neoclassicism, even some of the character types and stock scenes of Restoration comedy, but their characters were mostly less aristocratic and their concerns more middle class. In England the leading comic authors before 1800 were Richard Brinsley Sheridan (*The School for Scandal*) and Oliver Goldsmith (*She Stoops to Conquer*). Both are still revived.

France and the Well-Made Play. The most popular comic playwright in Europe and America before 1850, however, was Eugène Scribe, who created more than three hundred plays for Parisian theatres, including the Comédie Française (after *Hernani* had made a place for romantic drama there). Their translation and international production made French comedy a model for the world. Scribe's technique—for example, careful preparation, meticulous networks of relationships, apparent chains of cause and effect—gave the impression of tight causality when,

Spotlight

A production of *A Streetcar Named Desire* at South Carolina State University.

Tennessee Williams's *A Streetcar Named Desire*, 1947

One of Tennessee Williams's twenty-five full-length plays, *A Streetcar Named Desire* is the realistic, domestic drama that cemented his stature as a great American dramatist. *Streetcar* portrays a universe shot through with violence: the descent into insanity, sexual and emotional abuse, suicide, torn families, and homophobia. There are also significant expressionistic devices in *Streetcar*: the use of polka music as well as jungle sounds that only Blanche seems to hear. There is even a strange crone who appears periodically hawking flowers for funerals, wailing, "*Flores por la mortes.*"

The Story of the Play

Blanche Dubois arrives at her sister Stella's apartment in a New Orleans slum, having come because she has nowhere else to live: She is trying to find a safe haven. Blanche is outwardly a southern belle, ridiculously genteel; within, she is a wounded sufferer—of alcoholism, of loneliness, of despair. She is appalled by Stella's surroundings and by her husband, Stanley Kowalski, whom she calls "common."

Stanley, however, is much more than common. He is a patriarch (Stella is pregnant); he is also a materialist, a Philistine, and a brutal realist. He sees, correctly, that Blanche threatens his relationship with Stella (a mutually powerful sexual one) and his "possession" of Stella.

Stanley's friend Mitch is attracted to Blanche, and Blanche sees in him a last chance to find a protected place for herself. She and Mitch seem headed toward marriage, but Stanley tells Mitch what he has learned from other men about Blanche's past: that she was fired from a teaching job because she seduced a seventeen-year-old; that she was notorious for one-night stands in cheap hotels. Blanche tells Stella more truths about herself: that she nursed their mother through the horrors of a lingering death; that she lost the family home, Belle Reve, because she had no money; that the "sensitive young man" she has often talked about so romantically was in fact her husband, whom she found in bed with another man and who, when she said he disgusted her, killed himself.

Mitch fails to appear for a date; he has abandoned her because of what Stanley told him. Stanley buys Blanche a bus ticket out of town. Then, when Stella is in the hospital having the baby, Stanley rapes Blanche (the extent of her acceptance a matter of performance).

Some time later, Stella is home again. Blanche is disoriented, hallucinating that an old boyfriend is coming to save her. Instead, a doctor and nurse called by Stella come to take her to a mental institution. She goes on the doctor's arm, murmuring, "I have always depended on the kindness of strangers."

in fact, the plays were built around multiple lines of action that touched mostly by chance or coincidence. The expression the **well-made play** was applied to these techniques, first as a compliment and later (twentieth century) as a term of contempt. Nonetheless, it worked brilliantly for Scribe's audiences and served as an example to writers such as Ibsen. In a few plays, Scribe used these techniques to touch on contemporary problems, reviving the term *problem play*. Problem plays, although technically comedies, at least acknowledged contemporary social flaws; their resolutions, however, avoided suggesting how society could correct itself. (Ibsen's *A Doll's House* is, at base, a problem play, but its ending, in which a wife leaves her domineering husband and her children, slamming the door on them with "a sound heard all over Europe," could never be found in Scribe: It is too socially revolutionary.) Scribe could also write witty dramatic prose and sparkling farce.

England. In England, Oscar Wilde wrote perhaps the best, and still the most often revived, light comedy since the Restoration, *The Importance of Being Earnest,* an apparently frivolous look at upper-class mores and duplicity. George Bernard Shaw then dominated European and American comedy until the 1930s. A realist and a socialist, Shaw was paradoxically both the best comic playwright of the period and the most serious one as well, his plays full of verbal fireworks and the collision of real ideas—poverty, industrialism, war, nationalism—although their subjects were ostensibly the old ones of love, marriage, and money. Noel Coward continued verbal, elitist English comedy of wit through World War II. The three playwrights continue to be widely revived around the world.

The United States. In the United States, George S. Kaufman and Moss Hart created off-beat characters and a more democratic approach to comedy, but they remained socially conservative and somewhat sentimental. They wrote large-cast plays that commercial Broadway could afford even in the Great Depression. However, as costs rose, casts shrank, and smaller casts became the rule.

MUSICAL THEATRE Music has always been part of the theatre; as we have seen, it was a major component of melodrama. Various kinds of "ballad opera" marked the pre-Romantic period (e.g., Gay's *The Beggar's Opera*). By the early nineteenth century, *operetta* (romantic, story-based play with music) was popular in Paris; in London the works of William S. Gilbert and Arthur Sullivan (*The Pirates of Penzance*) dominated British musical theatre in the last quarter of the nineteenth century. In working-class areas, music halls grew out of public houses (saloons), and *music hall* became a term for lower-class musical variety, which included a master of ceremonies, songs, comedians, and dancers. In the United States, the similar vaudeville and burlesque were established during the first half of the nineteenth century. Burlesque, originally a comic form for mixed audiences (e.g., *Po-Co-Hon-Tas,* a send-up of a fashionable play about Native Americans) became overwhelmingly a male entertainment after Lydia Thompson's "British Blondes" toured America in 1869. Thereafter, burlesque featured spectacle, song, dance, and female bodies. Striptease was added after World War I, pushing burlesque to the outskirts of respectability. Vaudeville, on the other hand, flourished as a family entertainment and served as an example and a recruiting league for the Broadway *revue,* a nonstory mix of comedy, music, and dance with opulent spectacle and lots of more or less clothed female bodies (e.g., the many *Ziegfeld Follies*). Many of the stars of vaudeville moved to radio and the movies in the 1930s when vaudeville itself died, done in by movies and the Depression.

Musical theatre in the United States, however, took another direction. Incorporating songs and dance into story in new ways, it became the outstanding theatrical export of a nation that itself was coming to dominate the world with its popular culture.

The American Musical. As a distinctly American musical form developed after about 1900, the American musical separated itself from European operetta on the one hand and the musical revue on the other. From its beginnings, nonetheless, it had a double appeal in music and spectacle; the latter was often the female body, gorgeously costumed, often dancing—the "chorus girl."

Composers. Most of the top Broadway composers of the first half of the twentieth century wrote for operetta or revue (or both) even while (perhaps unconsciously) helping to create the new, story-based, integrated form that became American musical comedy. They worked with *lyricists* (writers of words to songs) and *librettists* (writers of the play or "book"). These composers and some of their works included:

- Victor Herbert (1859–1924), *Babes in Toyland,* 1903; *The Red Mill,* 1905; *Naughty Marietta,* 1910 (operettas)
- Jerome Kern (1885–1945), *Oh, Boy!,* 1917; *Sally,* 1920; *Show Boat,* 1927
- Sigmund Romberg (1887–1951), *Blossom Time,* 1921; *The Student Prince,* 1924; *The Desert Song,* 1926
- Irving Berlin (1888–1989), *Music Box Revue,* 1921; *Annie Get Your Gun,* 1946; *Call Me Madam,* 1950
- Cole Porter (1891–1964), *Anything Goes,* 1934; *Red, Hot and Blue!,* 1936; *Kiss Me, Kate,* 1948
- George Gershwin (1898–1937), *Lady, Be Good,* 1924; *Strike Up the Band,* 1930; *Of Thee I Sing,* 1931 (first Pulitzer Prize for a musical); *Porgy and Bess,* 1935
- Richard Rodgers (1902–1979), *Garrick Gaieties,* 1925, 1926; *On Your Toes,* 1936; *Pal Joey,* 1940; *Oklahoma!,* 1943; *Carousel,* 1945; *The Sound of Music,* 1959

Neither these composers' backgrounds nor their music was entirely "American," however. Herbert was born in Ireland, Romberg in Hungary, and Berlin in Russia. Their musical training was often European and classical, not American and popular—Gershwin with a private teacher; Romberg and Herbert in Europe; Kern at the New York College of Music and in Europe; Porter at Yale and Harvard. What distinguished their music as the century progressed, however, was the adoption of the rhythms of popular dance music. Such music had its roots in nineteenth-century black musical forms that, by 1900, had their own

FIGURE 18.6

Irving Berlin's *Annie Get Your Gun*

Irving Berlin wrote both music and lyrics for Broadway's 1946 hit *Annie Get Your Gun.* The show includes the song *There's No Business Like Show Business.* Here, a production by the Nevada Conservatory Theatre, Las Vegas.

literature and their own artists and that were known throughout the United States. Probably popularized in theatrical types that were themselves patronizing to blacks (e.g., the minstrel show, blackface vaudeville acts, "coon singing"), this music—cakewalk, ragtime—was already in the American grain by the time the American musical was ready to begin its evolution. Over the next half-century, jazz, blues, and then rock were also welcomed. Such music's creators, however, were not adequately credited, and black composers rarely made it to Broadway. (Exceptions included Will Marion Cook and Eubie Blake.)

This new American music was sung by new American characters. The characters of operetta had been stock European figures, usually with upper-class backgrounds (Romberg's *Student Prince* is typical); the characters of the new musical were untitled—although sometimes rich—and American.

Lyricists. Essential to such change were the lyricists who wrote the words to the songs and, sometimes, the scripts of the musicals. With increasing frequency, the top composers were associated with the same lyricists in musical after musical, and the lyricists clearly shaped the tone and often the style of the music. In no composer is this clearer than Richard Rodgers. Until 1940 his lyricist was the witty and inventive Lorenz Hart, and their musicals show Hart's unsentimental mind (*Pal Joey*). Rodgers later connected with Oscar Hammerstein II, and the musicals became more romantic, sometimes saccharine—*The Sound of Music,* for example. Hammerstein had had much the same effect on Jerome Kern, with

FIGURE 18.7
America's Early Theatre
The Walnut Street Theatre, Philadelphia, opened in 1809 and claims to be the oldest continuously operating theatre in the United States. Here, an exterior view of about 1820. Many of America's most important actors appeared on its stage over the years.

whom he collaborated after 1925; the result was *Show Boat,* a more serious and sentimental musical than Kern's earlier work with others. George Gershwin, on the other hand, worked throughout his career with his brother Ira. Cole Porter wrote his own lyrics.

Melody and Song. Both the operetta and the revue faded after the 1920s; the "book musical" (drama with music, but not operetta, first seen in the second decade of the twentieth century) took their place. Still usually frivolous and with songs often more stuck in than developed from the action, such musicals were meant as entertainments whose scripts were excuses for glorious melody. As a result, they produced many of the great songs of the American theatre. Jerome Kern, for example, poured out beautiful melodies seemingly endlessly; George Gershwin, in his short life, wrote many songs that became standards. What is perhaps most significant about these composers is that they were primarily *song*writers. Many of them wrote songs on order for a moment in a script ("song cue here!")—love songs, novelty songs, southern songs, patter songs, "showstoppers." These songs became part of the national cultural life at a time when many middle-class homes had a piano, and sheet music was sold at the five-and-dime. Songs were detached from the musicals and popularized via sheet music and radio, and they were sung and played in nightclubs and supper clubs—and in homes.

The Integrated Musical. Only gradually did a more serious dramatic purpose appear, foreshadowed in *Show Boat,* fully realized in *Pal Joey* and *Oklahoma!* The movement thereafter—that is, after 1940—was toward a serious comedy with a happy ending, usually centered on romantic love, mostly dealing with contemporary people, and having song arising from character and moving the plot along (hence **integrated musical**).

Gender and Race. It should be noted that all the composers and lyricists named above were white men; so were most musical producers and directors. (A few white women—Dorothy Fields, Betty Comden—were notable lyricists; Mary Rodgers was a composer.) Many of the composers and lyricists were also European immigrants or children of immigrants; most revered European culture but were caught up in American commercial culture. Their assumptions were reflected in the musicals, which, until at least the 1970s, were mostly about a white America obsessed with romantic love and material success. The "glorification of the American girl" was a very white male undertaking.

Mostly invisible but essential to the music were black musicians of both sexes. Although individual white composers often acknowledged a debt to African American music, the industry did not, and some black musicians resented such co-optings as Gershwin's *Porgy and Bess,* a white's version of southern black life, using the white's version of black music. Yet Gershwin's work is now an American classic, and one that has provided great roles for black musical performers.

THEATRES AND PRODUCTION PRACTICES

As we have seen, the most important factor in the development of commercial theatre was demographic: a larger and larger potential audience as cities grew and population increased. In the nineteenth century, theatre became the most popular public art in Europe and America, at least equal to contemporary movies or television. Satisfying this huge audience changed theatre buildings, scenery, acting, and costumes. The number and capacity of theatres increased; so did the size and complexity of stages and support areas. (The forestage, however, shrank.) At the same time, detail in scenery, costumes, and acting increased as a result of the shift from language as the core theatrical experience to a greater emphasis on scenic spectacle.

The eighteenth-century division between "legitimate" (monopoly) and "illegitimate" (proto-commercial fair and boulevard) theatre became a more complex segmentation by class and by taste within commercialism itself. By the late 1800s, cities had become enormous and public transport was needed to get from one part to another, deepening the divide between middle-class and working-class theatres. At the same time, the economic thrust toward profiteering and monopoly made producers and theatre owners the new masters of the theatre, able (briefly, as it turned out) to dictate what would be played and who would play it, and centralizing the theatre nationally while maintaining far-flung circuits.

Physical Theatre

With Romanticism, theatres had begun to expand and multiply as early as the late eighteenth century. London's Covent Garden Theatre, for example, doubled its capacity between 1730 and 1793. The first Chestnut Street Theatre in

Philadelphia (1794) seated 1,200 but was quickly enlarged to 2,000. More than thirty theatres were built in Germany from 1775 to 1800, thirty-five more by 1850.

The standard configuration remained box, pit, and gallery until almost the end of the nineteenth century. However, as seeing the play became dominant in the romantic age of spectacle, the audience was banned from the stage and the best seats shifted from boxes to the orchestra (the old pit). As Romanticism gave way to Realism, however, theatres tended to become more intimate, with continental seating and well-defined proscenium stages without forestages. Smaller theatres for realistic plays had relatively simple scene-shifting facilities, but those designed for spectacle had advances made possible by new technology—elevator stages and powered turntables.

Overall, these physical changes after 1750 were democratizing ones, removing a favored elite from the stage, bringing the best seats down among the audience, adopting Wagner's model of a theatre where all seats were equally good. At the same time, much of what was staged in the romantic period was less verbal and more visual, muting the old upper-class reliance on language as a mark of class. However, as theatres themselves stratified socially, the lower-class ones moved still further away from language—music hall, variety, vaudeville, and burlesque—and the now middle-class ones in places such as London's West End and New York's Broadway tended toward a drama that relied on language, albeit in prose instead of poetry. New theatres built for Realism were more intimate, again built for hearing as much as for seeing.

Production and Performance Practices

In 1750, scenery comprised wings, drops (painted fabric hung from overhead to the stage floor), borders, and ground rows (low, freestanding flats on the stage floor), the whole arrangement called **wing-and-drop scenery**. It adapted well to Romanticism, with the edges of wings, borders, and ground rows cut into the shapes of leaves, branches, and other natural objects; wings set at angles and sometimes set asymmetrically; and drops giving distant landscape and sky or imitations of walls, room interiors, and such things as caves. Three-dimensional details were added only where so-called *practicables* were needed—a bridge that actors actually crossed, for example. Increasingly after 1750, scenery and special effects were governed by the desire to represent reality pictorially; hence the term *pictorial illusionism*. Increasingly, too, the level of detail was raised to particularize settings (not simply "a room in a palace" but a particular room in a particular building). Historical and geographical detail were also added; by 1850, even in the United States (which lagged behind Europe), historical accuracy in costumes and sets was so popular that a term, **antiquarianism**, was used for it. By the 1880s, antiquarianism had become so entrenched that productions of Shakespeare sought to reproduce the real Juliet's tomb for *Romeo and Juliet*, the real Ardennes forest in France for the Forest of Arden in *As You Like It*. Costumes for such productions were copied from period paintings and museum collections.

FIGURE 18.8

Theatrical Properties

An auction of theatrical properties in a caricature of 1821 shows things for use on stage. Note masks, a skull, a miniature balloon, and so on.

With the emergence of Realism in the commercial theatre, scenery became still more three-dimensional and detailed—a literal copy of a restaurant, for example. By 1900, as well, audiences often sat in darkened auditoria, following Wagner's model, increasing their attention to the stage and increasing the sense of a stage "picture" framed by the proscenium. The now unused forestage shrank to a narrow "apron."

Lighting Eighteenth-century lighting was still done by candles or oil lamps. Various attempts to improve it with lenses and such things as liquid-filled bottles didn't work; the principal lighting was from candelabra hung over the stage. They lighted only certain areas, however, and then not well, probably causing actors and designers to use contrasting makeup and bright or glittery costumes; candelabra also inhibited the use of overhead scenery. After 1830, lighting in big, urban theatres was often done with gas, the audience area lighted by enormous central clusters of gaslights that generated so much moisture as a by-product that a fog could develop near the ceiling. Gas and, later, limelight (a chemical caused to incandesce by heat) allowed for crude spotlighting, with other principal lighting from footlights along the front of the stage and border lights overhead.

About 1880 the first electric lights appeared in theatres (the first all-electric theatre was the Savoy in London, home of Gilbert and Sullivan). Electricity made the artistic manipulation of light finally possible, and it extended the life of theatre buildings by reducing the risk of fire that had plagued theatres until then. Electric control also coincided with the darkening of the house, changing the visual relationship between audience and performance.

Actors and Acting Commercial theatregoers loved great acting as much as they loved spectacle and sentimental schlock. Steam, gas, and then electric power made national and then international stardom possible: Stars had their names and pictures in publications read by thousands, thanks to steam-powered printing machines.

Stars became identified with a role they played again and again: England's Henry Irving played a now-forgotten melodrama, *The Bells,* for thirty-four years; Eugene O'Neill's father, James, was identified with the role of the Count of Monte Cristo all his life; Joe Jefferson was identified with Rip Van Winkle. Such stars could become rich; it is said that Sarah Bernhardt had an income equal to that of her nation's prime minister.

Perhaps because of its enthusiasm for individuality and "genius," Romanticism also produced oddities—child stars who played adult roles, female stars who played men's (so-called breeches) roles. More important, Romanticism created a space and then an appetite for spectacular acting. Edmund Kean started a new age when he appeared in London in 1814, abandoning dignity and control in favor of flamboyance and passion. To see Kean act was to "read Shakespeare by flashes of lightning," a contemporary said. Romantic acting was thereafter marked by passionate outbursts and novel interpretations. In melodrama, different levels of passion were seen, and, just as there were blood-and-thunder melodramas and gentlemanly melodramas, so, too, there were blood-and-thunder theatres (the Bowery in New York in the 1840s) and more genteel theatres (New York's Park Theatre), and actors to suit each. Great actors moved across these extremes: Charlotte Cushman played both the Bowery and the Park, chilling audiences at the first with the death of Nancy Sykes in an adaptation of Dickens's *Oliver Twist* and charming them at the Park in ladylike roles. Probably the greatest American actor of the nineteenth century, she played Romeo, a crazed Scottish witch, a bloodcurdling English avenger, and most of the female roles of Shakespeare—all to raves.

FIGURE 18.9

Stage Practices

A comic glimpse into theatrical practices of the 1820s: note the shield for the footlights, the proscenium door, and the lighting fixture in the auditorium. Here, an interrupted performance of *Macbeth* when the balcony collapsed.

The acting style was very vocal, highly gestural, and not often tied to what we would now call motivation and objective. The emphasis on language—big speeches, flowery vocabulary—moved actors toward vocalism. An emphasis on physical illustration of big moments moved them toward gesture—"physicalization," but not in a way bound by close imitation of life. Many melodramas, for example, included in their stage directions what gesture the actor was to use ("recoils in horror"), and many also ended a big scene or act with the word *tableau,* a posed group picture that was to be held to make the maximum impact on the audience. Such posing and holding had no motivation; it was a purely aesthetic device, unconnected to character.

Subsequent acting, however, moved toward Realism as such plays as the comedies of Scribe provided contemporary roles with less flamboyance. Even later, Realism required a still less formal style. In the United States, this style took over an earlier one called *local color acting,* that is, the playing of rural types with identifiable accents and distinctive, often cute, quirks. However, a truly realistic acting style did not reach the American commercial theatre until at least the 1930s.

THE DECLINE OF COMMERCIAL THEATRE

Shortly after 1900, the theatre was faced with commercial competition of a kind it had never known—the movies. *Birth of a Nation,* the first feature-length film (1915), was a sensation and a box office hit. Sound came in 1927. By the late 1930s, *Gone with the Wind* was on the way to grossing more than $70 million; vaudeville stars were moving to another new medium, radio; and theatres across the United States were closing or turning into movie houses. Television became a commercial reality in the United States in 1948. These new rivals ravaged the American theatrical circuits and the "road," ending vaudeville and burlesque, and driving the last nails into the coffins of stock companies.

The effect on Broadway was also severe and drawn out. At the end of World War I (1918), Broadway saw two to three hundred productions a year. Costs were reasonable (as little as $2,000 for a small show, rarely more than $10,000). Ticket prices were low—$3 bought the best seat in the house. Tourists and New Yorkers flocked to the theatres.

By the end of the 1930s, however, the vigorous commercial theatre of the 1920s was in trouble. Despite occasional bright spots, Broadway's commercial theatre continued to decline through World War II and beyond. Increasingly, New York theatres were abandoned, torn down, or converted to movie houses or "girlie shows." Many others were dark (closed) as often as they were open.

Several other causes may be given for this decline. The Depression (1930s) hit theatre hard. Theatrical unions grew strong enough to demand higher wages—from a theatre less able to pay them. After World War II, the price of land in Manhattan soared, making theatre buildings extremely expensive to rent or buy. Fire regulations grew more strict, and the cost of remodeling a building to meet the new codes went up. As the cost of producing plays escalated, so did ticket prices; therefore, some former patrons found themselves priced out of the theatre. Clearly, the commercial theatre was in trouble, and its death was regularly—if inaccurately—predicted. It survived, but its glory days lay back before 1900 when theatre was the primary source of popular entertainment.

FIGURE 18.10

The New Rival—Film

Short movies became popular early in the twentieth century, but in 1915, D. W. Griffith released his feature-length *The Birth of a Nation*. Movies drained the mass audience out of the theatres, ending stock companies, vaudeville, and most of the road. This is a still from *The Birth of a Nation*, the assassination of Lincoln in Ford's Theatre, from the souvenir program of 1915. The lavish souvenir program suggests how important this premiere was.

RESPONSES TO COMMERCIAL THEATRE

We saw in Chapter 17 that reformers founded little and art theatres, which sought small and elite audiences. However, the triumph of commercialism also spawned attempts to create noncommercial theatres that rivaled the commercial in size and production values. In many cases, these involved government subsidy and pointed toward the foundation of a national theatre in the cultural capital.

The Theatre Guild

The United States has developed no national theatre in either the political (Washington) or the cultural (New York) capital. Instead, some organizations have made more modest efforts to offer productions not limited by a need for maximum profit. The first was the Theatre Guild in the 1920s, which supported works by American playwrights dealing with serious artistic or political issues (e.g., Eugene O'Neill) and serious (and, at the time, still controversial) foreign playwrights such as Ibsen and Shaw. Its early success almost persuaded Broadway that a commercial-sized audience existed for serious drama. By the Depression, however, the Guild was losing ground; as its own finances became precarious, it moved toward commercial practice. By the 1940s, the Theatre Guild was almost indistinguishable from the Broadway producers against whom it had originally rebelled.

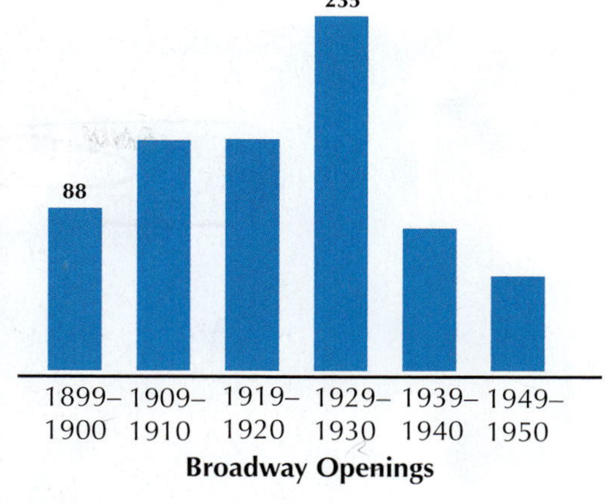

FIGURE 18.11

Changes in Commercial Theatre, 1900–1950

The number of Broadway openings has fallen since 1900. Data from *Variety*.

The Group Theatre

In the 1930s, another new organization, the Group Theatre, was at first a militant voice for non- or anti-commercial theatre in New York, driven by a strong leftist slant. Its repertory focused on social issues, especially poverty and oppression. Perhaps more important was its popularizing of an Americanized version of Stanislavski's acting techniques (the American Method), which became the American realistic style and dominates American stage and film. The Group Theatre also popularized a design style now called Simplified or Selective Realism. Financial and political problems ended the Group Theatre during World War II.

The Federal Theatre Project

Launched in 1935, the Federal Theatre Project (FTP) was a program of the federal government aimed at aiding theatre artists who had been thrown out of work by the Depression. Part of the program's excitement came from its national character (units were established in almost every state); part came from its commitment to cultural diversity (there were, for example, both Jewish and black theatre companies); and part came from its innovative artistic practices. In New York, for example, the first *living newspaper* in the United States premiered. A kind of staged documentary, living newspapers soon spread throughout the country, dramatizing society's most pressing problems: housing, farm policies, venereal disease, war. During an anticommunist government probe, however, living newspapers were denounced as communist plots. In 1939, the government failed to appropriate money for the FTP, and so ended the nation's first far-reaching experiment in support of the arts. Before its demise, however, the FTP introduced a number of major new artists and theatres, among them Orson Welles.

National Archives of the United States

FIGURE 18.12
The Theatre Guild: Classics with Important Actors
Shakespeare's *Othello* with Paul Robeson and Uta Hagen. Robeson was an international star as singer and actor. Hagan became one of the most important acting teachers in the United States.

Regional Theatre

The regional theatre movement is usually dated from 1947, when Margo Jones opened a professional theatre in Dallas, Texas. Her goal was not only to decentralize the theatre (to bring professional productions to the heartland of the United States) but also to encourage the production of original and classic plays. She nurtured the talent of Tennessee Williams, for example. Before Jones's death in 1955, there were professional theatres in Washington, D.C.; Houston, Texas; and Milwaukee, Wisconsin.

KEY TERMS

Check your understanding against this list. Brief definitions are included in the Glossary; persons are page-referenced in the Index.

actor-manager 289
antiquarianism 304
commercial theatre 288
gentlemanly melodrama 294
integrated musical 303
melodrama 291
producers 289
royalties 296
sentimentality 291
signature music 293
star system 289
well-made play 299
wing-and-drop scenery 304

CHAPTER

19

Eclectic Theatre, c. 1950–c. 2000

OBJECTIVES

When you have completed this chapter, you should be able to:

- Discuss how modernism and postmodernism differ
- Discuss the history of commercial and not-for-profit theatre of this period
- Identify and discuss the principal noncommercial trends of this period
- Identify and discuss three political theatre movements of this period
- Define and discuss Absurdism
- Identify and discuss two avant-garde theatres of this period

CONTEXT

A false and short-lived sense of stability came to America after World War II, represented (wrongly) by television shows like "Father Knows Best" and a brief focus on what at the time was called conformity (*The Organization Man*). At the same moment, Europe and much of the East were struggling with ruined cities, lack of food, and social upheaval. By 1950, the United States and the Soviet Union were enemies; Europe was divided by the "Iron Curtain," and small nations around the globe were being made pawns in the new United States–Soviet conflict; and the old colonial empires of Europe were unraveling. The United States went to war in Korea in 1950 as part of that conflict, and again at the beginning of the 1960s in Vietnam—a war that would tear the nation apart and end the idea of stability. That idea of stability, so essential to the nineteenth century, had become the victim of two upheavals—one, World War II itself and its effects; the other, changes in science, technology, and mass communications. These affected even the ideas of art, bringing an end to modernism and initiating so-called postmodernism (see below).

Societal Changes

Thousands of American soldiers, most overseas for the first time, brought back new ideas and expectations from World War II. The GI Bill allowed thousands of (mostly) men to enter college for the first time. Thousands of black soldiers returned to the United States changed by their experience, for they had lived and fought in a Europe where Jim Crow did not exist. American women who had worked in factories and offices during the war and who had experienced financial and social independence could see for themselves the possibilities of lives beyond the suburban front door.

Seemingly suddenly, as well, popular culture, represented by a pounding music derived from mostly hidden black sources, changed America, and the European icons that had so long dominated were replaced. History itself fell off the charts as a way of knowing. By the 1970s, the common coin was not Shakespeare and the Bible and the European canon, but television and advertising and rock 'n' roll and then hip-hop. Art, the secular religion that was once going to save humanity, lost all definition and crumbled into Andy Warhol's "Art is whatever you can get away with."

Technological Changes

Television, computers, and the Internet brought other revolutions. By the late 1950s, television sets were commonplace in American homes and became a binding social force as households watched favorite programs on three major networks. Personal computers appeared in the 1970s and were essential by the late 1990s. The Internet, widely accessible by the early 1990s, changed the ways and the speed with which people got news, music, personal messages, and entertainment.

Changed forever were people's quantity of information and quantity of points of access, making it possible for everybody to be in touch from home, from a car, from the street. The results have been, first, self-definition by ethnic, political, religious, sexual, and social groups whose members had before not been able to find one another; and, second, a shift from "engagement" or direct individual experience to observation, or the life of the couch potato—virtual experience. Electronic communications thus "democratized" institutions by making it difficult to hide information or to ignore constituencies; they gave power to any individual with a computer. This surfacing of previously hidden identities and invisible individuals arguably created a furor over "political correctness," an outward sign of an increasingly democratic society—that is, one in which everybody has a voice.

As well, the new technologies increased the speed of communication and wiped out distance. The idea of a center from which "truth" would radiate, essential to the old order of things, crumbled. Unpredictably, one of the effects was the greatly speeded-up life cycle of the avant-garde: If people could know instantly what was new and shocking, it ceased to be new and shocking.

A computer-driven movement toward substitute or virtual experience was marked by, paradoxically, an interest in "interactivity" and a substitute reality more "real" than Realism. Interactivity gave individuals at last the illusion of control over subject matter (e.g., computer games, computerized narrative) and led, for example, to more interaction between audiences and performers. Substitute reality led to a perhaps temporary enthusiasm for "reality TV," shows that seemed unscripted, performed by people without actor training (although close examination suggests that many such shows were, in fact, carefully scripted and their performers very self-aware). Both of these tendencies changed the idea of theatre and its practice.

Scientific Changes and Popular Worldview

Postmodernism is a crude term for another set of changes that accelerated beginning in the 1950s and grew out of the findings of two major scientists who had worked at the beginning of the twentieth century, Albert Einstein (the theory of relativity) and Werner Heisenberg (the uncertainty principle). Their results suggested that objects—the material world—were neither as solid nor as certain as they appeared in the world as defined by Isaac Newton's "laws." When popularized by the 1950s, these new ideas led to major societal and intellectual changes: the collapse of hierarchies, the equalizing of individuals and ideas, and the loss of certainty. The assumptions underlying these postmodern attributes include:

- doubt of the concepts of objectivity and truth
- doubt of the concept of absolute meaning
- belief in bottom-up participation rather than top-down dictation
- belief in differences and shades of meaning rather than black/white opposites
- suspicion of ideas of progress, objectivity, reason, certainty, and personal identity
- belief in a "truth" shaped by cultural bias, myth, metaphor, and political content.

FIGURE 19.1

Postmodernism

Mixing periods and reinterpreting text are part of a postmodern approach to performance. Here, each of the three acts of Thornton Wilder's *The Skin of Our Teeth* is given a new interpretation. Act one is presented in the style of a black-and-white film (left). Act two captures the energy and vibrancy of a 1960s beach scene (top right), while act three presents the cataclysmic aftermath of 9/11.

Jason Ayers

Some postmodern art came to be characterized by parody, satire, self-reference, irony, and wit. Other postmodern works emphasized the impossibility of communication or political or social improvement—a general nihilism.

Postmodern plays, as they evolved after the 1960s, were often not unified in tone, time, or style. Instead of linear actions organized by psychology and causality, postmodern theatre created unity through image, allusion, and metaphor; it appropriated the images and stories of popular culture and used them in subversive ways. Inevitably, postmodernism created reactions to itself, especially after the mid-1980s, in flights toward hierarchy, inequality of ideas, and certainty—most obviously, the powerful rise in fundamental religions around the world. It may be that the theatre of this period, or at least the commercial theatre, came to represent such flight, as well—that is, it was often backward-looking in its certainties of idea and style.

Theatrical Changes: The Theatre Scene

Given the stunning changes following World War II in society and worldview, science, and technology, it was inevitable that changes in art and in theatre would emerge. And, in fact, the older practices that had held theatre practice together grew weaker, under assault by many new alternatives. Thus, if anything can be said to characterize the theatre (both commercial and noncommercial) from about 1950 to about 2000, it has been its **eclecticism**—its tolerance of many styles and practices. The theatre buildings of the period were variously shaped and located. Theatrical productions were variously conceived, with wildly different styles. Plays were of mixed forms, mixed media, mixed theories.

Several of the theatrical venues that we take for granted today became widespread during these years. Dinner theatres, established in the early 1950s, had their heyday in the 1970s and were in decline by the mid 1980s. Community theatres, emerging from earlier art theatres and little theatres, continued to increase in number and importance, growing from about 3,500 right after World War II to about 15,000 by the mid-1970s. Off-Off Broadway emerged in the late 1950s as a "complete rejection of commercial theatre" and was housed in small spaces like coffee houses, church basements, and warehouses. Important, too, was the explosion of educational theatres during these years. Veterans returning from World War II flooded to college campuses, multiplying their enrollments. It was during these boom years that most colleges established their own theatre departments, with their own graduate and undergraduate degrees in theatre. With theatre departments and degrees came active producing programs on campus, a trend that quickly trickled down to high schools and earlier grades and established

FIGURE 19.2

Eclecticism

Barriers between forms and styles are rejected in the eclectic view of what theatre can be. Theatre is everything from traditional professional theatre to activist political street theatre. Here, the anti-war protest for the first anniversary of the Iraq War by the Bread and Puppet Theatre group.

Nancy Kaszerman/ZUMA Press

educational theatre as a major production venue in the United States. Most important of all was Off-Broadway, usually dated from 1952, when Tennessee Williams's *Summer and Smoke* appeared there—the first major hit in thirty years in a theatre below Forty-second Street in Manhattan. From then through the 1960s, Off-Broadway served as a showcase for new talent and "experimental" plays. By century's end, however, Off-Broadway had moved toward commercialism and eclipsed Broadway in the number and quality of nonmusical plays.

Nonetheless, the center of American theatre was elsewhere. Although much of American and European theatre after 1950 continued to be commercial (the "mainstream"), there was also a strong avant-garde movement through the early years of the period, and growing numbers of not-for-profit professional theatres appeared across America and Canada. The avant-garde groups remained vital for a while, many getting new life from resistance to the Vietnam War. However, they did not become the mainstream any more than the avant-garde of 1890–1900 had done, although they influenced the mainstream importantly.

FIGURE 19.3

Not-for-Profit Theatres Expand

The Perseverance Theatre in Juneau, Alaska, staged this adaptation of Herman Melville's novel *Moby Dick* as a fusion of Melville with the whaling tradition of the Iñupiat Eskimos. Performed by a multiethnic cast of Alaskan actors, the production later toured to Anchorage, Fairbanks, and Barrow, the northernmost settlement in North America.

After the 1950s, the center of American culture moved away from the theatre and toward pop culture, especially music and television. The theatre persisted as a moderately successful kind of commerce. It had offshoots in other activities, but, by the new millennium, it had little avant-garde. Consciously or not, people who might once have tried to reform it now recognized that it was an impotent activity—an entertainment, a business, a way of life for a few, an artifact.

AVANT-GARDE THEATRE

The 1950s introduced the most recent *ism* to the theatre—Absurdism. Plays called "absurdist" by critics (not by their authors) appeared just after World War II in Europe, when several new playwrights (now better understood as early postmodernists) were so grouped together by critics. **Absurdism** (fl. 1950s–1960s) was itself a blend of earlier *Dadaism* (fl. 1920s), with which it shared an emphasis on life's meaninglessness and art's irrelevancy; *surrealism*, with which it shared an emphasis on the subconscious; and *existentialism*, a theory of existence and behavior. Absurdism's additional commitment to irrationality and nihilism was a response to a world that had just experienced the Holocaust, the wartime destruction of Europe, and the atomic attack on Hiroshima. "Absurd" meant not "ridiculous" but "without meaning." Absurdists abandoned story and dramatic unity based on causality. The plays were often constructed as a circle (ending just where they had begun, after displaying a series of unrelated incidents) or as the intensification of a single event (ending just where they had begun but in the midst of more people or more objects). Usually, the puzzling quality of the plays came from the devaluation of language as a carrier of meaning: In the plays, what *happened* on stage often transcended and contradicted what was *said* there. Absurdists included Samuel Beckett (*Waiting for Godot)*; Eugene Ionesco; Edward Albee; and Arthur Kopit; they influenced later playwrights like Harold Pinter.

The 1950s and 1960s also saw a powerful counterculture that persisted into the 1980s. Partly the product of the Vietnam War, partly the product of political leftism, it challenged established values. This counterculture expressed itself in theatre through a new wave of avant-gardism that began Off-Off-Broadway and in other tiny New York theatres but quickly decentralized.

The innovators in the United States after World War II were partly like the older ones—that is, they were committed to reforming the art of theatre—but different in that some were overtly political. "Political" here, however, must be taken in a large sense, for it included not only the politics of the anti–Vietnam War movement but also the emergence of groups that had until then been unidentified or invisible—African Americans, Asian Americans, Latinos, women, homosexuals.

The now-old-fashioned arts reformers were again trying to make theatre important and serious—that is, to claim a place for it near cultural power. The political reformers were trying to use the theatre to carry vivid messages, to raise consciousness, to incite action. Both kinds, in the process, tried to rethink the relationship of theatre to life, of theatre to commerce, of actors to audience, and of text to performance. As in the period of the American art theatres, a national periodical became the observer and the voice of these ideas: *TDR* (formerly the *Tulane Drama Review)*.

The trajectory of this avant-garde movement can be suggested by briefly tracking the history of one of its most important organizations, the Living Theatre.

The Movement in Miniature: The Living Theatre. The Living Theatre, founded in 1947 by Julian Beck and Judith Malina, started as an art theatre in New York. The last of the modernist theatres, it looked back toward the earlier avant-garde in Europe and did plays by such Europeans as Pablo Picasso, Luigi Pirandello, and Bertolt Brecht. In the late 1950s, however, the group shifted toward new American works like *The Connection*, a realistic look at the (then) little-known drug culture, and *The Brig*, a harsh treatment of military prison. By the late

Living Theater

1960s, following a European tour, it became a political theatre, reorganizing into a commune to promote a revolution through "benevolent anarchy." According to Beck and Malina, "Our intentions are to further the revolution, meaning the beautiful, non-violent, anarchistic revolution." With a change in goals came a change in its approach to theatre. It quickly became famous for the direct participation of the audience, for performances that turned into protest marches, and for such shock tactics as nudity and obscenity. It had moved from modernism to postmodernism.

Probably its most famous production during this period was *Paradise Now*, which began with actors milling about the audience. Throughout the four or more hours of performance, actors verbally abused any spectators who seemed apathetic or hostile, shouting slogans and obscenities at them. Such confrontations, sometimes in the nude, were common in performance, and often, at the play's end, the group urged spectators to join it in taking the revolution out of the theatre and into the streets. When the performers did so, they were occasionally arrested and charged with things like disturbing the peace, indecent exposure, and interfering with law enforcement.

Following another overseas tour, the group returned to the United States in the 1970s. With radicalism on the decline (from the drawdown of the Vietnam War and the muting of civil-rights agitation), the Living Theatre entered a new phase, splitting itself into four "cells," each in a different city and each with a different emphasis: politics, the environment, the culture, and the spirit. Although the group remained active, by the 1980s its influence on American theatre and culture had abated, the victim of waning interest in revolution, to be replaced by other groups whose concerns were more fashionable.

The Living Theatre, then, tracked the major shifts of the avant-garde, from its early roots in European practice, through a period of revolutionary politics, into expanding interests and locations, and finally into self-induced disappearance. It continued into the new millennium, but almost invisibly. Its importance lies in its aftereffects and in the energy and innovativeness of its two founders. The Living Theatre embodied both major strands of twentieth-century American avant-gardism—politics and art.

Two Strands: Political and Artistic Theatre

POLITICAL THEATRE Early during this period, **street theatre** and **guerilla theatre** were names given to political performances that went to the audience, the first into the streets, the second in hit-and-run "guerilla" raids on nontheatrical spaces wherever people could be found (e.g., elevators, department stores). Big in the 1960s, these two were soon replaced by other sorts of political theatre, each tied to a major social movement: black theatre, tied to the Black Power movement; women's theatre, tied to the feminist movement; and gay and lesbian theatre, tied to the gay rights movement. Although these shared many basic assumptions, they differed in several ways.

Black Theatre. Although African American performers in America date from well before the Civil War, and African American theatre companies were firmly

Spotlight

Here, *Gem of the Ocean* at Tisch School of the Arts in New York City.

Scene Design by Benny Sato Ambush. Photo: Ella Bromblin

August Wilson: A Century of African American Life

August Wilson set out to write a ten-play series, with one play devoted to the black experience in each decade of the twentieth century. Collectively known as the Pittsburgh Cycle, named for the city where they are set, the plays were produced in New York after development in not-for-profit theatres. The pattern of three or more regional productions allowed Wilson to hone the dramas for Broadway and Off-Broadway.

The first, *Ma Rainey's Black Bottom*, appeared in 1985, the last, *Radio Golf*, in 2005. Within those twenty years, Wilson became one of the most important playwrights of his generation. His plays stand as a landmark in the history of black culture, American literature, and Broadway theatre. Perhaps the most honored playwright in the past quarter century, Wilson was awarded two Tony Awards, seven New York Drama Critics Circle Awards, a Pulitzer Prize, and the Olivier Award (the British equivalent of the Tony), among many other prestigious awards.

The plays, and the decade which they characterize are: *Gem of the Ocean* (1900s), *Joe Turner's Come and Gone* (1910s), *Ma Rainey's Black Bottom* (1920s), *The Piano Lesson* (1930s), *Seven Guitars* (1940s), *Fences* (1950s), *Two Trains Running* (1960s), *Jitney* (1970s), *King Hedley II* (1980s), and *Radio Golf* (1990s). They were not written or produced in this order, however.

These plays are connected by several shared traits. All but one play is set in the black neighborhood of Pittsburgh's Hill District; characters from one play occasionally appear in others; the characters usually speak in the street dialect of the Hill, but Wilson manages to make the dialogue sound poetic and even musical; most are focused more on character than plot; and supernatural elements abound. The guiding spirit of the cycle seems to be Aunt Esther, a woman said to have lived for more than three centuries.

Quite soon after his death in 2005, a Broadway theatre was renamed in his honor—the August Wilson Theatre.

established within black communities well before World War II, they were mostly unknown in mainstream theatre (where African Americans were often played by whites in blackface).

Two important plays seen by both white and black audiences shortly after World War II, however, heralded a change. In 1959, Lorraine Hansberry's *A Raisin in the Sun* was produced on Broadway. This study of African American family life, in which the tensions between women and men were sympathetically and sensitively dramatized, won the Drama Critics Circle Award. The same year, French playwright Jean Genet's *The Blacks* was produced Off-Broadway; it reversed the traditions of the minstrel show and used African American actors in whiteface to reveal abuses of white power. Although many African Americans

FIGURE 19.4

Black, Feminist Theatre: *For Colored Girls Who Have Considered Suicide/ When the Rainbow is Enuf*

Playwright Ntozake Shange's *For Colored Girls* began as a choreopoem—a series of monologues with movement—in California. It moved to Broadway but remained controversial within the black community because of its negative portrayal of black men. Here, *For Colored Girls* at the University of Missouri at Columbia.

rejected the play's thesis—that blacks will come to power only by adopting the tactics of their white oppressors—few failed to realize that the play represented a turning point in the theatrical portrayal of black people.

Revolutionary **black theatre** grew out of the racial turmoil of the 1950s and 1960s, when blacks turned in large numbers to the arts as a way of demanding change and repairing their ruptured society: The black theatre movement dates from 1964 and the Off-Broadway production of LeRoi Jones's *The Toilet* and *Dutchman*, both of which presented chilling pictures of racial barriers, human hatred, and the suffering that results from racism. Thereafter, the stereotypical stage Negro was increasingly replaced by more honest, if often less agreeable, black characters. Throughout the 1960s and early 1970s, Jones (now Imamu Amiri Baraka) remained the most militant and best-known black playwright.

Other African American plays studied the politics and economics of life within the African American community. Douglas Turner Ward's *Day of Absence* (1967) poked fun at whites as they were outwitted by cleverer blacks, whose disappearance for a single day led to the collapse of the white social structure. Alice Childress's *Mojo* (1970) suggested that African American men and women could work out their differences and exist happily as equals if they loved and respected each other.

By the mid-1970s, African American authors could criticize their own community. Ntozake Shange's *For Colored Girls Who Have Considered Suicide/When the Rainbow is Enuf* (1976) explored the double oppression of being black and female. It was an unflattering portrait of some black men as brutalizing black women as they themselves had been brutalized by whites. Originally staged in an African American theatre, this powerful "choreopoem" (a postmodern form) eventually moved to Broadway, where it earned a Tony Award.

With new plays came calls for a new criticism. Some African American critics took the position that their audiences saw and understood art in ways different from whites. Those artists and critics sought an aesthetic that was moral and corrective, one that supported plays that, in a direct and immediate way, affected the lives of African American theatregoers. An African American critic explained, "The question for the black critic today is not how beautiful a melody, a play, a poem, or a novel is, but how much more beautiful [that] poem, melody, or play [has] made the life of a single black man."

With the gradual improvement in the position of black people and the increasing conservativism sweeping the United States by the mid-1980s, the energy of the black revolutionary theatre subsided. Although some African American theatres and revolutionary playwrights and criticism persisted, black playwrights increasingly moved into mainstream theatres, taking black critics with them.

Women's Theatre. Whereas black theatre and drama arose from the social upheavals of the late 1950s and 1960s, **women's theatre** was a phenomenon of the 1970s. Increasing numbers of people, mostly female, banded together into theatrical units that aimed to promote the goals of feminism, the careers of women artists, or both. By the mid-1970s, more than forty such groups were flourishing; by 1980, more than a hundred had formed. Unlike black theatres, which were usually found in high concentrations of blacks in cities, women's theatres sprang up in places as diverse as New York City and Greenville, South Carolina.

The theatres ranged in size from those depending on one or two unpaid and inexperienced volunteers to organizations of professionals numbering in the hundreds. Budgets, too, varied widely, with some groups existing on a shoestring and the good wishes of friends, and others displaying a financial statement in the hundreds of thousands of dollars. Organization, repertory, working methods, and artistic excellence were highly diversified, but the groups all shared the conviction that women had been subjected to unfair discrimination based on their gender and that theatre could serve in some way to correct the resulting inequities.

Like the African American theatres, the women's theatres attempted to serve different audiences and to serve them in different ways. Some groups, like the Women's Interart in New York City, existed primarily to provide employment for women artists. Such groups served as a showcase for the works of women playwrights, designers, and directors. Because their goal was to display women's art in the most favorable light, artistic excellence was a primary goal of each production. Critical acceptance by the theatrical mainstream was the ultimate measure of success. But other groups, like the now-defunct It's All Right to Be Woman Theatre (also in New York City), believed the problems of women to be so deeply rooted in society that only a major social upheaval could bring about their correction. Such groups were revolutionary and tended to adopt tactics designed to taunt, shock, or shame a lethargic society into corrective action. These groups cared not at all for the approval of established critics because they believed that traditional theatre was a male-dominated, and hence oppressive, institution.

FIGURE 19.5

Commercial Women's Theatre

Beth Henley's Pulitzer Prize-winning *Crimes of the Heart* was first produced at the 1979 Humana Festival at the Actors Theatre of Louisville and was produced later on Broadway. Here, a production at Heritage Repertory Theatre in Charlottesville, Virginia.

Two techniques in particular came to be associated with revolutionary women's theatres: a preference for collective or communal organization and the use of improvised performance material, much of it uncommonly personal.

By 1990, however, leading feminist playwrights had moved to other matters, and women's theatres were in flux. Some had ceased producing, and some had moved away from feminism. Others moved in directions newly pointed to by feminism itself—emphasizing differences among women. They renewed explorations of the function of gender in life and art, investigating through performance the ways in which society and theatre construct gender.

Although hundreds of feminist plays were written, none became widely known. Their influence, however, is visible in commercial works such as Wendy Wasserstein's *Uncommon Women*; Marsha Norman's *Getting Out*, and Beth Henley's *Crimes of the Heart*.

Gay and Lesbian Theatre. Many U.S. cities had had self-aware gay and lesbian communities long before the 1960s, but these were largely covert, "in the closet." Homosexual acts were illegal in most of the United States; public homosexual conduct, even language, was sometimes punishable under laws against indecency and obscenity. Therefore, plays about homosexuality usually fell under the heading of prohibited speech. The exceptions were guarded, almost coded—for example, Lillian Hellman's *The Children's Hour* (1934). This situation changed in the 1960s, however, as court rulings extended free speech and concepts of privacy.

In 1968, Mart Crowley's *The Boys in the Band* was produced Off-Broadway and became the first homosexual hit comedy in a mainstream venue. Sympathetic to the lives and problems of gay men, Crowley's play made a place in commercial theatre for plays in which homosexuality was acceptable and nonthreatening—and

FIGURE 19.6

Lesbian Theatre

Diana Son's *Stop Kiss* (1998) was an exploration of a lesbian relationship. A tentative first kiss and growing relationship brings the violence of gay-bashing into the unsuspecting lives of the main characters. It was first produced at the Public Theatre in New York. Here, a recent production at Theatre South Carolina.

funny. Self-deprecating and sometimes self-destructive wit positioned homosexuals as victims, however, and thus ran the risk of sentimentality.

The gay rights movement itself dates from 1969, with the Stonewall Riot, when police raided the gay bar called the Stonewall Inn and were resisted by those they came to arrest. **Gay and lesbian theatre** is usually dated from 1976, when John Glines opened his theatre in New York City. The Glines theatre was dedicated to producing plays by and about gay people, including lesbians. Specifically lesbian theatres surfaced in the 1980s (e.g., Split Britches). Also by the 1980s, sympathetic gay plays grew common in mainstream theatre, the more so when the AIDS epidemic became national news, and "AIDS plays" became a subgenre (e.g., *As Is*, 1984).

The rapid acceptance of gay and lesbian plays in the commercial theatre probably came in part from the longstanding acceptance of homosexuality within the theatre community and in part from theoretical problems slightly different from those in black and women's theatre. In gay and lesbian theatre, coherent theoretical bases were elusive because of real problems of definition. What is a gay play—a play about gay men? By a gay man? Does a play by a gay or lesbian author but with a different subject fit? Is a negative play about gay men a gay play? What of those plays of the past by homosexual authors (e.g., Oscar Wilde, Tennessee Williams) that have no ostensibly homosexual content? Partly to deal with such theoretical problems, the idea of queer theatre and queer studies evolved, where *queer* is both an umbrella and a political term, a weapon seized from "the enemy" and turned around. Queer theatre announces itself (that is, it does not speak in code) and has pride in itself (that is, it is not apologetic).

ARTISTIC THEATRE Unlike political theatres, which sought to change society, some avant-garde theatres strove to change the art of the theatre. Such groups wanted to explore—either alone or in some combination—the nature of theatre, its relation to other kinds of performance and media, its arrangements for production, and the role of both script and audience in a performance. Probably closer to the earlier European avant-garde than to the political theatres in their goals, these artistic theatres nonetheless differed profoundly from both the earlier art theatres and the political theatres contemporary with them. (The Living Theatre began as artistic, but quickly moved to become political.)

Joseph Chaikin and the Open Theatre. Among the most influential of such theatres was that of Joseph Chaikin, who proposed an "open" theatre to distinguish it from the "closed" (rigid, text-bound, uncreative) theatres of Broadway. Believing that most theatres were overwhelmed by nonessentials, Chaikin sought a performance in which the primary focus was on the actor and groups of artists working together.

Thus, ensemble became the cornerstone of the **Open Theatre**, and actors were trained to work as a group rather than as individuals. To accomplish such an ensemble, Chaikin used a variety of theatre games and improvisations designed to develop sensitivity to group rhythms and dynamics, to increase mutual trust, and to replace competition for the audience's attention with cooperation among the group. The playwright, too, was considered a member of the ensemble and was encouraged to develop texts for the group out of the ideas of the group. Typically the writer would provide a scenario (an outline of the situation) and the group would improvise dialogue and action. The improvisations would be repeated several times, and the writer would select the best of them, add new materials as needed, rearrange sections, and finally develop "the text."

Although the plays varied enormously, they tended to share some combination of these characteristics:

- a unity achieved through exploring a central idea or theme (rather than a story)
- a rather free and often disconnected treatment of time and place
- the use of *transformations*, a technique in which actors played first one character and then another without corresponding changes in costumes or makeup and without clear transitions provided by dialogue, and
- a reliance on actors to provide their own environment by "becoming" the setting and sounds (For example, an actor plays a sheep in a field, another a snake on a tree; several become ambulance sirens.)

Although the Open Theatre existed for only ten years (1963–1973), its influence was lasting and profound. It focused attention on the centrality of the actor in performance; it demonstrated the willingness of audiences to substitute their imaginations for the usual setting, lights, and costumes; it popularized theatre games and improvisation as tools for training actors and as a source for group-inspired plays; and it showed that the usual theatrical hierarchy (a director leading a team of theatre specialists) was not the only way to organize theatrical production. Its techniques and theories are now part of the theatrical mainstream.

Performance Art. **Performance art** probably began in European art circles early in the century among the Dadaists, and it found echoes in the *happenings* of the 1960s. (Happenings were nonlinear and deliberately meaningless events that tried to redefine what was meant by theatre.) The resurgence of performance art in the 1980s made it the last energetic expression of the avant-garde. It is a form that defies traditional categories like theatre or dance or painting and that varies widely among its practitioners. As its name suggests, it depends on both performance and art, and despite its diversity it tends to share certain traits:

- preference for a nonlinear structure, one unified more often by images and ideas than by stories
- emphasis on visual and aural rather than literary elements
- tendency to mix elements of several arts, especially music, dance, painting, and theatre

Performance art involves a combination of time, space, the performers' bodies, and a relationship with an audience. That is, the performance occurs at a particular time and place, with specific performers and audience, and the art lasts only as long as the performance lasts. Performance art produces no lasting object like painting or music. Although performance art includes many group works, a large proportion of the works are conceived and performed by individual artists working alone, often resembling stand-up comedians like Lenny Bruce. George Carlin and Robin Williams (as a live stand-up comic, not a television or movie actor) continued the Bruce tradition.

Performance art probes the boundaries between life and art and between the several arts. Its frank experimentation has made it controversial not only among those who resist blurring the boundaries of arts but also among those who resent its often graphic portrayal of (to them) repugnant ideas or activities (e.g., feminism, homosexuality, pornography). Performance art is rarely realistic, but many of its devices (the solo performer, the confessional mode, the lack of deliberate technique) seek to authenticate its reality. In a sense, it is the ultimate reduction of American Realism. It is also part of the social shift that has made reality TV and tell-all interviews popular.

The Influence of the Avant-garde

The political avant-garde remained vital only as long as political and social uneasiness were high. In the 1980s, however, the United States got over the most extreme divisions of Vietnam and became an apparently more optimistic and less questioning place: Quick wars in Grenada and Panama and the first Iraq invasion were popular; society seemed not to want to probe or protest anymore. Material comfort became supremely important. Political avant-gardism became like kicking a pillow. By the late 1980s, theorists were proclaiming avant-gardism dead.

Avant-gardism may have dwindled not only because a historical shift undercut its political strength, but also because postmodernism's redefinitions of art undercut its aesthetic strengths. Avant-gardism, as well, was primarily reactive, and by the mid-1980s there was little to react against. By the 1990s, the decade of e-commerce and big money, only local vestiges remained.

Nevertheless, several practices pioneered by the avant-garde of the 1960s and 1970s appeared, if modified, in the commercial theatre, which

- displayed greater freedom of language, dress, and subject; nudity and profanity were readily accepted, and previously taboo subjects were now freely treated—e.g., *Torch Song Trilogy* (1983, homosexuality), *'Night, Mother* (1983, suicide), *As Is* (1985, AIDS), *Love! Valour! Compassion!* (1994, gay life in the age of AIDS)
- awarded prizes to plays by African American authors—e.g., *A Soldier's Play* by Charles Fuller (Pulitzer, 1982); *The Piano Lesson* (Pulitzer, 1990) and *Fences* (Tony Award for Best Play, 1987), both by August Wilson (see Spotlight, p. 319)
- awarded prizes to plays by female and Hispanic playwrights in larger numbers than before—e.g., Margaret Edson, *Wit* (Pulitzer, 1999), Edwardo Ivan Lopez, *Spanish Eyes* (1990).

PROFESSIONAL THEATRE

Whereas most avant-garde theatres operated on modest budgets, the **professional theatre** was marked by its relatively large budgets and by artists who made their living in the theatre. Professional theatres comprised not only the commercial theatres, which existed to make a profit, but also a growing number of not-for-profit theatres.

New York City remained the center of American professional theatre by virtue of the sheer number and scale of productions staged there each year. Between 1950 and 2000, New York was the home of Broadway's thirty-nine theatres, Off-Broadway's approximately seventy-eight spaces, and the myriad small "studio" venues. What these spaces shared was their "professional" status—that is, they were covered by union contracts that guaranteed that the performers and other theatre workers were paid contracted-for amounts and thus were professional. Although Broadway salaries were probably the highest in theatre in the country, many salaries Off-Broadway and in major regional theatres could be significant, too.

By 2000, professional productions included those in most Broadway and off-Broadway theatres; touring productions ("the road"); and productions staged in Las Vegas, Los Angeles, Chicago, Atlanta, and other large cities.

Although there were many more not-for-profit professional theatres than commercial ones, the distinction between the two types of organizations was one of tax status. Each commercial production was a fully taxed, one-time venture, whereas not-for-profits were ongoing ventures that received tax incentives to allow them to accept charitable contributions.

Early on, it was typical for plays established on Broadway to be produced later in regional (not-for-profit) theatres. After the late 1960s, there emerged a different synergy between the commercial theatre and the not-for-profit theatre,

FIGURE 19.7

Spectacle Sells

Andrew Lloyd Webber's *The Phantom of the Opera* won seven Tony Awards in 1988 and continues its long run. It originally opened in London's West End in 1986.

with entire productions transferred from a not-for-profit to a commercial Broadway run. This trend of transferring not-for-profit productions to Broadway began with Washington, D.C.'s Arena Stage, when its production of *The Great White Hope* moved to Broadway in 1967. It won a Tony Award, the New York Drama Critics Award, and the Pulitzer Prize for drama. By 2000, a connection between not-for-profit productions from around the country and the Broadway stage was commonplace.

Commercial Theatre

BROADWAY Except for a slump in attendance in the late 1980s, attendance at Broadway trended upward throughout the period, but the number of new productions was significantly lower: about 55 openings in 1950 and 1960, but only 31 in 1998 (compared with 88 in 1900 and 235 in 1930). Throughout the period, too, costs of production continued to rise: The musical *My Fair Lady* in 1956 cost $401,000, a figure considered staggering at the time. In 1964, the original production of *Fiddler on the Roof* cost $380,000, but its revival in 1976 cost almost double that. The musical *Rent* opened in 1994 at an estimated cost of ten million dollars.

As production costs rose, long runs and higher ticket prices became more important. One theatre businessman estimated that a play that took ten weeks to break even in 1956 would have taken twenty weeks by the mid-1970s, and that a musical that took fifteen to twenty weeks to break even in 1956 would have taken

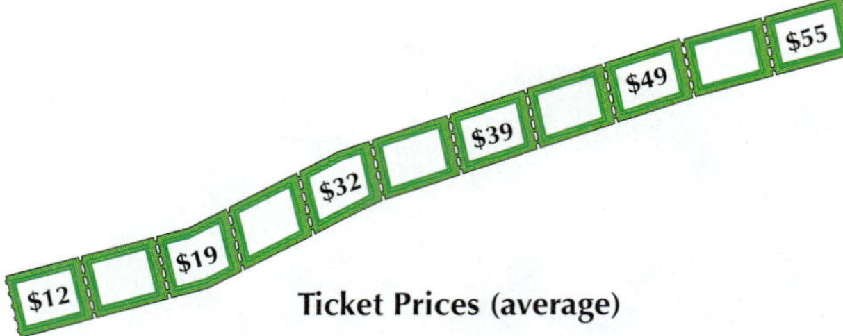

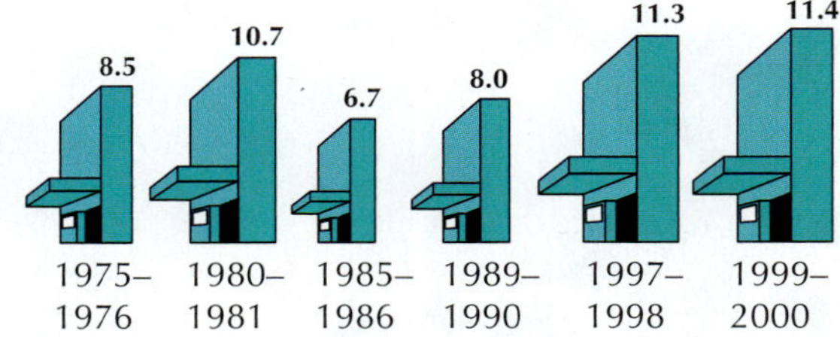

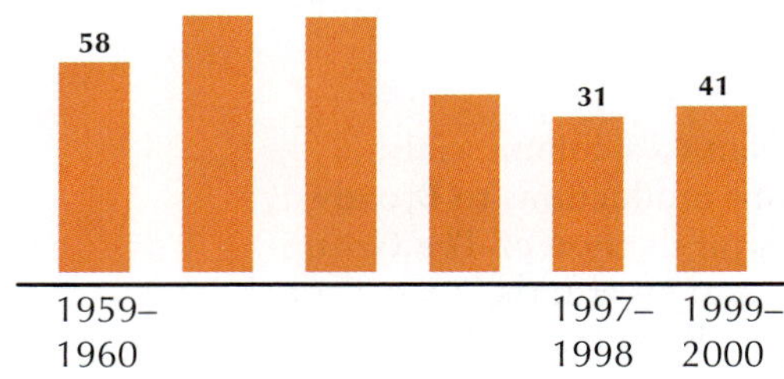

FIGURE 19.8

Changes in Broadway

Since 1950, ticket prices have soared as Broadway production costs have risen; the number of Broadway openings has declined, but attendance has increased. From data in *Variety*.

a year or more by the mid-1970s. The average ticket cost about $10 in 1975, about $30 by 1985, more than $45 by 1995, and about $55 by decade's end.

As costs and prices rose, audiences and repertories got more conservative. By the late 1990s, revivals made up an increasing percentage of productions, more and more musicals were produced, and nonmusical plays grew rarer (and appeared mostly off-Broadway).

The Plays

Musical Theatre. After World War II and through the early 1960s, Broadway composers and lyricists brought the integrated story musical to its optimal form:

- Frederick Loewe (1901–1988): *Brigadoon*, 1947; *My Fair Lady*, 1956; *Camelot*, 1960
- Jule Styne (1905–1994): *Gypsy*, 1959; *Funny Girl*, 1964
- Leonard Bernstein (1918–1990): *Candide*, 1956; *West Side Story*, 1957.

They were mostly optimistic—*Hello, Dolly!*, *Mame*—and continued traditions from before the war, but the production of *Hair* in 1967 was an acknowledgement that time had moved on—in its music, its counterculture characters, its idealism (and the influence of the Living Theatre). Developed in a not-for-profit theatre, *Hair* told of hippies, drugs, and the war, and the show's popularity led to the acceptance of practices earlier considered unacceptable in commercial theatre: nudity, four-letter words, irreverence, to cite only the most obvious. What *Hair* was to the 1960s, *A Chorus Line* was to the 1970s: Also developed at a not-for-profit theatre in New York, the script for this performance, developed by actors during rehearsal with a writer (the technique courtesy of the avant-garde), told of the difficulties faced by professional dancers. Its success launched a Broadway love affair with dance. In both shows, actors performed on stages mostly devoid of scenic pieces (with another probably unconscious nod to the avant-garde).

The 1970s and 1980s were dominated by the composer-lyricist Stephen Sondheim. His lyrics for *Gypsy* and his lyrics and music for *Follies* took a bittersweet look at the musical stage itself. All his work integrated character and song, so that songs often could not be detached from the drama (a great change from the days of George Gershwin and Cole Porter, when show tunes became "standards" without reference to the shows from which they came). To some in the audience, the gain in dramatic power was won at the cost of tunefulness and the old zesty, punchy musical show.

Musicals of the 1980s also emphasized spectacle. An influx of British musicals (*Cats*, *The Phantom of the Opera*) had encouraged a shift toward elaborate costumes and high-tech effects. The musicals of the 1990s continued Broadway's love affair with dance, including such dynamic tap shows as *Bring in Da Noise, Bring in Da Funk*, which featured black composers and performers. Then expensive and elaborate Disney productions appeared, beginning with the lavish and somewhat literal *Beauty and the Beast* (1994), followed by *The Lion King* (1997), which used large puppets and symbolic rather than realistic scenery to achieve stunning visual effects. (Again, avant-gardism, all but dead as a movement, lived on as an influence.) Disney continued to produce on Broadway into the millennium, signaling a shift in commercial organization toward the corporate and the warmed-over—all had been Disney movies first. The age of sheet music and home piano had given way to the age of the CD and karaoke and the commercial tie-in.

By 2000, much Broadway musical theatre was looking backward, with frequent revivals of hits from earlier seasons: *Oklahoma!*, from 1944; *Cabaret*, 1966; *Flower Drum Song*, 1958; *The Boys from Syracuse*, 1938; *The Pajama Game*, 1954; *Chicago*, 1975; *Grease*, 1972; and, from Off-Broadway, *The Threepenny Opera* (1954, originally from the Berlin avant-garde of 1930). These examples seem to suggest that Broadway was, by intention or not, introducing new generations to Broadway hits of the past.

Comedy. Commercial theatre also relied on comedy to ensure box-office revenues. Through most of the period, Neil Simon was the playwright most successful—phenomenally successful—with audiences. Such major plays from the 1960s and 1970s as *The Odd Couple* established his reputation as the master gag writer of the theatre and were transferred to movies and television. And in 1991, he won the Pulitzer Prize for *Lost in Yonkers*. No other comic American writer showed either Simon's ability or his staying power, but the British writer Michael Frayne was successful with a series of imported comedies, the best of which, *Noises Off*, was a masterly farce about the theatre itself.

Two of Wendy Wasserstein's plays cemented her reputation as a writer of successfully commercial comedies. *The Heidi Chronicles* transferred from a not-for-profit Off-Broadway run to Broadway in 1989, winning several major prizes. Wasserstein wrote five more successful plays before her death in 2006 at age 55.

Serious Drama. Some playwrights from the 1940s continued writing: Lillian Hellman, Tennessee Williams, Arthur Miller. Edward Albee was a new voice

Off-Broadway in the 1950s who became a commercial success on Broadway in the 1960s with works like *Who's Afraid of Virginia Woolf* and *A Delicate Balance*. His later plays were less commercially successful but were often critically so and closer to the avant-garde. He remained a major force in American drama well past the end of the century, still winning top artistic awards. In 1994 he earned a Pulitzer Prize for *Three Tall Women*.

In the 1970s and 1980s, David Mamet (*Glengarry Glen Ross*) and Sam Shepard (*Buried Child*) both won major prizes, and each wrote other important works. Several other important playwrights were the heirs of the advances made by the political avant-gardes:

- Women's theatre—included in the 1980s Beth Henley (*Crimes of the Heart*) and Marcia Norman (*'Night, Mother*). In the 1990s Paula Vogel emerged as a major figure (*Baltimore Waltz, How I Learned to Drive*).
- African American theatre—included Charles Fuller (*A Soldier's Play*) and August Wilson (*Fences*); Wilson emerged as the major American playwright of the last two decades of the twentieth century.
- Gay theatre—included the outstanding serious drama of the 1990s, *Angels in America*, by Tony Kushner, which won prestigious prizes in both 1993 and 1994. The play's principal subjects were homosexual life, only recently real to most Americans; AIDS, an epidemic little more than a decade old when the play was written; love and personal loyalty; and, through the real historical figure Roy Cohn, political and moral corruption. The play also established Kushner, long well known in gay theatre, firmly in the mainstream commercial theatre.

FIGURE 19.9
Sam Shepard
Sam Shepard was one of the most important playwrights of the 1970s and 1980s. Shepard won the 1979 Pulitzer Prize for his macabre exploration of the disintegrating American dream, *Buried Child,* shown here at Theatre South Carolina.

Jason Ayers

Despite these playwrights, the American commercial theatre would have been impoverished had it not been for imports. From the 1950s through the 1990s, some of Broadway's best productions had already succeeded abroad. England's Harold Pinter intrigued—and sometimes baffled—American audiences with his absurdist-influenced plays. The feminist British playwright Caryl Churchill (*Cloud Nine* and *Top Girls*) became a major presence, as did Tom Stoppard with such plays as *Rosencrantz and Guildenstern Are Dead* and *Jumpers*. South African Athol Fugard's anti-apartheid plays (*Master Harold and the Boys)* also came to New York by way of London.

Not-for-Profit Theatre

After a slow start in the late 1940s, professional not-for-profit theatres surged in the 1960s, with new not-for profits in places like Minneapolis, Los Angeles, Baltimore, New Haven, and Louisville. In a departure from current New York practices, some of these theatres built spaces without proscenia, preferring theatres in the round (e.g., Dallas and Washington, D.C.) or thrust stages (e.g., Minneapolis). More than sixty such companies existed across the country by the mid-1970s and several hundred by the late 1990s.

An example of the strength and endurance of the not-for-profit theatre is the **Stratford Festival** in Ontario, Canada, one of the biggest theatre operations in North America. Begun in 1953, the festival was originally a three-play summer theatre housed in a tent and devoted exclusively to Shakespeare. By the end of the1990s, the festival's four permanent theatres housed ten to fifteen plays each season; Shakespeare was still the leading playwright, but other period plays, several musicals, popular current plays, and new plays were also included. The festival has an extensive education program for schools during the academic year.

Not-for-profit theatres also opened in New York City, offering an alternative to the commercial theatres there. Of these, the most successful was the Roundabout Theatre Company. Opened in 1965, it went bankrupt in the 1970s but recovered and prospered in the 1980s, earning its first of many Tony awards. By the late 1980s, it had New York's largest subscription audience and regularly sent shows to Broadway. During the 1990s, it moved to a permanent theatre on Broadway, added a second theatre, and earned many, many awards. And like the Stratford Festival, the Roundabout sponsored a strong educational-outreach program.

THE DECLINE AND CULTURAL DISPLACEMENT OF THEATRE

Despite its successes, American theatre in the last half of the twentieth century was giving out warning signals. The robust avant-garde of the 1960s through 1980s was all but dead by the 1990s. Dinner theatre was in decline. On the bright side, not-for-profit theatres, educational theatres, and community theatres remained healthy. But the Broadway theatre—the theatre most people think of when they think of theatre—was struggling against rising costs, rising ticket prices, and declining audiences.

Some of theatre's problems came simply from increasing competition for the entertainment dollar. Just as radio and moving pictures had begun to compete with theatre for audiences before World War II, television, DVDs, computers, and cell phones all competed for attention after it—and mostly, they won. Television, not commercially successful until the late 1940s, had a set in nine of ten American households by the late 1960s. Although cable television had only about 15,000 subscribers in the 1950s, it had 65 million by the late 1990s. Computers, which required a room to house their vacuum tubes in the 1960s, sat on desks by the 1980s, thanks to the transistor and the microchip. They allowed e-mails and Internet communication by the 1990s, when DVDs and cell phones also became widespread. Such technologies could bring movies, sports, and spectacles into a living room—some could bring them into a car or up to the top of a mountain by 2000—and for less money than a theatre ticket.

But the changing technologies also seemed to lead (or maybe simply to reflect) a change in the needs and desires of people. The desire to participate with a group brought together for a single event—a theatre audience—seemed to give way before individual enjoyment in front of a machine or even interacting with that machine. Theatre, a product of an oral culture, seemed increasingly out of place in a world dominated by an electronic one.

KEY TERMS

Check your understanding against this list. Brief definitions are included in the Glossary; persons are page-referenced in the index.

Absurdism 316
black theatre 320
eclecticism 315
gay and lesbian theatre 323
guerilla theatre 318
Living Theatre 317
Open Theatre 324
performance art 325
postmodernism 313
professional theatre 326
Stratford Festival 331
street theatre 318
women's theatre 321

CHAPTER 20

U.S. Theatre, 2000–2010

OBJECTIVES

When you have completed this chapter, you should be able to:

- Explain some ways in which theatre has reacted to terrorist attacks
- Describe the nature and advantages of limited-run commercial productions
- Explain how some formerly underrepresented groups have moved into the theatrical mainstream
- Describe Broadway during the past decade
- Understand the importance of not-for-profit theatres in the development of new plays
- Characterize Las Vegas theatre and the road in the past decade

CONTEXT

As Western nations worried that the rollover from 1999 to 2000 would destroy the computers necessary to their economies, no one could predict when a truly new era would begin. With hindsight, we know a new era started, at least for many, on September 11, 2001, when terrorists flew two passenger planes loaded with jet fuel into the matching towers of the World Trade Center in lower Manhattan. The world watched on television as the towers, for some time the tallest buildings in the world, first burned and then collapsed. Later the rest of the story surfaced—a third plane crashed into the Pentagon and a fourth ditched in a Pennsylvania field, probably because of heroic action by the passengers against the hijackers.

America received the sympathy of much of the world. Soon, other countries—England and Spain foremost—suffered bombings on public transport, lesser in scope but nearly as terrifying. Many Europeans and some U.S. citizens, once united in sympathy and shared defense, recoiled when the U.S. government took precipitous action: invading Iraq (which the American public later discovered had no discernible involvement in terrorist acts or weapons of mass destruction); enforcing broad government secrecy; restricting international travel; torturing presumed enemies and jailing them without trial; and secretly eavesdropping on domestic communications. One phrase uttered by a White House official stood for the disaffection the United States suffered throughout much of the world: "If the president does it, it is not a crime."

Govermental rashness was not the only problem in the United States: Americans were overweight and used a disproportionate amount of the world's energy and raw materials, but millions were dying of starvation in the southern hemisphere. The United States was rich but was also crime-ridden and violent. American capitalism "triumphed," but huge businesses went bankrupt overnight, the stock market yo-yoed and then crashed, economies around the world suffered, and states from South America to central Europe questioned the free market. Contradictions, complexities, and uncertainties thus marked the first decade of the new millennium. The most historic change of this decade was the election in 2008 of Barack Obama, an African American, as President of the United States.

THEATRICAL CHANGES

The arts do not respect the calendar, and so they were little changed by the opening of the new millennium. Several general trends in the theatre noted in Chapter 19 continued:

- the importance of the not-for-profit theatre in new play development
- the continued profit potential of long-running musicals in the commercial theatre
- the absorption of avant-garde techniques and styles into mainstream performance
- an incremental growth of new voices in the commercial and not-for-profit theatres, namely the voices of women, African Americans, Hispanics, and gay people
- the continuation of most visible venues of mainstream American theatre in New York and other large cities
- the continued rise of Broadway ticket prices
- the continued performance by community theatres, with varying degrees of skill, of successful musicals and comedies from past seasons

Educational theatre, however, was seriously undermined by significant cuts in funding as a result of the world recession that began in late 2007. Many public school districts, under the stresses of lowered budgets and federally-mandated testing, eliminated arts training, including theatre. Colleges and universities also suffered: some programs were reduced or eliminated.

Theatre *did* react to a new millennium characterized by audacious terrorist acts and the responses of Western governments. The response of theatre to millennial changes in politics and offense to public values was sometimes tentative, sometimes coincidental, sometimes international.

Theatrical Responses to 9/11

Five productions may stand for the theatre's responses to 9/11 and United States actions thereafter.

FIGURE 20.1

Metamorphoses

The play, first staged at Northwestern University, moved to the not-for-profit Lookingglass Theatre in Chicago under the title *Six Myths*. When it moved to New York, it was renamed *Metamorphoses*. Here, a scene from a later production at Virginia Commonwealth University.

METAMORPHOSES Mary Zimmerman had worked for some years in Chicago on a stage adaptation of tales by the Roman writer Ovid. She called the play *Metamorphoses*. The stories unfolded in and around a shallow pool of water. The result was a gentle, humorous, often moving short evening of tales. Many dealt in magical ways with love that lasts past death. The production came to New York City's Second Stage Theatre, a not-for-profit, in October 2001. The *New York Times* reviewer Ben Brantley wrote, "It was then less than a month after the terrorist attacks of Sept. 11, and the show's ritualistic portrayal of love, death and transformation somehow seemed to flow directly from the collective unconscious of a stunned city. 'Metamorphoses' became a sold-out hit, and every night you could hear the sounds of men and women openly crying." *Metamorphoses* later had a successful commercial run on Broadway, opening in February 2002.

GUANTÁNAMO *Guantánamo: "Honor Bound to Defend Freedom"* was a documentary play, originating in Britain, that was produced in New York by the Culture Project in August 2004. The play is made of crisscrossing monologues, sometimes surprisingly witty, from the actual words of five British detainees released from the U.S. military prison at Guantánamo, Cuba, along with letters of other captives and testimony from family members, lawyers, and public officials. For example, a British citizen of Middle Eastern descent after a year in custody writes to his father, "After all this time I still don't know what crime I am supposed to have committed." Later his father says with dignity, "I am not asking for mercy from anybody. I am asking for justice."

The production received significant notice in the United States, despite "occupying an uneasy middle ground between melodrama and the lecture hall: violence and torture on the one hand, sedentary palaver on the other" (*New York Magazine*). Since the New York production, the play has been staged across the United States.

THE LYSISTRATA PROJECT As a peace action, Kathryn Blume and Sharon Bower organized "The Lysistrata Project: The First-Ever Worldwide Theatrical Act of Dissent." Thus, March 3, 2003, saw 1,029 performances of the ancient Greek satirical play *Lysistrata* staged in fifty-nine countries and all fifty U.S. states. In Aristophanes' comedy, Lysistrata convinces the women of Greece to withhold sex to force the men to negotiate a peace. In the play, unlike real life, the blackmail works and the war is ended. "The Lysistrata Project" saw readings and stagings of varied accomplishment, some with amateur performers and some with a few of the best-known actors in the world.

The director of the Rude Guerilla theatre of Long Beach, California, said, "This is a kinder, gentler protest than the ones with the signs on the streets.... What we have here is a 2,000-year-old play about making love, not war." Academy Award–winning actor F. Murray Abraham, appearing in a reading of *Lysistrata* in Brooklyn, said "It's a great tragedy that we haven't learned anything in all that time. Let's hope some of these people in power are listening." The *Washington Post* reviewer opined, "Yesterday's stagings of Aristophanes'

FIGURE 20.2
"The Lysistrata Project"
A global "act of dissent," *Lysistrata* was performed more than one thousand times. Here, in an undergraduate production at the University of South Carolina, Lysistrata leads the women of Athens to withhold sex to persuade their men to end the war.

satire were a wink-wink, nudge-nudge approach to antiwar activism." Yoko Mizushima Sato, who organized a Tokyo reading, said, "We . . . need the comedy of Aristophanes now, just as we need a massage when we have a stiff shoulder."

Black Watch Out of the National Theatre of Scotland in 2006 came *Black Watch*, a view of the Iraq War by soldiers in a Scottish regiment. The play moves between postwar interviews in pubs and reenacted deployment scenes depicting the crushing boredom of war spiked by moments of terror, all spiced by the music of regimental folk songs and bagpipes. The *New York Times* called *Black Watch* "an essential testament to the abiding relevance—and necessity—of theatre." The reviewer offered a description of a moment from early in the drama: "A group of young men sits around in a pub looking wary, joking rough and ragging an enemy in their midst, an interviewer asking variations on the question they are most tired of hearing: "What was it like in Iraq?' And then, without preamble, the red felt surface of the pool table tears and a hand punches through, followed by the full body of a man in combat fatigues who is followed by another. . . . And you know that for these men, these bodies are always there, in the pub, in the pool table, in whatever place they happen to be." *Variety* called *Black Watch* "both a hymn to soldiers and an indictment of the foolishness that makes their jobs necessary, shot through with odd, affecting grace notes of music and dance."

The production toured Scotland, the United States, Australia, Scotland, and the United States again, and then played London, where it won four 2009 Olivier Awards, the London equivalent of the Tony Awards.

ALL MY SONS In 2008, a commercial revival of Arthur Miller's 1947 play *All My Sons* opened on Broadway. The story is straightforward. Shortly after World War II, a midwestern family comes apart as a long-held secret is revealed: The father, who became wealthy as a supplier to the military, had knowingly shipped defective airplane engine parts, causing the deaths of twenty pilots. One of the pilots may have been the family's eldest son, a pilot who is missing and presumed dead. The shame of one man's profiting by death in war was not lost on an audience in the era of the Iraq War and the government's granting no-bid contracts for rebuilding.

The revival was staged with postmodern hallmarks: projections, expressionistic sound effects, a nonrealistic background, and direct address to the audience. For instance, the play begins with the actors entering the playing area in costume and facing the audience while a lead actor addresses the audience, reading Miller's description of the play's setting, "The back yard of the Keller home... August of our era." The actors then exit and the play begins. The acting was psychologically real. The fistfight between father and son near the close of the play was fierce, brutal, and frightening.

FIGURE 20.3

Star Power

Crowds flocked to see *All My Sons* in a strong production with a theme that struck audiences as timely. The fact that the Arthur Miller play had four star actors helped to draw audiences.

Commercial theatre, not-for-profit theatre, and grassroots political theatre attempted to help their audiences come to terms with important issues of the times. The response, then, of the theatre to the terrorists' attacks and the Iraq occupation was in many ways sympathetic, antiwar, and suspicious of government.

The Assimilation of Identity Theatres

Despite the actions taken overseas in the name of the American people, life went on at home fairly unchanged. In the theatre, however, those political theatres formerly identified by race or gender (now often referred to as **identity theatres**) were further assimilated into the mainstream.

WOMEN Women were accepted as important playwrights and directors, including such playwriting talents as Claudia Shear *(Dirty Blonde)*, Suzan-Lori Parks *(TopDog/Underdog)*, Lynn Nottage

(Ruined), Marsha Norman *(The Color Purple)*, and Sarah Ruhl *(Eurydice, The Clean House, In the Next Room)*. These plays and others by women playwrights were mostly developed in the not-for-profit theatre and then staged on Broadway or Off-Broadway and throughout the United States.

Two women playwrights, Suzan-Lori Parks and Lynn Nottage, won Pulitzer Prizes. In Sarah Ruhl's *The Clean House*, a Brazilian cleaning lady tells long jokes directly to the audience—in Portuguese. Suzan-Lori Park's *Topdog/Underdog* portrays two African American blood brothers named Lincoln and Booth. One is a card shark and Abe Lincoln impersonator in white-face makeup; the other has been a petty thief but wants to graduate to a more sophisticated con, three-card monte.

Female directors also guided major productions: Julie Taymor *(Spider-Man)*, Susan Stroman *(Young Frankenstein)*, Phyllida Lloyd *(Mamma Mia!* and *Mary Stuart)*, Emily Mann *(Anna in the Tropics, Translations)*, Anna D. Shapiro *(August: Osage County)*, and Diane Paulus *(Hair)*. The training of these directors was highly varied. Taymor, Shapiro, Paulus, and Mann come from the not-for-profit theatre. Lloyd learned the craft first at the British Broadcasting Corporation (BBC), followed by directing at government-subsidized regional theatres in England, at opera houses internationally, and in London's commercial theatre center, the West End. Stroman began as a choreographer of musical comedies, then moved to directing.

Ella Bromblin

FIGURE 20.4

Inspiration

Sarah Ruhl's comedy, *The Clean House*, was inspired by a remark overheard at a cocktail party. Here, a production at Tisch School of the Arts.

Tisch School of the Arts; Photo: Ella Bromblin

FIGURE 20.5

Wilson's Last Play

A dream-like moment from *Gem of the Ocean*, a play in the ten-play cycle by August Wilson that chronicles the decade-by-decade experiences of African Americans in the last century. *Gem of the Ocean*, produced on Broadway in 2004, was the last play written but it is chronologically the first play in the cycle.

African Americans Plays by and about African Americans grew even more common in mainstream theatres. These scripts included nearly all of the works of the late August Wilson (see Spotlight p. 319) and plays by Suzan-Lori Parks, Stew, and Anna Devere Smith.

Black plays and productions featuring African Americans also appeared on Broadway in greater number, including the musical *Passing Strange* and the historical monoplay *Thurgood*. Sarah Jones's one-woman show *Bridge & Tunnel* had a successful Broadway run.

"Bridge-and-tunnel" is a dismissive term for people who travel to Manhattan from the surrounding boroughs of New York. (Manhattan is an island mostly reached by bridges and tunnels.) The play, set at a public poetry reading, is a comic collage of people of many nationalities and both genders, getting by and searching for dignity and meaning while living in the outer parts of the city. With minimal costumes, Jones appears as a Chinese-American mother, a Russian-Jewish father, a Nigerian political refugee, and Mitzi, an eighty-seven-year-old German immigrant.

A musical adaptation of Alice Walker's novel *The Color Purple* played Broadway from 2005 through 2008 and toured the United States. Lorraine Hansberry's classic 1959 African American drama, *A Raisin in the Sun*, was a successful revival on Broadway with a cast that included Sean "Diddy" Combs. Broadway saw not only a revival of Tennessee Williams's *Cat on a Hot Tin Roof* with an all–African American cast but also a race-blind production of William Inge's *Come Back, Little Sheba* starring African American television actress S. Epatha Merkerson as the lead in an otherwise white cast. African American *audiences*, however, have not generally grown much, except for the gospel plays of the chitlin' circuit (see Spotlight).

Latinos/Latinas Latino/a playwrights including Nilo Cruz, Eduardo Machado, Sylvia Bofill, Ricardo Bracho, Ed Cardona, Jr., and others gradually

Spotlight

Tyler Perry as Madea. Photo: Lions Gate Films/Picture Desk Inc./Kobal Collection

The Chitlin' Circuit and Tyler Perry

The noted African American Harvard professor, Henry Louis Gates, Jr., borrowed the term *chitlin' circuit* to describe a contemporary touring theatre of plays made by, for, and about African Americans. The chitlin' circuit flourishes away from Broadway, Off-Broadway, and the not-for-profit theatre. It's professional in that everyone involved gets paid, but it's entirely nonunion. It's made loads of money for many involved.

The characters in chitlin' circuit plays are as standardized as those of *commedia dell'arte*. Typical roles include an outspoken fat woman, a beautiful woman of questionable morals, an over-the-top swishy gay man, and a handsome stud. The comedy is crude, full of insults and trash talk. At some point a gospel song is belted out. At stake in the plot is the loss of a family member or friend to drugs, gangs, prison, or prostitution. The happy ending often comes about from prayer and sometimes even from divine intervention in the form of angels or ghosts.

The audiences, as Gates noted, "are basically blue-collar and pink-collar, and not the type to attend traditional theatre." Gates continues, "However crude the script and the production, they're generating the kind of audience response that most playwrights can only dream of."

Some chitlin' circuit participants prefer to call their endeavors *urban theatre*, perhaps adapting the term from black radio stations that describe the music they program as *urban music*.

The cross-over financial star of the chitlin' circuit is clearly Tyler Perry. In 1998, he staged his first play, *I Know I've Been Changed*, at Atlanta's House of Blues. He sold out eight nights at the House of Blues and two more nights at the 4,500-seat Fox Theatre. Soon Perry was doing two to three hundred performances a year, playing to thirty thousand people a week. Perry wrote, directed, produced, composed, did makeup and set design, all to keep the budget tight.

Perry's innovation on the chitlin' circuit formula was to play the mother character himself, all six-foot-five of him, in drag. This character, Madea, takes the idea of the strong black mother's holding the family together a gigantic step further. Madea carries two guns in her handbag and will whip them out if necessary. She smokes grass and is blunt-spoken.

In 2005 and 2006, Perry made his first two Madea films for a total budget of $11 million; each opened at number one, and together they grossed more than $110 million. His eleven stage plays have grossed more than $150 million, and DVDs of his movies and plays have sold more than eleven million copies. He even had a best-selling book in 2006, *Don't Make a Black Woman Take Off Her Earrings: Madea's Uninhibited Commentaries on Love and Life.*

moved toward the mainstream. Many of the plays by these authors and others were developed at INTAR, a New York City Latino theater producing in English.

Nilo Cruz won the Pulitzer Prize for *Anna in the Tropics*. Set at the start of the Great Depression of the 1930s, the play takes place in a cigar factory in Tampa's Spanish-Cuban area. During work, a reader or *lector* reads Tolstoy's *Anna Karenina* aloud to the employees. First staged in a not-for-profit theatre in Miami, the play was publicized by a local reviewer whose work led to the Pulitzer and a Broadway production in 2001. Cruz's plays are produced at many leading not-for-profits.

Latino/a artists are now produced in the commercial theatres. The energetic musical *In the Heights*, by Lin-Manuel Miranda and Quiara Alegría Hudes, about a mixed Hispanic New York City neighborhood graduated from Off-Broadway to a commercial Broadway production and quickly turned a profit.

Gays and Lesbians Plays with stories of special interest to gay people continued to cross over from not-for-profit theatres to commercial Broadway houses. Doug Wright's *I Am My Own Wife*, for example, is a biographical one-person show about the German transvestite Charlotte von Mahlsdorf. She survived life under

Joan Marcus Photography

FIGURE 20.6

In the Hispanic Neighborhood

Lin-Manuel Miranda conceived, wrote the music and lyrics, and starred in this invigorating look at Latino life *In the Heights*. The book writer was Auiara Alegria Hudes.

both the Nazi and East German socialist regimes. The question: Was she a gay hero for living an open life as a cross-dresser in these repressive regimes or a gay villain because of unsavory acts she undertook to survive? Another Broadway critical and financial success, Richard Greenburg's comedy *Take Me Out*, concerns a star baseball player—handsome, well spoken, well paid, and masculine—who announces he is gay. Banter among the players in the locker and shower rooms is never the same.

Tom Stoppard's historical drama about the closeted homosexual poet A. E. Housman, *The Invention of Love*, also played on Broadway. Meanwhile, plays with gay themes, including *Rent* and *The Laramie Project*, were being produced at churches and regional, community, and college theatres.

The Tectonic Theatre Project conducted interviews with inhabitants of Laramie, Wyoming, in the aftermath of the brutal killing of Matthew Shepard. An openly gay college student, Shepard was enticed from a bar by two men and then robbed and beaten to death, his body left by the side of a rural road. In the resulting documentary play, *The Laramie Project*, eight actors portrayed more than sixty characters in a series of short scenes.

Into the Mainstream Perhaps two productions will serve to highlight the transition of identity theatres into the broader theatrical culture. Tony Kushner, working with Jeanine Tesori, wrote the musical *Caroline, or Change*. Caroline, an African American maid working for a middle-class Jewish family in Louisiana in 1963, is instructed to keep any loose change she finds in the son's pockets during laundry as a way of teaching the boy to be more careful. The bits of money mean little to the family but become significant for Caroline's household. A crisis develops when a twenty-dollar bill is found in the laundry. Kushner, author of *Angels in America*, is a gay man; both he and Tesori are Jewish. The musical was directed by George C. Wolfe, a gay African American. Significantly, almost no commentator noted any conflict in a white man's and woman's telling an African American story.

Assimilation of African American playwrights into the mainstream was not always without controversy. In 2009, a revival of August Wilson's *Joe Turner's Come and Gone* was staged on Broadway. The play's setting is a Pittsburgh boardinghouse that serves as a makeshift home for a changing mix of African Americans during the "great migration" (the first decade of the twentieth century), when descendants of former slaves moved toward the industrial cities of the North seeking jobs and new starts in life. Some people active in African American theatre, however, bemoaned that the $1.7 million production was directed by a white man, Bartlett Sher. At stake was not so much interpretation as cultural knowledge. Cast members noted to journalists that Sher was sensitive to his lack of knowledge of African American life and customs, bowing to the actors' personal experience.

In his lifetime, August Wilson would not approve a white director for any of his plays; this insistence is, in part, why no films have been made of his stories. The reason for demanding African American directors was to get them work. But the playwright's widow, Constanza Romero, personally approved the production and director, saying, "My work is to get these stories out there and to help ensure that audiences walk out of the plays with a deeper understanding for these American stories and for the ways our cultures intertwine."

Constanza Romero's work—getting the stories out there—has been at the heart of identity theatre's goals. But both the commercial and not-for-profit theatres increasingly acknowledge and showcase the unity of the human experience in people of many races and both genders.

A Faded Avant-garde

As theatre by and for women, African Americans, Latinos, and gays moved to the theatrical center, the avant-garde continued to fade from U.S. stages. A potent sign of the avant-garde's eclipse was the revival in New York City of the Living Theatre under the leadership of its cofounder, Judith Malina. It reproduced two of its signature hits, *The Connection* (1959) and *The Brig* (1963). Seen originally as seminal and ground-breaking avant-garde works presented in new and exciting ways, in revival these two plays were received as relics belonging to another age.

Sara Krulwich/The New York Times/Redux Pictures

FIGURE 20.7

New Take

First seen on Broadway in 1979, *Sweeney Todd* was significantly reconceived for its Broadway revival in 2005. The cast was reduced in size to ten, who also doubled as the orchestra. Here, Patti Lupone played the tuba when she was not performing the lead female role.

Still, a limited avant-garde continued in a small number of troupes. Mabou Mines toured a postmodern production of Henrik Ibsen's 1879 *A Doll's House* with a much altered script, mock period music, an interpolated puppet opera, and, most stunningly, all the male roles played by very short actors: midgets and dwarfs. The tall female actors could barely sit on the tiny furniture made to accommodate the men. The casting and staging exaggerated outrageously the themes of the original play. In the script, the men are small-minded; here they were literally small. The setting became almost literally a doll house in which adult women do not fit.

Elements of much of the late twentieth-century avant-garde kept cropping up in otherwise mainstream productions, accepted by audiences with little note. A revival of Stephen Sondheim's opera-like musical *Sweeney Todd* was staged without a traditional orchestra; instead, the performers played the accompaniment on a variety of instruments when not actually singing. The female lead played the triangle and the tuba. Frank Wedekind's 1891 play about teenage sexual tumult, *Spring's Awakening*, was adapted into a musical of almost the same name, with the dialogue scenes set in the original late-Victorian period but the songs styled as twenty-first-century rock. Both shows played on Broadway after initial productions at not-for-profit theatres.

In big ways and small, unity of tone and progression continued to be breached in twenty-first-century theatre—that is, eclecticism marked much of theatre in the new millennium. When the discontinuities served story and idea, the result seemed invigorating (*Spring Awakening*). At other times, the stylistic ruptures seemed like fashionable gambits, ineffective and cloying.

COMMERCIAL AND NOT-FOR-PROFIT THEATRE

Broadway

Long-running musicals continued to dominate Broadway and populate the road. Four shows running on Broadway in January 2000 were still playing at the beginning of 2010. Other financially successful musicals opened during this period. The 2008–2009 season alone saw three mega-musicals open: *Shrek The Musical, Billy Elliot: The Musical* (a British import based on a popular film), and *9 to 5* (based on a 1980 film). None of these musicals had anything much in the way of stylistic breakthroughs, timely themes, or songs that anyone wanted to sing outside the theatre. Broadway's successful musicals could be characterized as expensive carnival rides, colorful and fast-paced diversions that were quickly forgotten. Nevertheless, they made a lot of money.

In 2009, a commercial Broadway revival of the 1950s musical *West Side Story* was notable. The musical reworks Shakespeare's *Romeo and Juliet*, placing it in 1950s New York City. The feud between the Capulets and the Montagues is replaced by gang wars between Irish and newly arrived Puerto Rican youths. At the age of ninety-one, the author of the original book, Arthur Laurents, directed the production. His springboard for this revival was to translate some dialogue and two songs into Spanish. Actors from Spanish-speaking countries of the Americas were recruited for the production.

A growing number of star-studded, limited runs of comedies and serious plays had impressive Broadway success. They were characterized by short playing periods and were loaded with familiar names from television, movies, and theatre including *Macbeth* with Patrick Stewart, *The Vertical Hour* with Julianne Moore, *A Moon for the Misbegotten* with Kevin Spacey, *Cyrano de Bergerac* with Kevin Kline and Jennifer Garner, *God of Carnage* with James Gandolfini, *The Country Girl* with Morgan Freeman, and *The Odd Couple* with Nathan Lane and Matthew Broderick. For producers, salaries for their stars were expensive, but name recognition made sizable audiences more likely.

The success of limited-run productions with stars seems to suggest a trend: productions with stars who do not want to commit to a long run and thus miss out on more lucrative work in film and television. In the 2008–2009 season, twenty-nine such productions opened.

Successful new American plays, however, were rare on Broadway. David Auburn's *Proof* revolved about a mentally damaged but brilliant daughter of a recently deceased mathematics genius and tried to answer the question, Did he

Joan Marcus Photography

FIGURE 20.8
A New Idea
West Side Story returned to Broadway in 2009 with some dialogue and two songs translated into Spanish by Lin-Manuel Miranda, a creator of *In the Heights*. Here, one gang dances to Leonard Bernstein's music.

leave important findings behind in his unpublished papers? *Doubt: A Parable* by John Patrick Shanley dramatized the standoff between a nun and a priest over whether a male student at their Catholic school had been or was being molested. Charles Busch had a Broadway success as the author of a conventional comedy, *The Tale of the Allergist's Wife*, about an upper-middle-class woman's midlife crisis. All had long runs.

In his seventy-fourth year, the prize-winning playwright Edward Albee saw the premiere of *The Goat, or Who is Sylvia?*, an unlikely comedy about a man who falls in love with and has sex with a goat. The play ends when the main character's wife drags the dead goat through the front door of their swank apartment. Successful on Broadway, *The Goat* is being staged across America. Albee, then, had continued his ability to shock audiences, a quality evident in his first plays, staged in the late 1950s.

Not-for-Profits

In the new millennium, the nation's not-for-profit theatres continued to develop new plays and theatre artists. This trend, clear in the late twentieth century, became even more pronounced: Many new plays are now developed in workshops, readings, and initial productions in America's regional theatres. From the

1999–2000 season through the 2007–2008 season, 341 productions opened on Broadway. Of these, 175—more than half—originated in the not-for-profit theatre.

Las Vegas

The millennium saw Broadway and Off-Broadway musicals open in Las Vegas hotel-casinos, often with excellent results, at least financially. Perhaps the best example of the synergy that has developed between Broadway and Las Vegas is *The Phantom of the Opera*, performed in the Venetian hotel-casino in a new theatre space specially designed to mirror the Paris opera house in which the musical is set. The Las Vegas production, retitled *Phantom—The Las Vegas Spectacular*, has been shortened from the two-hour-plus playing time in New York to ninety-five minutes, with ten performances a week instead of Broadway's eight. *Phantom*'s physical production has been overhauled and highly computerized to take advantage of Las Vegas's superior technical facilities.

Mamma Mia! was performed more than two thousand times in Las Vegas. *Hairspray* has also played there, as did *The Producers, Avenue Q*, and *Spamalot*. The original Broadway creative team for each musical—director and all designers—was involved in re-creating these Broadway hits.

Las Vegas is primarily a tourist town. Its population turns over every three days, on average, with visitors of all social classes from Europe and the Americas. Many English-speaking tourists are not regular theatergoers; non-English-speakers often find spoken drama too difficult. As a result, Las Vegas theatre focuses on brand-name musicals that are presold because of long Broadway runs. The shows are often shortened because the casino owners, who house and bankroll the shows, want theatergoers to get up from their seats and get back to gambling.

Off-Broadway musical hits also have found a temporary home in Las Vegas. *Blue Man Group, Dragapella, Caveman,*

FIGURE 20.9
Las Vegas
Flashy signs are everywhere in Las Vegas. Here, the Venetian hotel advertises *Phantom* while a passing cab promotes a magician appearing at another hotel-casino

Menopause: The Musical, Forever Plaid, and *Tony 'n' Tina's Wedding* had strong runs in smaller hotel-casinos. These shows are not the brand names of popular Broadway musicals, but they have easily sold attributes. For example, at *Tony 'n' Tina's Wedding* the audience and actors mingle and interact over food at the wedding "reception"—it's a strange sort of dinner theatre.

Las Vegas is also home to six Cirque du Soleil productions, each a hybrid of crowd-pleasing high-tech scenery, costumes, lights, clowning, a modest suggestion of a storyline, and traditional circus acts. Their look and feel is often otherworldly and dream like. While not what is usually meant by drama, such productions are highly theatrical.

Las Vegas theatre, then, is a millennial reflection of a trend noted in commercial Broadway productions and road shows. It epitomizes the shift from theatre art to theatre entertainment: shortened productions, often trivial musicals, a reliance on spectacle, and the downplaying of the spoken word.

The Road

The road continued to prosper financially and continued to be derivative. At the end of the 2008–2009 season, at least twenty-five shows were traveling the United States, almost all musicals. Many of these productions took in more than one million dollars a week: *Wicked* (the story of the good and bad witches of *The Wizard of Oz*), *Dirty Dancing, The Color Purple, Mary Poppins, Monty Python's Spamalot*, and *Jersey Boys* (built around the songs and biographies of Frankie Valli and the Four Seasons). Two shows, *Wicked* and *Jersey Boys*, had *three* touring companies each crisscrossing the United States.

THEATRICAL TRENDS IN THE NEW MILLENNIUM

Time is needed for historians and critics to sift through the apparent successes and failures of an era, highlighting some as significant and letting others retreat to the shadows as fads.

The business of theatre is another matter. Figures can be tallied to provide a year-by-year financial picture of Broadway productions. The good news is that during the severe recession that began in 2007 Broadway survived, even prospered. The 2008–2009 season was financially strong. (See Figures 20.10 and 20.11).

The financial details of not-for-profit theatres are seldom reported. The major not-for-profit theatres in New York City, however, have cut costs but have maintained their subscriber base and have suggested that individual ticket sales have been substantial.

In many countries of Europe today, theatre is supported by the government. In the United States, not-for-profit theatres receive little federal government support, on average less than 1 percent of a theatre's budget. Instead, aesthetically and socially ambitious U.S. theatres rely on donations from wealthy individuals and grants from charitable foundations. Even then, ticket prices for live theatre

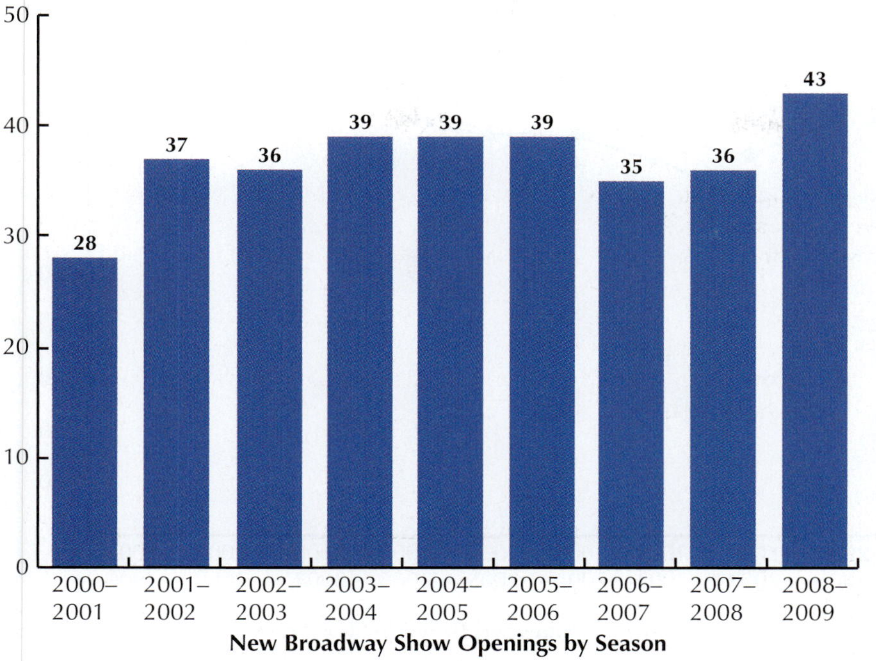

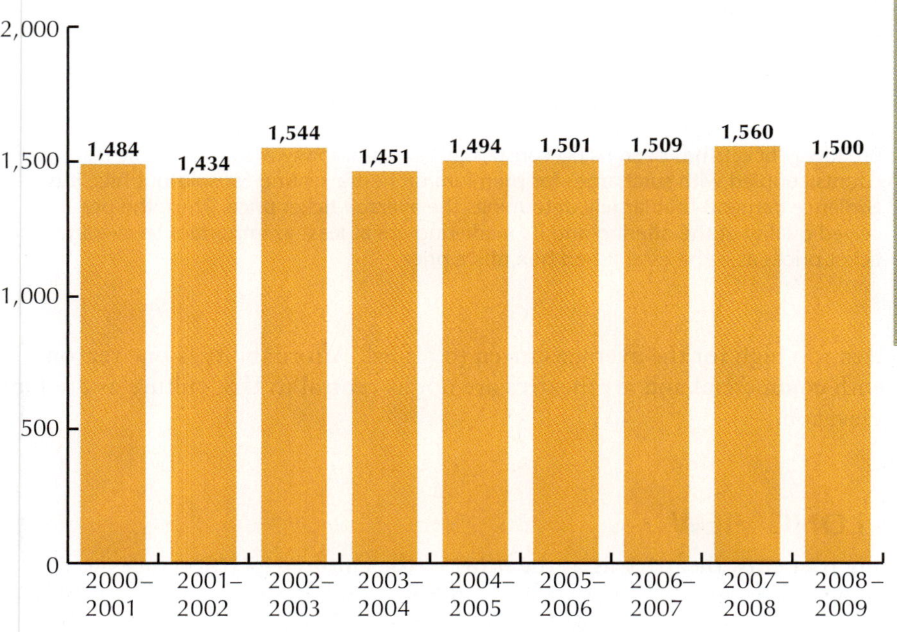

FIGURE 20.10

A Snapshot

In these nine years, the number of new productions each season has been trending slightly upward (top). Playing weeks, a better measure of how active is the Broadway theatre, have been essentially flat (bottom). Playing weeks omit periods when theatres didn't offer performances. So, if the 40 Broadway theatres were fully occupied for 52 weeks in a year, the maximum Broadway playing weeks would be 2080 weeks. Even if a new show wants to move into a theatre, it must wait for the previous production to move out its equipment. Then, the new production must load in lights, scenery, costumes, related equipment, and complete technical and dress rehearsals. This process can take four to six weeks. Sometimes there is no production ready to occupy a theatre when the previous production closes and the theatre is "dark." For the last nine years, Broadway has played about 72 percent of its potential playing weeks.

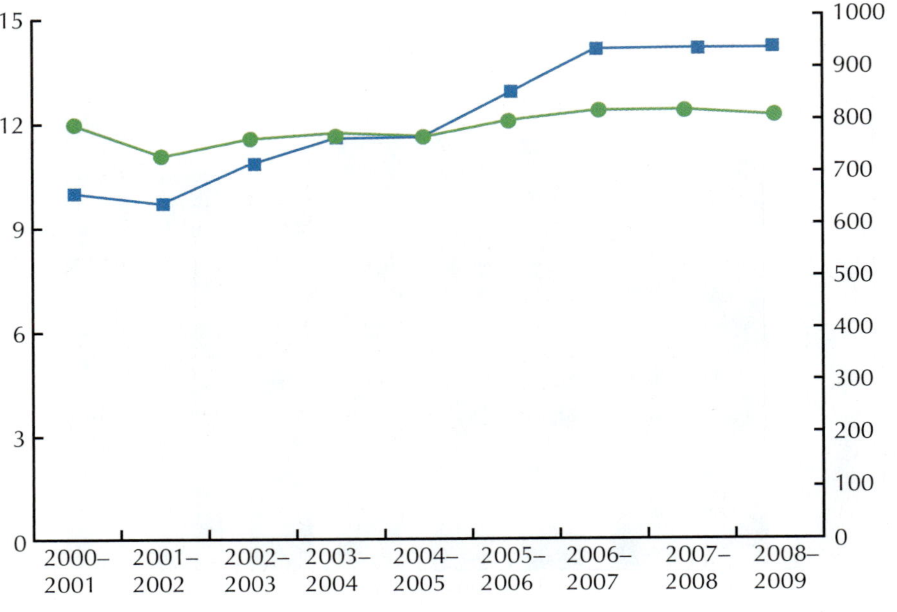

FIGURE 20.11

Broadway Revenues and Tickets Sold

Over this nine-year period, about the same number of tickets were sold each year but the average ticket price rose from $56.01 to $77.64. The published ticket price of Broadway tickets has been rising constantly. Yet, with many readily available discounts coupled with surcharges for premium orchestra seating for sold-out hits, it is audience demand that largely determines the average ticket price. Thus, the perceived quality of the offering and its marketing are at least as important to average ticket prices as is the established box office price.

are often too high for the average citizen to afford. Affordability is one reason that both commercial and art theatres are not as central to U.S. culture as are film and television.

THE LONG VIEW

In many past eras, theatre was at the heart of the culture—performances were civic, religious events that engaged much of the populace. In some eras, royal patronage protected and encouraged plays and the companies that produced them. In the age of Elizabeth I, a penny admitted a spectator to the plays of Shakespeare and his contemporaries. Until the 1700s, there was no division between "commercial" and "artistic" theatre; rather, the division was social and cultural, between court and popular theatre. Since c. 1800, however, a rift has developed between a commercial theatre and an art theatre. The commercial theatre has been characterized by sensationalism and thrills, the art theatre by attempts at artistic and social significance. In the United States now, a division between the commercial and the not-for-profit theatre has become particularly distinct. Today, most commercial Broadway theatres and the musicals they send on the road are entertainments, business ventures. Like rides at amusement parks, they have little to say about the culture and little artistic ambition. Developing new plays and producing historical, classic plays are now the province of not-for-profit theatres. Educational theatres, especially at the college and university level, echo the not-for-profits, while community theatres tilt toward Broadway.

And theatre itself is now a sidebar to Western culture, loved by some but ignored by many.

KEY TERMS

Check your understanding against this list. Brief definitions are included in the Glossary; persons are page-referenced in the Index.

identity theatres 338
limited run 345

CHAPTER

21

Global Theatre

OBJECTIVES

When you have completed this chapter, you should be able to:

- Explain how traits of ritual differ from similar practices in Western theatre
- List traits shared by most African dramas
- Differentiate among ritual, paratheatricals, and theatre
- Cite major differences among the theatres of West, East, and South Africa
- Describe kinds of theatre and drama from Turkey, India, and China
- Differentiate between Kabuki, Kyogen, and Noh

The focus of this book has been the self-aware narrative theatre derived from that of ancient Greece that is now the dominant theatre of Europe (including the former Soviet Union), North America, and Central and South America. But there are other important traditions of theatrical performance outside this one—the theatres of Africa, the Middle East, and Asia, for example. This chapter introduces some representative work within these traditions.

CONTEXT

Cross-Cultural Currents

By 1960, many nations around the world had theatre as part of their cultures. Many, such as Turkey and Greece, had state-supported national theatres as well as commercial theatres in larger cities. Language limited the internationalization

Elbin Cleveland

Farley Richmond

FIGURE 21.1

Masks

Masks and other elements associated with Western theatre are also found in some rituals, ceremonies, and performances of non-Western cultures. Here, a painted mask from Korea (left) and a mask from India (right).

of these theatres, however; many nations continue to have active, sophisticated theatres that are little known outside their own boundaries.

There was some crossing of international boundaries, however. Foreign plays such as *Marat-Sade* (originally German) had a huge impact in England and the United States. The play's director, Peter Brook, became an international figure, directing in Iran as well as Britain and the United States. The Polish director-theorist Jerzy Grotowski had considerable influence in the 1960s and 1970s as director and teacher. International festivals in places as far apart as Scotland, Costa Rica, and Iran (which held a festival of Islamic theatre in the 1990s) brought together productions from all over the world. Japan did a commercial production of a musical version of *Gone With the Wind*. At the same time, the great "museum" theatres—Kabuki and Noh in Japan, Kathakali in India, Beijing opera in China—maintained their places and were seen by increasing numbers of foreigners, with their art internationalized by tours and by replication by foreign artists—Beijing opera in San Francisco, Noh and Kabuki at the Institute for Advanced Study in the Theatre Arts in New York.

It is not always possible now to identify a purely Western or purely indigenous form, so intertwined have they become in some locations. It is not even possible, especially in former colonial areas like Africa, to say what, if any, theatre existed before the Western idea of theatre arrived. This introduces a second major issue, the one with which this book began: What is theatre?

Theatre and Theatre-Like Activities

In many cultures outside the West, various rituals, ceremonies, and performances share elements that we now associate with theatre: masks, costumes, dance and music, and some sort of text.

Because of these shared traits, some scholars have blurred the distinctions between theatre and theatre-like activities. Two important kinds of theatre-like activities are **rituals** and **paratheatricals**.

RITUALS In Africa, pre-Columbian America, Southeast Asia, and parts of the Pacific, many social and religious forms have been grouped together under the term *ritual* because they tend to share certain elements. Many of their shared elements, however, are often not those that in the West we typically associate with theatre. Major elements shared by rituals are listed here and then compared with practices more usually found in Western theatre.

Major elements shared by rituals are:

- Communal bonding of all those present
  - In ritual, the identifying element is "community."
  - In Western theatre, the identifying element is "art."
- No clear separation of audience and performer
  - In ritual, those in attendance participate in the activities.
  - In Western theatre, audiences typically watch and listen to activities performed by others.

- Indifference to permanently established space
  - Rituals take place in spaces made specially for the ritual but seldom permanently altered.
  - Western theatre typically has a space set aside and configured specifically to accommodate the event.
- Diffused focus
  - Rituals may take place over several miles of countryside, without an audience and with some people able to catch only occasional glimpses of the activities.
  - Western theatre typically takes place in one place arranged so that the audience's attention is focused on the event.
- Little or no "scenery" (visual clues to location)
  - Rituals make no attempt to re-create a location other than the actual location of the event.
  - Western theatre typically strives to represent and identify some place other than the theatre itself.
- Purposes that are cultural
  - Ritual aims to do things like heal, honor, or mourn.
  - Western theatre typically aims to do things like teach, entertain, or make money.

Both Western and indigenous scholars still debate whether rituals should be considered a kind of indigenous theatre.

FIGURE 21.2
Storytelling
This Tlingit/Haida storyteller, Gary Waid, relates Alaskan myths such as the tale of the raven and king salmon.

Paratheatrical Forms In addition to these still-debated rituals are other indigenous forms that are clearly related to theatre and that have received much attention from scholars. Important and representative among such forms are the following:

- **Storytelling.** Often with music (or at least drumming) and mime; for example, the *griot* of West Africa and the *meddah* of Turkey
- **Cultural Transmission.** The passing on of knowledge in cultures without writing. This varies enormously, from simple but expert pantomime of birds and animals to elaborate instruction in traditions through pantomime, song, and dance

- **Dance.** Often with narrative and elaborate theatrical effects, especially costumes and masks—for example, the elaborate temple dances of Southeast Asia
- **Puppet Theatre.** For example, the shadow puppets of Turkey and the large Bunraku puppets of Japan

Neither ritual nor the paratheatrical forms are discussed in this chapter as forms of theatre, although elements of them appear clearly in several indigenous theatres that we do discuss.

THE EAST

Major traditional theatres have appeared in a number of cultures of the East. The cultures themseves have often been conservative and religious, with the result that arts—including theatre—have often been preserved centuries after their initial creative energies were gone. Elites within the cultures have often prized these arts, seeing in their preservation an expression of their own continuity. As a result, the modern nations that have emerged from these ancient cultures now typically display a dual theatrical sensibility: One track is re-creative and backward-looking, displaying the sensibility of a museum; the other is creative and forward-looking, displaying the sensibility of Western art. Neither track is "better" than the other.

Generally, Eastern traditional theatres are nonrealistic and share certain common elements:

- Highly stylized, dancelike movement
- Nonrealistic makeup or masks
- Non-Western dramatic form, meaning that they are not based on Aristotelian ideas of action, unity, and the interrelated parts of the play
- Acting styles far removed from Western ideas of impersonation, often with radically different uses of the voice (so that Westerners have called some forms "operas"), for which years of rigorous training are required

Despite similarities, however, traditional Eastern forms are so different from one another that one looks as foreign to an Easterner from another culture as it does to a Westerner. A quick examination of the theatrical traditions of India, Japan, and China will reinforce this observation.

India

The multilingual culture of India was already old when Alexander the Great reached it in 327 BCE. However, it is the modern state of India that maintains an important tradition of theatre, as well as a minor modern theatre and a world-famous film industry.

SANSKRIT THEATRE Sanskrit was the spoken and written language of India, then of its ruling and intellectual classes, until a thousand or so years ago. It was the language of an important treatise on the theatre, the *Natyasastra*, and of the drama.

The Natyasastra. Probably derived from oral tradition and ascribed to the "mythical" authority Bharata, the *Natyasastra* was a long treatise on theatre and drama, analogous to Aristotle's *Poetics*, probably written down between 200 BCE and 200 CE. The *Natyasastra* is a valuable source of theatrical evidence, revealing an ancient India of touring professional acting companies that included both men and women; of permanent theatres built of wood and stone, with elevated stages and close connections to temples; and of rigid caste limits, restricting this kind of theatre to the elitist Brahmin caste.

FIGURE 21.3
Chinese Theatre
A character from the Beijing Opera performs in traditional costume and makeup.

The Drama. Sanskrit drama included at least a thousand plays in the period 200–800 CE. Of these, the plays of Kalidasa are best known in the West, and his *Sakuntala*, which reached Europe in the early nineteenth century, is the most often seen. In seven "acts," it follows a highly romantic love action between a king and the modest Sakuntala and includes the intercession of gods, a curse, and a ring that is lost and then found in the belly of a fish. *Sakuntala* is a play of many scenes, places, and moods, unified not by action but by *rasa*, the state of perception and emotion (in this case, love) induced in the audience. Like much of Sanskrit drama, it took as its source the *Mahabharata*, which, with the *Ramayana*, is the great source work of Hindu culture.

Popular Offshoots of Sanskrit Theatre: Kuttiyatam. Sanskrit, already the language of a small elite, became archaic after about 800; popular languages took its place. In many places in India, Sanskrit theatre absorbed or was absorbed into other forms; the results were highly varied. The most important extant form is **Kuttiyatam**, still performed in southern India.

Kuttiyatam performances go on for several, sometimes many, days. Like Sanskrit theatre, they include totally integrated dance, poetry, music, story, and impersonation. Although aesthetically based in the *Natyasastra*, Kuttiyatam violates Sanskrit purity (its clowning has been called obscene, for example) but offers the possibility of adaptation and change, which pure Sanskrit drama did not.

NON-SANSKRIT THEATRE: KATHAKALI Because of the great importance of movement, especially highly controlled and traditional movement, most Indian theatre has close affinities with dance. Certain forms are often called *dance drama* or *dance theatre* because the dance element is so important. Because they include story and impersonation, some of these forms can be included here; of them, a spectacular example is **Kathakali**, which, like Kuttiyatam, had its origins in southern India.

Kathakali, like many Indian dramatic types, uses stories from the *Ramayana* and the *Mahabharata*. These are sung by one group of performers while others dance to the accompaniment of loud, fast drumming. No raised stage is used and

Spotlight

The female lover (innamorata) of the commedia dell'arte may have been the first role played by a professional female actor in Europe since the Roman mime.

Women on the Global Stage

Japanese Kabuki began as a female form about 1600, only to have women banned from it (for "immorality") three decades later, when men took over the female roles. At the same time, there were no actresses in Islamic lands and had been none since at least the seventh century, and probably none in China (although there had been actress-"courtesans" in the court). Only India in the non-Western world had a continuing tradition of female performers.

Until almost the time of the female Kabuki, Europe had also barred women from the stage: only female religious, performing in religious houses, had acted during the Middle Ages. In ancient Rome, women had appeared only in the mime, the popular but not very respectable form that disappeared from Europe after the empire moved east. The Greek and Roman festival theatres had had only male actors.

Then Europe changed. A woman, probably Italian, appeared on a public stage about 1500, the first to perform before a mixed audience in a thousand years. The first woman performed in a Madrid *corral* a generation later. The French theatre waited another twenty years for a woman, the English another fifty after that. By the eighteenth century, women were on stages all over Europe—but few other places except India. In the Muslim world, theatre remained rare, but, where they were allowed, women performed veiled, or non-Muslim women (Jews in Egypt, for example) acted. Generally, however, women in the Muslim world acted only after 1900, when "modernization" movements began. The traditional theatres of Japan and China remained all-male even longer.

In most cases, once women were allowed on the stage, they came quickly to be linked in common myth with immorality (e.g., the female Kabuki players). The myth also worked the other way: men used the theatre as a place to target women. Many later theatres—the serf theatres of Russia, the nineteenth-century European ballet, the English and American musical ("chorus girls")—became meat markets for "stage-door johnnies."

Why was the woman actor of 1500 Italian? Because, as some scholars speculate, the Italian acting families that toured Europe c. 1500 were remnant mimes from Byzantium? But why did women appear in Europe, and only after a thousand years of invisibility? And why did they not, except for the brief Kabuki interval, appear at the same time in Asia or the Islamic world? For answers, we probably have to look at the European Renaissance and the lack of a similar movement elsewhere, although this will raise other issues: Why the theatre and not politics or art or religion? Why, if women were to emerge from the seclusion the medieval cultures preferred for them, did they see the theatre as the means? Was it because of the theatre's outsider status? Were they in effect going from seclusion to exile?

there is no theatre structure: Performers work outdoors on a flat earth square about sixteen feet on a side. The only light is an oil fire. There is no scenery. While the singers recite the text and the drummers pound, the dancers, in astonishing makeup and elaborate but almost abstract costumes, mime, sign, and dance, impersonating characters with intricate hand symbols, facial expressions, and body movements. All Kathakali performers are male, and the dancers' training takes many years.

Western-Influenced Theatre British residents of India built Western theatres as early as the eighteenth century and began to perform Western plays, to which some Indians were invited. In the nineteenth century, Western theatre became one of the foci of antitraditionalism, and a Western style of Indian drama emerged.

The popular modern Indian form is film, not theatre, and outside cities like Calcutta and Bombay, professional secular theatre does not flourish. The Indian theatrical tradition is religious; the modern state—with its capacity for funding the arts—is secular. The gulf between the two is great.

Japan

Japan, situated on a chain of islands in the Pacific Ocean off the Asian mainland, developed early under Chinese influence and then, after about the fourteenth century CE, rejected China and its ways.

Several forces created traditional Japanese theatre: a feudal society with an emperor nominally at its top; a warrior ethic that made the samurai warrior a model and placed the military ruler at the actual head of state from the sixteenth through the mid-nineteenth centuries; and religion, including native Shinto ("the way of the gods"), Chinese Confucianism, and, above all, a form of Indian Buddhism, Zen.

Dance was probably fundamental to all Japanese theatre. Important dramatic theatre developed from or alongside it, incorporating movement forms that demanded special training. Like Indian theatre, then, Japan created an important dance form (Bugaku) and dramatic forms that were nonrealistic, preserved more or less in their ancient forms for hundreds of years. Two of these forms, Noh and Kabuki, are of particular interest.

Noh **Noh** has been called "the oldest major theatre art . . . still regularly performed." Poetic and austere, it is a theatrical expression of Zen Buddhism. Its originators were a father and son, Kanami (1333–1384) and Zeami (1363–1444), both professional actors attached to a temple. They wrote most of the more than two hundred extant Noh plays, creating a body of work with certain rigid characteristics:

- A three-part structure of *jo, ha*, and *kyu*
- A form based on the interaction of two characters—the *waki*, an accidental confidant, and the ***shite***, the protagonist—with a chorus
- Classification of plays into five subject categories: god, man, woman, insanity, and demon

Japan Information and Culture Center, the Embassy of Japan, Washington, D.C.

FIGURE 21.4

Japanese Noh

The "oldest major theatrical art... still regularly performed," Noh is typified by compressed, poetic drama and symbolic, nonrealistic staging with close ties to Zen Buddhism. Here, a performance of *Izuttsu* (*The Well Curb*), a three-part play.

Traditionally, a Noh performance took all day and consisted of five plays—one from each category, in the preceding order—and an introductory dance, the *okina*, which used an ancient Sanskrit (Indian) text.

Noh plots are simple; their abundant exposition seems natural to a form that is concerned not with events but with the effects of past events. Profoundly influenced by Zen Buddhism, however, Noh's ideology is intuitive, not rational, and its goal is an understanding reached by a mental leap from appearance to reality.

Modern Noh performances rarely include five plays because of the plays' length and difficulty. The style and staging, however, remain largely unchanged:

- A small, raised stage, with all entrances made along a raised passage (***hashigakari***) at one side; at the rear is a wall with a pine tree painted on it
- Onstage musicians (three percussionists and a flute) and chorus, soberly costumed and unmasked
- Male performers, with the male voice undisguised for female roles
- A very deliberate tempo
- Masks for certain characters
- Elaborate and beautiful costumes, but no scenery, and rare, often symbolic properties

Noh had an important offshoot: **Kyogen**. Of later (fifteenth-century) creation but based in much earlier forms, Kyogen is a comic drama performed between Noh dramas. It seems a contradiction, for it mocks the very austerity and aristocratic spirituality that make Noh what it is. The reason usually given is that Kyogen was written by commoners at a period when commoners attended Noh performances; Kyogen expressed their attitudes. Kyogen used the Noh stage but no orchestra or chorus.

KABUKI Although related to Noh, the far more robust and spectacular form—**Kabuki**—that appeared in the seventeenth century quickly established itself as a different and far more popular form. Early censorship actually strengthened the form, leading to much more active and diverse texts (when music and dance were temporarily suppressed) and much more carefully defined acting (when first women, then young men, were banned from the stage).

In its developed form, Kabuki featured long and fully developed actions unfolding in many acts, with many characters and scenes. It was also marked by illusionism, with its direct imitation of contemporary (seventeenth-century) life.

The Kabuki also developed its own theatre and style, which included:

- A large raised stage with a raised walkway to it, the ***hanamichi***, through the audience (originally, there were two such walkways and a connecting walkway at the rear).
- Spectacular scenery, including a revolving stage, introduced c. 1750 (the first in, the world); trapdoors; and a front curtain.
- Elaborate but fundamentally illusionistic makeup.
- Complex, beautiful costumes, including a spectacular feature called ***hikinuki***—costumes so constructed that at a gesture they completely change, literally turning themselves inside out to reveal, for example, a man in armor where a woman had stood.
- All-male companies, with the art of the female impersonator carried to great detail; as a result, Kabuki became above all an actor's, rather than a playwright's, art. Great Kabuki actors have been declared national treasures, like great paintings or great buildings.

Japan Information and Culture Center, the Embassy of Japan, Washington, D.C.

FIGURE 21.5
Japanese Kabuki
This eighteenth-century woodblock print depicts a Kabuki theatre with one raised walkway through the audience. Men play female roles; scenery, costumes, and staging are often spectacular.

Kabuki stories were drawn from many sources and were often heroic and "romantic." Whereas Noh is a theatre of resignation and withdrawal from the world, Kabuki is a theatre of confrontation and an embracing of the world.

Western-Influenced Theatre The abrupt influx of Western ideas into Japan in the nineteenth century corresponded roughly with the rise of dramatic Realism in the West. The result was the somewhat exotic blossoming of several imitations of Western theatre, some of them not very well understood by their practitioners. Recently, for example, hits have emphasized plays as diverse as a musical version of *Gone with the Wind* and the plays of Shakespeare. A small avant-garde drama exists, but theatre is not a truly popular art; like India, Japan is in love with film.

China

China's culture, like India's, is an ancient one that developed in a region of diverse geography and languages. Chinese opera is the dominant theatrical form in China.

CHINESE OPERA The Western designation of Chinese theatre as "opera" suggests one of its major characteristics: reliance on song and musical accompaniment. Chinese music is very different from Western music, and the style of production is very different from that of Western opera, but the name persists. Significantly, too, it accurately reflects the minor role of dance in Chinese theatre.

Classical Chinese theatre as it is now understood—called **Beijing opera** after the city where it appeared—developed in the nineteenth century. It is typified by:

- Multiact dramas
- All-male actors
- Song and music virtually throughout
- Division of characters into four major types: male, female, painted face, and clown (*painted face* referring to those using elaborate makeup, e.g., demons and warriors)
- A reliance on traditional sources for stories and characters

Beijing opera in the nineteenth century became an enormously popular form. Although the tradition of itinerant actors continued (troupes rarely stayed at the same theatre more than a few days, even in big cities), permanent theatres were built. Leading actors moved from one theatre to another in the way that Western opera stars move; the repertory was generally so well known that without rehearsal, they could step into a part in any theatre. The performances themselves

FIGURE 21.6

Eastern Elements in Western Theatre

This production of John Fletcher's *The Woman's Prize* or *The Tamer Tamed*, originally set in Italy, has been give an Asian interpretation by Butler University. Note the use of masks in both images.

relied on centuries-old conventions, on stages all of the same type. Outstanding elements included:

- A raised, pillared stage with an audience on three sides and entrances left and right
- No scenery, and restriction of large properties to chairs and tables (which could be used as walls, mountains, and so on)
- An acting style removed from reality, the result of up to twenty years of rigorous training in every gesture and slightest facial movement
- An onstage orchestra and property man
- Symbols and signs—for example, carrying a whip symbolized riding, and running with small flags symbolized wind
- Almost unbelievable acrobatics—used, for example, in battle scenes

One name stands out in later Beijing opera: Mei Lan Fang (1894–1943). A superb actor of women's roles, he toured extensively in the West, restored some classical elements to Beijing opera, and was a force for the preservation of the form through World War II. His memoirs are an important record of actor training and theatre history.

OTHER CHINESE THEATRE The fall of the last dynasty loosened antitraditional feelings; antitraditionalists turned West. *Uncle Tom's Cabin* was one of the first non-Chinese plays produced (1911). Others followed, bringing disturbing innovations: popular, rather than classical, language; non-Confucian social and moral questions; all-spoken (not sung) drama; and, after 1924, women in female roles. The first coeducational theatre school was created in 1930.

With the communist rise to power in 1949, Chinese theatre went into a period of change, some of it under Russian influence (evident in the introduction of classical ballet, for example). A model revolutionary opera, *Taking Tiger Mountain by Strategy*, was produced, incorporating conventions of Beijing opera but relentless in its revolution ary emphasis. A very small avant-garde movement has appeared in China; however, the repressions of 1989 and after have endangered it. With expression rigidly controlled, avant-gardism is likely to withdraw into formalism.

THE ISLAMIC WORLD

With the appearance of the prophet Muhammed in the late sixth century CE, a new religion, Islam, spread rapidly from the Arabian peninsula: north into the Near East; west along all of Mediterranean Africa and down the East African coast; and east into India and Southeast Asia. For complex reasons, the world of Islam was hostile to theatre (although not to storytelling, puppetry, and dance). As well, it drastically limited the public life of women, including their appearance on the stage.

Islamic peoples developed a highly sophisticated literature, especially in Persian and Arabic, along with other arts; theatre, however, was largely ignored until the nineteenth century. Turkey was an exception.

Turkey

Contemporary Turkey has both professional theatre companies that perform Western and Turkish plays and a vigorous film industry. Turkey also had a popular, traditional theatre that has now effectively disappeared. A popular comic form called *orta oyunu* persisted into the twentieth century. Although its origins are not known, scholars suggest that it may be a continuation of Byzantine mime. Some similarities to Italian commedia dell'arte—comic regional types, improvisation, stock costumes, and characters—suggest influence but may be the result of a common root or may be coincidence.

Other Islamic Theatre

The development of an Islamic theatre apparently came about because of European domination of certain Islamic areas: France in Lebanon; Great Britain in Egypt, Syria, and what is now Jordan; and Italy in Somalia. Following European example, young dramatists began to write and produce plays in Damascus and Cairo, and Cairo became the center of a theatre heavily dependent on music.

A few women had appeared on the infant Islamic stage—most of them Christians and Jews—but after World War I, a liberal movement in Islam loosened some restrictions. In Cairo, a government-funded theatre was set up in 1948.

Nonetheless, theatre in Islamic countries cannot yet be called vigorous, although film flourishes, especially in Egypt. Particularly since the rise of Islamic fundamentalism in the 1970s and the economic hardships of the same period, theatre has had the status of a minor, and perhaps a threatened, art.

AFRICA

Africa is a huge and diverse continent. The colonial period, although brief (c. 1870–1965), changed Africa radically. People with different languages, religions, and cultural backgrounds found themselves under one (European) government. In fact, the boundaries of modern countries of Africa often were set up by European colonizers for the convenience of the colonizers, without regard to the integrity of the indigenous groups living within them.

The colonial influence is important in part because of the effect that language has had on African life, and so on theatre. For example, many people in Africa have found themselves needing three languages in order to thrive: a local language in which to conduct their daily lives; a national language (like Kiswahili in East Africa), which diverse indigenous people speak as a way of communicating across tribal groups; and an international language (usually the language of their colonizers—English, French, German, Portuguese) with which they conduct much of their business, especially international business. Plays in Africa have been written in all three sorts of language.

However, because most people in Europe and the United States read or speak only Western languages, plays written in local and national African languages remain largely inaccessible to people in the West. For this reason, this discussion sketches only the English-language theatre within Africa.

African Universities

African universities were important to the theatre after 1960 because many had created departments of drama, often with advanced degrees. These sometimes, as in Botswana, provided the only live theatre to be seen; therefore, unlike American colleges and universities, African institutions were central to the country's theatre rather than peripheral. Indeed, where university theatre was strong, African theatre tended to be strong.

It was also partly from the universities that a new South African theatre came. In academic venues, multiracial casts were sometimes possible, even under apartheid; there, as well, both whites and blacks opposed to apartheid could seek ways to express, their dissatisfaction. Undergirded by scholarship and criticism in the universities, and extended professionally by a government-funded film industry (jobs for actors, directors, and technical people), the South African theatre had strong black, white, and interracial companies by the end of apartheid (c. 1992).

African Drama

At independence (1955–1965), African playwrights were writing Western-style plays in both formerly French (francophone) and British (English-speaking) Africa. Few were known outside of Africa, however, not least because they could find neither production nor publication overseas. At the same time, writers often had trouble at home if they chose the former oppressors' language instead of a local one; thus, not merely was the content of plays sometimes political, but the very language in which the playwright wrote was also political. Nor was the life of an outspoken writer in many postindependence African countries easy: Self-censorship could block performance, but government repression could also cost playwrights their freedom—or even their lives.

Directed and photographed by Jessica Kaahwa, Kampala, Uganda

FIGURE 21.7
African Theatre
This drop with its death imagery provides a simple but evocative setting for a production in Africa.

African theatres also share a tendency to use amateur rather than professional actors and to work willingly in a variety of performance spaces. In these ways, too, African theatres tend to differ from European and American ones. Probably these traits emerged in part from the practicalities of college theatres, but also from the limited budgets available for producing theatrical works in Africa and from the influence of various indigenous practices (rituals, paratheatrical forms).

Nonetheless, a highly varied African drama has emerged. Three outstanding African dramatists can serve as examples.

Wole Soyinka A Nigerian, Wole Soyinka won the Nobel Prize for Literature in 1986. Soyinka's first play was produced while he was at the Royal Court Theatre in London; his later plays, including both those on African themes and those oriented toward European culture, have gained him international acclaim and gotten him into trouble with his government (*The Trials of Brother Jero, Death and the King's Horseman*). Soyinka ultimately went into exile to escape government repression, although he made a brief return in 1998 after the government changed. Despite Soyinka's international reputation, he suffers a typically African criticism from some quarters: He writes in English, not an African language; he sometimes uses non-African models (e.g., his own version of Euripides' *The Bacchae*). To some, he is "too European"—although if he did not write in English and did not have a European literary orientation, it is unlikely that he would be known outside his language group.

Athol Fugard The most famous of South African playwrights *(Master Harold and the Boys, The Captain's Tiger),* Athol Fugard is white. An actor as well as a writer, he acted in and directed his own small-cast, anti-apartheid plays. Most had mixed-race casts and were realistic in style. Fugard was able to dodge government censorship with comedy, obliqueness, and a lack of preaching: His plays presented apartheid in individual, often superficially funny, cases. Fugard's career has been a long one, spanning the worst of apartheid and its aftermath.

Ngugi wa Thiong'o A Kenyan, Ngugi wa Thiong'o wrote both plays and novels about the problems of independence and Kenya's casting off of colonialism. He was particularly interested in the problems of his own Kikuyu people. Plays such as *I Will Marry When I Want* (written with Ngugi wa Mirii, 1980) had powerful—and dangerous—implications for policy in independent Kenya, made more so by Ngugi's sometimes writing in Kikuyu when the government was trying to downplay tribal cultures. As a result, Ngugi had difficulties with the government; his theatre company was forbidden to play in 1982, and he was in detention for several years. He decided to live outside the country and left Kenya.

Many other African playwrights, as their nations moved away from their colonizers and their literature, came to share traits that set their plays apart from Western drama. Much influenced by Brecht's epic theatre, these included:

- An epic quality: large casts, sweeping themes, loosely structured plots, free-ranging space and time
- A didactic purpose
- A mixture of realism and nonrealism, with music, dance, and drumming

- An extensive use of recognizable cultural elements, such as proverbs, gestures, history, and symbols
- An openness to dramatic symbolism, especially symbolic characters

Theatre for Development

Much world theatre of the last twenty years has reacted against remnants of colonialism, especially in Africa and India. One example is **theatre for development**—that is, a use of theatre to define and help solve local problems. Originally conceived as a top-down educational form in which an elite (government or university) would develop a script, rehearse actors, and send them out to perform, it is now conceived cooperatively. The top-down model is now seen as paternalistic, Western, and colonial.

Instead, a few actors now go into a village to live. With local people, they develop and rehearse a script in the local language about a local problem (AIDS, marriage laws, pollution). Everybody is encouraged to participate, which includes watching rehearsals. Everybody is invited to contribute. Discussion follows public performance, but the process itself is seen as more important than the performance. Theatre thus becomes a way of studying a problem, devising a solution, and showing how to effect it—a way of "performing" real life to understand it. This bottom-up model assumes that people who have problems will be able to identify them and suggest ways of solving them.

Theatre for development is not without its critics. Perhaps because it has been most often practiced by activists of the political left, theatre for development is

FIGURE 21.8
Athol Fugard
Fugard was the most important white South African playwright through the apartheid years and after, dealing with censorship and restrictions through guile and humor. Here, a scene from *Master Harold and the Boys* at Triad Stage.

often opposed by those on the right. Others argue that expecting uneducated villagers to analyze their problems and suggest feasible solutions is naïve and unrealistic, and so unproductive. Still others maintain that, although theatre for development may be socially useful, it is neither artistic nor aesthetically pleasing and so is not really theatre at all.

This situation raises the overriding question of this book: What should be the role of theatre in a developing society?

KEY TERMS

Check your understanding against this list. Brief definitions are included in the Glossary; persons are page-referenced in the Index.

GLOSSARY

What follows is a compilation of *Key Terms* found at the end of each chapter as well as a few additional terms used in the text. Numbers at the end of each entry refer to the page(s) where a fuller discussion can be found.

Abstraction An artistic depiction that is different from a literal, photographic representation of the thing depicted, usually by being more generalized, less particular. (55)

Absurdism A style of drama popularized in France after World War II that viewed human existence as meaningless and treated language as an inadequate means of communication. Major authors include Samuel Beckett and Eugène Ionesco. (316)

Academy A group formed to further a specific artistic or literary end; for example, the French Academy and the rhetorical academies of the Renaissance. (217, 246)

Acting Creation of a character in action, through impersonation, for an audience. In formal acting, the actor seeks the truth of theatrical convention; in realistic acting, the actor seeks the truth of everyday life. (98–116)

Action According to Aristotle, a causally linked sequence of events, with beginning, middle, and end; the proper and best way to unify a play. More popularly, the single and unified human process of which a drama is the imitation. To some modern critics, an interaction (between dramatic protagonist and others). (34–35)

Actor-manager A starring actor who is head and nominal artistic director of a company; for example, Sir Henry Irving in the late nineteenth century in England. (289)

Actors Equity See *union.*

Advertising Paid-for materials and media to spread awareness of a product. (66)

A-effect See *Alienation effect.*

Aesthetic response Audience reaction to art object as art, not as idea, meaning, and so on; implies some idea of "beauty." (8)

Aesthetics Study of the nature of beauty. (133)

Afterpiece A short play that followed the main attraction. (255)

Agent Professional who represents theatre artists for a percentage of their income. (67)

Alienation effect (A-effect) Customary, but perhaps misleading, translation of the German *Verfremdungseffekt,* "to make strange." Term now almost always associated with Bertolt Brecht's epic theatre, which aims to distance the spectator from the play's action in order to force conscious consideration of the political and social issues raised by the play. Shortened often to *A-effect.* (280)

Alley stage Performance area shape that puts audience on each side, with the performance area, usually a long rectangle, between. (73)

Amateur theatre A producing organization in which most participants are not paid or are paid only token amounts well below professional levels. Usually community and educational theatres are amateur theatres. (80)

Amphitheatre In Roman theatre, a large public space for paratheatrical entertainments, like animal fights. (195)

Angle perspective Multipoint perspective; results when several vanishing points are located away from the center of the stage so that vistas appear toward the wings. (250)

Antagonist The opponent in an agon, or contest; in drama, either of two opponents in conflict, or the character who opposes the protagonist. (37)

Antiquarianism The study of the details of past civilizations, often with a view to reproducing historically accurate settings onstage. Movement was popular toward the end of the eighteenth century and is viewed as a precursor to Romanticism. (304)

Applause Positive response to performance by clapping hands. (18)

Apron That part of a stage that extends in front of the proscenium arch. (71)

Arena stage A stage in which the audience completely surrounds the playing area. Also called *theatre in the round.* (72–73)

Art Activity done for its own ends, separable from both life and practicality, although it may be applied to very practical as well as aesthetic purposes. (8–10)

Art theatre movement A theatrical movement of the late nineteenth and early twentieth centuries that tried to separate itself from commercial theatre and the reliance on box office. (282–286)

Audience Those who watch or listen to a performance. (4)

Audition A session at which a theatre artist, usually an actor, displays his or her craft in order to secure a job. (113–114)

Auditorium "Hearing place"; audience section of theatre. (53)

Automated fixtures Flexible focusing and special effect fixtures. By a remote signal these instruments can move from area to area on the stage and change color. They are standard equipment in rock concerts and light shows. (154)

Avant-garde Art thought ahead of the mainstream, experimental. (259, 282–286)

Backdrop Painted two-dimensional hanging, usually as part of a scenic background. (327)

Balance On the proscenium stage, the visual equalizing of the two halves of the stage picture as seen from the audience. In any stage moment, the attempt to achieve a sense of equal weight between the people and objects on stage. More a metaphor than an actuality. (133, 135)

Balcony Elevated audience area. (71)

Ballad opera A "minor" form of musical drama especially popular during the eighteenth and nineteenth centuries in England and featuring political satire interlarded with familiar tunes for which new and topical lyrics were devised; for example, John Gay's *The Beggar's Opera.* (299)

Beat A rhythmic unit in a play; defined variously by different actors and directors. (137)

Beijing opera Traditional Chinese theatrical form, spectacular, nonrealistic. (362–363)

Biomechanics The concept and the complex of techniques devised by Vsevolod Myerhold to train actors so that their bodies could be as responsive as a machine. (279)

Black theatre A theatre movement of the 1960s and after, primarily for black audiences, actors, and playwrights, originally connected with the Black Power movement, a political ideology. (318–321)

Blocking Stage movement for actors, given in rehearsal (usually) by the director. (130)

Body language Communicable emotional states understood from posture and other conscious and unconscious use of the body. See also *gesture.* (106)

Book 1. The spoken text of a play or musical; early musicals with stories and dialogue were called *book musicals.* 2. Several flats hinged together and folded together form a book of flats. 3. To book a production is to schedule a performance of it. (77, 87)

Border Curtain, or less often flats or cutouts, suspended at intervals behind the proscenium arch to mask the overhead rigging. Particularly important in Italianate settings. (237)

Boulevard Historically, the permanent home of the old fair theatres of eighteenth-century Paris, and later of the illegitimate houses where melodrama and comic opera flourished during the nineteenth century. Now refers to the district of the commercial theatres in Paris and means roughly what the word *Broadway* implies in the United States. (251, 256, 260, 262)

Box Historically the favored, and most expensive, seats in a theatre. Made by sectioning off parts of a gallery, boxes were spacious and outfitted with armchairs, in contrast to the crowded galleries, whose seats consisted of backless benches, and to the pit, where originally no seats were provided. (73)

Box, pit, and gallery Eighteenth- and nineteenth-century arrangement of audience with a ground-level pit, up to five levels of boxes or galleries surrounding it, with the cheapest seats at the top. (253)

Box set Interior setting represented by flats forming three sides (the fourth wall being the proscenium line); first used around 1830 and common after 1850. (267)

Breeches role Role in which an actress portrays a male character and dresses like a man, presumably adding sexual titillation to dramatic interest. (306)

Broadway In popular parlance, the area of New York City on and adjacent to the street named Broadway, where the commercial theatre of the United States is concentrated. (75)

Burlesque In eighteenth- and nineteenth-century theatre, a form of "minor" drama popular in England and featuring satire and parody. In the United States of the late nineteenth century and the twentieth century, a kind of entertainment originally dependent on a series of variety acts but later including elements of female display (including striptease) in its major offerings. After moving to the fringes of respectability by the 1940s, burlesque disappeared in the United States by the late 1950s. (299–300)

Business Activity performed by actor(s) at given points in a performance; for example, the business of lighting a cigarette or cooking a meal. See also *lines of business*. (136, 240)

Byzantine "Of Byzantium," the eastern Roman Empire, c. 300–1453. (202–203)

Casting The process of selecting a specific actor to play a specific role. (129)

Casting call Public announcement of auditions or interviews for casting of a play. (129–130)

Casting director Mediates between actors and producer(s), for whom he or she works; makes initial sifting of acting pool. (67)

Catharsis Aristotle cited as the end cause of tragedy "the arousal and catharsis of such emotions [pity and fear]," a statement popularly understood to mean that tragedy "purges" fear and pity from the audience; but alternative interpretations suggest that tragedy arouses and satisfies such emotions within its own structure and characters. Highly controversial and elusive concept. (182)

Causality Belief that human events have causes (and therefore consequences); as a result, events are seen as joined in a chain of cause and effect. (35, 110)

Causal plot Plot of linked, internally consistent cause and effect. (35)

Centering Actor's term for localization of human energy source in the body, usually in the abdomen. (105)

Character One of Aristotle's six parts of a play, the material of plot and the formal cause of thought; an agent (participant, doer) in the play whose qualities and traits arise from ethical deliberation. In popular parlance, the agents or "people" in the play. (36–37)

Chariot-and-pole system An elaborate system for changing elements of the scenery simultaneously. Devised by Giacomo Torelli in the seventeenth century, the system involved scenery attached to poles that rose through slits in the stage floor from chariots that ran on tracks in the basement and depended on an intricate system of interlocking ropes, pulleys, wheels, and windlasses for their simultaneous movement. (238)

Chorus In Greek drama of the fifth century BCE, a group of men (number uncertain) who sang, chanted, spoke, and moved, usually in unison, and who, with the actors (three in tragedy and five in comedy), performed the plays. In the Renaissance, a single character named Chorus who provided information and commentary about the action in some tragedies. In modern times, the groups that sing and/or dance in musical comedies, operettas, ballets, and operas. (170–172)

City or Great Dionysia The major religious festival devoted to the worship of the god Dionysus in Athens. The first records of tragedy appeared at this festival in 534 BCE, and so it is called the home of tragedy. See also *festivals*. (172)

Classical Specifically refers to that period of Greek drama and theatre from 534 BCE to 336 BCE (the advent of the Hellenistic period). Loosely used now to refer to Greek and Roman drama and theatre in general (a period dating roughly from the sixth century BCE through the sixth century CE, about twelve hundred years). (176, 178)

Climax The highest point of plot excitement for the audience. (35)

Cloak and sword play (capa y espada) Romantic Spanish plays of love and dueling—swashbucklers. (277)

Closet drama Plays written to be read, not performed. (265)

Comedy A form (genre) of drama variously discussed in terms of its having a happy ending; dealing with the material, mundane world; dealing with the low and middle classes; dealing with myths of rebirth and social regeneration; and so on. (43, 233)

Comedy, middle See *middle comedy.*

Comedy, new See *new comedy.*

Comedy, old See *old comedy.*

Comedy of manners Refers most often to seventeenth- and eighteenth-century comedies whose focus is the proper social behavior of a single class. (253)

Comic opera A "minor" form of musical drama popular first in the eighteenth century and characterized then by sentimental stories set to original music. Later used to mean an opera in which some parts were spoken (in contrast to "grand opera," where everything was sung). (250)

Commedia dell'arte Italian popular comedy of the fifteenth through seventeenth centuries. Featured performances improvised from scenarios by a set of stock characters and repeated from play to play and troupe to troupe. See also *lazzi*. (239)

Commercialism A movement after about 1860 that saw the financing of theatre move from the state, a wealthy individual, or the church to companies or individuals that wished to make a profit through the sale of tickets. (288)

Community theatre Theatre performed by and for members of a given community, especially a city or town. Usually amateur, sometimes with professional directors, designers, and business staff. (82, 288)

Complication Ascending or tying action. That part of the plot in which the action is growing tenser and more intricate up to the point of crisis (turning point), after which the action unties and resolves in a section called the *dénouement*. (35)

Composition Arrangement of visual elements for aesthetic effect. (133–136)

Computer-assisted design (CAD) Use of powerful computer programs to draft, elevate, rotate, color, etc., designs. (148–150)

Confidant(e) In drama, a character to whom another leading character gives private information. (37, 232)

Conflict Clash of characters, seen either as objectives that create obstacles for one another, or as actions, neither of which can succeed unless the other fails. (35)

Confraternity In France, a religious brotherhood, many of which sponsored or produced plays during the Middle Ages. One, the Confraternity of the Passion, held a monopoly on play production in Paris into the 1570s. (209)

Constructivism A nonrealistic style of scenic design associated with Vsevolod Myerhold and marked by the view that a good set is a machine for doing plays, not a representation of familiar locales. Incorporated simple machines on stage and often revealed the method of its own construction. (279)

Continental seating First devised by Wagner in the late nineteenth century for his theatre at Bayreuth; eschews a central aisle in favor of entrances and exits at the end of each aisle. (266)

Convention (dramatic, theatrical) A way of doing things agreed on by a (usually unstated) contract between audience and artists; for example, characters' singing their most important feelings and emotions is a convention of musical comedy. (54)

Copyright Legal concept of intellectual property rights. (97)

Corpus Christi plays Medieval cycle plays and cosmic dramas (see entry) often performed during a spring festival established in the fourteenth century in honor of the Christian Eucharist. Also see *festivals*. (206)

Corrales Spanish theatres of the late Middle Ages, sited in open courtyards among houses. (255)

Cosmic drama Long dramatic presentations popular in the Middle Ages that depicted religious events from the creation to the Last Judgment. Short plays were combined until the total presentation could last several days or weeks and occasionally a month or more. See also *cycle play*. (207)

Cothurnus High boot with platform sole for tragic actor, Hellenistic Greece. (183)

Court theatre A theatre located at the court of a nobleman. After the Renaissance, Italianate theatre, whose perspective was drawn with the vanishing points established from the chair of the theatre where the ruler sat, making his the best seat in the house. (226)

Crisis Decisive moment at the high point of a rising action; turning point. (35)

Criticism The careful, systematic, and imaginative study and evaluation of works of drama and theatre (or any other form of art) *dramatic*, of plays; *performance*, of live performances. (1, 62)

Cue Immediate stimulus for a line, an action, or an effect. (87, 138, 140)

Culture The set of beliefs, values, and lifestyle of a group. (19–22)

Cycle play Medieval (especially English) dramas covering the "cycle" of history from the creation of the world to doomsday. See also *cosmic drama*. (207)

Dadaism Art movement of the first third of the twentieth century that rejected logic and tradition; often satirical, sometimes intentionally contradictory, silly. (317, 325)

Decision In Aristotelian criticism, the most highly characterizing trait of a dramatic agent; the trait that translates idea into action and thus, in Aristotelian terms, unites with plot (in the sense here of action). See also *plot* and *action*. (35, 37, 42)

Decorum In neoclassical theory, the behavior of a dramatic character in keeping with his or her social status, age, sex, and occupation; based on the requirements of verisimilitude (see *verisimilitude*). (233)

Dénouement That part of the plot that follows the crisis (turning point) and that includes the untangling or resolving of the play's complications. (35)

Deus ex machina Literally, "the god from the machine," a reference to a deity who flew in at the conclusion of some Greek tragedies (particularly those of Euripides) to ensure the play's appropriate outcome. Popularly, any ending of a play that is obviously contrived. (179)

Dialect Regional or ethnic speech, sometimes necessary for an actor in a particular role. (107)

Dialogue Character interaction through language. (93)

Dimming Through an instrument for controlling the intensity of light, manipulating the amount of electricity that reaches individual lamps. (153)

Dionysia A Greek religious festival in honor of the god Dionysus. The City Dionysia and the Rural Dionysia both included drama as a part of the celebration, but the city festival was clearly the dominant one of the two. See also *festivals.* (171–172)

Discovery According to Aristotle, any passage from ignorance to knowledge within a play, by means of (for example) sign, emotion, reasoning, action. Good discoveries grow out of suffering (awareness) and lead to reversal (change of direction). (34)

Discovery space Permanent or temporary space in the Elizabethan (Shakespearean) playhouse that permitted actors and locales to be hidden from view and then "discovered" (or revealed) when needed. Location, appearance, and even invariable existence of the space are hotly disputed. (218)

Dithyramb A hymn of praise, often to the god Dionysus, performed by a chorus of men or boys; a regular part of the religious festival of Athens after 509 BC. (170)

Domestic tragedy A serious play dealing with domestic problems of the middle or lower classes. In the eighteenth century, a reaction against "regular" or neoclassical tragedy. See also *purity of genres.* (255)

Double 1. To play more than one role. 2. *The Theatre and Its Double*, an influential book by Antonin Artaud, calls the Western theatre merely a shadow or double of the (to him) true and vital Eastern theatre. (280)

Downstage That part of the stage closest to the front. In early Italianate theatres, the stage floor was raked (slanted) up from the front to the back; therefore, to move forward on the stage was literally to move "down the stage." (135, 238)

Dramaturg Dramatic advisor and researcher for theatre or production. (63)

Dress rehearsal A final rehearsal in which all visual elements of production, including costumes, are used. Typically a rehearsal that strives to duplicate, insofar as possible, an actual performance. (138)

Drop Backdrop. Large curtain, usually of painted canvas, hung at the rear of the stage to provide literal and visual closure for the stage setting. (304)

Eccyclema In classical Greece, a machine used to thrust objects or people (often dead) from inside the skene into view of the audience. Probably some sort of wheeled platform that rolled or rotated through the skene's central door. (178)

Eclectic(ism) Gathering of materials from many sources; popularly, a mixture of styles and methods. In twentieth-century theatre, the idea that each play calls forth its own production style. (315)

Educational theatre Theatre by and (in part) for students in an elementary, secondary, or collegiate setting. (81–82)

Emblem A device (usually an object or picture of an object) used as an identifying mark; something that stands for something else. In the Middle Ages, a key stood for St. Peter, a crooked staff for a bishop. (199)

Encore Part of performance repeated in response to audience applause. (18)

Ensemble A performing group. Also, a group acting method that emphasizes unity and consistency of performances. (273)

Environment The visual and spatial surrounding of the play, influenced by such matters as mood and visual meaning. (126)

Ephemeral art Art that cannot be repeated exactly. (11)

Epic theatre Term originated by Erwin Piscator and popularized by Brecht to describe a theatre in which the audience response is objective, not subjective, and in which such narrative devices as film projections, titles, and storytelling are used. See also *alienation effect.* (279–280)

Episodic plot Plot whose incidents are connected by idea or metaphor or character, not by cause and effect. (36)

Exposition Necessary information about prior events, or a part of a play given over to communicating such information; because it is a "telling" and not an enacting of narrative, it is usually nondramatic. (33)

Expressionism A style of theatre popular in Europe after World War I and typified by symbolic presentation of meaning, often as viewed from the standpoint of the main character; distortions of time, space, and proportion are common. (278)

Façade stage One that puts the actors in front of a neutral (nonrepresentational) surface. (177)

Fair theatre "Illegitimate" theatres in France and England performed at large, periodic fairs. (256)

Farce Form of comedy "stuffed" with laughs that arise not from verbal wit or human profundity but (usually) mechanics: business, mix-ups, mistaken identities, etc. (43)

Feminist theory (of theatre) An attempt to explain the effects of gender in the workings of theatre and drama and, through them, on society and culture. (61)

Festivals In Greece, religious worship took place in private and at major public festivals. In and around Athens, there were four festivals devoted to the god Dionysus. At three of these, records of drama appeared during the fifth century BCE. At the festival of no other gods can such records be found. See *City Dionysia*, *Rural Dionysia*, and *Lenaia*. During the Middle Ages, there were Christian festivals at which dramas were often produced. See also *Corpus Christi*. (169, 187–191, 205)

Flat A structure upon which scenery is painted, consisting of a wooden frame and canvas covering; usually of a size to be carried by one or two persons for shifting. Used in both Italianate staging and box sets (see entries). (178, 237)

Floodlight Broad-beam stage instrument that "floods" a large area with light. (153)

Flying Method of handling scenery for quick shifting by raising it out of sight over the stage with one of various systems of ropes, pulleys, counterweights, machines, and so on. Also, the illusion of flight in actors and properties through the use of concealed wires and the same system of ropes and pulleys. (210)

Focus The point or object that draws the eye of the audience to the stage picture. (133)

Foil A minor character intended to set off another character through contrast. (37)

Follow spot Powerful, hard-edged lighting instrument mounted so that an operator can "follow" action with the light. (154)

Footlights Light sources arranged along the front of a stage (between actors and audience) to throw light upward from stage level to eliminate shadows from harsh overhead lighting. Rarely used with modern lighting systems, but standard equipment with candle, oil, gas, and early electrical systems (c. 1650–1920). (154)

Forestage That level part of the stage in front of the scenery, especially in Renaissance stages, which used a slanted floor for forced perspective in the scenic area. See also *apron*. (71)

For-profit Professional theatre that is fully taxed and gets its income from ticket sales and related sources. (27)

Fourth wall (Realism) Nineteenth-century concept of a completely Realistic performance space that the audience looked into through a removed or invisible "wall" (the proscenium plane). (272)

French scene Scene division between entrance or exit of major character(s). (137)

Front of house (FOH) Everything on the audience side of the proscenium or boundary of the acting space; e.g., promotion and publicity for performances, house management, box office sales. (71)

Gallery The highest audience areas in nineteenth-century theatres (box, pit, and gallery), hence, the cheapest seats; the balconies. (218)

Gay and lesbian theatre Theatre of, by, and often for a gay and lesbian community. (323)

Gel In stage lighting, a medium for coloring the beam of light. (153)

Generic criticism Criticism by identification of genre (comedy, tragedy, etc.) (42)

Genre In dramatic criticism, a category of plays: comedy, tragedy, melodrama, farce. Popularly, any category. (42)

Gentlemanly melodrama Later melodrama for middle-class audiences with upper-middle-class subjects and settings. (294)

Gesture In one sense, any human act that conveys meaning (i.e., a speech is a gesture). In a more limited sense, a planned physical movement that conveys meaning, like waving a hand or pointing a finger. (106)

Given circumstances Basic facts that define the world of the play; conditions of place, period, social level, and so on. (54)

Given circumstances (of characters) In Stanislavskian vocabulary, those aspects of character that are beyond the character's or actor's control: age, sex, state of health, and so on. (110)

Glory In medieval and Renaissance art, a cloud or sunburst in which divinities appeared. In the theatre of those periods, a flown platform made to look like a cloud or sunburst. (210)

Golden Age The great age of any culture. In Spain, the period c. 1550–1650, the greatest age of Spanish drama; in France, the age of Louis XIV; in England, the age of Elizabeth and Shakespeare. (217, 224–226)

Graeco-Roman period That period in Greece and Greek lands when Roman domination had arrived, usually dated from c. 100 BCE to the fall of the Western Roman Empire, c. 550 CE. In theatre architecture, those Greek theatres that were remodeled to bring them in closer accord with the Roman ideals. (Not to be confused with Roman theatres built in Greek lands.) (185)

Great Dionysia see City Dionysia.

Griot West African storyteller. (355)

Groove A shallow channel in the stage floor in which a flat rode, for quick scene changes; a bank of several grooves would allow one flat to be pulled aside while another was pushed on in its place, seemingly in the same plane. (271)

Ground plan The "map" of the playing area for a scene, with doors, furniture, walls, and so on indicated to scale. (128)

Ground row A piece of scenery at stage level, often used to hide stage-level machinery or lights or to increase the sense of distance. (304)

Guerilla theatre Didactic political theatre done in nontheatrical spaces—streets, factories, subways—without previous announcement; hit-and-run performances like guerrilla attacks. (318)

Guild Religious and, sometimes, trade or professional organization in the Middle Ages that became the producer of civic medieval theatre. (209)

Hamartia Aristotle's concept of error or failure of judgment by the tragic hero (sometimes translated inaccurately as "tragic flaw"). (182)

Hanamichi In the Japanese Kabuki theatre, a walkway through the audience used by actors to get to and from the stage. (361)

Happening Quasi-theatrical event of the 1960s, done outside the commercial theatre, usually done in nontraditional spaces and having no plot (in the Aristotelian sense); often, audience members moved through the event at their own rates and in their own sequences. (325)

Happy idea The basic premise on which a particular Greek old comedy was based. For example, the happy idea in *Lysistrata* is that women can prevent war by withholding sex. (176)

Hashigakari: In the Japanese Noh theatre, a walkway at the side of the stage for the actors' entrances and exits. (360)

Heavens 1. Area above the stage: in the Elizabethan theatre, the underside of the roof that extended over the stage. 2. In the nineteenth century, the highest gallery. (218)

Hellenistic period 1. That period of Greek history dating from the coming of Alexander the Great (c. 336 BCE). 2. In theatre architecture, those Greek theatres built during the Hellenistic period. (181–183)

Hero 1. A figure embodying a culture's most valued qualities (for example, Achilles in *The Iliad*) and hence the central figure in a heroic tragedy. 2. Popularly the leading character in a play or, more precisely, the leading male character in a play. 3. In melodrama, the male character who loves the heroine. See also *protagonist*. (43, 173, 216, 292–293)

Heroic Of or relating to a hero; by extension, exalted. Heroic couplets are two lines of rhyming iambic pentameter, probably an English attempt to reproduce the French Alexandrine, the approved verse for neoclassical tragedy. Heroic acting stressed the vocal and physical grandeur of the actor. Heroic tragedy, popular during the seventeenth and eighteenth centuries, customarily treated the conflict between love and duty and was written in heroic couplets. (43, 216, 259)

Hikinuki: In Japanese Kabuki performance, the sudden transformation of a costume into a completely different one. (361)

Hireling In professional companies of the Renaissance and after, an actor or technician hired by the shareholders to work for a set wage at a set task. (220)

Hit or flop Supposed condition of a commercial theatre that has no middle ground and no economic tolerance for plays that may earn back their costs slowly. (80)

Householder Member of an acting company who owns a share of the theatre building itself. (215)

Humanism A philosophy that believes that people should be at the center of their own deepest concerns. (215)

Hut In Elizabethan public theatre, small space below roof, probably for machinery. (218)

Idea In Aristotelian criticism, the moral expression of character through language; more generally, the intellectual statement of the meaning (see entry) of a play or a performance. (37–40)

Identity theatre Political theatre identified by race or gender. (338)

Illusion of the first time An expression used by an English critic (late nineteenth century) to describe the effect of good realistic acting: that is, the event seems to be happening for the first time to the character. (111)

Illusionism Scenic practices (with analogs in acting, directing, and other theatre arts) that rely on a belief in the theatrical imitation of the real world. (232)

Imagination In acting, inventive faculty of the actor. (See also *instrument.*) More generally, that faculty of mind or feeling, usually thought to be nonlinear, imagistic, metaphorical, and playful. (99)

Impersonation Pretending to be another. (10)

Impressionism A style of art that sought truth in fleeting moments of consciousness. Prevalent in the drama and theatre of the 1890s, Impressionism was noted for its moody and mysterious quality. (277)

Improvisation Acting technique or exercise emphasizing immediacy of response and invention rather than rehearsed behavior. (109)

Independent theatre movement In nineteenth-century Europe, the appearance of noncommercial theatres in several countries more or less simultaneously, most of them amateur or nontraditional and able to operate outside the usual censorship, "independent" of commercial demands. (272)

Instrument The actor's physical self. See also *imagination.* (105)

Integrated musical Musical with songs and dances that are organic parts of story and character. (303)

Intermezzi Italian entertainments usually given at courts and presented between other forms of entertainment. See *interlude.* (239)

Italianate staging A kind of staging developed during the Renaissance in Italy and marked by a proscenium arch and perspective scenery arranged in wing and shutter. (237–238)

Kabuki Traditional Japanese theatre of great spectacle and powerful stories, often heroic and chivalric or military. (360)

Kathakali Traditional Indian dance-drama form. (357)

Kuttambalam Theatre type used by an Indian Kutiyattam (see entry): square, roofed stage with audience on three sides.

Kuttiyatam Indian theatrical form, derived from Sanskrit drama. (357)

Kyogen Japanese theatre form: comic interludes between parts of a Noh performance. (360)

Language In Aristotle, one of the six parts of a play (also called diction); the formal cause of music, the material of thought; the words of a play. (40)

Latin music drama Medieval dramas performed inside churches by clergy. The dramas unfolded in Latin rather than the vernacular and were sung rather than spoken, thus the name. Also called *liturgical drama.* (205)

Lazzi: Stock bits of business designed to provoke a particular response, usually laughter, from the audience. Associated particularly with the commedia dell'arte and the French farce of the seventeenth century. (240)

Lenaia One of three major Athenian religious festivals devoted to the public worship of the god Dionysus at which drama was recorded. The home of comedy. See also *festivals.* (171, 175)

Light plot The lighting designer's graphic rendering of the arrangement of lights and their connections. (153)

Lines of business A range of roles in which an actor would specialize for the major part of his or her acting career (e.g., young lover, walking gentlewoman, comic servant). Particularly important during the seventeenth and eighteenth centuries. (250, 251, 253)

Little theatre movement In the early twentieth-century United States, the appearance of noncommercial theatres throughout the country dedicated to art; many became community theatres. (284)

Limited run Short, predetermined playing period (Broadway) with major names. (345)

Liturgy The rites of worship of the church; liturgical drama: the kinds of plays that were done inside churches as part of the religious services and thus were performed in Latin, by the clergy, and were usually chanted or sung rather than spoken. Liturgical drama is also called *Latin music drama.* (204)

Living Theatre Important American avant-garde theatre, second half of twentieth century. (317)

Long run Uninterrupted sequence of performances of the same play, "long" by comparison with that of others like it: A dozen performances would have been a long run in the seventeenth century; on today's Broadway, a long run can last years. (345)

Lords' room Expansive space close to the tiring house in Elizabethan theatre. (218)

Ludi: 1. In Rome, festivals or *ludi* were given for public worship of a variety of gods and on various public occasions like military victories and the funerals of government officials. As drama was often included as a part of the festivals, they are important in a history of Roman theatre. 2. Early medieval term for plays. (187)

Machine play Any play written especially to show off the special effects and movable scenery in a theatre. Especially popular during the Neoclassical period, when regular plays obeyed "unity of place" and so had few opportunities for elaborate scenic changes. (246)

Mansion The particularized setting in the medieval theatre that, together with the platea, or generalized playing space, constituted the major staging elements of the theatre. Several mansions were placed around or adjacent to the platea at once—thus "simultaneous staging." See also *platea.* (204)

Marketing That part of an organization that focuses outward on consumers; oversees public relations and advertising. (65)

Marxist theory Theory of theatre or drama based on Karl Marx's economic and political ideas. (61)

Masque Spectacular theatrical form, especially of the Renaissance and the Neoclassical periods, usually associated with court theatres (see entry) or special events. Emphasis was put on costumes and effects, with much music and dancing; amateur actors frequently performed. For example, Ben Jonson's many court masques. (223)

Master artist A term, coined by Richard Wagner, to identify the person responsible for the unification of a complex work of art like a music drama; someone who controls every aspect of a performance. (266)

Master artwork *Gesamtkunstwerk.* Both term and concept popularized by Richard Wagner, who argued that such a work would be the artistic fusion of all major artistic elements, including music, into a single work under the artistic supervision of a single master artist. (266)

Master of secrets That craftsman/artist of the medieval theatre charged with the execution of special effects in the dramas. (210)

Meaning Intellectual content suggested or inspired by a play or a performance. All plays have meaning, however trivial, and most plays and performances have several meanings. Best thought of as "range of meaning" or "world of meaning." (41–42)

Mechane Machine, or machina. In classical Greece, a crane by means of which actors and objects could be flown into the playing area. (179)

Mediator One who comes between—in theatre, somebody who stands between audience and performance, affecting audience perception. (60)

Medieval That period of world history dating roughly from the fall of the Western Roman Empire (c. 550 CE) to the fall of Constantinople and the beginning of the Renaissance (c. 1450). In drama, the period between 975, the first record of drama, and c. 1550, when religious drama was outlawed in many countries throughout Europe. (219–230)

Melodrama Literally "music drama." A kind of drama associated with a simplified moral universe, a set of stock characters (hero, heroine, villain, comic relief), rapid turns in the dramatic action, and a dual-issue ending. Leading form of drama throughout the nineteenth century. (291)

Method The American version of Stanislavski's "system" of actor training. (110)

Middle Ages An early name for the period dating roughly from the fall of Rome to the Renaissance. (203)

Middle comedy That transitional kind of Greek comedy dating from c. 404 BCE, the defeat of Athens by Sparta, to 336 BCE, the beginning of the Hellenistic period. Less topical than Greek old comedy, middle comedy dealt more with domestic issues and everyday life of the Athenian middle class. (180)

Milk an audience When a performer tries to evoke a response from an audience beyond that which it seems inclined to give. (18)

Mime 1. A kind of drama in which unmasked actors of both sexes portrayed often bawdy and obscene stories. In Rome, it became the most popular kind of drama after the first century CE. 2. Form of silent modern theatre. (184, 194)

Miracle play Medieval play treating the lives of saints. (206)

Modernism Name for art of a period (roughly 1890–1950) identified by radical experimentation with form and nonrealism. (61)

Monopoly Legal control or exclusive domination of a theatrical locale; the courts of both France and England in the late seventeenth century, for example, granted licenses to a limited number of theatres that thus gained monopolies. (250, 252, 256, 260, 262, 265)

Morality play Allegorical medieval play, like *Everyman*, that depicts the eternal struggle between good and evil that transpires in this world, using characters like Vice, Virtue, Wisdom, and so on. (206)

Motivation In Stanislavskian vocabulary, the internal springboard for an action or a set of behaviors onstage. (110)

Music One of Aristotle's six parts of a play: the material for diction. Popularly, the kind of art form having harmony and rhythm. (33, 39)

Musical An American musical comedy, a form traceable to the mid-nineteenth century and now typified by a spoken text or book (see entry) with songs and (usually) dances and a singing-dancing chorus. (299–303)

Musicians' gallery A space for musicians. In the Elizabethan theatre, it is above the stage. (218)

Mystery plays Usually drawn from biblical stories, these medieval plays were often staged in cycles, treating events from the creation to the Last Judgment. Often staged in connection with Christian festivals, some mysteries were quite elaborate and took days or even weeks to perform. (206)

National Endowment for the Arts (NEA) Federally (U.S.) funded arts-support entity. (28)

Naturalism A style of theatre and drama most popular from c. 1880 to 1900 that dealt with the sordid problems of the middle and lower classes in settings remarkable for the number and accuracy of details. Practitioners included Émile Zola, André Antoine, and Maxim Gorky. (268)

Natyasastra: Ancient Indian (Sanskrit) work on theatre aesthetics. (357)

Neoclassicism A style of drama and theatre from the Italian Renaissance based loosely on interpretations of Aristotle and Horace. Major tenets were verisimilitude, decorum, purity of genres (see these three terms), the five-act form, and the twofold purpose of drama: to teach and to please. (232, 243–257)

New comedy That form of Greek comedy dating from the Hellenistic and Graeco-Roman periods and treating the domestic complications of the Athenian middle class. A major source for Roman comedy. (182)

New Stagecraft A movement in stage design in the United States that favored simplified, often abstract, settings. It was, in effect, a reaction to overly realistic settings. Lighting played an important part in the design. Designers of the New Stagecraft often sought alternatives to the proscenium stage like the arena or thrust configurations. (283)

Noh Austere, poetic drama of medieval Japan, based in Zen Buddhism. (359)

Not-for-profit Professional theatre whose income comes only partly from ticket sales, the rest from donations and grants; given federal tax breaks. (27)

Obie Awards given annually to performers, playwrights, designers, and productions that made significant contributions to the Off-Broadway theatre scene. Name comes from the first letters of Off-Broadway. (90)

Objective In Stanislavskian vocabulary, a character's goal within a beat or scene; the goal of a motivation. (110)

Obstacle Barrier, difficulty; in acting, something preventing the reaching of an objective. (35)

Off-Broadway Popularly, those small, originally experimental but now often quite commercial theatres that are located outside the Times Square/Broadway area. Theatres with a seating capacity of fewer than three hundred that pay lower wages and fees than the larger Broadway houses. (77)

Off-Off-Broadway Popularly, the very small nontraditional theatres located in churches, coffeehouses, and so on that fall considerably out of the commercial mainstream. Theatres with highly limited seating capacities that may be granted exemptions from a wide variety of union regulations and scales. (78)

Old comedy That form of Greek comedy written during the classical period (see entry) and featuring topical political and social commentary set in highly predictable structural and metrical patterns. (176)

Onkos The high headdress of the Roman, and perhaps Hellenistic Greek, actor. (183)

Orchestra 1. That area of the Greek and Roman theatre that lay between the audience area and the scene house. 2. Originally the circular space where actors and chorus danced and performed plays; later a half circle that was used as a seating space for important people and only occasionally as a performance area. 3. In modern times, the prized seating area on the ground level of a theatre and adjacent to the stage. (71, 177, 189)

Open Theatre Important American avant-garde theatre, 1960s and 1970s; major influence on acting and production. (324)

Orta oyunu: Traditional Turkish comic theatre form. (364)

Pace Apparent rate of performance; partly a matter of speed with which the performance goes forward, but also related to intensity of action and complication and the artistic ways (actor's intensity, for example) that the action is realized. (136)

Pageant In the medieval period, a movable stage, a wagon on which plays were mounted and performed in parts of England, Spain, and occasionally continental Europe. By extension, the plays performed on such wagons. (209)

Pageant wagon See *pageant*.

Pantomime In the Roman theatre, a dance/story performed by a single actor with the accompaniment of a small group of musicians, particularly during the Christian era. In the eighteenth and nineteenth centuries, a "minor" form of entertainment marked by elaborate spectacle and often featuring commedia characters and a scene of magical transformation. (194, 255)

Paratheatrical Related to or parallel to the theatrical. Used to refer to activities tangential to theatre: circus, parades, and so on. (354)

Patent An official document that confers a right or privilege to the bearer. In several countries during the seventeenth and eighteenth centuries, only men who held patents from the king could open and operate theatres. (252, 265)

Patio Ground-level audience area in the Spanish corrales (see *corrales*).

Performance In life, the execution of an action (or the action executed) or a behavior taken in response to a stimulus. In art, the action of representing a character in a play, or, more generally, any public presentation. (4–6)

Performance art An avant-garde form that blends several arts (most often music, painting, dance, and theatre) into a visual, more than literary, expression of an often very personal truth. (325)

Performance criticism Analysis and explanation of performance (rather than of drama alone). (45–47, 62–63)

Performance theory Systematic description of the nature of performance (rather than of written drama alone). (60–62)

Performing art Any art that depends on a live performer in the presence of a live audience, for example, theatre, dance, opera, musical concerts. (4)

Periaktoi: Stage machines in use by the Hellenistic period in Greece. An early method of scene changing that consisted of a triangle extended in space and mounted on a central pivot so that when the pivot was rotated, three different scenes could be shown to an audience. (189)

Period movement Actors' movements imitative or suggestive of the way people moved, or are thought to have moved, in another historical period. (106)

Perspective Simulation of visual distance by the manipulation of size of objects. (235)

Phallus Simulation of the male sex organ. In Greek old comedy and satyr plays, phalluses were enlarged and otherwise made prominent for purposes of comic effect. (180)

Physical theatre The theatre building: its architecture and decorations, including the audience, stage, and backstage areas. (47–49, 71, 235, 250, 303)

Picturization Directorial creation of stage groupings ("pictures") that show or symbolize relationships or meanings; storytelling through stage pictures. (131)

Pit 1. Area of the audience on the ground floor and adjacent to the stage. Historically an inexpensive area because originally no seats were provided there and later only backless benches were used. By the end of the nineteenth century, a preferred seating area (now called the orchestra section). 2. Now refers often to the area reserved for members of the orchestra playing for opera, ballet, and musical comedy. (218, 253, 266, 293)

Platea The unlocalized playing area in the medieval theatre. See also *mansion*. (204)

Play reader Mediates between playwright and producer(s) by reading and judging submitted scripts; employee of producers(s). (67)

Plot 1. In Aristotle, one of the six parts of a play and the most important of the six; the formal cause of character; the soul of tragedy; the architectonic part of a play. 2. Popularly the story of a play, a novel, and so on. (33–36)

Point of attack The place in the story where a dramatic plot begins. Typically, Greek plays, like *Oedipus Rex*, have a late point of attack, and medieval and Shakespearean plays, like *King Lear*, have an early point of attack. (34)

Political theatre The kind of theatre devoted to achieving political and social rather than artistic goals. (84)

Possession of parts During the seventeenth and especially the eighteenth centuries, the practice of leaving a role with an actor throughout a career. Under the system, a sixty-year-old woman playing Juliet in Shakespeare's tragedy was not unheard of. (251)

Postmodernism A critical approach that doubts the possibility of objectivity and that favors, consequently, the open acknowledgement of socially constructed meanings and investigates the implications of those meanings. (61, 313)

Presence Being there—the actuality of the live actor; also, loosely, the onstage magnetism of the actor. (10)

Preview Public performance given prior to the official opening of a play, often to test the audience's response. (138)

Private theatre In Elizabethan and Stuart England, indoor theatres that were open to the public but were expensive because of their relatively limited seating capacity. Located on monastic lands, these theatres were outside the jurisdiction of the city of London. Initially they housed children's troupes, but later the regular adult troupes used them as a winter home. (218)

Probability In drama, the internally closed system that allows each event in a play to seem likely and believable for that play (for example, the appearance of God in a medieval cycle play). (265)

Producer Executive who arranges financing and who oversees a commercial production. (25, 289)

Professional theatre As used in this book, the term means that the participants—director, choreographer, actors, designers, and stagehands—work (and are therefore paid) under the aegis of a union. Here, the term does not refer to the quality of a particular production. (75, 326)

Prologue In Greek drama, that part of the play that precedes the entrance of the chorus. In other periods, a short introductory speech delivered by an actor, either in or out of character, to set the scene, warm up the audience, defend the play, or entertain. (176)

Properties Objects used on stage—furniture, cigarettes, dishware. (148)

Proscenium (theatre, arch) Theatre building in which the audience area is set off from the acting area by a proscenium arch that frames the stage, protects the perspective, masks the backstage area, etc. The audience views the onstage action from one side only. (71)

Protagonist In Greek theatre, the first (or major) actor, the one who competed for the prize in acting. Later, the leading character in any play (the "hero"). (37, 178)

Psychological realism A kind of theatre that relies on a view of human behavior as defined by late nineteenth- and twentieth-century psychology. (273, 282)

Public relations The business of causing the public to understand and esteem an event, institution, or cause. In theatre, it usually includes activities like advertising plays, developing essays for programs, designing posters, and inducing the public to have goodwill toward the theatrical organization before and after, as well as during, a specific production. (66)

Public theatre In Elizabethan and Stuart England, outdoor theatres like the Globe. Because larger than the indoor theatres, public theatres tended to be relatively inexpensive and so attract a general audience. (218)

Purity of genres Neoclassical tenet that elements of tragedy and those of comedy could not be mixed. The injunction was not merely against including funny scenes in tragedy but also against treating domestic issues or writing in prose, these elements being of the nature of comedy. (233)

Quem Quaeritis: A liturgical trope that opens, "Whom do you seek?" and that has early connection to drama, most especially in Ethelwold's *Regularis Concordia*, in which the trope is accompanied by directions for staging. (204)

Raisonneur In drama, a character who speaks for the author. (37)

Raked stage Stage slanted up from front to back to enhance the perspective. Stages began their rakes either at the front of the apron or at the proscenium line. (237)

Rasa: Important element of Sanskrit aesthetic theory—the inducing of an appropriate emotion in the audience. (357)

Realism The style of drama and theatre dating from the late nineteenth and early twentieth centuries that strove to reproduce on stage the details of everyday life with a view to improving the human and social condition. (267–268)

Regional theatre Theatre outside New York City in the United States and Canada; term usually restricted to professional, nontouring companies. (346)

Rehearsal The practicing of plays, either whole or in part, in order to improve their performance. (114)

Renaissance Literally, "rebirth"; refers to a renewed interest in the learning and culture of ancient Greece and Rome. Beginning in Italy, the Renaissance spread throughout western Europe from c. 1450 to c. 1650. (215–217)

Rendering Theatrical designers' finished drawings or paintings intended to show how the item(s) will look when built and placed on the stage. (148)

Repertory A set group of performance pieces done by a company. Also, the practice in such a company of alternating pieces so that they are done in repertory. Loosely, a resident professional theatre company in the United States, a repertory theatre. (72, 74–80, 130)

Representational A style of performance and design that lays emphasis on re-creating onstage aspects of daily life; the audience members are thought of as passive onlookers. Contrasts with presentational (see entry), a style that stresses presenting an event for an audience. (177, 182)

Restoration The period of English history that dates from 1660, when King Charles II was restored to the throne. (251–256)

Reversal According to Aristotle, a change in the direction of action or in the expectation of character. Reversals result in complex plots, preferred over simple plots for tragedies. (34)

Reviewer A person who views an artistic event and then writes his or her descriptive evaluation of it for immediate publication. (64–65)

Revival A new production of a play after its initial run. (328)

Rhythm Regular and measurable repetition. (134)

Rigging The combination of ropes, lines, pulleys, pipes, and so on that permits the manipulation of scenic units backstage. (71)

Rising action Action of increasing complication. (35)

Ritual theory a theory that asserts that drama derived from religious rituals (in Greece, for example, religious rituals devoted to the worship of the god Dionysus). (6, 169, 170, 354)

Road A complex of theatrical circuits for travelling and performing plays outside of New York City. (77)

Road show Production for the road. (77)

Roman A period in theatre and drama dating from c. 364 BCE to c. 550 CE and customarily subdivided into the Republican period (c. 364 BCE–27 BCE) and the Empire (c. 27 BCE–c. 550 CE). (186–198)

Romanticism A style of theatre and drama dating from c. 1790 to c. 1850 and marked by an interest in the exotic, the subjective, the emotional, and the individual. Began in part as a reaction against the strictures of neoclassicism; grew out of the eighteenth century's sentimentalism (see entry). (260–267)

Royalties Payments made to authors (and their representatives) for permission to reproduce, in text or in performance, their artistic products (plays, designs, etc.). (96, 294)

Run-through A kind of rehearsal in which the actors perform long sections of the play (or the whole play) without interruption, usually for the purpose of improving the sense of continuity, shaping the whole, and so on. (137)

Rural Dionysia One of three Athenian festivals devoted to the public worship of the god Dionysus at which drama appeared. See also *festivals.* (171)

Sanskrit drama Drama of ancient India, e.g., Kalidasa's *Sakuntala.* (356–357)

Satyr play A short, rustic, and often obscene play included in the Dionysian festivals of Greece at the conclusion of the tragedies. (172)

Scaffold In medieval staging in England, the localizing structure in or near the platea. See also *mansion.* (209)

Scenario In general, the prose description of a play's story. In the commedia dell'arte, the written outline of plot and characters from which the actors improvised the particular actions of performance. (240)

Scrim Mesh used in scenery; becomes transparent when lighted from behind, opaque when lighted from the front; useful for transformations, misty effects, and so forth. (277)

Script Play text. See also *text* and *book.* (103)

Scrolling color changer A device placed in front of a standard lighting instrument that can, through a remote signal, change the light from one color to another. (154)

Secular plays Plays that treat matters of this world rather than the next. Often used in discussions of the medieval period to distinguish between religious and worldly plays. (210–212)

Secularism Belief in the validity and importance of life and things on earth. Often contrasted with spiritualism, otherworldliness, or religiosity. The Renaissance period was marked by a rising secularism. (215)

Semiotics The study of signs, things that stand for other things. When applied to language, art, and criticism, semiotics focuses attention on the meanings that audiences create from the words or images of a playscript or a performance. (62)

Sense memory Recall of a sensory response—smell, taste, sound—with both its cause and the actor's reaction; important to the creation of a character's behavior in some theories of acting. (108)

Sentimental comedy A kind of comedy particularly popular during the eighteenth century in which people's virtues rather than their foibles were stressed. The audience was expected to experience something "too exquisite for laughter." Virtuous characters expressed themselves in pious "sentiments." (255)

Sentimentalism Prevalent during the eighteenth century, sentimentalism assumed the innate goodness of humanity and attributed evil to faulty instruction or bad example. A precursor of the romanticism of the nineteenth century. (250–251)

Sentimentality The arousing of feelings out of proportion to their cause. (291)

Shareholder Member of a sharing company who owned a part of the company's stocks of costumes, scenery, properties, and so on. Sharing companies were the usual organization of troupes from the Renaissance until the eighteenth century (and beyond), when some actors began to prefer fixed salaries to shares. (24)

Sharing company One made up of shareholders. (24)

Shite: In Noh theatre, the protagonist. (359)

Shutter Large flat, paired with another of the same kind, to close off the back of the scene in Italianate staging; an alternative to a backdrop; sometimes used for units at the sides. When pierced with a cutout, it became a "relieve" and showed a diorama. (237)

Sight lines Extreme limits of the audience's vision, drawn from the farthest and/or highest seat on each side through the proscenium arch or scenery obtruding farthest onstage. Anything beyond the sight lines cannot be seen by some members of the audience. (72)

Signature music Music associated with certain characters or certain types of characters, particularly in the melodramas of the nineteenth century. Stage directions indicate "Mary's music," "Jim's music," and so on. (293)

Silhouette The outline of a body or costume—its mass. (151)

Simultaneous staging The practice, particularly during the Middle Ages, of representing several locations on the stage at one time. In medieval staging, several mansions (see entry), representing particular places, were arranged around a platea, or generalized playing space. (204)

Single-point perspective A technique for achieving a sense of depth by establishing a single vanishing point and painting or building all objects to diminish to it. (237)

Skene: The scene house in the Greek theatre. Its appearance can first be documented with the first performance of the *Oresteia* in 458 BCE. Its exact appearance from that time until the first stone theatre came into existence (probably in the late fourth century BCE) is uncertain. (177)

Slice of life Critical notion closely associated with Naturalism and used to describe plays that avoided the trappings of Romanticism and the obvious contrivance of well-made plays in favor of a seemingly literal reproduction of daily life on the stage. (269)

Spectacle One of Aristotle's six parts of a play, the part of least interest to the poet but of most importance in differentiating the dramatic form from the narrative and the epic. In everyday parlance, all visual elements of production and, by extension, particular plays, scenes, or events in which visual elements predominate. (41)

Spine In Stanislavskian vocabulary, the consistent line that connects all elements of a character through a play. See *through line.*

Spotlight Stage light with hard-edged focus intended to highlight a person or object in its beams. (154)

Springboard A director's initial reaction to a play, a "taking off place"—perhaps visual, perhaps rational—that leads to an interpretation for play production. (126)

Stage left The left half of the stage as defined by someone standing onstage facing the audience. (135)

Stage right The right half of the stage as defined by someone standing onstage facing the audience. (135)

Staging "Getting the play on its feet;" the director's shaping of movement and timing in rehearsal; see also blocking. (130)

Standing ovation An audience stands and claps in order to show supreme approval of a performance. (18)

Star Dominant actor whose name and presence draw an audience. (289)

Star system Company organization in which minor characters are played by actors for the season, while central roles are taken by stars (see entry) brought in for one production; still common in opera, sometimes seen in summer theatres. (289)

Stock company Theatre company in which actors play standardized roles and (originally) owned shares of stock in the company. (216, 220, 290)

Storm and Stress Sturm und Drang; a theatrical movement in Germany during the 1770s and 1780s that was marked by its militant experimentation with dramatic form, theatrical style, and social statement. (264)

Story Narrative; coherent sequence of incidents; "what happens." A general, nontechnical term that should not be confused with *plot.* (50)

Stratford Festival Major Canadian not-for-profit with four theatres in Stratford, Ontario. (331)

Street theatre Theatre, often political, that takes place outside traditional theatre spaces and without traditional theatrical trappings. (318)

Striplights Series of connected lights located overhead or in the wings; usually used to bathe the stage in light; also light border. (154)

Style 1. Distinctive combination of elements. 2. In Aristotelian terms, the way in which the manner is joined to the means. 3. Particulars of surface, as distinguished from substance. 4. "The way a thing is done" in a time and place. (55)

Suffering According to Aristotle, an awareness. The material out of which discoveries are made. (182)

Superobjective In Stanislavskian vocabulary, the "life goal" of the character. (110)

Surprise An unexpected discovery or event. In dramatic surprise, the surprise, although unanticipated, must be seen in retrospect to be quite probable. (50)

Surrealism A style popular immediately following World War I that rejected everyday logic in favor of a free expression of the subconscious (or dream) state. (279)

Suspense An increasing sense of expectation or dread, provoked by establishing strong anticipations and then delaying outcomes. (50)

Symbolism A style of theatre and drama popular during the 1890s and the early twentieth century that stressed the importance of subjectivity and spirituality and sought its effects through the use of symbol, legend, myth, and mood. (277)

Table work Reading aloud of the script by cast and director before staging begins. (137)

Take a bow To appear in front of the audience to acknowledge its applause, usually at the end of a play. Women customarily curtsy and men bow. (18)

Take an encore From the French encore, meaning "again." A performer repeats a part of a performance or offers an additional piece in performance at the insistence of an audience, which claps until the encore is begun. (18)

Technical director The person charged with coordinating backstage activities preparatory to production, including the coordination required to transform the scenic designer's vision into finished settings. (150)

Technical rehearsal Rehearsal devoted to the practice and perfection of the various technical elements of the show (lighting, sound, flying, trapping, and so on). (138)

Text The written record of a play, including dialogue and stage directions; a playscript. (30, 45, 118)

Theatre for development Use of theatrical techniques for both community involvement and community instruction. (367)

Theatre history Theatre's past. Also, a study of the theatre's traditions, including its plays, performers, designers, buildings, and methods of payment. Also, a field of scholarly endeavor devoted to such studies. (159–368)

Theatre in the round See *arena theatre.* (72)

Theatre of cruelty Phrase popularized by Antonin Artaud to describe a kind of theatre that touched the basic precivilized elements of people through disrupting normal "civilized" expectations about appearance, practice, sound, and so forth. (282)

Theory Any systematic attempt to explain a phenomenon; *dramatic*, of play texts; *performance*, of live performances. (1, 60)

Three unities In neoclassical (Western) dramatic theory, the unities of time, place, and action. (233–234)

Through line In Stanislavskian vocabulary, a consistent element of character running through a scene or a play. (111)

Thrust stage Dominant kind of staging during Shakespeare's time in England that is being revived in many contemporary theatres. Also called three-quarter round because the audience surrounds the action on three sides as the stage juts into the audience area. (72)

Timing Actor's sense of tempo and rhythm. (136)

Tiring house The building from which the Elizabethan platform, or thrust, stage extended. A place where the actors attired themselves. (218)

Tony Annual awards made by the directors of the American Theatre Wing in memory of Antoinette Perry to recognize outstanding contributions to the current New York theatrical season. (319, 321)

Tragedy In popular parlance, any serious play, usually including an unhappy ending. According to Aristotle, "an imitation of a worthy or illustrious and perfect action, possessing magnitude, in pleasing language, using separately the several species of imitation in its parts, by men acting, and not through narration, through pity and fear effecting a catharsis of such passion." At this point in theatrical history, almost indefinable. (233)

Transformation 1. Technique popularized in the 1960s whereby an actor portrayed several characters without any changes in costume, makeup, or mask, relying instead on changing voice and body attitudes in full view of the audience. 2. In medieval and Renaissance theatre, seemingly magical changes of men into beasts, women into salt, and so on. 3. In English pantomime, magical changes made by Harlequin's wand. (112, 255)

Trap Unit in stage floor for appearances and disappearances; varies from a simple door to complex machines for raising and lowering while moving forward, backward, and sideways. (218)

Trope An interpolation in a liturgical text. Some believe medieval drama to have been derived from medieval troping. (204)

Unified art work A work in which all elements are brought together to form an artistic whole; associated with the theories of Richard Wagner. See *master artwork*. (266)

Union An alliance of persons formed to secure material benefits and better working conditions. Major theatrical unions are USAA (United Scenic Artists of America, for designers); Equity (Actors Equity Association, for actors); and IATSE (International Alliance of Theatrical Stage Employees, for theatre technicians). (75–76)

Unit see beat. (137)

Unit set A single setting on which all scenes may be played. (147)

Unity Cohesion or consistency. When applied to a text, it refers to the method of organizing: unity of plot, unity of character, unity of action. When applied to design, it refers to how well all the visual elements fit together to achieve an artistic whole. (146, 182, 192, 196, 234, 247, 269)

Upstage The sections of the stage closest to the back wall. Comes from a time when stages were raked, or slanted, from the front to the back, so that upstage meant quite literally walking up the stage toward the back wall. (135, 237)

Utility player Actor hired to play a variety of small roles as needed. (250)

Vaudeville 1. In America in the nineteenth and twentieth centuries, vaudeville was popular family entertainment featuring a collection of variety acts, skits, short plays, and song-and-dance routines. 2. In France in the eighteenth and nineteenth centuries, vaudeville referred to *comédie-en-vaudeville,* short satiric pieces, often topical, that were interspersed with new lyrics set to familiar tunes and sprinkled with rhyming couplets (vaudevilles). The form in France is roughly equivalent to the ballad opera (see entry) in England. (299–300)

Verisimilitude Central concept in Neoclassical theory and criticism. Literal meaning is "truth-seemingness," but used historically, at a time when truth referred to the general, typical, categorical truth. Not to be confused with Realism. (250–252)

Villain Character in melodrama who opposes the forces of good (represented by the hero and the heroine) and who, at the play's end, is punished for his evil ways. Typically, the villain propels the action of a melodrama. (293)

Vomitory Audience entrance (Roman audience) into middle of auditorium through passage under part of audience area. (72)

Wagon Wheeled platform that moves on and off a stage, particularly a proscenium stage; also, in medieval theatre, a movable scenic unit and playing area, or pageant (see entry). (209)

Waki In Noh theatre, the second character, usually a confidant. (359)

Well-made play A play written by or in the manner of Eugène Scribe and marked by careful preparation, seeming cause-and-effect organization of action, announced entrances and exits, and heavy reliance on external objects or characters to provide apparent connections between diverse lines of action. Now often used as a term of derision. (299)

Wing-and-drop scenery An illusionistic arrangement, common from the Renaissance through the nineteenth century in Europe and the United States, of paired wings along the sides and a drop along the back of the stage. See *wings*; see *drop*. (304)

Wings 1. Scenic pieces (flats) placed parallel to the stage front, or nearly so, on each side of the stage; combined with overhead units for "wing-and-border" settings. 2. The offstage area beyond the side units of scenery—"in the wings." (From which is derived wing space, the amount of room offstage at the sides.) (71, 237)

Women's theatre A theatre whose repertories and practices are devoted to the advancement of women. Such theatres offer some combination of theatre by women, for women, and about women. (321–322)

Wright "Maker," as in playwright. (86)

Yard Another name for the pit in the Shakespearean theatre; where patrons stood on the ground in front of the stage. (218)

Zanni In commedia dell' arte, the group of comic servants that includes Arlecchino, Trufaldino, etc. (259)

INDEX

Note: This is primarily an index of names, terms, and titles. Historical subjects within periods (e.g., Elizabethan acting) are not so indexed but can be located using the appropriate headings (e.g., acting). Technical and historical terms are also listed in the glossary (which is not indexed). References on successive pages appear with the page number followed by ff. (e.g., action, 37ff.).

PHOTO CREDITS

P. 10, Ahmanson Theatre; p. 22, Ahmanson Theatre; p. 23, Ahmanson Theatre; p. 29, *As You Like It*, Theatre South Carolina, Photo: Jason Ayers; p. 41, Mark Taper Forum; p. 44, *The Skin of Our Teeth*, Theatre South Carolina, Photo: Jason Ayers; p. 60, *Hair*, Joan Marcus Photography; p. 70, *Bloody Bloody Andrew Jackson*, Center Theatre Group, Los Angeles, Kirk Douglas Theatre, Photo: Craig Schwartz; p. 81, *Journey of the Fifth Horse*, Fifth Floor Theatre, directed by Michael Sexton, scenery by Laura Jellinek, costumes by Caitlin O'Conner, lighting by Mike Inwood; p. 85, *Mother Courage and Her Children*, Theatre South Carolina, Photo: Jason Ayers; p. 90, *Canticle*, Walker Theatre, directed by Ruben Polendo, scenery by Jason Simms, costumes by Caitlin O'Connor, lighting by Adam Greene; p. 98, *South Pacific*, Lincoln Center Theatre, Joan Marcus Photography; p. 106, *Bloody Bloody Andrew Jackson*, Center Theatre Group, Los Angeles, Kirk Douglas Theatre, Photo: Craig Schwartz; p. 108, Mark Taper Forum, Photo: Craig Schwartz; p. 109, Center Theatre Group (Los Angeles), Ahmanson Theatre, Photo: Craig Schwartz; p. 111, Mark Taper Forum, Photo: Craig Schwartz; p. 115, Mark Taper Forum, Photo: Craig Schwartz; p. 117, *The Trojan Women,* Theatre South Carolina, Photo: Jason Ayers; p. 127, Joan Marcus Photography; p. 141, *Tartuffe*, Theatre South Carolina, Photo: Jason Ayers; p. 183, Ancient Roman, "Relief of a Seated Poet (Meander) with Masks of New Comedy," probably 1st century B.C.; white marble, H: 44.3 cm; w. 59.5 cm; d. at right foot of poet 8.5 cm. © Photo: Trustees of Princeton University. May not be reproduced without permission in writing from Princeton University Art Museum, Princeton, NJ 08544. Princeton University Art Museum. Museum purchase, Caroline G. Mather Fund. Photo Credit: Bruce M. White. y1951-1; p. 186, Robert Sisson/National Geographic Image Collection; p. 241, *Miracle at Naples* by David Grimm, Huntington Theatre Company, directed by Peter DuBois, Photo: T. Charles Erickson; p. 243, *The Country Wife*, Theatre South Carolina, Photo: Jason Ayers; p. 311, *The Trojan Women,* Theatre South Carolina, Photo: Jason Ayers; p. 319, *Gem of the Ocean*, Fifth Floor Theatre, directed by Benny Sato Ambush, scenery by Sara Walsh, costumes by Jennifer Nweke, lighting by Zack Brown; p. 333, photographs and collage by Tim Donahue; p. 339, *Clean House*, Atlas Theatre, directed Giovanna Sardelli, scenery by Jason Simms, costumes by Malgosia Turzanska, lighting by Greg Goff; p. 340, *Gem of the Ocean*, Fifth Floor Theatre, directed by Benny Sato Ambush, scenery by Sara Walsh, costumes by Jennifer Nweke, lighting by Zack Brown; p. 352, Jack Vartoogian/Front Row Photos.